SAINT AN
AND H
BIOGRAPHER

THE BIRKBECK LECTURES
1959

Ḡec vita prefixa in principio oper[is]
Anselmi impreſſ[a] Coſſon 1560 per Brickmann

INCIPIT PREFATIO SEQUENTIS OPERIS

QUONIAM occultas & anteceſſorū nſorū temporibus
inſolitaſ rerū mutationeſ nſiſ diebuſ in anglia
accidiſſe & coaluiſſe conſpexim̄ · ne mutationeſ
ipſe poſteroſ ſcientiā penitus lateret quedā ex illiſ
ſucciniere excepta literarū memorie
tradidimus · Sed qm̄ ipſum opus in hoc maxime uerſat· ut ea
que int̄ regeſ angloꝝ & anſelmū archiepm̄ cantuarioꝝ facta ſ̄
in concuſſa ueritate deſignet· queq̄ omnib·puta illoꝝ hiſtoriam
ſcire uolentib· tunc temporiſ innoteſcere potuerit licet inculto pla-
no tam̄ ſermone deſcribat · nec adeo qcquā in ſe cōtineat qd ad pri-
uatā cuerſatione · uel ad moreſ ipſiuſ anſelmi q̄litate · aut ad mi-
raculoꝝ exhibitione ponere uideat· placuit quibuſdā familiarib·
meiſ me ſua prece ad hoc pducere · ut ſicut deſcriptione notarū
rerū poſteriſ · ita deſignatione ignotarū ſatagere tā futuriſ quā
& pſentibus aliqd officii mei muniſ impendere · Ơſ eo qd offen-
& ſummope cauebā · dedi opā uoluntati eoꝝ p poſſe more gere ·
ſe Opuſ q̄ ipſii de uita & cuerſatione anſelmi archiepi cantu-
arienſ̄ exitularū · taliſ dō adiuuante curaui diſponere· ut quiſ
aliud opuſ qd pfignauim̄ ex maiori parte de eiuſdē uiri con-
uerſatione ſubſiſtat· ita tam̄ in ſua materia integre narrationiſ
formā pretendat· ut nec illud iſti · nec iſtud illiuſ p mutua ſui
cognitione multū uideat indigere · Plene tam̄ acc̄ei ſcire uo-
lentib·· nec illud ſine iſto · nec iſtud ſine illo ſufficere poſſe pro-
nuncio · Explicit prefatio; INCIPIT LIBER PRIMUS

DE VITA ET CONVERSATIONE ANSELMI CANTVARIENSIS ARCHIEPI;
INSTITVTA VITA & cuerſationiſ ANSELMI cantuarien-
ſiſ archiepi literarū memorie tradituruſ · pmo omniū uocata
in auxiliū meū ſūma dī clementia & maieſtate· quedā breui dicā
de ortu ac morib· parentū ei · ut hunc lector aduertat de qua
radice pdierit· qd in ſtudiiſ naſcenturꝫ pliſ pmodū fulſit· Pater
ei guudulfuſ · mater ermenberga uocabatur· Vterꝗ; iuxta
ſeli dignitate nobiliter nati· nobiliter ſunt in auguſta ciuitate

-1-

THE BEGINNING OF THE 'VITA ANSELMI' IN EADMER'S MANUSCRIPT

# SAINT ANSELM
## AND HIS BIOGRAPHER
### A STUDY OF MONASTIC LIFE AND THOUGHT
#### 1059–*c*.1130

BY

## R. W. SOUTHERN

*Chichele Professor of Modern History
in the University of Oxford*

## CAMBRIDGE
### AT THE UNIVERSITY PRESS
#### 1966

CAMBRIDGE UNIVERSITY PRESS
Cambridge, New York, Melbourne, Madrid, Cape Town, Singapore, São Paulo, Delhi

Cambridge University Press
The Edinburgh Building, Cambridge CB2 8RU, UK

Published in the United States of America by Cambridge University Press, New York

www.cambridge.org
Information on this title: www.cambridge.org/9780521103312

First published 1963
Reprinted 1966
This digitally printed version 2009

A catalogue record for this publication is available from the British Library

ISBN 978-0-521-06532-0 hardback
ISBN 978-0-521-10331-2 paperback

TO
MY WIFE

# CONTENTS

vii

# PART II

CONTENTS

# PREFACE

THIS book is a study of Anglo-Norman monastic life and thought during the period from 1059 to about 1130 at two distinct but complementary levels: the level of the high speculative genius of Anselm, and that of the more commonplace but observant Eadmer, his biographer. Taken together, the writings of the two men embrace almost every side of contemporary monastic experience: theological, devotional, personal, historical, political and (in some small measure) economic. All these aspects of monastic life must be surveyed so far as they fall within the range of the combined literary product of the two authors. In doing this, I have had it before my mind that this is not a book primarily about theology, though theology necessarily plays a large part in the story. Nor is it primarily about any, or even all, of the specialized subjects which have just been mentioned, but about the experiences which they promoted and served to crystallize. In most of these fields Anselm of course is far ahead of Eadmer in originality and power of thought. But Eadmer is more representative of the monastic community as a whole, and it is this characteristic which gives him his special importance. Anselm and Eadmer shared a common rule of life. They were the servants of a community whose rights and interests came before every other practical claim to their allegiance during the years in which they were associated. It is difficult for us now to realize how much this community of rule and life formed the thought and actions of those who came under its influence. Anselm is an original thinker of great stature, and we can easily forget that he was not always original nor always a thinker, and that much of what he held most strongly was the common property of men of much less intelligence. It is for these men that Eadmer speaks.

This is not to say that Anselm failed to speak for them. On the contrary, his actions and his spoken words, so far as they have come down to us, reflect the common monastic environment of the time more clearly than his treatises, and they were the inspiration of much that Eadmer wrote. But as a theologian, Anselm habitually rose above the common thoughts of his day, and he did not often draw Eadmer after him. Eadmer, however, sometimes took flight on his own account: as a reporter of contemporary events, as a champion of Anglo-Saxon devotion in a new age, and most conspicuously in his biography of Anselm, he made discoveries in literary form and religious expression of some importance. Occasionally Eadmer's flights of speculation and his sensitivity took him beyond the positions of Anselm and gave him a solitary eminence in his time. In one small way he is more interesting even than Anselm, for he was always more aware of his surroundings, whether they lay immediately before his eyes or presented themselves at a distance to his historical imagination, than ever Anselm was. He was a more articulate observer than any other English monk of the period immediately after the Norman Conquest.

It is this complicated interaction of the two men which gives their friendship its interest, and illuminates the history of English Benedictinism in its half century of unshaken confidence and achievement after the Norman Conquest. This history cannot properly be written in terms only of its greatest men. The broad foundation of commonplace is important, if only because the commonplace also has its revolutions and its slowly moving tides. The greatest evil of the commonplace is dullness, and I do not know whether Eadmer will seem to others to rise sufficiently above mediocrity to become interesting. For myself, he has stood the test of concentrated observation remarkably well. Perhaps I have said more about him than—in the company of Anselm—he deserves. By contrast, I fear I have said more about Anselm than my own competence warrants. Those who are better equipped theologians than I am will soon see this. My only excuse must be that if I have said too much, it would have been easy to say more; and I have tried to say no more than was necessary to give a fair impression of Anselm's personality, his habitual modes of thought, and the general nature of his contribution to the thought and piety of his day. Whether I have succeeded in any of these aims I must leave it for others to judge.

The subject has drawn me on step by step. In one form or

another it has occupied me intermittently for over twenty-five years. It was in 1933 that I first suggested to Sir Maurice Powicke that I might prepare an edition of the letters of St. Anselm, and I began to collate the Paris manuscripts in the autumn of that year. This work came to a stop when I learned that Dom Schmitt was already working on the edition which has happily been completed this year. Thereafter I turned to other things, but Anselm has held first place in my scholarly affections since those days. Looking back on all that has happened since then, this book seems a small fragment to save from the wreckage of so many years. But however small, it would not have survived without the help of many friends: in the first place, the Rector and Fellows of Exeter College, among whom as a Junior Research Fellow I began this study; after them, my colleagues at Balliol who have provided large opportunities for continuing this work; then the Master and Council of Trinity College, Cambridge, who by inviting me to give the Birkbeck Lectures in 1959, helped me to take a fresh view of some parts of the field; and finally the friends on whom I have especially relied for advice, information and encouragement. Among these I may here mention Sir Maurice Powicke, Professor V. H. Galbraith and Dr. R. W. Hunt, who have helped me in innumerable ways; Professors W. C. Kneale and Henry Chadwick, who have read various parts of the work in typescript; Mr. and Mrs. R. F. I. Bunn, Mr. C. J. F. Williams, and my wife, who have read all the proofs and saved me from many errors. To all of them I offer my humble and hearty thanks.

# ABBREVIATIONS

Anselm's letters are referred to as follows: Ep. 1[i, 1]. The first number is the number in the edition of Dom Schmitt; the second is the number in Gerberon's edition, reproduced in Migne, *Patrologia Latina*, vol. clviii–clix.

*Anglia Sacra*: Henry Wharton, *Anglia Sacra*, 2 vols., 1691.

*ASC*: *Anglo-Saxon Chronicle* (references are to C. Plummer, *Earle's Two Saxon Chronicles Parallel*, Oxford, 2 vols. 1892, 1899).

*BGPM*: *Beiträge zur Geschichte der Philosophie des Mittelalters*, begründet von Clemens Baeumker.

Bouquet: *Receuil des historiens des Gaules et de la France*, ed. M. Bouquet and others, 1738–1904.

Cantor: N. F. Cantor, *Church, Kingship and Lay Investiture in England*, 1089–1135, Princeton, 1958.

C.C.C.C.: Corpus Christi College, Cambridge, (*Descriptive Catalogue of the Manuscripts* by M. R. James, 2 vols, 1912).

*CDH*: *Cur Deus Homo*.

*CSEL*: *Corpus scriptorum ecclesiasticorum latinorum*, Vienna, 1866–.

*DB*: *Domesday Book*.
*Domesday Monachorum*: *The Domesday Monachorum of Christ Church Canterbury*, ed. D. C. Douglas, 1944.

*EHR*: *English Historical Review*.

*Fl. Wigorn*: *Florentii Wigorniensis monachi chronicon ex chronicis*, ed. B. Thorpe, 2 vols., 1848–9.

*GP*: William of Malmesbury, *Gesta Pontificum Anglorum*, ed. N. E. S. A. Hamilton, Rolls Series, 1870.

*GR*: William of Malmesbury, *Gesta Regum Anglorum*, ed. W. Stubbs, Rolls Series, 2 vols., 1887–9.

*HN*: Eadmer, *Historia Novorum in Anglia*, ed. M. Rule, Rolls Series, 1884.

Jaffé-Wattenbach: Ph. Jaffé, *Regesta pontificum Romanorum*, 2nd ed., G. Wattenbach, S. Loewenfeld, F. Kaltenbrunner, P. Ewald, 1885–7.

*Mansi*: *Sacrorum conciliorum nova et amplissima collectio*, ed. J. D. Mansi.

*MARS*: *Medieval and Renaissance Studies*, ed. R. W. Hunt and R. Klibansky, 1941–.

*Memorials of St. Dunstan*: *Memorials of St. Dunstan*, ed. W. Stubbs, Rolls Series, 1874.

*MGH*: *Monumenta Germaniae Historica.*

*MGH, SS*: *Monumenta Germaniae Historica, Scriptores.*

*Muratori*: *Rerum Italicarum Scriptores*, ed. L. A. Muratori (New edition, ed. G. Carducci and V. Fiorini, 1900–).

Ordericus Vitalis: Ordericus Vitalis, *Historia Ecclesiastica*, ed. A. le Prévost and L. Delisle, 5 vols., 1838–55.

*PL*: J. P. Migne, *Patrologiae Latinae cursus completus.*

Porée: A. Porée, *Histoire de l'Abbaye du Bec*, 2 vols., 1901.

*Regesta*: *Regesta Regum Anglo-Normannorum*, vol. 1, 1913, ed. H. W. C. Davies and R. J. Whitwell; vol. 2, 1956, ed. Charles Johnson and H. A. Cronne.

*R. Bén*: *Revue Bénédictine.*

*RS*: Rolls Series (Chronicles and Memorials of Great Britain and Ireland during the Middle Ages).

*RTAM*: *Recherches de Théologie ancienne et médiévale*, 1929–.

*SB*: *Sitzungsberichte.*

Schmitt: F. S. Schmitt, O.S.B., *Sancti Anselmi Cantuariensis archiepiscopi Opera Omnia*, i–vi, 1938–61.

*VA*: *Vita Anselmi*. (The references are to book and chapter and may be found either in the edition by Rule in the Rolls Series (see *HN* above) or in my edition in Nelson's Medieval Texts, 1962. When there is a reference to a note on a passage of the *Vita*, or to a page, it will be found in my edition.)

Wilmart, *Opuscula*: *Edmeri Cantuariensis cantoris nova opuscula de sanctorum veneratione et obsecratione* (*Revue des Sciences religieuses*, xv, 1935, 184–219, 354–379).

Wilmart, *Auteurs Spirituels*: Dom A. Wilmart, O. S. B., *Auteurs spirituels et textes dévots du moyen âge latin: études d'histoire littéraire*, 1932.

# PART I

# CHAPTER I

# ANSELM'S EARLY YEARS

## I. ANSELM'S FAMILY AND LOCAL BACKGROUND

ANSELM was born in 1033 in the Alpine town of Aosta, on the southern boundary of the kingdom of Burgundy. When he was born, the old régime (as we may call it) seemed to be entirely solid. The dominating figures in Europe were the Emperor Conrad II, who had recently added Anselm's own country of Burgundy to his empire, and Odilo abbot of Cluny, under whom Cluny came to stand for all that the western world most admired in monasticism. The pope, Benedict IX, was a distinguished Roman aristocrat, about whom so much evil was later believed that he put the name of Benedict out of circulation as a papal title till the fourteenth century; but contemporaries remained in happy ignorance of his posthumous ill-fame and accepted him as part of the order of things without comment. In Byzantium, the great reign of Basil II had recently ended. He had extended the effective power of the Greek Emperors from the Dalmatian coast to the eastern boundary of modern Turkey, a greater area of centralized government than anything known in Europe before the rise of modern Russia; and this victorious advance, to all outward appearances, was still continuing in the earliest years of Anselm's life. Yet when Anselm died seventy-six years later the Greek Empire was only a shadow of its former self. At its southern boundaries were western Crusading states. The maritime power of the Italian cities was beginning to dominate the Mediterranean. The successor of Conrad II, his great-grandson Henry V, was a hated tyrant whose ruthless energy and splendour could not conceal the antiquated nature of his power. The successor of Pope Benedict IX, by contrast, though a weak and vacillating man, governed a spiritual empire which was a more effective, because more loyal, instrument than anything any western ruler had ever commanded.

3

By 1109 the monasteries of Cîteaux and the Chartreuse were already presenting a challenge to the leadership of Cluny; Abelard and St. Bernard were young men; there was a large literature of canon law and political controversy, fields where silence had reigned almost unbroken in Anselm's youth.

The span of his life covered one of the most momentous periods of change in European history, comparable to the centuries of the Reformation, or the Industrial Revolution. As a mere constellation of talent in different fields Anselm, Gregory VII and William the Conqueror were the greatest men in Europe during this period. Anselm was slightly younger than the other two; he outlived William by twenty years and Gregory by twenty-four years. He survived to have the unexpected task of trying to reconcile their work. It was a task for which he was in no way prepared, and the perplexities into which it led him will concern us at a later stage in this story: for the present it is sufficient to mark its unexpectedness. William and Gregory were men of action of a kind rare at any time, but almost unknown in the Middle Ages: they were creators who dealt intuitively with confused situations, having little in precedent or business routine or learned construction to guide them. Gregory had an energy of purpose and clarity of vision in practical affairs for which no parallel can be found in these centuries. William had an undaunted mastery of the problems of the secular world—that is to say, of other men's wills—in both fighting and ruling, unapproached in creative power by any other medieval ruler after Charlemagne. Anselm, who spent half his life in positions requiring business ability, never learnt to love business or to transact it with even tolerable efficiency. He had more opportunities than most men for observing the transformation of western Europe in his lifetime, but there is no sign that he took much notice of it or saw himself in any way as an instigator of change. After the age of twenty-seven he looked out on to the world unwillingly and with distaste. He sought no wide influence. He was at his best talking to a group of pupils, not one of whom made an immediate mark as a scholar or writer of first-class importance. Yet in the long run, as one whose thoughts

4

became part of the life of other men, Anselm outdistanced all his contemporaries. There is no side of the great change in the mind and face of Europe that came about in his lifetime which he did not in some way touch or stimulate.

Like most of the men of his generation who made an original contribution to the world, he had to struggle out of a cramping environment. William the Conqueror and Gregory VII, among the rest, seemed by birth and early circumstances destined to the frustrations of men with minds greater than their situations. In Anselm's case, his destiny seemed likely to consist of propping up a declining family fortune by ecclesiastical preferment with the help of a provincial education. It was possibly to this education that he owed an ingenious, though mercifully infrequently displayed, intimacy with the works of Horace and Virgil. There are a few passages in his letters which show that he had a taste for the playful exchange of classical allusions which, if developed, might have made his works as painful to read as those of his namesake and older contemporary, Anselm of Besate. This familiarity did him no kind of good. In the few passages where Anselm displays his classical learning his brand of learned obscurity is no better than that of other writers of his time.[1] It may be to this early education also that he owed the literary mannerisms which are most conspicuous in his earliest writings. But he showed no interest in law and rhetoric, which were the foundations of north Italian education. Aosta, with its ancient Roman tradition, its literary and scholastic conservatism, its notaries, its cathedral and canons—among whom, there is some reason to think, his family had destined him to take his place—all this seems to have meant nothing to him. Although he crossed the Alps four times in later life, he never revisited his native town. On the first occasion there were some practical reasons for this: the detour, though short, would have taken him into enemy country. But on his second journey, only age, weariness and indifference can account for his neglect. He never seems to have spoken of his native town with any affection. He escaped from it when he was a young man, quarrelling with his father, and became in all essentials a man of northern France at the

[1] The worst example is Ep. 57 [i, 48], addressed to Lanfranc.

5

time when this area was first emerging as the pre-eminent force in the life of Europe.

Although he did not speak of Aosta, he sometimes spoke of the mountains, with affection. Eadmer preserved a touching expression of his pleasure at finding himself in a mountain village in south Italy, where 'exhilarated with the hope of future quiet' he exclaimed 'Here is my rest; here I will dwell'.[1] On another occasion he told Eadmer a story which shows that some of his later moral and intellectual dispositions were early developed. Above the town of Aosta were the glittering mountains, of Jupiter as they were called, and he not unnaturally imagined them to be the home of God. One night in a dream he climbed the mountain and came to the court of God. In the valley, as he passed, the women were carelessly reaping the corn, and he resolved to accuse them to their Lord. Coming to the court of God, he found Him alone with His steward, the household being engaged on the harvest. He sat down at the Lord's feet, and was fed with white bread—not the black concoction of the countryside—which the steward brought him. And the next day, when he awoke, he confidently asserted that he had been in Heaven and had fed on the bread of God.[2]

There is nothing much here that could not have happened to anyone. But it evidently made a deep impression on Anselm, for he told the story to his biographer fifty or sixty years later. And in a childish way it portrays the direction of his whole life when it becomes visible to us—the clarity and simplicity of his objective, his horror of sin, a certain unquestioning literalness of outlook, are all there in old age as they had been in childhood. The hill of God lay before him in later life inviting a moral and intellectual ascent. Although it was no longer a physical object, it was astonishingly real to him. Unbelief in any form puzzled him, especially when it took the form of putting temporal advantage before the work of God. 'Are they not Christians?' he would say, 'And if they are Christians, why should they break faith because of any temporary gain? The thing is impossible.'[3] The things which he saw intellectually, he saw with the clarity of the childhood vision, especially

---

[1] *VA* II, xxx.        [2] *VA* I, ii.        [3] *VA* II, xiv.

the pure summit which was the home of that Being who alone without qualification *is*. He could scarcely credit that others should disbelieve, or act as if they disbelieved, either in the Supreme Essence, or in any other Substance hidden from the senses but visible to the eye of the spirit.

The mountains left their impression on him, but we must not exaggerate the peaceful seclusion of his early years. Aosta was a strategical point on one of the most important routes in Europe. The Great St. Bernard, at the foot of which it lies, was one of the two main passes of the western Alps. Along this route merchants and pilgrims, and with them a steady stream of gossip and rumour, ceaselessly flowed. Anselm was well placed to know what was going on, and one of the stories of Rome in the time of Leo IX, which he later told his companions, must have reached him as a traveller's tale when he was a boy.[1] More than rumours, the valley also gathered round it the conflicting ambitions of some of the most important rulers in Europe. The town of Aosta itself lay at the extreme south of the kingdom of Burgundy, where it marched with Lombardy. In the year before Anselm was born, the last independent king of Burgundy, of the line that had established itself on the ruins of the Carolingian Empire, had died. During the next six years, the king of Germany, Conrad II, succeeded in establishing his son and successor as king of Burgundy. From this time the valley of Aosta acknowledged the authority of the German king. But the real power had passed into other hands—not however into the hands of Anselm's family, which showed signs of declining fortune in his lifetime.

In later life he sometimes talked to Eadmer about his family. Unfortunately he did not say enough, or Eadmer did not record enough, to give us a clear impression of their position in the world; but we can learn something from Eadmer's report, and more from a single letter in which Anselm has preserved some revealing details. His mother, Ermenberga, was a native of Aosta; his father, Gundulf, came to live in his wife's town.[2] Ermenberga must have been socially the more important of the two, and perhaps an heiress. Their only children were Anselm

---

[1] See *MARS*, iv, 213–16, and below, p. 141.      [2] *VA* i, i.

and his sister, Richeza.[1] The most significant fact about the family connexions, however, is supplied in one of Anselm's letters, written late in life to Humbert, Count of Savoy. In this letter Anselm speaks of the Count with fulsome respect, thanking him for his condescension in recognizing their consanguinity and declaring that 'my relatives rejoice to call themselves your vassals'.[2] This is little enough to go on, but it gives a clue to the position of Anselm's family in their native land, and may perhaps help to indicate the stock from which Anselm came.

First of all, the position of the Counts of Savoy is to be noticed. When the kingdom of Burgundy came into the hands of the kings of Germany after the failure of the royal house in 1032, it brought them very little in the way of royal authority. Here, as elsewhere, the decay of the sub-Carolingian kingdom was a symptom of the feudal struggle out of which new local families were emerging. In the valley of Aosta, and in the whole troubled and contested area between Lyons and the upper Po valley, the family which was gaining the upper hand throughout the eleventh century was the ambitious house of Savoy. By engulfing comital rights, episcopal nominations and monastic advocacies, and by building up chains of vassalage, it was slowly hammering out for itself an enduring political authority.[3] Anselm's family were related by blood and vassalage to this great family.

How they were related remains obscure. But in the obscurity we can see a family which by its name, if nothing else, invites attention. For a brief period at the beginning of the eleventh century there was a family, known to historians as the Anselmid family, which appeared to be competing with the forbears of the House of Savoy for effective power in this region of the dissolving kingdom of Burgundy. The progenitor of this rival to the House of Savoy was a certain Anselm, who died early in the eleventh century leaving three sons and a daughter in

[1] See Ep. 268 [iii, 67] where Anselm writes to Richeza: 'ego enim sum unicus frater vester'. There may of course have been other brothers who had died.
[2] Ep. 262 [iii, 65].
[3] For the feudal struggle in this area, see C. W. Previté Orton, *The Early History of the House of Savoy* (1000–1233), 1912.

important positions: one of his sons, who also bore the family name of Anselm, was bishop of Aosta and died in 1026; another was Burchard, archbishop of Vienne, who died after 1031; and a third was Ulric, advocate of his brother's archbishopric. Their sister, Ancilia, married Count Humbert Whitehands, the ancestor of the House of Savoy.[1] The later fortunes of the Anselmid family are obscure, but it is clear that, while the family of Humbert Whitehands throve and established its ascendancy through the whole district of the western Alpine passes, the Anselmid family failed to consolidate its advantages and came to nothing. Whether St. Anselm belonged to this family must remain uncertain, but his possession of the family name, his relationship with the Counts of Savoy, and his association with the Alpine area in which this family flourished, make it not improbable.

In any case, what little we know of Anselm's family all points to a condition of decayed nobility. At a later date, various members of his family tried, without much success, to make use of their kinsman's high ecclesiastical position. A cousin, Folceraldus, made his way to Bec while Anselm was abbot, and seems to have tried, and failed, to make this home a permanency.[2] Two other relatives, Haimo and Rainaldus, also visited Bec, and then disappear from sight.[3] Among these relatives, the most persistent claimant for Anselm's notice was Burgundius, the husband of his only sister. He showed signs of wanting to come to Canterbury; but Anselm warned him off in no uncertain terms.[4] Being thwarted in this direction, he then prepared to go in the wake of the Crusaders to Jerusalem. Anselm encouraged this plan, but wrote to his sister, 'if your husband returns and wishes to come to me, I expressly forbid him to do so'.[5] Evidently he was not at all well off. Burgundius either did not return or died soon after his expedition, and this left Anselm with the problem of providing for his sister. He tried to arrange for her to be received as a nun at the Cluniac house of Marcigny, and all seemed to be

---

[1] Previté Orton, pp. 10–11, 19–21, 27, 67–8.
[2] Epp. 55 [i, 46], 56 [i, 47], 110 [ii, 20], 111 [ii, 21], 209 [iii, 25].
[3] Ep. 120 [ii, 28].　　　　　　　　　[4] Ep. 258 [iii, 63].
[5] Epp. 264 [iii, 66], 268 [iii, 67].

arranged when the abbot of Chiusa stepped in to forbid the arrangement.[1] What objection this great sub-Alpine monastery could have is uncertain; but her only son had been a monk of Chiusa from childhood and the monastery may have expected to succeed to the family property. In any event, the plan for providing for his sister broke down, and Anselm was reduced to supplying her wants as occasion arose; but for her son he was able to do something more substantial.

This nephew, who bore his own name, was the only member of his family, after his mother, with whom he had any close relations. He visited the young man at the monastery of Chiusa on his way to Rome in 1098, and brought him back to England with him.[2] He was not a very bright young man. Anselm was still writing to him during his second exile, when he cannot have been less than twenty-five years old, urging him to practice writing every day, especially in prose, to prefer a plain and logical style to an obscure one, and to talk Latin whenever possible.[3] This is good advice for anybody, but it is not the kind of advice Anselm was wont to give to those for whom he felt the warmest regard. The young Anselm rose to positions of importance and died as abbot of Bury St. Edmunds, but he owed his rise to the fame of his uncle. His small niche in literary history, however, he owed to himself and to his advocacy of the new Marian devotions in an England that provided a fertile soil for these developments.[4] As a youth at Chiusa he believed himself to have been the object of a miraculous intervention on his behalf. He had spilt some wine while assisting at the celebration of Mass and in his terror he prayed to the Virgin. The stain was removed. The incident in itself was a trifling one, but it gave a direction to his whole life. He became the assiduous propagator of every type of Marian devotion, and especially of the Feast of the Conception of the Blessed Virgin, which he found tenuously established in England, and helped to turn into a European movement. This interest gave him a link with Eadmer, who was the first im-

[1] Ep. 328 [iv, 114].                    [2] VA ii, xxix.
[3] Ep. 290 [iv, 31]. Much the same advice is repeated in a later letter, Ep. 328 [iv, 114].
[4] I have discussed in detail the evidence for what follows in 'The English Origins of the "Miracles of the Virgin" ', MARS, iv, 1958, 183–200.

portant writer on this theme in Europe. But the young Anselm shared none of the speculative interests of his uncle, or even of Eadmer. His contribution to the literature of his favourite theme probably consisted of a collection of miracle stories, which achieved a vast popularity but had no literary or scholarly merits. He was an enthusiast without any perceptible distinction of mind.

The family and local background which these scattered facts disclose is complicated and obscure. Perhaps they played a larger part in Anselm's development than we can now discover, but such facts as survive point to a very casual and superficial influence which had no power to direct his life.

It was in about 1056 that Anselm broke loose from his native town.[1] His mother, to whom he was devoted, had died; and with his father, a secular and spendthrift man, he had nothing in common except a mutual dislike and incompatibility. Eadmer does his best to make Anselm appear a humble and dutiful son. But we must be cautious in crediting the virtues ascribed to young men who grow up to be saints. We only know that Anselm quarrelled with his father and left home with very little preparation. Whatever plans he had are entirely obscure. In earlier years he had felt an urge to become a monk, and then a scholar: but these ambitions had come to nothing, and in 1056 he may have had no larger purpose than escape. The footsteps of a young man in this situation can scarcely be expected to follow any very rational plan, but no doubt he had some reasons for the direction he took.

He crossed the Alps in great discomfort and some danger, when it would have been easier to go south into Italy. This however is intelligible. In Lombardy his only relations were his father's family, and they would be unlikely to help him. The kingdom of Burgundy to which his mother's family belonged lay mainly across the Alps, and they were his most likely means of support. Moreover if, as seems possible, members of the family were to be found in the region of Lyons and Vienne, this would account for his oblique movement south-west to reach the Mont Cenis pass instead of going

[1] For what follows, see *VA* I, iii.

directly over the Great St. Bernard. Support he must have found, for he could not have lived long on what he brought from his father's house. Yet, if his movements were guided by the need for support, they also had a larger significance. His choice of direction was a momentous one for his later development.

## 2. THE INFLUENCE OF LANFRANC

Eadmer reports that Anselm spent nearly three years, partly in Burgundy and partly in France. The statement is admirably precise in its chronology, but it is silent on the subjects about which we should most like to hear. What did a young man, awakening to intellectual life in the mid-eleventh century, wish to learn; what did he look for; what masters did he have? These are questions about which our notions are lamentably dim. But though the ground-work of schools and masters and scholastic exercises is obscure, we can see something of the scene which met Anselm's eyes as he came northwards through the country between the Loire and the Seine. The intellectual scene here was dominated by Berengar and Lanfranc who were doing something—with eager confidence on the one hand, and a certain reluctance on the other—which was new. They were applying the scholastic disciplines of grammar and logic, which had been agitating the schools of northern France for the last fifty years, to the discussion of a serious theological problem. The combination, which marked an epoch in the history of European thought, was being effected at the moment of Anselm's arrival in these parts.

It was the reputation of Lanfranc which brought Anselm to Normandy and to Bec. He became Lanfranc's pupil at the moment when the dispute with Berengar was at its height. He had at this time no thought of becoming a monk. His interest was in learning; and the months which followed his arrival at Bec were a time of severe and sustained intellectual labour. Lanfranc established so great an ascendency over his pupil that (as he told Eadmer) if Lanfranc had told him to stay in the forest between Rouen and Bec and never come out, he would have obeyed without hesitation.[1] Extravagant though this statement

[1] *VA* I, vi.

12

now seems, it was at the time a quite practical possibility and we must take it as being literally true. Lanfranc was Anselm's only master: behind him we can discern no large influence nearer than St. Augustine and after him, but more faintly, Boethius. To us, who know how the careers of the two men developed, the contrast between Lanfranc and Anselm is so striking that it is hard to take this phase of discipleship quite seriously. We see Lanfranc as a statesman, prudent, forceful, practical, not overweighted with scruples, nor too much concerned with fine theoretical points. We can acquit him, I am sure, of any gross deceits such as those with which his name has been too long associated;[1] but he knew the importance of ambiguity in practical affairs, and he knew that if men are to be governed they must not be expected to perform the impossible. There can be no doubt that he greatly preferred William the Conqueror as a collaborator to Pope Gregory VII; that he was more willing to tolerate the king's rough dealings with ecclesiastical discipline than the pope's intransigeance; that practical order was more important to him than a theoretical correctness of procedure. Lanfranc was a man who, having made his reputation as a scholar, only rose to his full stature in the world of practical affairs. In this he was the opposite of Anselm, whose virtues as a philosopher condemned him to comparative failure as a statesman. As archbishop, Anselm was always more concerned to ensure that every detail within his personal responsibility should be unimpeachable, than that any broad general plan should work with reasonable smoothness. To sacrifice no grain of truth to expediency, to judge details of conduct not by the test of relative advantage or disadvantage but by the principles which they illustrate, to apply an equal strictness of inquiry to every problem, and to leave nothing ambiguous which can be made plain—these are the virtues which Anselm habitually displays. It was not so much a question of choice as of instinct. Lanfranc did not choose one path and Anselm the other. They simply exhibited in their personalities two divergent modes of thought and action.

---

[1] See R. W. Southern, 'The Canterbury Forgeries', *EHR*, lxxiii, 1958, 193–226, for the literature on Lanfranc's supposed complicity in making the forged privileges of Canterbury.

These differences are clear to us, but we must not think that contemporaries saw things as we do. Especially we must beware of thinking that characteristics which are clear in later years were already clear in 1059. In this year Anselm was a young man of twenty-six; Lanfranc was about fifty. Anselm was rather old to become a devoted and enthusiastic pupil, but he still (it would seem) had academically everything to learn. As for Lanfranc, he was not yet the statesman; he was the leading scholar and philosopher in Europe. His claims to this position now seem feeble enough and they will probably not seem much stronger even when all the scattered fragments (and they are many) have been collected.[1] But the consensus of contemporary opinion is very impressive: 'he relit the light of the arts in the West'; 'he restored and renewed the art of dialectic'; 'he was raised up as a guide and a light to lead the minds of the Latins to the study of the trivium and quadrivium, which had fallen into neglect and profound obscurity'.[2] It was undoubtedly in this light that Lanfranc appeared to Anselm in 1059. There is no sign that he was disappointed by what he found.

If, however, we ask what Anselm owed to Lanfranc's influence, we ask a question which Anselm gives very little direct help in answering. There are no quotations and no acknowledgments in his works to help the inquiry. This appearance of aloofness from contemporary influences and interests has always intrigued Anselm's readers. It is deceptive. It takes no very close study of his works to discover characteristics which derive directly from Lanfranc and from the situation in which Anselm found himself in 1059. It will be convenient to distinguish these as follows:

### (i) *Method*

Anselm's works show him as a logician of great originality and power. But this originality should not, as it sometimes

---

[1] On these fragments, see B. Smalley, *The Study of the Bible in the Middle Ages*, 2nd ed., 1952, p. 69–72 and R. W. Hunt, 'Studies on Priscian in the 11th and 12th Centuries', *MARS*, i, 1943, 206–8.

[2] For these contemporary quotations, and for much of what follows, see my discussion on Lanfranc and Berengar in *Studies in Medieval History presented to F. M. Powicke*, 1948, 27–48.

does, obscure the fact that he was also extremely well grounded in the basic textbooks of eleventh century logic—the works, that is, of Aristotle and Boethius which later became known as the *Logica Vetus*. Anselm never wrote a commentary on these works: his talents were not of this kind. But he did write an introduction to dialectic, which presupposes a close familiarity with these textbooks. Unfortunately he gave it a misleading title, *De Grammatico*, which has put later scholars on to a false scent. This is the more unfortunate because of all his works it is the most difficult to understand and therefore the easiest to misinterpret. Consequently it has encountered the most hostile and even contemptuous criticism. To his enemies it has appeared an exhibition of futility, and to his friends a work to be excused on the grounds of its unimportance. Lately it has been argued that it is neither futile nor unimportant; and, by one of those revolutions in taste which have unexpected effects on the interpretations of the past, it has been discovered that Anselm was discussing questions which modern linguistic philosophers find interesting.[1] It is still too early to say what lasting effect these discoveries will have on the evaluation of the *De Grammatico*, but at least it can no longer be regarded as nonsense. Moreover, it may be said without paradox that it is difficult to understand precisely because it is elementary, and must therefore be read within the framework of eleventh century scholastic exercises. Looked on in this way it is exactly what Anselm calls it: 'an introduction to dialectic'. It is an introduction of a peculiar kind: it is not a commentary, or a summary, but a dialogue between a master and pupil, raising in an apparently casual fashion the main logical problems of the day: the relation between substance and accidents, between words and the things they represent, between the formal shape of an argument and the verbal expression of it, between dialectic and grammar, between genuine and sophistical arguments. It is an 'advanced' introduction, for those who have come to the end of the beginning and can start to use the contents of their textbooks. It seems that Anselm, even as a schoolmaster, could not help doing things in an

---

[1] See D. P. Henry, 'Why "Grammaticus"?', *Archivum Latinitatis Medii Aevi*, xxviii, 1958, 165–80.

original way, intelligible no doubt to his immediate pupils, but puzzling to those who do not know their basic books and assumptions.

It is highly unlikely that Anselm's *De Grammatico* would have survived if it had not been preserved among his other works of more lasting interest. Apart from them, it would have gone the way of the other school books of the day, of which only fragments survive. Among these lost school books are the *Dialectica* of Lanfranc and his *Quaestiones*, which are now known only because they appear in eleventh century library catalogues. But to contemporaries it was precisely as a logician that Lanfranc especially shone. Of this side of Lanfranc's work the only traces are in contemporary judgments, in Lanfranc's glosses on St. Paul, and in his treatise against Berengar. These however are enough to show that his professed reluctance to introduce dialectic into theological questions was not due to any lack of proficiency in the art. Quite the contrary. His was the modest disclaimer of an expert in the subject, who thereby hoped to expose the brash over-confidence of his opponent. And that Lanfranc *was* the expert in the subject appears not only from the way in which he is careful to point out the logical structure behind the arguments of St. Paul, not only from his familiarity with the logical writings of Boethius which he shows in writing against Berengar, not only in the words of contemporaries, but even in the terms in which he disclaims any intention of using dialectic in theological questions:

Even if the matter in dispute is such that it could be more clearly explained by the rules of this art (of dialectic) I prefer so far as I can to conceal my art by equipollency of propositions, lest I seem to rely on art rather than truth and the authority of the holy Fathers.[1]

This remark is often quoted as an example of Lanfranc's anti-dialectical tendency: it is not so often observed that the whole manner of the excuse expresses the pride of the expert, and indeed is only intelligible to someone who has an advanced knowledge of dialectic.

Lanfranc could not have turned Anselm into an original

---

[1] *Liber de Corpore et Sanguine Domini* cap. vii, (ed. J. A. Giles, ii, 160).

logician because he was not one himself. But it is doubtful whether Anselm's talent as a logician would ever have developed without the stimulus of the dialectic of which Lanfranc was a master. In its limitations as well as its virtues this art was an essential part of Anselm's intellectual equipment.

(ii) *Books*

The direct references in Anselm's works to other men's books can be very briefly listed. In the Prologue to the *Monologion* and in his *Epistola De Incarnatione* he refers to Augustine's *De Trinitate*.[1] In the *De Grammatico* he has many references—more numerous than all his other references here or elsewhere to all other authors put together—to Aristotle's *Categories*.[2] In the *Cur Deus Homo* he quotes Aristotle's *De Interpretatione*.[3] In the *Epistola De Incarnatione* he describes (in order to refute) the views of Roscelin and other modern dialecticians.[4] That is all. Indirectly, there is ample evidence of an entire familiarity with a large range of St. Augustine's works and of the whole body of Aristotelian logic transmitted in the translations and commentaries of Boethius; but it is not possible to speak with confidence about other influences except those of the Bible and the Rule of St. Benedict. In Anselm's correspondence there is convincing evidence that he was familiar with, and could use in a casual way, the works of Horace, Virgil, Lucan and Persius; and to this list of classical authors we should perhaps add Terence.[5] What is more revealing in these letters is Anselm's interest in procuring unusual texts from English libraries, and using his English connexions to obtain a more correct text of Bede's *De ratione temporum* than he had at Bec.[6] His letters about copying books show that he had the instincts of a careful and acquisitive librarian. Eadmer also draws attention to his

---

[1] Schmitt, i, 8; ii, 20, 35.  [2] Schmitt, i, 154, 162–5.
[3] Schmitt, ii, 125.  [4] Schmitt, ii, 4.
[5] For Horace, see Epp. 2 [i, 2], 57 [i, 48]; for Virgil Ep. 2 [1, 2]; for Persius Epp. 19 and 20 [i, 19, 20]; for Lucan Ep. 115 [ii, 25]. A possible reminiscence of Terence is in *Cur Deus Homo*, II, xvi. It should be added that most of these quotations are not common tags, but imply a ready familiarity with the poets.  [6] Epp. 42 [i, 34], 43 [i, 35], 60 [i, 51].

care for textual accuracy, and this too was a habit in which he followed in Lanfranc's footsteps.[1] The list of books mentioned by Anselm, though it must be absurdly incomplete as a picture of his reading, is not entirely uninformative. The wide range of his knowledge of St. Augustine and Boethius would not have been possible except in a carefully stocked library. He could be selective because he knew the important books, and could cut through the trivialities of contemporary discussion. Without his knowledge it is impossible to write central works on central themes in any subject. The relative absence of quotations in Anselm's works is a reflection of his confident command of the literature of Christian theology, and not of the paucity of his sources. No one who reads him will doubt this. He was not a bold or impetuous innovator. His inclination was to cling to authority and custom; and in his most personal and original works we shall find traces of a large literature and of a familiar tradition on which he builds. Far more than their surface appearance would suggest, his works required for their conception and writing access to a good library, and to a library kept fresh by use. There were not many places in Europe in the mid-eleventh century where these conditions were fulfilled. In some places there were the books, but not the active use which made them intelligible; in other places there were school books, with little patristic theology; in others again, the Fathers without up-to-date scholastic handbooks. It was Lanfranc who made Bec a place where the combination of all these elements required for Anselm's works was to be met with. It was Lanfranc who provided the materials and the technical equipment for their use.

It is unfortunate for Lanfranc's reputation that the library of Bec has almost entirely disappeared. Lanfranc's work as a collector of books must be sought at Canterbury, his later creation. The evidence there is impressive, and something must be said about it in another chapter. For the present it is important only to notice that in his creation (it is hardly less) of a library at Canterbury, Lanfranc was following a model he

---

[1] *VA* I, viii. For Lanfranc, see *Vita Lanfranci*, cap. 48 (ed. Giles, *Lanfranci Opera*, i, 310).

18

had already established at Bec: the twelfth century catalogue
from Bec, and the similarity between the few remaining volumes
from Bec and those from Canterbury, tell the same story of a
single guiding plan.[1] Lanfranc's books reveal his character
and aims as much as anything in his public life. The simple
and stately volumes, beautiful in their clarity and astonishing
in their accuracy, are a monument to Lanfranc's orderly and
practical spirit. They do not display the foibles of the biblio-
phile or of the searcher for out-of-the-way texts; they are books
to be used by a scholar. They contain the central works of
Latin Christianity, and the more closely they can be associated
with Lanfranc the more central they are. Every one of the
few volumes from Canterbury which Dr. Dodwell is prepared
to ascribe definitely to the time of Lanfranc is a work of one
of the four chief Latin Fathers—Ambrose, Augustine, Jerome
or Gregory—and several of these volumes bear signs of the
care with which Lanfranc read and annotated them.

A study of Lanfranc's annotations would be worth making,
not for their ideas—for they rarely contain anything beyond the
barest grammatical and structural explanations—but because
they are the best indication of the range of his learned influence,
and the repute in which he was held. They show him not only
as a great library builder but a great influence in the library-
building of others. The texts which he assembled were copied
far and wide, even with the peculiar system of marginal
annotation for which he seems to have been responsible;[2] and
many scribes gathered the fragments of Lanfranc's teaching
from the margins of his manuscripts. This teaching was not

---

[1] The identity of plan can be made out only in a very fragmentary way,
but the few surviving pieces of evidence are extremely suggestive. On this
subject see C. R. Dodwell, *The Canterbury School of Illumination* 1066–1200,
1954, pp. 6–20 and Plate 4.

[2] Z. N. Brooke was the first to point out that in Lanfranc's manuscript
of canon law (Trinity College, Cambridge, MS. B. 16.44) there are a large
number of symbols in the margin, in the form of an 'a' with two dots,
thus: .a. (*The English Church and the Papacy*, 1931, p. 68). These marks
are often found in Canterbury manuscripts of the period, and in some of
the few manuscripts of Bec. It would seem that Lanfranc brought this
system of annotation from Bec and that it became established at Canterbury.
When Canterbury manuscripts were copied for other libraries these marks
were often copied with the text, with the result that they can be found in a
very large number of English manuscripts of the twelfth century.

exciting. It consisted mostly of such comments as this on Job XXII, 6 *Abstulisti enim pignus fratrum tuorum*:

Pignus, pignoris: filius vel consanguineus.
Lucanus: 'Pignora nulla domus, nulli coiere propinqui.'
Pignus, pigneris: quod pro debito aliquo debetur.[1]

This was the kind of work for which Anselm had no talent: *tu scis* (he later wrote) *quia molestum mihi semper fuerit pueris declinare*.[2] Lanfranc was a schoolmaster, Anselm a man of original genius. But he needed Lanfranc's books, accurate in their texts, systematic in their collection, carefully read and annotated, for the development of his genius.

### (iii) *The Beginnings of Discussion*

Just as it is difficult to recognize the school-logic of the period or the use of a substantial library behind Anselm's works, so it is difficult to see a connexion between Lanfranc's angry dispute with Berengar and the development of Anselm as a theologian. Both the spirit and the substance of Anselm's works seem far removed from this controversy. Unlike some other pupils of Lanfranc who rose up to defend or expound the master's views, Anselm never mentioned the subject. The violent vituperation, which disfigured both sides, found no reflection in the placid surface of Anselm's early works, in which the spirit of contention is wholly lacking. Yet it would be strange if Anselm's aloofness from the controversy and its results were as complete as the first impression would suggest. It must have been the reputation which Lanfranc was making in this controversy which drew Anselm to Bec. This controversy was inflaming popular passions as no theological issue had done for hundreds of years; and to come to Bec at this moment was to take a side. Lanfranc was either on the point of going, or more probably had just returned from, the Lateran

---

[1] This comes from a series of glosses on the book of Job preserved in two manuscripts, Tours 317, f. 190v. and Bodleian, Laud misc. 5, f. 11. In the Tours MS., they have the heading: 'Dicta Lanfranci archiepiscopi in Job'. The most likely explanation for their origin is that they were marginal annotations by Lanfranc, and that they were found sufficiently interesting to be extracted from their context and circulated separately.

[2] Ep. 64 [i, 55].

Council of April 1059, at which the humiliation of Berengar had been accomplished, when Anselm arrived. Anselm's choice of Lanfranc at this moment must have been made with the whole sequence of events in the controversy fully in view. Moreover, in the years which followed, when Berengar defended his views against his opponents and Lanfranc replied, the dispute continued to be the centre of theological interest. The works of the two rivals are confused, ill-tempered and painful to read. But the faults of the authors must not obscure the importance of their conflict. It brought a renewal of serious theological debate, and it demonstrated once and for all the relevance of logic and grammar as instruments in the discussion of theological problems. It is hard to think that a young man could anywhere have found more to think about than at the centre of this controversy.

Anselm never mentioned the controversy in his later writings, but he benefited from it. He felt the freedom which it brought. Theology could never again be simply a matter of collecting and arranging the thoughts of earlier and greater writers. However important, essential even and basic, this process might be, it was not the end. Different though they were in temperament and outlook, Lanfranc and Berengar were an effective combination in promoting the rights of the secular disciplines—grammar and logic in the first place—as instruments in the settlement of doctrinal disputes. They were effective because they were so different. Berengar, the sanguine assertor of the rights of dialectic, both claimed to be, and in an important sense was, the upholder of conservative views on the theological issue. Lanfranc, who would probably have preferred the approaches of theology and dialectic to remain at the timid level exemplified in his own glosses, in the end went further than Berengar or any previous writer in explaining the Eucharist in language borrowed from the science of logic. It was Lanfranc who first distinctly described the change in the Eucharistic elements in terms of the Aristotelian categories of substance and accidents.[1] Despite all his uncertainties of

---

[1] This is a point which, I think, has not been sufficiently appreciated in the literature on the subject: I have tried to amplify it in *Studies in Medieval History presented to F. M. Powicke*, pp. 39–41.

language, and all his expressions of reluctance to intermingle the sacred and secular disciplines, it was he who made Boethius and Aristotle the instruments of explanation of the Christian mystery. It was a bold step, which Lanfranc with his conservative temper would scarcely have taken without the stimulus of popular support and the favour of such powerful advocates at the papal court as Cardinal Humbert. Yet it was he who took the step and effectively introduced a new factor into theological discussion.

Lanfranc's victory over Berengar was the first victory of Aristotelian thought in a matter of wide general importance in the Middle Ages. Anselm himself was not Aristotelian in his philosophical outlook; he was an old-fashioned neo-Platonist. But this did not prevent him accepting the application of Aristotelian logic to theological questions as a matter of course. And it was not merely in the general atmosphere of discussion that Anselm belonged to the period after the Eucharistic dispute. There are in his works echoes of the arguments and procedures developed by both sides in the course of this conflict.

We have seen that Lanfranc in his reply to Berengar expressed a preference for conducting his argument by means of equipollent propositions rather than by formal syllogisms, lest, as he said, he should seem to rely on art rather than on truth and the authority of the Fathers. It is not at all easy to find in Lanfranc's works examples of the procedure he had in mind, but it is fairly clear what he meant. It may briefly be illustrated by the following argument. If we wish to show that 'whatever is true is just', we can either set the argument out in some form of syllogism as:

> Whatever is true is right,
> But whatever is right is just,
> Therefore whatever is true is just,

Or we can proceed by showing that various statements are strictly equipollent or equivalent to each other, as:

A true statement is one which describes things as they really are;
A statement which describes things as they really are describes things justly;

A statement which describes things justly has the quality of justice;
A true statement therefore has the quality of justice;
But a statement which describes things as they really are has the
   quality of truth;
Therefore that which makes a statement true also makes it just;
Therefore whatever is true is just.

The reason why Lanfranc claimed to prefer the second
method of argument is that the first method is more obviously
a creation of art than the second; it is magisterial, intellectual,
dialectical.

The second method, by contrast, proceeds by way of
enlarging a definition; it is closely tied to the explanation of a
text or a word. Hence there is in it less of the master. Now,
although it is difficult to find examples of this method in
Lanfranc's works, it is to be found everywhere in Anselm. He
has a strong preference for proceeding by definitions and
equipollent propositions rather than by means of syllogisms.
The example just given is taken with little alteration from
Anselm's *De Veritate*.[1] Instead of the syllogistic form:

> All A is D
> But all B is A
> Therefore all B is D

the kind of argument he prefers takes the form:

> A = B = C = D
> Therefore A = D.

Lanfranc professed to base his preference for this method on
modesty and caution, but there was another reason for his
preference which he might have mentioned. The science of
logic was not clearly distinguished from that of grammar, and
all the scholars of his generation—including Berengar and
Anselm—were grammarians before they were logicians. They
were grammarians at heart. That is to say, they were concerned primarily with the definitions of words and the explanations of texts. It was therefore very natural to prefer a method
of argument which started from a text or a word, and to regard

---

[1] Schmitt, i, 178: *De Veritate*, cap. 2.

23

with some suspicion a method which drew conclusions from general propositions.

Before leaving this subject we may notice an argument on Berengar's side which throws some further light on the intellectual atmosphere in which Anselm grew to maturity. The argument on which Berengar placed most reliance was one which may be stated thus:

No statement is valid in which the subject is destroyed by the predicate or vice versa.[1]

Berengar applied this principle to the words of consecration in the Mass, *Hoc* (indicating the Eucharistic Bread) *est corpus meum*. According to the grammarians of the day pronouns stood for the substance of things considered apart from their accidents. Hence the pronoun *Hoc* indicated the substance of the Bread. But on Lanfranc's view the substance of the Bread ceased to exist as a result of the words of consecration. Thus in the statement *Hoc est corpus meum*, the subject of the sentence (the substance of the Bread) would be destroyed by the predicate. But since this would invalidate the statement from a logical and grammatical point of view by leaving the predicate without a subject, Berengar felt that he could safely leave his attack on the nascent doctrine of transubstantiation to the force of this one argument alone.

We are not concerned either with the validity of Berengar's argument or with Lanfranc's attempt to answer it. We are concerned only with the light which it throws on the intellectual processes of the time. Here we have an attempt to deduce from grammatical structure alone a truth about the nature of the sacramental reality. Although the argument was peculiar to Berengar, it belonged to a class of puzzles which attracted much attention in the eleventh century: what is the relation between words and the reality they express? between logical

---

[1] The argument is stated in various slightly different ways in the course of the controversy. In its first appearance it has the form: 'Non enim constare poterit affirmatio omnis, parte subruta'. (Lanfranc *De Corpore et Sanguine Domino*, cap. vii, where his reply is quite inadequate). Berengar repeats it and amplifies it in his *De Sacra Coena*: 'omnis enuntiatio amissa parte altera utra, predicatum dico atque subiectum, constare non poterit' (p. 234). See further *Studies presented to F. M. Powicke*, pp. 44–7.

necessity and necessary being? between the *ordo disserendi* and the *ordo naturae*? Anselm in due course formed a view on these problems of his time. His famous argument for the existence of God is a special case of one of these problems. It is an attempt to deduce from the definition of a word something about the reality it expresses. In form the argument is closely similar to that of Berengar. Berengar had asserted the continued existence of the substance of the consecrated Bread as a consequence of the grammatical structure of the sentence *Hoc est corpus meum*. In a similar way Anselm tried to show that in the sentence 'God does not exist' the necessary implication of the subject is destroyed in the predicate, and therefore this sentence must be invalid and strictly meaningless. Whether either he or Berengar succeeded in making good their claim is another question, but formally at least what they are doing was precisely the same.

Nevertheless between Lanfranc and Berengar on the one side and Anselm on the other, there was a great gulf. Lanfranc and Berengar were scholars applying a technique of argument and exegesis to the discussion of a theological question that had arisen accidentally. Their rival views, though fiercely canvassed, are foreign to the main body of their work. They might have changed sides, and nothing in their other writings would warn the reader that something was wrong. Able and powerful men though they were, they were by no possible extension of the words either philosophers or theologians. Anselm on the other hand was both a philosopher and a theologian. Everything that he wrote so far as it touches on either philosophy or theology is coherent, and, to speak bluntly, alive. Even when his ideas seem wrong, they have a power of persuasion which seems to be independent of their truth. This force arises, partly at least, from the clarity and coherence of Anselm's thoughts. These were qualities which Lanfranc achieved only in practical affairs. Hence, although Lanfranc gave Anselm his impulse to work, equipped him with the necessary tools, and pointed the way to the combination of theology and dialectic, the two men had intellectually little in common. But this was something hidden from both of them in 1059.

Lanfranc left Bec in 1063. The two men never ceased to

address each other with affection and respect, but, though
Anselm continued 'his servant in subjection, his son in affection, his disciple in doctrine', Lanfranc's part in the formation
of his pupil was finished. There was one critical moment when
Anselm sent the archbishop his first work, the *Monologion*.
Lanfranc showed his disapproval very clearly and there is no
sign that Anselm sent him any of the other works which he
wrote during the next ten years. When Lanfranc died, there is
good reason to think that Anselm wrote the long and eulogistic
epitaph which has been preserved.[1] It praises his generosity,
his austerity, his love of justice and mercy, the loss suffered by
the Church through his death, the duty and the profit of
prayer for his soul. But a single colourless line served to recall
the teacher. It had once been his greatest title to fame, but it
was so soon sinking into oblivion. Lanfranc incurred the
penalty of a scholar who had become great in another sphere.
When Berengar died, the two best poets of the day celebrated
in lofty epitaphs his fame as a philosopher and poet.[2] His
scholarly reputation suffered less from his condemnation and
later obscurity than Lanfranc's from his success and great
position. We must regret that Anselm, who thirty years earlier
had been Lanfranc's greatest pupil when his master's reputation
resounded throughout Europe, did not take the opportunity of
his death to recall the teacher of those days. But in the interval
he had perhaps gone too far to look back.

---

[1] The epitaph is in *PL* CLVIII, 1049–50. It is preserved only in a MS.
from Bec, Vat. Reginensis 499, but it is almost certainly referred to by
Ordericus Vitalis, iii, 309: 'Beccensis autem Anselmus supra scriptam
compatriotae sui memoriam heroico carmine volumini lacrymabiliter indidit.'
Presumably he intended to give the text of this epitaph, as he did of many
others, in his History, but for some reason failed to do so.

[2] Hildebert, *Epitaphium Berengarii*, *PL* CLXXI, 1396–7; Baudri de Bour-
gueil, 'Super domnum Berengarium' in *Les Œuvres poétiques de Baudri*, ed.
P. Abrahams, 1926, p. 82.

# CHAPTER II

# THE MONK OF BEC

## I. THE YEARS OF SILENCE

THIRTY years separate the Anselm who came to Bec from the Anselm who heard of Lanfranc's death. Another four years were still to pass before he became Lanfranc's successor as archbishop. But by 1089 Anselm's first period of authorship was over, and the new more contentious conditions in which he was to pass the remainder of his life were already in sight. The previous thirty years are the period of his brightest and freshest work. Theologians may prefer the later *Cur Deus Homo*, but those who examine Anselm's works less for the contribution which they make to major issues than for the light which they throw on his mind and character will prefer the works of the earlier period. It was while he was at Bec that he wrote under the strong impulse of new thoughts and sentiments, and in the first consciousness of his powers.

It is unlikely that anything we now possess was written before 1070, when he was already thirty-seven years old. For these works, the years between 1059 and 1070 were a time of preparation. They may be divided into two periods of unequal length.

## (i) *1059–60*

The transformation of the pupil of Lanfranc into the monk of Bec did not take place without a crisis in Anselm's life. In coming to Lanfranc, he had committed himself to a life of scholarship, and to the revival of his early intellectual ambition. But on the heels of this, an even earlier love revived. As a child he had wanted to become a monk, and now in a rather naïve way the hard labour of scholarship suggested that with no greater sacrifice of ease he might win a greater reward.[1] It

---

[1] *VA* I, v.

27

was thus, as he told his biographer, that his monastic inclinations revived. Various choices now presented themselves. He could become a monk at Bec: but then (he reflected) the presence of Lanfranc would make his newly acquired learning quite useless—there was no room for them both in one community. Or he could become a monk at Cluny. It is a striking testimony to the contemporary prominence of Cluny, that this should have appeared the only possible monastic alternative. But then (he reflected), if Bec gave him no chance to shine as a scholar, Cluny with its arduous routine would leave him no energy to do so. He was the first of many to express this criticism of Cluny's over-filled day, but by the time that others took up the cry, his own voice was on the other side.[1]

The third possibility which occurred to him was that he might become a hermit, and historically this is the most interesting of all his reflections. For if he had gone into Italy, instead of coming north in 1056, the chances of the hermitage being his final choice would have been much increased. There is very much in his later writings which suggests that the life of solitude and contemplation was more suited to his natural inclination than the life of a monastic community. In this inclination he was expressing a strong contemporary impulse. There is no more significant pointer to the re-orientation of religious tastes in the late eleventh century than the new light in which the eremitical life came to be seen. Instead of the lonely warfare against the evil spirits and the savage mental conflict of which we hear in earlier literature, we begin to hear of the sweetness of solitude, the pleasant springs and refreshing breezes, and the unhindered communion with God.[2] Such phrases are an unconscious testimony to a spiritual revolution, and it was from Italy that the breeze blew which carried the message all over Europe. The old cities of Italy, Ravenna,

---

[1] See below, p. 349.
[2] The founder of the eremitical movement in Italy was St. Romuald who was born at Ravenna about 950. His life was written by Peter Damian, and the following description of one of his hermitages taken from this work gives an indication of the new spirit: 'Postremo repertus est . . . locus eremiticae conversationis satis congruus, montibus undique vallatus et silvis; in medio vero ampla quaedam planities non solum proferendis frugibus apta, sed perspicuis etiam fontium aquis rigua.' *PL* CXLV, cap. XXXV.

Venice and the cities of the south, with their Byzantine connexions and their unadventurous intellectual life, seem to have had the power to produce a succession of men like Romuald, the founder of the hermitage at Camaldoli, and Peter Damian, to proclaim the joys of the life of solitude. Anselm would have been at home with such men, but he would have lost the intellectual discipline of the north which elicited the peculiar powers of his mind. By the end of his life the message of solitude had spread far and wide, but at the time of which we speak it is roughly true that, though the geographical picture was becoming blurred, the Cluniac ideal of monastic life dominated the north, and the eremitical life flourished chiefly in Italy.

The fourth choice which presented itself to Anselm seems to have been closely connected with the eremetical ideal: he thought he might live on his patrimony and dispense alms to the poor. He may here also have been influenced by recollections of the south; for it is in Italy that we find hospitals and hermitages, both harbingers of later religious ideals, growing up side by side, and presenting an alternative to the corporate life of the Benedictine monastery.[1]

These possible choices provide a sort of map of the opportunities open to a spiritually ambitious young man in the middle years of the eleventh century. All Anselm's considerations, however, came to nothing. Like many another, he discovered that the arguments for different courses of action were too nicely balanced for the exercise of choice. 'My will was not yet tamed,' he said later; and in a fit of self-disgust he threw himself on the authority of Lanfranc and Maurilius, archbishop of Rouen.[2] The archbishop, himself a monk, had already in the previous year encouraged a former member of his household, Gundulf, to become a monk of Bec.[3] With

---

[1] The chief founder of hospitals in Italy at this time seems to have been St. John Gualbert, the founder of the monastery of Vallombrosa. Like Anselm he had been torn between the monastic and the eremitical life, and like Anselm finally chose the former. See his *Life* in *MGH.SS.* xxx, ii, 1087: 'Quae usque ad suum tempus per Tusciam erant hospitalia? . . . Hospitalia tot et tanta huius exemplo et exortatu iam videmus nunc per Tusciam edificata et ecclesias vetustissimas tot renovatas, ut nos cogant dicere "Ecce vetera transierunt et facta sunt omnia nova".'

[2] *VA* i, vi.          [3] *Gundulfi Roffensis episcopi Vita*, PL CLIX, 815–16.

such advisers, there could be no doubt which way the decision would go. Like Gundulf, Anselm became a monk of Bec.


(ii) *1060–70*

In 1060, Anselm turned from both scholarship and solitude to the corporate life of religion, and for ten years we hear nothing that can confidently be said about him. He wrote nothing, or nothing which has survived. All the signs are of a total dedication to the duties of the monastic life. He never wrote a treatise on the Benedictine rule, and what he wrote professedly about the monastic life can be brought into a very small compass. But his thoughts and actions as they slowly unfold themselves bear impressive marks of his monastic dedication. The principle of obedience to authority was the foundation of his life and thought; and by this he did not mean obedience as a code of external action and mental submission as men ordinarily interpret the word. He meant a loyalty intensely conceived and meticulously observed. Something of what this implied in political action and in moral teaching we shall later observe.

Anselm lived for three years as a simple monk; then, when in 1063 Lanfranc went to Caen, he became prior at the age of thirty. This change brought a great alteration in Anselm's position in the community. It brought him also some hostility. The situation which had made him, in his 'untamed' state, hesitate to become a monk at Bec was now at an end. He was left with no scholastic rival in the community. But it is likely that the ambition to shine which had caused his hesitation was now dead. Certainly he seems to have made no attempt to rival Lanfranc in his fame as a teacher. In Lanfranc Bec had lost its great luminary, and for a time it must have seemed once more a poor and undistinguished community. Anselm's only pupils appear to have been members of the community; it was probably only much later that strangers came to him for the solution of their problems. He seems to have abandoned, or only unwillingly given his mind to, formal teaching. We hear no more of the school of Bec in the form in which it had developed under Lanfranc.[1] The children in the monastery of course still required instruction, but this was not a task for which Anselm had any aptitude. His talent was for those of more mature years within the community, whose wax was neither too soft nor too hard.[2] Eadmer did not know him in those days, so he cannot give us a clear idea of the times and occasions at which Anselm talked with these pupils; but it is probable that many of his ideas were first expressed in sermons in the daily chapter, and that from them arose the discussions, which were later incorporated in the treatises.

Since Anselm wrote nothing until his ideas were fully formed, the stages in his intellectual development cannot be established, but these years must have been a time of steady application to the works of St. Augustine. It was his claim that in his earliest work he was doing little more than re-think the thoughts of Augustine:

It was my intention (he says in writing to Lanfranc about the *Monologion*) throughout the whole of this disputation to assert nothing which could not be immediately defended either from canonical writers or from the words of St. Augustine. And however often I look over what I have written, I cannot see that I have asserted anything other than this. Indeed no reasoning of my own, however conclusive it seemed, would have persuaded me to be the first to presume to say those things which you have copied from my work in your letter, nor several other things besides. St. Augustine proved these points in the great discussions in his *De Trinitate*, so that I, having as it were uncovered them in my shorter chain of argument, say them on his authority.[3]

This was his defence when Lanfranc criticized his first work and advised him to add references to his authorities. We may sympathize with Lanfranc. No doubt he had never known the works of Augustine as Anselm knew them; the references which were clear to Anselm were hidden from him. Yet it is

---

[1] There is no sign under Anselm that secular scholars who had no intention of becoming monks came to study at Bec as they had under Lanfranc. For this feature of Lanfranc's school we have the evidence of Alexander II and his nephews; of Anselm himself; of Ordericus Vitalis, ii, 210; William of Malmesbury, *GP* 38; and Gilbert Crispin, *Vita Herluini*, p. 97 (ed. J. A. Robinson, *Gilbert Crispin, Abbot of Westminster*).
[2] *VA* i, xi.       [3] Ep. 77 [i, 68].

puzzling that the name of Augustine is never mentioned in Anselm's earliest works, and that the single reference in the prologue to the *Monologion* was evidently a result of Lanfranc's protest. Why should Anselm have been so secretive? There is a psychological puzzle here, which is not entirely solved by pointing out that Anselm's method required that he should not quote authorities. Nor is it entirely solved by the reflection that the deeper the influence the more difficult it is to express, and the more inadequately it is expressed by quotations. This reflection would certainly be true, yet the ambivalence of Anselm's relations to St. Augustine remains one of the mysteries of his mind and personality. Augustine's thought was the pervading atmosphere in which Anselm moved; but he was never content merely to reproduce Augustine. From the beginning we can see that Anselm is wholly Augustinian in his general theological programme, but in the course of time he diverged very widely from some of Augustine's main positions. Anselm's language was formed on that of Augustine; but his sentences have a precision, elegance and balance that are quite his own. Anselm followed Augustine in his conception of the relations between Faith and Reason, but so far as he allows us to see he had never known doubt. The circumstances, education, and the habits of mind of the two men were wholly dissimilar. Augustine is full of a knowledge of the world and a sense of history: Anselm knew almost nothing of the world, and his system of thought is remarkable for its lack of historical sense and its entire reliance on logical consistency. If Augustine is like an ocean, tempestuous, variegated, and with contradictory currents, Anselm is a narrow channel, clear-cut, lucid, admitting no extraneous elements. Anselm's greatest and most characteristic phrases can always be traced back in the direction of Augustine, but the trail disappears before it reaches him: 'Fides quaerens intellectum'; '*Deus*: aliquid quo maius nihil cogitari potest'; '*Veritas*: rectitudo mente sola perceptibilis'; '*Iustitia*: rectitudo voluntatis propter se servata'; '*Libertas arbitrii*: potestas servandi rectitudinem voluntatis propter ipsam rectitudinem'.

One notable thing about these phrases is that they are all definitions of words except the first—and that is the definition of a programme wholly Augustinian, but expressed with a conciseness that did not come from Augustine. Anselm had the gift of precision; he had not the abounding flow of ideas of Augustine. Augustine is prodigal and scatters his thoughts unsystematically and with a lavish hand: Anselm has a smaller supply which he lays out to the best advantage. No treatise of Anselm, except the *De Grammatico*, can be discussed without reference to Augustine, yet everything has undergone a change, and this becomes more pronounced as time goes on. Anselm, at his first appearance as a writer, was and claimed to be an *Augustinus minor*; but he was an Augustine formed by the logic, grammar and monastic life of the eleventh century, instead of the terrible stresses caused by the ruin of the ancient world.

The first impression Anselm's writings make is one of youthful brilliance and intensity. Yet they are the result of a long preparation and intense study. We have nothing which Anselm wrote till he was nearly forty, and his greatest works came either when he was forty-five or over sixty years old. This is surprising. To judge from the example of those who are nearest to him in genius, his mind was of the kind which develops early. The clear, original thoughts of mathematical precision are not of the kind which normally require laborious preparation. They come early or not at all. The same is true of the intense expressions of friendship in Anselm's early letters. Anselm's strength did not lie, as did that of later medieval theologians, in the mastery of a vast and intricate mass of materials. This must take time. Yet even Thomas Aquinas and later Duns Scotus, who wrote when the materials to be co-ordinated were most abundant, had already produced great works of massive comprehension, and the latter was dead, before they reached the age at which Anselm began to write. But they lived when the path was clear. Anselm had to find his path; he had to find his master; and then his final monastic choice did not point towards authorship. The monastic vocation was intended equally as a renunciation of learned ambitions and as a turning away from a life of solitary contemplation. Strangely enough, in the event, it led to the brilliant expression of precisely those two sides of his nature on which he had turned his back—his love of 'letters' and his love of solitary contemplation.

## 2. THE PRAYERS AND MEDITATIONS

Anselm began quite suddenly, about 1070, to write things which he wished to preserve for posterity. The *De Grammatico*, which has much of the appearance of an early work, and some of his prayers may be a few years earlier than this date; but not much, if at all. We can be quite sure that no early works which he would have liked to preserve have been lost. To a remarkable degree he was able to determine both the form and content of what we know of his thoughts. They are as near perfect as he could make them. When he corrected a work, as he sometimes did, his second thoughts differ in only minute details from his first. He worked as an artist to whom form and content were very closely allied. There is none of that sprawling untidiness of composition which distinguishes so many medieval works. In Anselm's works, the few exceptions to this rule of perfectly finished literary production can be accounted for by exceptional circumstances. For example, the fairly wide differences in the recensions of the *De Incarnatione Verbi* were caused by the impatience of pupils who snatched his work and copied it before it was complete.[1] The only important example of Anselm making substantial additions to a work which he had once finished is the long prayer to the Virgin Mary.[2] Here the novelty and difficulty of the formulae he elaborated may account for the development. But even here the alterations are quite small compared with the wide differences in the recensions of other authors. They are simply a few new bricks inserted into an edifice already essentially complete.

This literary fastidiousness has nowhere been less evident

[1] See F. S. Schmitt, 'Cinq recensions de l'Epistola de Incarnatione Verbi', in *Revue Bénédictine*, li, 1939, 275–87. I think that Dom Schmitt exaggerates the number of recensions (see *MARS* i, 1941, 32–4), but this does not affect the principle. Anselm himself complains of the premature circulation of his work in the Preface to *Cur Deus Homo*, but no imperfect recensions of this work have yet been found.

[2] See A. Wilmart, 'Les propres corrections de S. Anselme dans sa grande prière à la Vierge Marie', *RTAM*, ii, 1930, 189–204. A different recension which may be earlier than any of those discussed by Dom Wilmart is in St. John's College, Oxford, MS 165 (see *VA* p. xxi).

to modern eyes than in the *Prayers and Meditations* printed under Anselm's name. The reason for this is very simple. Whereas the main theological treatises, and even the letters, made up a body of writings which offered little scope for imitation or adaptation, the devotional works opened up a field of expression in which Anselm had many imitators. They belonged to a class of literature where every man felt free, and rightly, to make what alterations and additions he pleased. Within a very short time of Anselm's death the genuine collection was enlarged by some prayers and meditations of his pupil Ralph; and in the fourteenth century, when Anselm's name had become a pass-word to fame for a host of anonymous writings, the collection was further and much more grotesquely swollen.[1] By the time the seventeenth century editor set to work, the tradition was hopelessly confused; unless he had been assisted by great good fortune in finding the right manuscripts, or great acumen in seeing through their confusions, his chance of cutting his way through the accumulation of centuries was small. The editor had neither good fortune nor good judgment. He printed what he found, and what he found was very much; seventy-four prayers (many of considerable length), twenty-one meditations and sixteen homilies were printed under Anselm's name. For over two hundred years, until some thirty years ago, it was impossible to tell the genuine from the false; they were all quoted, though sometimes without much conviction, to illustrate various sides of Anselm's thought. This was the state of affairs when the great Benedictine scholar, Dom Wilmart, took the matter in hand. When he had finished, only nineteen prayers, three meditations and no homilies remained—a total of twenty-two pieces out of a hundred and eleven. But what we now have is indisputably genuine. For the first time it is possible to form a true picture of Anselm as a devotional writer—a picture which was hidden even from his earliest successors.

[1] For the growth of the collection of prayers, see especially A. Wilmart's preface to D. A. Castel, *Méditations et Prières de S. Anselme*, Collection Pax, xi, 1923; for the homilies, of which none are authentic, A. Wilmart, 'Les homélies attribuées à saint Anselme', *Archives d'Histoire doctrinale et littéraire du Moyen Age*, ii, 1927, 5–29. For Ralph, see below, p. 206. The genuine Prayers and Meditations are in vol. iii of Schmitt.

Of the twenty-two prayers and meditations which are genuine, seven (six prayers and a meditation) had been written by 1071 when Anselm sent copies of them to Adelaide, a daughter of William the Conqueror; and it is possible that another meditation which he did not send was also in existence by this time.[1] In the following year he sent three new prayers to his friend Gundulf, who had gone to Canterbury with Lanfranc.[2] Within the next three or four years the collection became known outside Normandy, for we hear of it at La Chaise-Dieu in Auvergne, and at a monastery near Rheims.[3] The prayers were therefore beginning to achieve a certain circulation before any of Anselm's treatises were known, or even written. The exact size of the collection at this time is uncertain, but it is probable that most of the prayers were written before Anselm became abbot in 1078. There are a few later pieces. The prayer to St. Nicholas was probably composed about 1090, after the translation of the body of this saint to Bari;[4] and the important *Meditation on Human Redemption* was certainly composed in 1099 as a devotional summary of the *Cur Deus Homo*.[5] This last piece, however, is markedly different from the rest of the collection; it is more impersonal, more sober in its language, and more strictly theological in its content than the earlier meditations; it reflects the mood of Anselm's later years. The earlier pieces, however, with their effusive and personal tone reflect the period of Anselm's

[1] Ep. 10 [iv, 121]. For the Collection which this letter accompanied, see below p. 42.

[2] Ep. 28 [i, 20], with Prayers v–vii in Schmitt's edition.

[3] Epp. 55 [i, 46], 70 [i, 61].

[4] About Christmas 1092, when Anselm was settling down in England to revise his letters and to complete his treatise against Roscelin, he sent to Bec: 'Mittite mihi Orationem ad sanctum Nicolaum quam feci, et Epistolam quam contra dicta Roscelini facere inchoavi, et si quas de aliis nostris epistolis habet domnus Mauritius, quas non misit.' The context suggests that the Prayer was a recent work; and this suggestion is strengthened by the fact that the translation of St. Nicholas to Bari in 1087 gave a great impetus to his cult in the west. At Bec, moreover, there seems to have been a strong interest in the translation and the subsequent devotion. For these facts, which all point to a date *c.* 1090–2 for Anselm's prayer, see Wilmart in Castel, *Méditations et Prières de S. Anselme*, pp. xxv–xxvi; for a different view, see Schmitt, 'Zur Chronologie der Werke des hl. Anselm,' *R. Bén.* 1932, xliv, 322–50.

[5] *VA* ii, xliv.

earliest works; their similarities are with the style and method of the *Monologion* and *Proslogion* and of the early letters.

The recipients of the prayers were either monastic friends or ladies of noble birth. It was this conjunction of monastic piety and the religious impulses of great ladies which chiefly fashioned the private devotions of the Middle Ages, and it is interesting to see that those two influences were at work in the dissemination of Anselm's collection. The first and the last of the recipients of whom we hear in Anselm's lifetime were both great ladies, though of very different importance. The Conqueror's daughter, Adelaide, was scarcely more than a girl when she received the prayers in 1071. She was probably living near Bec under the guardianship of Roger of Beaumont, one of the chief magnates of the valley of the Risle.[1] Although not a nun, she was under some kind of religious vow, and she died without making any mark in history. By contrast, the last recipient, to whom Anselm sent the prayers in 1104, was the greatest woman of her time—Matilda, countess of Tuscany.[2] She was in a position to make the collection known, and a whole family of manuscripts in Austria and Italy has been shown to descend from her copy.

There were probably more manuscript copies of Anselm's prayers in existence in his lifetime, and for a hundred years after his death, than of any other work of his. Thereafter they were outdistanced by the demand for copies of his theological works in the Universities. But the prayers kept their place in

[1] The letter does not say that Adelaide is a daughter of William the Conqueror, but only that she is of royal birth and rich. Her relationship to the Conqueror is a conjecture of Dom Schmitt. That the Conqueror had a daughter called Adelaide is known only from Ordericus Vitalis, ii, 392. Orderic describes her thus: 'Adelidis pulcherrima virgo iam nubilis devote Deo se commendavit et sub tutela Rogeri de Bellomonte sancto fine quievit.' The chief castle of Roger of Beaumont was only a few miles from Bec, so Anselm probably had her as a near neighbour. Moreover, Orderic's words indicate that though she was under some religious vow, she was not a nun: Anselm's reference to her wealth would therefore not be out of place. Altogether there seems so much to support the conjecture that it may be taken as very probable indeed.

[2] Ep. 325 [iv, 37]. For the collection of Prayers sent to the Countess Matilda, see A. Wilmart, *Auteurs spirituels et textes dévots du Moyen Age latin*, pp. 162–72; and O. Pächt, 'The Illustrations of St. Anselm's Prayers and Meditations', *Journal of the Warburg and Courtauld Institutes*, 1956, xix, 68–83.

devotional literature until the end of the Middle Ages, becoming ever more diluted by spurious works, and perhaps in the end (as we shall see) more valued for their spurious, than for their genuine, pieces. By the end of the Middle Ages, Anselm's prayers had been almost submerged in the literature they helped to create. But in his lifetime, his prayers contained the fullest expression of that fervid and personal devotion, especially to the Virgin Mary, which was winning adherents everywhere in Europe. Anselm was not only among the first to express these sentiments, but he was the first to express them in a way which satisfied the needs of the educated laity, as well as the cloister. His words to Countess Matilda, which came to form a Preface to the whole collection, are the expression of a new liberty: 'The reader ought not to be concerned to read the whole, but only so much as he feels sufficient to arouse in himself the impulse to pray. This is why they are written.'[1] And to this, he later added: 'Nor is it necessary to begin always at the beginning, but wherever the reader prefers. The distinctions into paragraphs are made for this purpose, so that he can begin and end where he chooses, lest superfluity or the frequent repetition of the same place cause boredom.'[2]

This was the language of 1104, when Anselm was over seventy. Even at this late date his words were a notable addition to the theory of devotion. A generation earlier, when Anselm was beginning to write, he had been an innovator in a scene which had changed little during the previous two hundred years and more. This inheritance requires a brief survey in order to understand Anselm's contribution to its development.

## (i) The Traditional Pattern

The tradition of private prayer which Anselm and his contemporaries inherited was that of the Carolingian age.[3] That

---

[1] Ep. 325 [iv, 37].     [2] Prologus Orationum, Schmitt, iii, 3.
[3] The elements of this tradition may most conveniently be studied in A. Wilmart, Precum Libelli quattuor Aevi Karolini, 1940. The volume of introduction to these texts unfortunately never appeared, but a great deal may be learned from Wilmart's fundamental article, to which I am greatly indebted, 'Le Manuel de prières de saint Jean Gualbert,' R. Bén., xlviii, 1936, 259–99.

is to say, it was an inheritance in which the Psalter held an undisputed supremacy. The Psalter was *par excellence* the prayer book of clergy and laity alike, and the greater part of private prayer was centred on the recitation of the Psalms, imitating at a distance the regular psalmody of the monastic office. In response to the need for some simple order of psalmody suitable for private use, a number of schemes for regular repetition had been drawn up, which grew in popularity in the course of the eleventh century. These selections, interspersed with short prayers, could be used in conjunction with the public offices or separately; and it was not uncommon for pious and cultivated lay men and women to follow some daily scheme of this kind.[1]

The Carolingian inheritance was becoming diversified and in various ways specialized in the course of the eleventh century. But in essentials it embodied the ideas of the time when Alcuin had recommended to his master, the Emperor Charlemagne, a regular daily course of private psalmody, and had, with an enthusiasm which can never have been surpassed, recommended the Psalms for all the needs of private devotion:

In the Psalms, if you look carefully, you will find an intimacy of prayer, such as you could never discover by yourself. In the Psalms you will find an intimate confession of your sins, and a perfect supplication of the divine mercy. In the Psalms, you will find an intimate thanksgiving for all that befalls you. In the Psalms you confess your weakness and misery, and thereby call down God's mercy upon you. You will find every virtue in the Psalms, if you are worthy of God's mercy in deigning to reveal to you their secrets.[2]

This was the spirit of the private devotions to which the manuscripts of the tenth and eleventh centuries bear witness. The manuscripts of this period, in which the Psalms are set out for private use, commonly have suitable collects inter-

---

[1] King Alfred, as Asser tells us, carried about with him just such a book of devotion: 'libellum, quem in sinum suum sedulo portabat, in quo diurnus cursus et psalmi quidam atque orationes quaedam, quas ille in iuventute sua legerat, scripti habebantur' (Asser's *Life of King Alfred*, ed. W. H. Stevenson, p. 73: the book is also, more fully described on p. 21). For Alcuin's instructions to Charlemagne 'qualiter homo laicus qui adhuc in activa vita consistit per dinumeratas horas has Deo supplicare debeat' see *PL* CI, 509–10 (Duemmlcr, *Epistolae Alcuini*, *MGH*, p. 462, no. 304).

[2] *PL* CI, 465–6.

spersed with the text of the Psalms, and they are followed by a selection of prayers which preserve throughout all accidental changes certain common features. The collects are necessarily short, but a somewhat greater liberty of development is perceptible in the prayers which follow the main body of the book. Among these Carolingian prayers there is one group which catches the attention, because, unlike the majority of the prayers of the time, they are addressed not directly to God but to various saints, of whom the most regular are the Blessed Virgin Mary, St. John the Baptist, St. Peter, St. Paul, St. Andrew, St. Stephen and St. Benedict, generally in this order.[1] They form a well defined group and they follow a plan which is both simple and effective. The plan consists of picking out some incidents in the life of the saint and applying it to the speaker's needs. Thus St. Peter is addressed as the prince of the Apostles to whom the power of loosing and binding has been granted, and the prayer continues:

loose me, I pray, from all the bonds of my iniquities, and intercede for me that the Lord, your Master, may look on me as he looked on you; and may He who saved you from the deep waters, save me from the deep waters of wickedness.[2]

Thus in one sentence three separate incidents in the life of St. Peter are recalled and given a practical application.

The formulas are extremely brief and their intention is expressed with aptness and simplicity. There is reason to think that Alcuin himself may have been the author of this group of prayers;[3] and in any case they admirably combine the discipline and sobriety of Carolingian scholarship with the earlier freedom of the Anglo-Irish tradition. These texts served the purposes of private devotion for over two hundred years. It does not seem that these brief formulas had been much

[1] See the references given by Wilmart in *R. Bén.*, xlviii, 1936, pp. 283–5; to these may be added Bodleian MS. D'Orville 45, f. 40–1. The texts are printed in Bianchini, *Thomasii Opera*, 526–8.

[2] Bianchini, *op. cit.* p. 527.

[3] This is perhaps a hazardous suggestion, but, besides the wide circulation of these prayers which suggests an important origin, I note that the author of the prayer to St. Peter calls him *pastor et nutritor meus*, which would fit well with Alcuin. The unity of style and method in this group of prayers is very striking. They deserve the attention of an expert.

added to before about the middle of the eleventh century. Nothing, indeed, shows the conservatism of the preceding two centuries more clearly than the stability of forms of devotion which had no liturgical framework to ensure their permanence. This conservatism can be verified in the manuscripts of the period. If we wish to see the kind of book for private prayer which was accessible to Anselm in the early days at Bec we cannot do better than look at a manuscript in the Bodleian Library, D'Orville 45, which comes from the Cluniac Abbey of Moissac and was written in about the year 1067.[1] It contains an arrangement of Psalms and prayers, of which all the chief features go back to the ninth century. The main part of the volume is taken up with the text of the Psalter, preceded by the detailed directions for its use in private devotion drawn up by Alcuin, and followed by the group of prayers which I have already mentioned. Manuscripts of this kind, whether for the private devotions of monks or of laymen, are quite common about 1050. But by about 1050 there were signs of a change. The brevity of the prayers, above all of those to the Virgin Mary, no longer satisfied the ardour of the time. Maurilius, the archbishop of Rouen from whom Anselm sought advice before he became a monk at Bec, had expanded somewhat cautiously the old Carolingian prayer which ran as follows:

Singular in merit, sole, unexampled, Mother and Virgin, Mary, whom the Lord preserved inviolate in mind and body, in order that thou mightest be worthy to form the body of the Son of God, the price of our redemption, from thy body: I beseech thee, by whom the whole world has been saved, most mercifully to intercede for me, soiled and filthy as I am with all my iniquities, so that I who am worthy only to receive eternal punishment for my sins, may be saved by thy merits, most glorious Virgin, and attain the everlasting kingdom, through Jesus Christ. Amen.[2]

This prayer, which is preserved in many manuscripts from the ninth to the eleventh centuries had satisfied the needs of private devotion since the time of Charlemagne. But the urge for expansion, for a more profound self-abasement, and for a more

---

[1] For a long note on the date and origin of this manuscript, see the *Summary Catalogue of Western Manuscripts in the Bodleian Library at Oxford.*
[2] Wilmart, *Precum Libelli quattuor aevi Karolini*, p. 140.

glowing exaltation of the powers and privileges of the Virgin, ensured its rapid supersession in the second half of the eleventh century. Maurilius took it as his basis, and added thereto a long development containing much emotional, vivid and personal expression, without however adding to its theological content. The following phrases are a fair example of these additions:

Unhappy man that I am, I have entirely lost the grace of innocence and holiness. Again and again I have violated the holy temple of God. But what am I doing, pouring out my obscenities into undefiled ears. I tremble, Lady, I tremble; my conscience accuses me; I am ashamed to appear before thee in my vile nakedness.[1]

It is no reflection on the sincerity of these phrases to say that the religious conscience of the time was developing a great partiality for such outpourings. But the danger that they would degenerate into meaningless vapourings is only too clear. They often did. What was needed was someone who could speak this language of self-revelation with power, and add to it the gift of clear thought. These were just the qualities which Anselm could contribute.

## (ii) *The Anselmian Revolution*

Anselm began by observing the traditional pattern in one respect at least. When he sent his earliest prayers to Adelaide in 1071, they were an appendix to a selection of passages from the Psalms for her private use.[2] This florilegium has not been preserved. But the popularity of the Psalter in the Carolingian age had led to a number of such selections coming into general use, and it must be supposed that Anselm's was not very different from those which went under the name of 'St. Jerome' or 'St. Bede'.[3] Our interest lies in the sequel. To his Psalter, Anselm says that he has added seven prayers. So far this might be Alcuin speaking; and the saints addressed in these prayers are also the familiar saints of the Carolingian appendix

---

[1] *PL* CLVIII, 946. For the proof that this prayer, which very soon came to be included in the manuscripts of Anselm's prayers, was by Archbishop Maurilius, see Wilmart, *Auteurs spirituels et textes dévots du moyen âge latin*, 1932, pp. 480–1.　　　　[2] Ep. 10 [iv, 121].

[3] The selection of verses from the Psalter attributed to Bede is printed by Wilmart, *Precum libelli*, pp. 143–59.

to the Psalter. We cannot identify all these prayers with certainty, but the first was a meditation on the fear of death, and the others were prayers to the saints, probably St. John the Baptist, St. Peter, St. Paul, St. John the Evangelist, and certainly St. Stephen and St. Mary Magdalen.[1] The pattern of Psalms followed by prayers was familiar; but when we look at the texts, the traditional appearance turns out to be wholly illusory. In the first place the balance of the older books is entirely overthrown. Instead of the prayers being a brief appendix to a substantial body of Psalms, the substance now is not in the Psalms but in the appended prayers. So unimportant had the preliminary selection from the Psalms become, that no single manuscript of Anselm's prayers has preserved them in the setting in which they first appear. The prayers are always preserved as a separate work, either alone or with Anselm's other writings; and nearly always under his name. They are the first considerable body of medieval prayers to circulate neither anonymously nor under the patronage of some great ancient name, but with the name of their author, and in the corpus of his literary works. Far from being absorbed in anonymity, they drew to themselves the work of other men, whose prayers lived until our own day in the shadow of Anselm's name. But more important than any external differences between Anselm's prayers and those of the earlier period was the content of these texts. It was here that Anselm made his first decisive break with the past.

We may illustrate the difference by quoting the first sentences of his prayer to St. Peter, and compare their style and content with the Carolingian prototype already quoted:

Holy and most benign Peter, faithful shepherd of the sheep of God, prince of the apostles, prince of those so great princes, who

---

[1] Anselm says that he added seven prayers to his extracts from the Psalter. Of these, he describes the first in a way which leaves no doubt that it is the *Meditatio ad concitandum timorem* (Med. I); he also mentions prayers to St. Stephen and St. Mary Magdalen (Or. XIII and XVI in Schmitt). The others can only be conjectured, but the prayers to the Virgin Mary (Or. V–VII) can be excluded, since they were not yet written, and a number of other prayers are unlikely for various reasons, either because they appear to be later additions to the collection (e.g. Or. I–IV) or because their subject matter is unsuitable (e.g. Med. II, Or. XVII). In the final choice only one or two items remain doubtful.

dost bind and loose what thou willest, who dost make whole and raise up whom thou willest, who dost give the kingdom of Heaven to whomsoever thou willest: great Peter, great, endowed with so many and such great gifts, exalted with so many and such great dignities, behold I, the poorest and basest of homunculi, weighed down with many and grave burdens, stand in miserable need of the help of thy kindly power; but my mouth does not have words with which to express my need, nor does my heart have devotion to reach thy so great height from so great a depth.

Again and again I try to stir up my slothful mind and to draw it in from dissipating itself among vanities; but even when all its strength has been brought together, it cannot break through the shadows of its torpor, which the stains of its sins have brought upon it, and it cannot continue long in its intention. Alas, most wretched, wretched man that I am, this is the truth: it is no pretence; it is so. Who will help the wretched being who can neither express tribulation in his words nor find sorrow in his mind?[1]

There are many finer passages than this in Anselm's prayers, but this illustrates the change which has taken place since the earlier prayers were written. Most obviously, of course, there is the immense elaboration which weighs down every thought. Then there is the much greater sense of the independent agency of the saints in the work of salvation, and a new emphasis on the inexplicable primacy of the will, which finds expression in the thrice repeated *solvis quod vis, resuscitas quem vis, das regnum caelorum cui vis.* Moreover, although the plan of Anselm's prayer followed the well-established Carolingian pattern, taking incidents in the life of St. Peter and applying them to the sinner, there is a wealth of imagery previously unknown. That the Apostle should be the shepherd, and the sinner his erring sheep was inevitable; but that the image should be elaborated in such passages as this, was new and surprising:

The sheep is sickening to death: his ulcers swell, his wounds are reopened and grow putrid. The wolves have tasted his blood. They are waiting for him to be cast away. Faithful shepherd, turn your eyes on him; see that he is one of yours. If he has strayed, still *he* has not denied his lord and shepherd. If, through the filth, you cannot recognize the face of one washed white in the fountain of

[1] Or. IX (Schmitt iii, 30).

44

Christ, at least see that he confesses the name of Christ, who thrice asked 'Lovest thou me?' and then said 'Feed my sheep'.[1]

The verbal and biblical reminiscences, even in this short passage, are numerous and some are obvious. But whereas in the earlier prayer everything is immediately clear, here there is much which is too subtle, too complex and too personal to be apparent without close and thoughtful concentration. The prayer is wholly freed from the earlier liturgical associations, which enforced the need for plainness and brevity; it is transported wholly to the private chamber where length and complexity are not a disadvantage. It was entirely consistent with this retirement into privacy that Anselm should express and require from his reader a powerful mental effort for his full comprehension. This effort had a double character of mental excitation and personal abasement—two features of all prayer, but given a quite new intensity in Anselm compared with anything since the writings of St. Augustine.

Anselm strains every resource of language to express these two characteristic traits. Rhyme, assonance, antithesis, the frequent employment of parallel grammatical constructions and closely similar words to express opposing or complementary ideas—all these devices are very common in this prayer, as in all his earliest writings.

The love of antithesis was more than a literary affectation—it was the expression of a deep intellectual need for order and balance, and of a sharpness of vision in which there were no blurred edges. The rhymed prose, however, was a fashion which Anselm largely outgrew. All his earliest writings are highly mannered and they sometimes give the impression of a certain residual childishness of outlook. Anselm's style responded to the weight of his matter. In the early philosophical treatises it is at its best, still retaining its early elegance of form without the fault of over-elaboration and artificiality. Later, and especially after he became archbishop, his style became plainer. By the time he wrote the *Cur Deus Homo* it has no ornaments except those strictly required by the argument. But in his earliest writings he seems to have had a more primitive

[1] *Ibid.* p. 31.

45

sense of the importance of words and grammatical forms as an image of real things. This gives his writing a curious mixture of power and transparent artifice often to be seen in his prayers:

Anima mea, anima aerumnosa, anima inquam misera miseri homunculi, excute torporem tuum et discute peccatum tuum et concute mentem tuam. Reduc ad cor enorme delictum et perduc de corde immanem rugitum. Intende, infelix, intende sceleris tui horrorem et protende horrificum terrorem et terrificum dolorem.[1]

These words come from the beginning of the most turbulent of Anselm's early writings, his *Deploratio virginitatis amissae per fornicationem*. This was a piece not added to the Psalms which he sent to the daughter of William the Conqueror, but it may well be the earliest of his existing works. The nature of the sin which it discloses, the comparative theological immaturity, and the strong rhetorical influence in its style all point to an early date. It is a piece of writing more reminiscent of the later Donne than of the later Anselm:

Horror! Horror! What do I see, where no order, but everlasting horror, dwells? Only a confusion of wailing, a tumult of gnashing of teeth, a confused volume of groans. Woe, woe! again and again and again, woe, woe! The sulphurous fire, the tartarian flame, the billows of smoke, with what terrific roaring do I see you revolve! And you worms, living in the flame, what strange avidity of gnawing burns within you, whom even the fire of fires does not burn? You burning demons, raging with fire, roaring with ire, why are you so cruel to those who twist and turn among you? You torments of every kind, limited by justice, unlimited in suffering, will no limit, no remedy, no end ever quench you? Are these the ends, great God, prepared for fornicators and despisers of thy word, of whom I am one?[2]

These are not the words of a man whose mind had always been the placid mirror of sweetness and light. To explain them in any but their natural sense would be, though a false delicacy, to say that the writer was not a sinner but a trifler.

These prayers are Anselm's earliest works, and whatever else may be thought of them, they are certainly the work of a man with great literary gifts, great originality in transforming traditional models, great sensibility, and an overwhelming

[1] Med. II (Schmitt iii, 80).    [2] *Ibid.* p. 82.

sense of the grievousness of sin. One of the main characteristics of the Carolingian piety which they helped to make obsolete was its sobriety—a quality which had developed in reaction to the long drawn-out reiterations of the Irish and insular piety of a still earlier age. Anselm's prayers marked the moment of rebound. They introduced into a tradition still Carolingian in temper a new note of personal passion, of elaboration and emotional extravagance, which anticipated some of the chief features of later medieval piety.[1] They owed their power to an unusual combination of intensity of feeling and clarity of thought and expression. They show little sign of the exact and metaphysical mind which was soon to produce some of the classics of Christian theology: but when these later works had been written it was possible to see that they displayed many of the same qualities as the prayers.

It is very likely that most people will now find the plain severity of the Carolingian, and even the archaic repetitions of the still older Anglo-Saxon prayers, more congenial than the tense emotional and complex intellectual effusions of Anselm, which seem to oppress the spirit with their excess of feeling. But this would certainly not have been the judgment of the centuries after Anselm's death. Anselm's prayers opened the way which led to the *Dies irae*, the *Imitatio Christi*, and the masterpieces of later medieval piety.

### 3. THE EARLY TREATISES

Until he became archbishop, Anselm's life for over thirty years was one of monastic peace disturbed only by the occasional enmities inseparable from the life of men living in close proximity in a small community, and by material cares which weighed less heavily upon him, as some thought, than they

---

[1] Ever since Dom Wilmart discovered the spiritual writings of Anselm's older contemporary, John, abbot of Fécamp (b. *c.* 990; d. 1078), it has been customary to see in him a fore-runner of St. Anselm. Doubtless to some extent this is right; but I can see little in common between the solid, biblically heavily-laden, theological meditations of John of Fécamp and the poignant personal and intellectual effusions of Anselm. The comparison can easily be made by referring to the edition of John of Fécamp's works in J. Leclercq and J. P. Bonnes, *Un Maître de la vie spirituelle au XI siècle: Jean de Fécamp* (1946).

47

ought to have done. All his writings of this period are the witnesses of this peace: his intimate correspondence with friends at Canterbury and elsewhere, his prayers and meditations, his *Proslogion* and *Monologion*—themselves meditations on the nature of God—and his philosophical and theological dialogues, which were the product of his teaching in the cloister. In all this body of work there is scarcely a word of controversy. The only controversy was with the remarkable Gaunilo over the argument of the *Proslogion*, and it was conducted with such mutual regard and identity of purpose that it is hard to realize that a new philosophical issue had suddenly sprung into existence. Nothing could be more peaceful or more withdrawn from the storms and controversies which, in the realm of government, were rending the Empire and Papacy of Henry IV and Gregory VII, or which, in the realm of theology, in 1079 produced the final condemnation of Berengar of Tours. The idea that the task of the theologian was to reconcile apparent contradictions arose from the controversies of this time. It influenced the future in countless ways. But this was not Anselm's method: there is never in his works a moment of indecision, of poise between two opposites, and a final resolution of the point at issue. If ever there was a moment of irresolution we are not allowed to see it: in all his writings, he appears on the field already a victor, ready to explain, perhaps to demonstrate, but not to fight. None of the paraphernalia of *pro* and *contra*, of *distinguo* and *respondeo* had any place in his thought. For him the points about which others argued were the points which were settled before arguments began.

It may therefore seem strange that so much of his work was cast in the form of dialogue, which of all forms seems most to suggest the existence of opposing points of view. It was not so with Anselm. Indeed when Anselm came up against two concrete opponents, Roscelin and the Greeks, he dropped the dialogue form. For him, the dialogue was a form of art, used, as Plato had used it, to draw out his meaning and to give structure to thoughts which might otherwise have seemed to tumble out with too little disposition towards a system; it was not an expression of two rival bodies of thought. The protagonists in his dialogues were always a master and his pupil, never the representatives of two schools of thought.

Although most of the treatises which Anselm wrote at Bec are in dialogue form, the two earliest works, written shortly after the main body of his prayers and meditations, are extended meditations. They grew out of the earlier writings and have many similarities with them. They could be read, and to some extent they must be read, as religious exercises: we shall have especially to remember this in discussing the argument of the *Proslogion*, which begins in the manner of one of Anselm's earlier prayers:

Come now, little man, put aside your business for a while, take refuge for a little from your tumultuous thoughts; cast off your cares, and let your burdensome distractions wait. Take some leisure for God; rest awhile in him. Enter into the chamber of your mind; put out everything except God and whatever helps you to seek Him; close the door and seek him. Say now to God with all your heart: 'I seek thy face, O Lord, thy face do I seek.' [1]

But, however strong their connexions with his earlier prayers, the treatises we are now to examine were much more ambitious than anything previously attempted by Anselm. They place him at once in the front rank of theologians and philosophers, and despite all his depreciatory gestures it is impossible not to see that he knew this.

The passage in which Eadmer describes Anselm's first appearance as a theologian is the best introduction to these treatises. Eadmer's words at this point have almost the authority of autobiography, for there can be no doubt that Anselm was their source, and it is very likely that he read and at first approved what Eadmer had written:

He also composed another small book, which he called the *Monologion* because in this he alone spoke and argued with himself. Here, putting aside all authority of Holy Scripture, he inquired into and discovered by reason alone what God is, and proved by invincible reason that God's nature is what the true Faith holds it to be, and that it could not be other than it is. Afterwards it came into his mind to try to prove by one single and short argument the

---

[1] *Proslogion*, cap. i.

things which are believed and preached about God—that he is eternal, unchangeable, omnipotent, omnipresent, incomprehensible, just, righteous, merciful, true, as well as truth, goodness, justice and so on; and to show how all these qualities are united in Him. And this, as he himself would say, gave him great trouble, partly because thinking about it took away his desire for food, drink and sleep, and partly—and this was more grievous to him—because it disturbed the attention which he ought to have paid to Matins and to Divine service at other times. When he was aware of this, and still could not entirely lay hold on what he sought, he supposed that this line of thought was a temptation of the devil and he tried to banish it from his mind. But the more vehemently he tried to do this, the more these thoughts crowded in on him. Then suddenly one night during Matins, the grace of God shone on his heart, the whole matter became clear to his mind, and a great joy and jubilation filled his inmost being.[1]

The two works thus described, the *Monologion* and *Proslogion*, belong to the years 1077 and 1078. They are closely related in plan and subject-matter. They both consist, broadly speaking, of proofs of God's existence followed by meditations on God's qualities. But whereas the first, the *Monologion*, is concerned with the qualities of the Trinity, and is closely dependent on Augustine's *De Trinitate*, the *Proslogion* is chiefly concerned with the qualities of God as Unity; it is only very slightly dependent on Augustine, and it is altogether more personal and more vivid in expression than the earlier treatise.

There is also a notable difference in Anselm's intellectual posture in the two works: although they both contain proofs which Anselm regards as wholly convincing, the *Monologion* is a philosophical soliloquy, while the *Proslogion* is a prayer. The distinction is important. The *Monologion* was in form a highly original work, but in substance it had the authority of Augustine behind it. In it Anselm speaks, with the confidence of a man with all the best cards in his hand, with a secret source of authority; there is in his opening words a youthful confidence, as if it were the easiest thing in the world to prove, even to those of mediocre intelligence, that those things which we believe about God are necessarily true.[2] But in the *Proslogion*

[1] *VA* I, xix.    [2] *Monologion*, cap. I.

he was on his own; he had reached the furthest limits of his thought; he still trembled with the awe of a new discovery. The *Proslogion* contains Anselm's most original contribution to philosophy, but it should be approached, as Anselm approached it, through the *Monologion.*

### (i) *The Monologion*

The first words of the *Monologion* laid down a principle of inquiry from which he never afterwards departed.

Some of my brethren have persistently asked me to write down some of the things which I have proposed to them in talk for meditation on the divine essence and certain associated topics . . . with this condition that I should persuade them of nothing on the authority of scripture, but plainly and simply put down whatever the argument might require, without overlooking any objections, however fatuous.[1]

It would be hard to imagine a more complete break with the past than this. To Lanfranc, the whole enterprise appeared misguided. Yet the younger spirits were ready for the change. Anselm was not a reformer speaking odious truths to a generation unwilling to listen to him. He was a conservative, reluctantly writing what he would have preferred to leave to the spoken word, speaking perhaps what he would have preferred to leave unsaid, driven on by eager pupils. That the pupils were eager there is every reason to believe: their existence was not a literary fiction. They only needed the signal for a freer and more speculative approach to the problems of theology.

Anselm himself assumed an attitude of indifference towards the fate of his work. He sent it to Lanfranc asking him, as if casually, to approve it or to destroy it; and if he approved, to give it a name.[2] The casualness was deceptive. Lanfranc did not approve, though he did not condemn outright. He made suggestions which would have altered the whole nature of the work. Anselm did not follow them. Nor did Anselm destroy

---

[1] *Ibid.* prologus.

[2] Ep. 72 [i, 63]. Lanfranc's letter of criticism does not exist—it is interesting that Anselm, who preserved some other letters of Lanfranc, should not have preserved this—but its contents can be gathered from Anselm's reply, Ep. 77 [i, 68].

the work. Instead, he himself turned to the question of giving his treatise a name. Ostensibly, he had left the work without a title and without an author's name because it was unworthy of such ornaments; but another reason seems to have been the difficulty of finding the right name. At first he called it an 'Example of meditating about the substance of faith (*de ratione fidei*)', but he still left it anonymous. Then he called it a '*Monoloquium* on the substance of faith'. Finally he dropped the descriptive phrase and, introducing a literary refinement after the fashion of the time, abandoned the hybrid *Monoloquium* in favour of the more elegant *Monologion*.[1] And so, with many hesitations, but also with a considerable show of firmness, not to say obstinacy, this first treatise was launched into the world.

The work was quite unlike any other of recent times and substantially unlike any other work of any earlier period. The most striking point which separated it from other writings of this period was its entire lack of any quotation of authorities. This omission was not designed by Anselm as a *tour de force*: it was a deliberately chosen method and it sets him apart from all his contemporaries, except those who came under his immediate influence, and from the main line of development of medieval scholastic thought. By nature Anselm was anything but a rebel, but in this one respect he may be accounted one. The whole articulation of medieval thought came about through the collection of authorities, through the work of arranging and examining them, and through the task of harmonizing the vast and confusing mass of authoritative texts. The process of accumulation, of arrangement, and even —though as yet only feebly—of criticism, had already begun. It was against all this that Anselm set his face. There is no one in these centuries more conscious of his philosophic mission: he will not repeat other men's words.

Anselm at first called the *Monologion* an example of meditating about the substance of faith, *de ratione fidei*. This is an ambiguous phrase, and he soon dropped it from the title of his work. Nevertheless it was a phrase to which he reverted on several occasions and it contains the best description of what

[1] For the stages in the development of the title, see *VA* i, xix n.

he was trying to do throughout the whole of his writings. It therefore requires careful examination.

First of all then the *Monologion* is an *exemplum meditandi*, a meditation. This was a form of writing which Anselm made peculiarly his own. 'Meditatio' and 'meditare' are words which occur very rarely in the Rule of St. Benedict, and then with a sense very different from that in which they are used by Anselm: they refer to such activities as learning the Psalter, or preparing the Lessons or the music for the Offices, not to the free excursion of the mind among problems of theology.[1] St. Augustine also has very little to say about meditation. It is not until the twelfth century, and especially among writers of the Cistercian school, that meditation came to have a well defined place as a philosophical activity.[2] But we need not go into the technical meaning attached to the word to see that it suggests a form of reasoning which claims a certain freedom of development, letting the mind take what turns it will, ignoring the exigencies of scholastic debate. All this is well brought out by the twelfth century writer Hugh of St. Victor in his account of the place of meditation among the arts:

Meditation has its foundation in reading, but it is constrained by no rules or order of reading. It rejoices to run freely in an open space where it can fix its gaze on the truth without hindrance, and investigate now this, now that problem until nothing is left doubtful or obscure.[3]

It was Anselm who did more than anyone else to fix this later, freer tradition of meditation, and to use it as a basis both for extended private prayer and for philosophical inquiry. The inquiry was scarcely distinguishable from the prayer, since

[1] *Regula*, cap. 8, 48, 58. (See the note on these passages in B. Linderbauer, *S. Benedicti Regula Monachorum herausgegeben und philologisch erklärt*, 1922). For the use of the word 'meditation' in this sense, see Bede, *Hist. Eccl.* III, vi: 'meditari . . . id est, aut legendis scripturis, aut psalmis discendis operam dare' (ed. Plummer, p. 136).

[2] See, for example, Alcher of Clairvaux, *De Spiritu et Anima* (printed among the works of St. Augustine, *PL* XL, 779) cap 28: 'Sensus parit imaginationem, imaginatio cogitationem, cogitatio meditationem. Meditatio acuit ingenium, ingenium rationem; ratio conducit ad intellectum, intellectus ad intelligentiam, intelligentia per contemplationem ipsam veritatem admiratur, et per caritatem in ea delectatur.'

[3] *Didascalicon*, iii, 10 (ed. Buttimer, p. 59).

the aim of both was to shake off the torpor of the mind and see things as they are in their essential being.

Secondly, the *Monologion* is a meditation *de ratione fidei*. What this phrase means is not very easy to say. It comes from St. Paul, who in the Epistle to the Romans admonishes his readers, if they have the gift of prophecy, to prophesy *secundum rationem fidei.*[1] St. Paul seems to mean by this that their words are to be accommodated to the measure of their faith, but this cannot be Anselm's meaning. Perhaps the best translation would be 'a meditation on the rationale of the Faith', and this is a fair description of most of Anselm's theological works.

Anselm soon dropped the phrase *de ratione fidei* from the title of his work. He probably did so only for reasons of literary elegance. But he must have known that the conjunction of the two words 'reason' and 'faith' raised a problem. It was inevitable from the nature of his inquiries that he should soon say something about the relations between them, if only to allay the misgivings and suspicions which his method and the absence of authorities in his work aroused.

*Faith and Reason*

This is a subject on which a great deal of confusion can be avoided by making an immediate distinction between two senses of the word 'faith': in the first sense it is a mode of knowledge, an activity; in the second, it is an object of knowledge, a state of affairs capable of being expressed in a set of propositions. We know 'by faith' and what we know is 'the Faith'. About faith in the first sense Anselm has very little to say. He has no psychology of belief; he feels no difficulties. The holding of the propositions of the Catholic faith was an obligation on all who had been baptized:

Our Faith is to be defended by reason against unbelievers, not against those who profess to rejoice in the name of Christians. From the latter, it may justly be demanded that they hold inviolate the pledges made for them in baptism . . . The Christian ought to progress through faith to understanding, and not through understanding to faith. Let him rejoice if he is able to attain understanding; and if he cannot, let him revere what he cannot apprehend.[2]

[1] Romans xii, 6.                [2] Ep. 136 [ii, 41].

54

This is a blunt statement of his position and should be kept in mind, but it is open to some misunderstanding. It suggests that knowing by faith is a mere passive act of receptivity; but it is this only at a very low level of understanding. The man who believes is impelled to raise his mind to God. He does this by means of reason. But reason is itself a spiritual gift, by which man is made in the image of God: reason is not a machine for performing a plodding series of mechanical acts; it is a kindling of the spirit, a throwing off of the chains of the flesh, a rising above the world of material things. Hence it is not inappropriate that Anselm uses in his philosophical discourses the same phrases of mental excitation which he uses in his prayers. This is most evident in the *Proslogion*. Here prayer and philosophy are most intimately combined; yet the philosophical starting point is strictly a problem of grammar and logic, and not one of faith in the narrow sense at all. It was not an accident that he chose this moment to assert the necessity of faith for understanding, and to coin the famous phrase which better than any other describes his theological programme: *Fides quaerens intellectum*.[1] Reason is the activity of faith. Hence, at the most primitive level, those who fail to discern the reality of universals fail before they begin to think: they are slaves of their corporeal images; they are like bats disputing with the eagle about the rays of the noonday sun; they are incapable of ascending to the plane of rational truth, which is the plane of incorporeal essences.[2] Indeed it is clear that if the objects of reason are incorporeal essences inaccessible to the senses, some sort of act of faith is necessary before the processes of reason can begin at all. If anyone does not admit the existence of such essences, he lacks both faith and an object in which to exercise his reason. Nothing can be done about him except oblige him to keep silence. One way of achieving this was by authority; the other way was to convict him of a logical contradiction in asserting that something is *not*, which by logical necessity *is*. Anselm hoped that he had

---

[1] This wonderful phrase was the original title of the work. It was later dropped for the more enigmatic title *Proslogion*, but the programme is expressed in the body of the work, though less attractively: 'Neque enim quaero intelligere ut credam, sed credo ut intelligam.'

[2] *Epistola de Incarnatione Verbi*, i (Schmitt, ii, p. 8).

achieved the second of these results. But whether or not he was justified in this hope, it is plain that faith and reason, considered simply as activities, are much more closely related than the dogmatic statement which has been quoted would suggest.

Similarly, the objects of faith and reason are the same. St. Augustine expressed this identity of aim in two images when he said that reason is to the heart as the eye is to the body, and faith glows in the eye of the heart as gold in the eye of the body.[1] Reason, therefore, is the eye of the spirit, and faith is the most glorious of the objects presented to it. But, just as the eye does not change the nature of the object presented to it, so the nature of faith is not altered by the scrutiny of reason. This view, with all the consequences which follow from it, is also Anselm's, and his attitude is sharply distinguishable from that of St. Thomas Aquinas. Professor Gilson has remarked that for St. Thomas when something has been proved it ceases to be an object of faith; it is an object of demonstration. For Anselm it is not so. Reason makes faith intelligible; it does not supersede it. Faith becomes intelligible in two ways. In the first place, the interrelation between the various tenets of faith becomes plain: system emerges from a mass of details. Secondly, the rationality of faith is established: that is to say, what is known by faith is shown to be rationally necessary.

Why then is faith not swallowed up in demonstration? For two reasons. Firstly, because (as we have seen) the demonstration is only convincing to a man in a state of spiritual elevation, which if not identical with faith is closely related to it. Secondly, because the demonstrations of reason are in varying degrees provisional. In Anselm's theology they are provisional in the same way that explanations in natural science are provisional. If the explanation accounts for all observed events in the field it purports to explain, it may be said to have a high degree of probability. But, even supposing that no unobserved events could exist, and that all observed

---

[1] Dedit tibi Deus oculos in corpore, rationem in corde (*Hom.* 32, 11); Sicut lucet aurum ad oculos corporis, sic lucet fides ad oculos cordis (De decem chordis, x); Fides gradus est intelligendi, intellectus meritum fidei (*Hom.* 32, 1). Many similar passages can be found in which this union of faith, reason and understanding is expressed in various ways.

events have been correctly observed, it would still be possible for another explanation to fit them and for the other explanation to be the right one.

Of course, scientific explanations are doubly provisional, because the facts are never either complete nor reported with complete accuracy. Anselm would not have admitted that the theologian was faced with this double hazard: the Faith, enshrined in the dogmas of the Church, is certain, and, within the limits of its subject-matter, complete. But to compensate for this, it is supremely difficult to grasp intellectually, and full of apparent contradictions between God's foreknowledge and man's free will, God's mercy and God's justice, the goodness of the Creator and the existence of evil, and so on. The distance by which any explanation, however bound together by 'necessary reasons', falls short of giving a complete explanation of these apparent contradictions in the Christian faith, is the measure of the provisional character of all reasoning on these subjects.

## (ii) *The Proslogion*

When Lanfranc failed either to approve or give a name to the *Monologion*, Anselm's reaction shows that the author in him in some degree predominated over the monk. He neither altered nor destroyed the work. Instead, he straightway wrote another which not only had the characteristic which Lanfranc had found offensive in the *Monologion*—an absence of all authorities—but even went further in the same direction, in that it could not be said in any sense to provide a simplified account of St. Augustine's thoughts. It is on this work that Anselm's philosophical, as distinct from his theological, reputation will always chiefly rest. It was written in a state of philosophical excitement which (it is probably safe to say) had never before been experienced so intensely in any Benedictine monastery, and was probably never again to be repeated in Benedictine history.[1] This excitement is chiefly to be associated with the first three chapters of the treatise in which the famous, so-called ontological, argument for the existence of God is set out.

[1] For the history of the discovery, see *VA* I, xix.

57

Although everything Anselm wrote is stamped with his personal quality, these chapters are in a special sense his own. The proof they contain was his own discovery; and it is the only philosophical discovery of the early Middle Ages which has survived to excite the interest of modern philosophers who have no other interest in the period.

Whether it is true or false, nothing is more surprising than the way in which this proof has united, at least temporarily, men of the most diverse temperaments and outlooks—a tenuous link across vast seas of spiritual difference. Among living philosophers none is perhaps further removed from Anselm in outlook, though perhaps not so far in qualities of mind, than he who remembers :

the precise moment, one day in 1894, as I was walking along Trinity Lane, when I saw in a flash (or thought I saw) that the ontological argument is valid. I had gone out to buy a tin of tobacco; on my way back, I suddenly threw it up in the air, and exclaimed as I caught it: 'Great Scott, the ontological argument is sound'.[1]

Leave out Trinity Lane, the tobacco and the 'Great Scott' (delightful evocation of an age more remote in spirit than the eleventh century) and substitute Bec, Matins, and *Deo gratias*, and it was just so that the argument came to Anselm in 1078 :

Behold, one night during Matins, the grace of God shone in his heart and the matter became clear to his understanding, filling his whole being with immense joy and jubilation.[2]

We can well believe that the argument came, as Eadmer describes, in a flash of illumination after days or weeks of frustrated gropings and reluctant distraction in the midst of the daily offices. Yet it did not come from nowhere. Its distant ancestor must be judged to be St. Augustine, but only in a remote and ineffectual way. Its immediate parents are the grammar and logic of Anselm's day, but applied with an otherwise unknown subtlety. As we shall see, what Anselm needed for this argument was a definition of God on which he could build a logical structure of a peculiar kind. He did not find this in Augustine, whose language—so similar to that of

---

[1] Bertrand Russell, *My mental development*, in P. A. Schilpp, *The Philosophy of Bertrand Russell*, 1944, p. 10.    [2] *VA* i, xix.

Anselm in some respects—lacked the precision of the logician. He could find in Augustine that:

God is not really known in the sound of these two syllables (*Deus*), but this sound, when it strikes the ears of all who know Latin, moves them to thinking of some most excellent and immortal nature. . . . For when God is thought of, our thought tries to reach something than which nothing is better or more sublime.[1]

This has the germ of what he needed—the concentration on the word *Deus*, and the connexion between this word and a nature 'than which nothing is better or more sublime'. But there is no basis here for a proof of God's existence. Strangely enough, the form of words Anselm needed for his proof were lying in a most unlikely place. He may have noticed them. In the Introduction to Seneca's *Quaestiones Naturales*—a rare book, but a book of which there were two copies at Bec in the twelfth century[2]—there is a definition of God: 'God is that than which nothing greater can be thought'.[3] Seneca used these words in a sense very different from Anselm: he was speaking only of physical magnitude, and was certainly innocent of any philosophical intention. But for Anselm, whether he found this phrase in Seneca or coined it himself, these words were full of exciting possibilities. They gave him a starting-point for his argument.[4]

He begins with the Fool, described by the Psalmist as one who thinks 'there is no God'. What, Anselm asks, is God? He is 'something than which nothing greater can be thought'. The Fool, then, has this *something* 'in intellectu' but denies that it exists 'in re'.

[1] *De Doctrina Christiana*, I, vii.

[2] G. Becker, *Catalogi Bibliothecarum antiqui*, p. 202, no. 104; p. 266, no. 136. Of these two volumes, the first came to Bec in the twelfth century; but the second may have been there in Anselm's time. The only other reference to this work in the catalogues printed by Becker is at St. Gall in the ninth century (p. 35).

[3] I am indebted to Schmitt, i, 102 n. for this quotation: 'Quid est Deus? quod vides totum et quod non vides totum. Sic demum magnitudo sua illi redditur, qua nihil maius excogitari potest' (*Senecae Opera*, ed. F. Haase, i, 159).

[4] The following paragraphs summarize the argument of the first four chapters of the *Proslogion*. I have tried to preserve what, for want of a better word, may be called Anselm's *tone*, but it is more difficult to do this here than in any other part of Anselm's writings.

59

Let us suppose the Fool is right. Then God does not exist outside the mind. But still it would be possible to think of another Being, also having the quality of being 'that than which nothing greater can be thought', who exists not only in the mind but also outside the mind. Such a Being would be greater than the Being existing only in the mind. The Being existing only in the mind is therefore not 'that than which nothing greater can be thought'; such a Being therefore is by definition not God. Thus the Fool asserts that 'God is not-God', which is nonsense. God, therefore, exists not only in the mind but also outside the mind.

Now we can go a step farther. God exists both 'in intellectu' and 'in re'. But many other things exist outside the mind which do not exist necessarily. There is no logical necessity in the existence of physical objects. Not so with God: he exists outside the mind, and *cannot* be thought not to exist outside the mind.

The Fool is now reduced to a very pitiable state. He thought he understood the meaning of words like 'God' and of sentences like 'God does not exist'. But if the argument is valid, it has been shown that he uses words without understanding the things to which they refer, and constructs sentences without understanding the verbal contradictions they contain. Not only has he no understanding of things, but he does not even grasp words and sentences in their basic grammatical and logical connexions. Although Anselm nowhere says so formally, we can see in the progression of his argument that there are three stages of knowledge:

*cogitatio* at the level of words and sentences (grammar and logic);

*intellectus* at the level of entities, the things to which words refer (philosophy);

*sapientia* in the apprehension of the Supreme Being (theology).

The Fool of course lacked *sapientia*, being by definition *insipiens*. Anselm has tried to show that he consequently lacks *intellectus* and even the power of *cogitatio*: he must be silent like a beast. Meanwhile, the right-thinking person has risen from understanding the word 'God' (*cogitatio*), to under-

THE MONK OF BEC

standing the thing for which the word stands 'God outside the mind' (*intellectus*), to a knowledge of God's necessary Being (*sapientia*).

It has been necessary to express the well-known argument in this way in order to bring out its grammatical and logical foundations. For it is clear that though Anselm's argument is to be placed in the same class as that of Descartes, yet Anselm's presuppositions, his method of proceeding, and even his conclusion is different from that of his successor. It is only in a careless way that Anselm's proof can be called a proof that God exists. It is rather a demonstration of the manner of God's existence; for that he has some kind of existence, the mere fact that it is possible to attach some meaning to the word 'God' is sufficient to show. What the proof undertakes to show is that the existence of God is external to the mind, and that it cannot be thought of in any other way.

That the argument can be refuted has been shown again and again. But the argument continues to attract defenders and opponents, and this suggests that the refutations are never quite complete, or that the argument has some hidden source of life. Instead, therefore, of entering on a refutation, we may ask what conditions would have to be satisfied for the argument, as Anselm states it, to be valid. In this way we may hope to discover something which, whether or not of any philosophical value, is of value for understanding the mind and presuppositions of Anselm.

It is evident at once that there are two conditions which have to be satisfied before the argument can have any claim to validity. The first condition is that when we say that something is 'greater' than something else, we can mean—and in this context *do* mean—that it is 'greater' in having a greater degree of being; and that 'existence only in the mind' and 'existence both in the mind and outside the mind' are related in respect of degrees of being. If this were not so, then the criticism of all who have attacked the argument from Anselm's day to the present would be clearly justified: God *in re* would not be greater than God *in intellectu*. He would just be something entirely different, even though the same word 'God' is used, in different senses, in both phrases. There must therefore be degrees of being, such that 'being in the mind' and 'being in the mind and outside the mind' are related as lesser to greater. Moreover, Anselm evidently attaches a special degree of being to that which not only exists *in intellectu et in re* but also cannot be thought of as not existing. The degrees of being are thus, in ascending order: *esse in intellectu* < *esse in intellectu et in re* < *esse in intellectu et in re et non posse cogitari non esse*.

The second condition is a consequence of the first: in the phrases 'it exists in the mind' and 'it exists outside the mind', it must be possible for the subject to be really, and not merely grammatically, the same in both sentences. If this were not so, we should be talking about different things in the two sentences; and to arrange them in series, as if the second sentence referred to the same thing as the first, would be to fall into the simplest form of blunder arising from an identity of grammatical structure.

For Anselm there is only a difference of degree between the existence of a thing and the existence of the idea of a thing. The idea in the mind and its object outside the mind are strictly related as ascending powers in a scale of existence. But this interchangeability between idea and thing is only plausible if there is a still higher degree of being, of which both the idea and its object are lower powers; and this higher degree of being can only be in the mind of God himself. We know from the *Monologion* that this is in fact what Anselm thought: things have their highest degree of being in the mind of God; a lower degree in their own objective existence; a still lower degree in our idea of them.[1]

This is of course a form of Platonism. There seems to be no proof that Anselm had read even that amount of Plato which was accessible in his day, but he had imbibed the elements of Platonic thought from St. Augustine, and there can be no doubt that his essential philosophical ideas are Platonic—so much so that he seems to think that any other type of philo-

---

[1] *Monologion*, xxxvi: Restat igitur ut (creatae substantiae) tanto verius sint in seipsis quam in nostra scientia . . . Cum ergo et hoc constat, quia omnis creata substantia tanto verius est in Verbo, id est in intelligentia creatoris, quam in seipsa. . . .

sophy must not only lead to heresy but even gives evidence of hopeless intellectual blindness.

The *Proslogion* is intended both as a meditation for the believer and a proof for the unbeliever. The proof for the unbeliever does not, as has sometimes been thought, depend upon the previous acceptance of certain theological truths, but it does depend on a previous acceptance of certain philosophical principles which appear on analysis to commit the unbeliever to a view of knowledge which necessitates the existence of God. A proof which demands, in however subtle and roundabout a way, assent to its conclusion before it begins will rightly be thought to be no proof at all in the ordinary sense of the word.[1]

Whether Anselm was conscious of this limitation in his argument we cannot tell. He seems to have thought that the account of knowing which his argument presupposed was the only possible one and that since the unbeliever could produce no other he would effectively be reduced to silence. This is a possible and—despite many difficulties of which Anselm could not have been aware—a consistent point of view: consistent both in itself and within the framework of the theological programme announced at the beginning of the *Proslogion*: *Fides quaerens intellectum*. The argument returns, and must always return in Anselm's thought to its point of origin, the Faith from which it starts. But, for the purpose of this argument, the Faith is not the Christian faith but a philosophical faith which Anselm seems, wrongly, to have thought an essential part of any coherent system of thought.

To most people all these preliminary conditions will appear unacceptable, and all refutations of the argument are based on the rejection of these preliminaries. In the common view, horses exist and unicorns do not exist; and it does not seem

---

[1] There is, however, at this point an interesting affinity between Anselm's argument and G. E. Moore's proof of an external world, which—having the same problem of arguing from what is 'inside the mind' to what is 'outside the mind'—ends in the same predicament; the proof is only a proof for those who, in the last resort, accept as a premiss the conclusion which the argument purports to prove (G. E. Moore, *Philosophical Papers*, 1959, p. 150).

an adequate description of the difference between the existence of the one and the non-existence of the other to allege that both exist, but one more than the other, because one exists *in re et in intellectu* while the other exists only *in intellectu*. Similarly most people who believe that God exists will not think that the existence of God is in any way affected by our ability or inability to think of Him as not existing. But since Anselm certainly himself accepted these preliminary conditions of his argument, we must ask what the status of the argument will be if his conditions are accepted. The answer is clear: the argument will then be irrefutable, but irrefutable only because it requires the conclusion to be accepted before the argument starts.

Anselm's philosophical outlook was not destined to command any wide body of assent, at least for a long time to come. It was not until the thirteenth century that the proofs for the existence of God engaged the serious attention of theologians and the weight of opinion was then against the validity of Anselm's argument.[1] Among Anselm's immediate friends and disciples no one except Eadmer so much as mentions the argument. Of the others Gilbert Crispin repeats the definition on which the argument was based, but he did not build upon it. We know that Lanfranc disapproved of the *Monologion*: we do not know what he thought of the *Proslogion*, but it is hard to think that—if he ever read it—he approved. In the immediate future the peculiar mixture of linguistic analysis and Augustinian philosophy on which the argument, as Anselm stated it, was based was replaced by newer methods and by a different conception of the purpose of theological study. Yet if Anselm's argument did not meet with acceptance, the two treatises *Monologion* and *Proslogion* made his name known far and wide. In 1085 he could no longer have spoken of himself as he did ten years earlier as a man unknown to the world. Within a year or two of their composition the two works were known not only in Normandy and in Canterbury, but at Poitiers, Tours, and Lyons.[2]

It is very common for authors to say that they have been

---

[1] The essential texts for the thirteenth century are collected in A. Daniels, *Gottesbeweise im xiii Jahrhundert mit bes. Rücksicht auf dem ontologischen Argument* (*BGPM*, viii, 1909). [2] Epp. 83 [i, 74], 109 [ii, 17].

obliged to write by the demands of their pupils, but there is no reason to doubt that Anselm is telling the truth when he says this. At Bec and elsewhere he had an eager audience. A generation had grown up in the monasteries of men who were connoisseurs in theological debate. Yet it did not produce monastic successors to Anselm. Philosophical interests soon became centred on the universities and the age of Anselm remained the highest point of philosophical culture in the history of the Benedictine Order. Unlike the later schoolmen, the monastic philosophers and theologians have left comparatively little record of their interests. Anselm's first critic therefore deserves a special mention. Gaunilo, monk of Marmoutier near Tours, is entirely unknown except for three or four pages in which he criticized Anselm's argument. These pages also would no doubt have been lost if Anselm had not given directions for the inclusion of the criticism and his reply to it in all future copies of the *Proslogion*. Since all the earliest copies include Gaunilo's criticism, it must have been written very soon after the composition of the treatise. It is so familiar a text that it is hard to realize how unlikely it was to survive. It is a very notable piece of writing. Though not quite conclusive as an attack on Anselm, it is urbane and intelligent, and strikingly anticipates later lines of attack on the ontological argument. Its existence is a warning against underestimating the level of philosophical cultivation in communities which have left little trace of their intellectual attainments.

Of all the arguments for the existence of God, the one which Anselm first formulated is the most refined and the least capable of a finally satisfactory statement. It draws its strength from an ambiguity, which appears to be an ambiguity in language, but is more deeply an ambiguity in human experience. If God exists, there must be a level of experience at which it is impossible to think of God as not existing. But at what level can this impossibility be made to appear? Must the demonstration await the experience of the Beatific Vision? Or can it, at the very opposite extreme, be made out at the level of linguistic-logical analysis? Whether valid or not, the first three chapters of the *Proslogion* were the first piece of writing in which this problem was raised and a solution proposed which will probably never be finally buried. It may be agreed that Descartes put it better, because more simply and with fewer philosophical presuppositions. He had the advantage, which Anselm lacked, of inheriting, if only to reject, a long philosophical tradition. The Augustinian and grammatical background of Anselm's thought, which made it possible for him to formulate the argument, also burdened it with limitations. But these pages of Anselm must be placed among the most deeply interesting pieces of reasoning ever written The early chapters of the *Proslogion*, in which the argument was first expressed, will never be read without excitement, nor thought about without appearing to be more cogent than they are. For the most extraordinary thing about the argument is that it loses nothing of its power, its freshness, or even in a curious way its persuasiveness, by being refuted. The *Proslogion* may not set forth a valid argument for belief in God, and even if it were valid it is doubtful whether it would ever persuade an unbeliever; but in its subtlety, and in a certain unsubstantial, ethereal quality which antagonizes men of robust common sense, it perfectly reflects the quality and mystery of Anselm's personality.

The *Monologion* and *Proslogion* were the product of two remarkable years in Anselm's life, 1077-8, his last years as Prior of Bec. In sheer force of philosophical originality he never rose to these heights again. For the next fifteen years before he became archbishop of Canterbury he was occupied in monastic administration and in the composition of four works (all of them Dialogues) which display his talent and originality, but could not in themselves have formed the basis of his reputation, as the *Monologion* and *Proslogion* standing by themselves could have done. They were years in which his reputation in the world slowly grew, in which the number of his pupils— men who had become monks at Bec mainly because of his influence and presence—increased, and in which his monastic peace was disturbed only by necessary journeys to courts and synods and tours of inspection of his lands in England. The last of these journeys was, as we shall see, fatal to this monastic peace.

## 4. THE LETTERS OF FRIENDSHIP

Anselm's earliest letters—that is to say the earliest of his letters which he thought worthy of preservation, for we cannot believe that he never wrote a letter before 1071—belong to the same period as the main body of his prayers and meditations. For the years between 1071 and his death in 1109 nearly four hundred of Anselm's letters have been preserved, a considerably larger number than we have from any of his contemporaries except Gregory VII. But this large body of letters consists of two quite distinct collections, distinct both in the manner of their preservation and in their general scope and interest. The first collection contains the letters which Anselm wrote between 1071 and 1093, while he was at Bec; the second collection contains his correspondence as archbishop from 1093 until his death. The first collection consisting of 147 letters, of which 139 are his own, was put together by Anselm himself; he corrected and occasionally altered the text; he expected these letters to be read, and in later life he sometimes advised monks of Canterbury to read what he had said in an early letter.[1] By contrast, the later and politically much more important letters were preserved somewhat haphazardly in drafts; and the collection, as we now have it, was put together after Anselm's death by someone who had not altogether mastered his material, and made mistakes of arrangement and duplications, which fuller knowledge would have enabled him to avoid.[2] To put

[1] See F. S. Schmitt, 'Zur Entstehungsgeschichte der handschriftlichen Sammlungen der Briefe des hl. Anselm v. Canterbury', *R. Bén.*, xlviii, 1936, 300–18. (cf. *MARS*, iii, 89–90.) In Ep. 335 [iii, 103] Anselm wrote to the monk Warnerus at Canterbury in 1104: 'Consulo tibi ut quaeras epistolam quam ego feci domino Lanzoni, quando novitius erat.' This is Ep. 2 [i, 2], which had been written over thirty years earlier. This letter is also quoted in Epp. 35 [i, 27] and 51 [i, 43]. In *VA* i, xx, Eadmer gives an extensive quotation from Ep. 37 [i, 29].

[2] The chief manuscript of the later letters, Lambeth MS. 59, from Christ Church, Canterbury, is a carelessly written volume with many erasures and corrections, misplacements, omissions and later additions. Its appearance and shortcomings are an eloquent testimony to the confusion of the materials with which its compiler had to work. I cannot believe that it was written, as Dom Schmitt suggests (*Scriptorium*, ix, 1955, 73–4) in the lifetime of St. Anselm. A date about 1125–30 seems to me much more likely. The verse

the matter briefly, the later letters are a business archive preserved as a tribute of loyalty to the archbishop's memory; the
earlier letters are personal letters, mostly letters of friendship
or instruction on the monastic life, put together by Anselm
himself because they contained matter he thought worthy of
preservation. They are very carefully written—for our taste
often too elaborately contrived—showing the same wealth of
rhyme, assonance and antithesis which we have already noticed
in the early prayers and meditations.

In preserving these letters Anselm was following an impulse
which is strong in many people at all times, but only very
occasionally rises to the level of producing a form of art—the
impulse to preserve moments of experience and expressions of
friendship which have no place in the more conventional forms
of literature. The letters he wrote at Bec are Anselm's most
personal contribution to a great age of letter writing. In the
Middle Ages there were two such periods: the first lasted from
the later years of the tenth century to the beginning of the
thirteenth century; the second from the middle of the fourteenth to the early sixteenth century. The first period opens
with the letters of Gerbert and closes with those of Peter of
Blois; the second opens with those of Petrarch and closes with
those of Erasmus. Needless to say the collections of letters
made during these two periods have very varied sources of
inspiration and are very unequal in interest; but they have this
in common, that their main purpose was not to contribute to
the conduct of business but to intellectual, or literary, or
religious instruction. Among them all, Anselm's letters are

at the end of the manuscript 'Que restant modici sunt scripta manu Thiderici'
provides no clue to the scribe of the manuscript, but only to the original
collector of the fragments of Anselm's writings with which the manuscript
ends. Still less can the writing of the manuscript be associated with Anselm's
letter, Ep. 379 [iv, 70] to Thidricus: there is not the slightest reason to
think that this letter refers to the making of this or any other collection of
Anselm's letters. It is, of course, beyond question that drafts of Anselm's
letters, and other letters, were preserved at Canterbury for reference purposes
in the conduct of business: for this, see also Ep. 357 [iv, 58]. But this is
very different from making a literary manuscript for permanent record. It
is necessary to make this point because false conclusions can be drawn from
Dom Schmitt's hypothesis: e.g. Cantor, p. 169–70, 'Anselm himself took
care to prohibit documents not altogether favourable to the reform cause
from publication in his collected correspondence'.

conspicuous for the extent to which they were simply expressions of friendship and spiritual communion.

It was Lanfranc's removal from Caen to Canterbury in 1070 which first turned Anselm into a letter-writer on a considerable scale, and gave him a congenial theme. Lanfranc took with him a handful of monks from Normandy to form a small nucleus of like-minded men in a community of largely hostile English monks. Anselm's earliest letters were written to these men, and though the range of his correspondents grew with the passage of time and the spread of his reputation, they remained the chief recipients of his letters; they received nearly fifty of his letters between 1071 and 1079, and nearly half his total correspondence before 1093.

Very often he had, in an ordinary sense, almost nothing to say. He was not much given to the exchange of news. The essential business, which kept messengers journeying to and fro between Canterbury and Bec, would seem often to have been transacted by word of mouth or in formal documents which have not come down to us. Factually, there was not much else which required to be said. There were gifts to be acknowledged and personal matters of business to be arranged; but above all these was the task of communicating himself to his friends. This he did in language which now seems to us, who are accustomed to read quite different meanings than he intended into the words which he uses, enormously overdone:

When I sit down to write to you, oh soul most dear to my soul, when I sit down to write to you, I am uncertain how best to begin what I have to say. Everything I feel about you is sweet and pleasant to my heart; whatever I desire for you is the best that my mind can conceive. For such as I have seen you to be, I have loved, as you well know; and such as I now hear you to be, I desire, as God well knows. And so, wherever you go, my love follows you; and wherever I stay, my desire embraces you. Why then do you entreat me through your messengers, exhort me in your letters, and constrain me by your gifts, to remember you? 'If I do not remember thee, let my tongue cleave to the roof of my mouth', if I prefer not Gundulf among my chief friends. For how should I forget you? How could he be removed from my memory, who is impressed on my heart like a seal on wax? [1]

[1] Ep. 4 [i, 4].

These words were written to Gundulf, a man ten years his senior, who had left Bec with Lanfranc in 1063, and whom consequently Anselm can seldom have seen during the eight years before the letter was written. How are we to interpret such language? At first sight the kindest judgment would seem to be that it is the embodiment of Gothic extravagance. These expressions are not expressions of friendship as we understand it. But still less are they expressions of the passionate love which such words would now suggest. They could not have been written in the next century, when language of this kind had been appropriated by the poets of romantic love between men and women. We are still in the period when love was essentially an intellectual concept. No doubt these words were written under the impulse of a strong emotion. But the nature of the emotion may be judged from a sentence at the end of the letter directing that another of Gundulf's companions, with whom Anselm had much less in common, was to regard everything in it as equally applicable to himself. This, then, was not a private letter intended for no other eyes than those of the recipient. It had a wider application, and it was intended ultimately to reach a large public. There can be no doubt that Anselm looked on these letters of friendship as more suitable and profitable for general reading than the later political letters, which have provided so much material for historians. This was partly no doubt because he looked on friendship as an important subject, and political negotiation as an unimportant one; but also because on the first subject he had something important to say, and on the second nothing. To understand this we must look at the background.

### (i) *The Traditional Pattern*

Like everyone else in his day, Anselm no doubt owed to Cassian the main outlines of his views on friendship.[1] There is no reason to think that he had read Cicero on Friendship, but from Cassian he would have learnt the classical doctrine of the three kinds of friendship: the first based on mutual pleasure,

---

[1] Cassian, Collationes, xvi: *De Amicitia* (ed. Petschenig, *CSEL*, pp. 437–62).

as of brothers, parents and children, husbands and wives; the second on common interest, as of merchants or soldiers or thieves; the third on the union of the souls of good men. That kind of love between man and woman, issuing in marriage, which we commonly regard as having a place apart, in interest and variety superior to all others, is here not only placed on the lowest rung but also is lumped together with various other kinds of domestic attachment. These attachments, being the work of instinct and not of conscious purpose, were lower in the scale of friendship than the association of partners in business or even in crime, which (considered apart from the result) was the product of the higher functions of the human soul. Given these presuppositions, the highest place was naturally reserved for that kind of friendship which finds expression in the union of will and intellect in a good purpose—that is to say the union of the souls of good men in the pursuit of virtue. This alone deserved the attention of spiritual men. Such friendship was indissoluble and independent of local circumstances and chance removals. It was based on a common will and a common aim; it was rooted in a contempt of worldly goods. It could not exist without identity of purpose, and it could be clouded by differences of opinion; but since the common purpose required a communion of minds, in which the slower and more stupid could sometimes hit the mark missed by the abler and more learned, such differences should not, in the friendship of good men, lead to a breach of charity. The ideal friendship was essentially moderate, rational and unemotional.

There are many expressions of this traditional doctrine in the letters of the period. Lanfranc, for instance, could write to his 'dearest brother and friend' Thomas, archbishop of York, that 'distance separates from mutual love only those who love because of earthly gain or bodily pleasures; but those who are joined in a sincere and Christian love suffer no division through bodily absence or local separation.'[1] What Lanfranc here calls 'sincere and Christian love' we may be inclined to call coolness, or even (knowing the circumstances) humbug. He no doubt loved his fellow archbishop with that discerning charity which implies no warmth of feeling; it is hard to think

[1] Ep. 13 (*Lanfranci Opera*, ed. J. A. Giles, i, 34).

71

that he ever needed his company. Here, as often in early medieval thought, we see the denigration of instinct and passion in the interests of intellect. Lanfranc was not alone in this. He did no more than express the traditional doctrine, sanctified by Augustine and many others, that 'those who are joined together in love are never separated, though one is in the east and the other in the west'. They are never separated because spirit transcends all local differences.

## (ii) *The Anselmian Experience*

Set against this background of moderate, rational and unemotional friendship Anselm's letters at once present a contrast and a puzzle. The contrast is obvious. Anselm seems to throw to the winds the *gravitas* of earlier writers in the pursuit of something more vivid and consuming. He avoids the risk of cold and lifeless urbanity by rushing to the opposite extreme of apparently boundless emotion:

My eyes eagerly long to see your face, most beloved; my arms stretch out to your embraces. My lips long for your kisses; whatever remains of my life desires your company, so that my soul's joy may be full in time to come.[1]

It is extremely difficult to give these words a sense which is at once plausible and sensible. The difficulty will be apparent when it is remarked that they were written to two young relations, aspirants to the monastic life, whom Anselm in all probability had never seen. Even if there were no other grounds for doing so, we must therefore, to some extent at least, exclude the natural sense of words in explaining this and similar passages. Equally, however, we may not explain them in a purely symbolic sense. They are distantly, but only distantly, reminiscent of the *Song of Songs*, which provided the best authority for the expression of spiritual love in terms of physical union. It cannot be doubted that they express a

[1] Ep. 120 [ii, 28]: 'Concupiscunt iam, dilectissimi mei, concupiscunt oculi mei vultus vestros, extendunt se brachia mea in amplexus vestros. Anhelat ad oscula vestra os meum, desiderat conversationem vestram quidquid restat de vita mea, ut in pleno gaudio futurae vitae vobiscum gaudeat anima mea'. For the word *conversatio*, see below pp. 332-3.

personal and passionate longing; but the nature of this longing, and the extent to which it was associated with its ostensible object in the person directly addressed, are not easily distinguished. We see in these expressions of friendship a familiar characteristic of Anselm's thought. He bends his mind to the contemplation of an ideal image, he attaches it to himself with passionate intensity, he defines its nature, and he gives it a name. Here the name is that of a friend. In his prayers and meditations, formed under the influence of a similar impulse, the name is that of a saint or of God. But in the latter, the reality of the ideal object was guaranteed in advance; in his letters of friendship it was a subtle blend of fact and imagination. When he wrote to his young relatives Anselm's ardent response was excited by their monastic vocation and not by their personalities, of which he knew nothing. The 'conversation' he desired was the community of monastic discipline; and the 'full joys of the life to come' referred at least as much to the joys of Heaven as to the pleasures of companionship on earth. The dignity of friendship lay in this: of all things belonging to the natural world it alone continues essentially unaltered in Heaven. Anselm did not hesitate to see health, strength, speech, and power of sight as elements of eternal blessedness. This was the theme of his best-known sermon. But these qualities are transformed in Heaven. Only friendship, the union of wills, is unchanged. Momentarily at least it can now be experienced as fully as 'in that holy society where there will also be unfailing and perfect friendship'.[1] It is in this context that we must understand Anselm's cry:

You have come; you have set me on fire; you have melted and fused my soul with yours: this soul of ours can now be rent asunder, it can never be separated.[2]

What Anselm desired was an identity of profession. In this he was following the classical doctrine which declared such identity to be the essence of friendship. But he desired some-

---

[1] *Liber de beatitudine caelestis patriae*, x (*PL* CLIX, 638). See also *PL* CLXXXIV, 359–60, for the other form of the sermon in which Anselm expresses this idea; and cf. *VA* I, xxxiii.       [2] Ep. 120 [ii, 28].

thing more than this. The distant realization of the ideal was not enough. Hence in the realm of friendship Anselm abandoned the time-honoured doctrine that absence was a negligible factor in the union of souls in friendship. His words on this subject have an intensity which it is difficult now to understand. We suspect a certain extravagance when he writes to Henry, prior of Canterbury, with whom, in the ordinary sense of the word, he seems to have had little in common:

Those whose minds have been fused together by the fire of love, not unnaturally, find it grievous when distance separates their bodies.[1]

He uses similar phrases after enjoying for a few months the company of the Englishman, Osbern, whom Lanfranc sent as an exile to Bec:

we cannot now be separated without tearing apart our joint soul and severing our heart.[2]

This fusion of souls and the *scissura animae* which takes place at separation are recurring themes in the letters of Anselm at Bec. They are used about persons and in situations astonishingly various: persons whom he has never seen, or not seen for many years, have the same treatment as those with whom he had long lived in intimacy. Physical presence and incompatibilities of temperament seem to have brought no disillusion; absence and distance no cooling.

The peculiar ardour of Anselm's imaginative projection of his personal ties no doubt bred misunderstandings in those who did not understand that the fire was primarily intellectual and that it fed on an incorporeal ideal. It was a product of philosophy rather than of feeling: the unity of souls in friendship was a dramatic realization of that unity in which all men are one. Anselm spoke with contempt of those philosophers who were so tied to the data of their physical senses that they could not rise to the intellectual comprehension of this unity. For himself, this unity was a present, painful and—if we are to trust some of his expressions—shattering experience. It was an experience

---

[1] Ep. 5 [i, 5].
[2] Ep. 39 [i, 31]; cf. Ep. 84 [i, 75] to Anselm's old friend Gilbert Crispin.

at the command of the most transient applicants, and never more elaborately so than when it was sought by a fugitive. One of the most curious of all the expressions of friendship was written on behalf of a certain Moses, a runaway monk returning to his monastery 'clothed from head to foot in the skin of your servant and brother Anselm':

If therefore I have at any time offended any of you, scourge the skin of Moses for my fault and in him deprive my mouth of food. For I have commended my skin to my brother Moses for him to keep it carefully as his own. Do not spare it on this account; but if you beat my skin for his fault, I shall require satisfaction from him; and if you spare it I shall be thankful.[1]

This was not a joke intended to turn away wrath by raising a smile. Nothing would be less in character than the light touch on such an occasion. Anselm's words are entirely serious. They express in a personal and domestic way his assurance of the perfect substitution of one man for another, which on a cosmic scale dominated his doctrine of the Atonement. Indeed his theology and his doctrine of friendship alike presuppose to an extraordinary extent the homogeneity of the human race and the ability of one man to stand in the place of another. If his language *appears* fanciful and extravagant, it does so because we do not share his philosophical views. And if it *is* fanciful, it was not intended to be so.

In intention Anselm's extravagance of language has nothing in common with the contrived fancifulness of the language of romantic love. Here, as so often, Anselm hovers between the old and the new. In his intellectual intention he is on the side of tradition; but in the vividness of his experience and the novelty of his language he points to the future. His friendships are far from those of romantic love. They are not even very near to the sentimental friendships of the cloister to which the example of Aelred of Rievaulx later gave a certain authority and

[1] Ep. 140 [ii, 45]. We may compare this with the action of the monks of Rochester at the death-bed of Anselm's friend, Bishop Gundulf, in 1108. As he lay dying he asked for corporal punishment for his sins; the monks refused to beat their dying friend, but promised that they would all undergo punishment on his behalf (*Vita Gundulfi*, PL CLIX, 834). Cf. also Anselm, Ep. 11 [i, 9].

charm. They are the expression of a union of wills, intellectually conceived and passionately expressed. The friend is more of an idea than a person. Even Anselm's contemporaries seem to have been disappointed to find that he meant something less or something different than appeared on the surface. They expected him to write and he was silent; they expected him to stay and he left. Hence the reproaches which his letters were partly intended to answer; hence the bitter sense of desertion which swept through the community of Bec when it learned that he was after all to be archbishop of Canterbury. No protestations of Anselm could entirely dispel the suspicion that his sentiments were less stable than he claimed. It is very noticeable that though the letters of the twenty years after 1070 sparkle with ardent and unconventional expressions of friendship, there is nothing similar after 1093. The break was decisive. Perhaps the shock of the dissension that broke loose at his leaving Bec helped to dry up this stream of thought. In any case it never flowed again. Anselm still retained the power to draw men to him, but it was as disciples rather than as intimate friends that they now appeared. The change has a parallel in his writings and in his altered circumstances. His world became larger and more hostile; he left peace and spiritual intimacy behind at Bec, and faced a sea of troubles both practical and speculative.

# CHAPTER III

# CUR DEUS HOMO

## I. THE BACKGROUND OF THE 'CUR DEUS HOMO'

THE *Cur Deus Homo* is Anselm's greatest intellectual achievement. Its composition marks the climax of his theological development. Standing at the beginning of the most creative period of the Middle Ages, it has an un-rivalled combination of sustained argument, intense moral force, and originality in general conception and in detail. Yet it was, perhaps rightly and at least understandably, a com-paratively neglected work. In its immediate circumstances it was written at an unpropitious time, under the stress of Anselm's early years as archbishop, in bickerings and controversies which we must later examine, and 'in great tribulation of heart'. It was finished in exile near Capua, in the mountain village of Liberi in 1098; but the greater part must have been planned and written in England before October 1097. Reading his great argument, we can understand Anselm's relegation of all secular business to his man of affairs, and his drowsiness while the petty disputes about knight service and feudal aids and the pallium raged round him in the royal court. Eadmer, who has described in vivid detail Anselm's indifference to the secular problems which beset him on all sides, has somehow missed the fierce intellectual fire which burned at the centre of his meditations. This is revealed in the *Cur Deus Homo*. Here we may trace his most mature reflections. But before doing so, it is necessary to say something about the stage we have reached in Anselm's life and in his relations with the outside world.

### (i) *Roscelin and the 'De Incarnatione Verbi'*

Anselm arrived in England early in September 1092. He came on the business of his monastery and in answer to the appeal of his sick friend Hugh earl of Chester. Hugh recovered, and,

77

after making arrangements for a new monastic foundation at Chester, Anselm's business hung fire. By Christmas he was at Westminster waiting for an interview with the king.[1] It was soon clear that he would have to wait a long time and he settled down with his friend Abbot Gilbert Crispin. He sent to Bec for various works—his letters, a prayer to St. Nicholas, and his unfinished reply to Roscelin's views on the Trinity. Having thus provided himself with work for several months ahead he disappears from our view until the dramatic events of the following March from which he emerged as archbishop. During the intervening months, he seems to have revised the text of his letters; but he was chiefly occupied with Roscelin, whose challenge had brought a new element into his life.

Until this time Anselm had been concerned only with answering his own questions and those of his monastic friends. He had taken no part in controversy. But the dispute with Roscelin brought Anselm once more into contact with a world from which he had been cut off for over thirty years—the uneasy world of secular masters and their floating population of pupils. For a short time as a young man Anselm had moved in this world; now he was confronted with it again. In this setting Roscelin was a very notable man. When his views were first reported to Anselm, probably in about 1090, he was a canon of Compiègne. But in 1092 he was certainly at Bayeux, perhaps as a canon of the cathedral, and it may have been his move to Normandy which forced him once more on Anselm's notice.[2] We are not concerned with Roscelin's later career except in so far as it illustrates the vitality and resources of the new secular masters. They were men whom neither official condemnation nor popular execration could silence, and for whom new patrons and new positions could always be found. They are one of the great new unchronicled phenomena of the time. Roscelin made enemies wherever he went, but he was irrepressible. The stages of his career, like his philosophical views, are obscure, but at every stage he was a centre of

---

[1] For these events, see *MARS*, iii, 1954, 87–8.
[2] Roscelin witnessed a charter on 7 May 1092 at Bayeux among the members of the chapter. (F. Picavet, *Quelques documents sur un de nos vieux maîtres: Roscelin de Compiègne*, 1912.)

controversy. After his appearance at Compiègne and Bayeux, we find him at Tours, at Loches and in England, teaching and making himself hateful, but always gaining adherents; and he disappears from view still undefeated, as a canon of Besançon. As a philosopher his name is written in water; but he taught Abelard, he corresponded with the earliest of the Oxford masters, and he started Anselm on a new phase of his theological career.[1] These facts are his chief monument.

He touched Anselm at a sensitive spot. It had been Anselm's chief contribution to theological method up to this date to make dialectic a natural and uncontroversial instrument for the discussion of the central Christian doctrines. He never praised dialectic as Berengar had done, nor did he boast of his untapped dialectical resources as Lanfranc had done, he simply used the methods of dialectic to clarify his problems and to define his terms. The perils which had seemed so evident to his older contemporaries fell away before him. But they were not destroyed. In particular the doctrine of the Trinity presented an immovable obstacle to all attempts at dialectical treatment. The God who is one Substance and three Persons defied the procedures of dialectic. It was tempting to say in the language of dialectic that the one Substance is to the three Persons as Substance is to its Accidents, but this kind of language was soon seen to be incompatible with the language of Athanasius. Yet, if this language was inadmissible, what better could be found?

Roscelin was the first master to bring this problem into the open. His views came to Anselm only at second-hand and in a single sentence, but they required an answer. He appears to have asserted that the three Persons of the Trinity were either so separate that they could be said to be three Gods, or so united that all three must have been incarnate in Christ. This was the kind of thing that dialecticians were bound sooner or later to say; but what made Roscelin's statement so challenging was the fact that he coupled his statement with the names of Lanfranc and Anselm. He claimed that he had convinced

---

[1] For Roscelin's relations with Abelard, see his letter in *PL* CLXXVIII, 357 (or in a better edition by J. Reiners, *Der Nominalismus in der Frühscholastik, BGPM* VIII, 1910, 62–80); for his correspondence with the Oxford master Theobald of Étampes, see the latter's letter in *PL* CLXIII, 767–70.

Lanfranc and that, given the opportunity, he could convince Anselm. So far as Lanfranc was concerned this claim was not very plausible, and it was beyond the possibility of proof. But, in Anselm's case the claim had some plausibility. Anselm was reported to have said—and he did not deny the report—that the Persons of the Trinity were to God what the qualities *albus, justus, grammaticus,* and so on, were to an individual man. In other words, the relationship was like that of Substance and Accidents. In the first draft of his reply to Roscelin Anselm attempted to justify this parallel by explaining the sense in which it was true. But it opened the way to so many misunderstandings that he suppressed this passage in his final version.[1] Nevertheless, the discovery of the unfinished draft has shown that Roscelin was not quite reckless in mentioning Anselm as a possible supporter of his views. One of the consequences of Anselm's parallel might reasonably seem to be the inseparability of the Persons of the Trinity in the act of Incarnation.

Anselm had briefly replied to Roscelin when he was first challenged on this subject in about 1090. He had then embarked on a more detailed reply, but he abandoned it when Roscelin recanted at the Council of Soissons. Rumours then got about that Roscelin's recantation was insincere, and though Anselm knew this only from hearsay he determined to finish his reply. This was the state of the argument when Anselm sent to Bec for his draft and completed it in the winter of 1092–3, under the title *Epistola de Incarnatione Verbi.*

The circumstances of its composition may help to explain why as a whole it is the weakest of his works. He had been forced to write on a subject not of his own choosing and in a manner which was uncongenial to him. He had no insistent impulse to write. Hence his delays and alterations of plan

---

[1] Dictum quoque mihi prius fuerat similiter, quia Francigena quidam—hunc autem novi, quia amicus meus est—assereret se a me audisse ita de Deo dici Patrem et Filium et procedentem a Patre et Filio Spiritum, quomodo albus et iustus et grammaticus et similia de quodam individuo homine dicuntur. (*Ep. de Incarn. verbi prior recensio,* Schmitt, i, 282. The substance of this passage survived Anselm's first revision of the work in MS Hereford P. 1.1—where however the report of Anselm's words is ascribed to Roscelin—but it has disappeared in the final version.)

unusual in his writings. There are naturally some striking and characteristic passages in it, such as the statement of his theological method, his emphatic assertion of the real existence of universals, and the comparison between the Trinity and the parts of the river Nile. But as a whole the work is not written with Anselm's usual lucidity, and it does not convey the intense experience communicated in his other works. Yet it has an important place in his intellectual development. Begun at Bec and finished at Canterbury, it links the two phases of his career, and it introduces the features which mark his later years—the intrusion of contemporary controversy and the presence of actual, not imaginary, enemies. In subject-matter also it marks a transition from the early to the later works. The earliest works had dealt with all aspects of the nature of God, *except* the Incarnation. It was this deficiency that the *Epistola de Incarnatione Verbi* and the *Cur Deus Homo* supplied. In the first of these works Anselm attempted to demonstrate against Roscelin, that *if the Incarnation was a fact* it must have involved the Incarnation of only one Person in the Trinity. But the question still remained: was the Incarnation a fact or, as the enemies of Christianity declared, a figment of the imagination? In the *Cur Deus Homo* Anselm undertook to demonstrate that the Incarnation was not a figment but a fact; and not just a fact but a necessary fact. The purpose of the work was therefore similar to that of the *Proslogion*, in which Anselm had undertaken to demonstrate that God is not only a Being, but a necessary Being, who cannot be thought of as not existing outside the mind. With the establishment of these two points the main outline of Anselm's theology would be complete; all that came after could only be an elaboration of thoughts already sketched.

It is evident, therefore, that though unwelcome and unforeseen circumstances provoked this phase of Anselm's theological writing, it was necessary for the completeness of his system that these works should be written. Without a consideration of the Incarnation his theology would have remained essentially incomplete: the theology of a Christian God unattached to the Christian dispensation. If Anselm's method of rational inquiry into the mysteries of the Faith was valid it had sooner or later to be applied to the main object of Christian belief. The step had to be taken, but Anselm's long delay in taking it—he was now over sixty—may be explained by the novelty of his understanding. So far he had restricted his method of rational proof to the area of metaphysical reality. Now he was extending it to the area of historical fact. It was a single, unique historical fact that he was concerned with, and one already guaranteed by Christian dogma. But we shall find pupils who thought that the same method of proof could be applied to other historical facts not yet determined by dogma. Even, however, with his self-imposed limitation, Anselm was undertaking the occupation of new and unknown ground, departing farther than ever before from St. Augustine. When he started to write against Roscelin he probably had no clear idea where this new phase of his theological writing was to lead him. But gradually the work gathered momentum, and the *Cur Deus Homo* was written with a flood of new thoughts such as he had not experienced since he wrote the *Proslogion* nearly twenty years earlier.

### (ii) *Theological speculation and the school of Laon*

It was impossible, however, in the 1090s to recapture the simplicity of the *Proslogion*, written in monastic peace and seclusion. Anselm was archbishop. He could shut out—perhaps he ought not to have done—the clamour of secular pleas. But he could not shut out the questions of his friends or even of those who were not his friends. They were becoming very insistent. When he was writing against Roscelin, he had an eye for 'the many whom I feel to be struggling with this problem'.[1] Similarly in the *Cur Deus Homo* he refers to 'many not only learned but even illiterate men who ask this question and require an answer'.[2] This large army of questioners of all degrees was no more imaginary than Roscelin himself. There is every reason to think that the area of theological inquiry had been immensely widened during the last few decades, both in the scope of the questions asked and in the number of people who were asking them.

Anselm must have been kept informed of the developments in theological debate by the many young men who came to Bec in his last years as abbot. Among the latest of these arrivals

---

[1] *Ep. de Incarn. Verbi* §1 (Schmitt, ii, 6).    [2] *CDH* I, 1 (Schmitt, ii, 48).

was the monk of Bec whom he summoned to England specially to help him in this theological work. In the *Cur Deus Homo* he named this monk as his interlocutor. In all his other dialogues the conversation is between an unnamed *Disciple* and *Master*: in the *Cur Deus Homo*, and only here, it was *Boso* and *Anselm* who spoke. The distinction has a certain importance. It was a tribute to an essential collaborator. Boso knew at first hand the questions that were agitating the minds of the younger generation. He had come to Bec in about 1090 to discuss problems which he found too agitating for his peace of mind, and he stayed because he found there an answer to his questions. He himself wrote nothing that has survived. Administration and ill-health may have quenched his philosophic fire, but he brought to Anselm the unease of the outside world, and it was he who chiefly provoked the writing of the *Cur Deus Homo*: *tu maxime inter alios me impulisti*, wrote Anselm.[1]

But what were the questions of the day and whence did they arise? We have already seen that Anselm's two works on the Incarnation are linked with his other theological writings by an inner logic of their own; yet they arise more immediately than his earlier writings from contemporary discussion. Roscelin provided one external stimulus, but there were others equally important. They are more obscure because they were more successful. They avoided notoriety. The darkness which surrounds the career of Roscelin is bright in comparison with the obscurity of the more influential masters who rose to fame in the last thirty years of the eleventh century—the men who took over from Lanfranc and Berengar, and prepared the way for Abelard and the masters of emergent scholasticism. The influence of those men on the future is only now beginning to have justice done to it:[2] their influence on the *Cur Deus Homo* has not been recognized at all.

[1] Schmitt, ii, 139.
[2] The pioneers in this work have been Miss B. Smalley and Dom O. Lottin. The former has dealt chiefly with the school of Laon in the context of Biblical exegesis; the latter in the context of theological discussion. But originally the two streams must have been one, as the references in many of the theological fragments show. The most comprehensive collection of these fragments is now to be found in O. Lottin, *Psychologie et Morale aux XII^e et XIII^e Siècles*, v, 1959, where there are references to earlier work.

Our ignorance at this point will always be profound, but it is not quite impenetrable. The *Cur Deus Homo* has the appearance of asking many questions which had never been asked before. Yet within a few years these same questions, or many of them, are commonly found in scholastic discussions. These discussions do not as a rule show any influence of Anselm's treatise: the questions are found in a quite different context, discussed in a different way, and generally with a different solution. The conclusion seems inescapable that the theologians of the schools did not get their inspiration from Anselm. Did he get any inspiration from them?

To keep this question within answerable limits it will be well to confine our attention to a single school where the novelties of the time are most easily discernible: the cathedral school of Laon. Here the broadening stream of theological discussion is most conspicuous. By about the year 1100 it was the chief resort in northern Europe for the education of ambitious youth, and the connexions of the school with official circles in England were especially close: William of Corbeil, clerk of Ranulf Flambard and later archbishop of Canterbury; the nephews of Henry I's justiciar Roger of Salisbury; the sons of the royal chancellor Ranulf; and several others who later became archdeacons and bishops; all these were at Laon while Anselm was at Canterbury.[1] They were sent there by relatives, who cannot be suspected of *avant-garde* tendencies, for a safe and reliable education likely to lead to future promotion, under a master who had no claim to brilliance. Master Anselm of Laon had nothing in common with St. Anselm, except his name, and strictly perhaps not even that.[2] He is an illustration of the fact that great academic reputations can be made, and great academic influence exerted, without a spark of genius. He had qualities that appeal to academic minds and easily influence academic institutions: methodical completeness, the

---

[1] The evidence is found in Herman of Tournai, *De Miraculis S. Mariae Laudunensis*, PL CLVI, 974—giving an account of the journey with relics of the church of Laon through southern England in 1113. For the date see J. S. P. Tatlock, 'The English Journey of the Laon Canons', *Speculum* viii, 1933, 454-65.

[2] In contemporary records his name is Ansellus (Anseaux); it is only in theological texts that the form Anselmus habitually appears.

careful absorption of the past, a distrust of new ideas. The school of Laon was theologically conservative, but in method it was the most advanced in Europe. Here lay the secret of its great influence.

It was probably the first secular school to make theology its speciality. This in itself was a point of great importance. It anticipated the infinite capacity for asking questions which is the chief external characteristic of the later schools. At Laon these questions seem to have been tied to biblical exposition: they were not yet systematic, still less did they range at will over the whole field of theology. But they were asked; and they were being asked at the time when the *Cur Deus Homo* was written.

Of the work of this school only fragments remain, but the fragments can now be numbered in hundreds. Their existence makes it possible to see in a general way how the practice of the schools, and especially of the school of Laon in the late eleventh century, made biblical commentary a channel for theological inquiry. It was precisely this that Lanfranc, and even Berengar, only a generation earlier, had tried to avoid; their commentaries were confined to discussions of the meanings and derivation of words, and analysis of the forms of argument. It was only accidently that they were concerned with the theological substance of the text. This reticence had disappeared by the end of the century. There is plenty of evidence that the Pauline Epistles provided the masters of Laon with opportunities for discussing the necessity of the Incarnation, the rights of the Devil, and other related topics. But it still remains to ask whether this flow of inquiry had any distinct influence on the *Cur Deus Homo* beyond providing the general atmosphere in which it was written. A chance survival makes it possible to answer this question.

There is only one chapter of the *Cur Deus Homo* in which Anselm states a traditional view in order to demolish it. This is the chapter dealing with the rights of the Devil (i, 7) and it is one of the most powerful pieces of argument in the whole work. It is also one of the most revolutionary. The form of the argument is especially masterly. It begins with a rough rejection of, and ends with a small concession to, a long tradition:

'As for that which we are accustomed to say'—and here Anselm quotes the traditional view that the Devil possessed a just power over man—'I do not see what force it has.'

Anselm then gives his reasons for this forthright rejection and in the last sentence of the chapter restates the rejected view with a slight modification, which makes it in a limited way acceptable. As a piece of controversial writing there is nothing quite like this elsewhere in Anselm; nor in its combination of argumentative force with moderation of statement is there anything to match it in contemporary literature.

I have called the argument of this chapter Anselm's, and this no doubt is right; but we must not overlook the fact that Anselm puts the whole argument into Boso's mouth. This is the only place where Boso abandons his rôle as interrogator and critic of Anselm's arguments and puts forward an argument of his own. Boso states, and demolishes, the traditional view; and Anselm receives his remarks without comment. In a writer so careful of literary form as Anselm, it is impossible to think that this is accidental.[1] It is reasonable to suppose that Boso took an important part in bringing forward the subject of the Devil's rights and in formulating, or helping to formulate, the objections to them. Boso, we know, was a newcomer to the monastic life, who had been unable to find anyone to answer his questions until he met Anselm. We do not know whom he had previously asked; but it would have been natural for him to have frequented one or other of the secular schools of the day, and this probability gives a special interest to the discovery

[1] Professor McIntyre, *St. Anselm and his Critics: a reinterpretation of the Cur Deus Homo* (1954), p. 70 noticed the anomaly of Boso's rôle here and suggested that the refutation of the traditional view should be transferred to 'Anselm'. But this suggestion is invalidated by the absence of manuscript support, and by the further difficulties that would arise at the end of the speech. There is, however, some reason to think that the whole of chapter i, 7 is an insertion into an already existing dialogue. In chapter i, 6 Boso formulates a number of questions and Anselm's first speech in chapter i, 8 gives his immediate reaction to these questions without referring to the argument of the preceding chapter. It seems therefore quite likely that Anselm did not originally intend to include an attack on the rights of the Devil in his dialogue, and this might explain Gilbert Crispin's ignorance of this part of the argument in his *Disputatio Judaei cum Christiano* (see below).

86

of a link between this chapter of the *Cur Deus Homo* and the theological teaching of the school of Laon.

Twenty-five years ago it was discovered that the statement at the beginning of the chapter, which Boso quoted for criticism, was embedded verbatim in a theological fragment from the school of Laon.[1] In this fragment the passage in parenthesis in the *first* sentence of the chapter is followed immediately by the *last* sentence of Anselm's chapter, but without the modification which the intervening argument had made necessary. The writer of this fragment showed no knowledge of the refutation. He wrote entirely from the point of view which Anselm rejected, and betrayed no consciousness that his opinion was under criticism. The scholar who discovered these parallels nevertheless thought that the Laon master was borrowing from the *Cur Deus Homo* without acknowledgment, even though he omitted the central argument. He supposed that this master had borrowed Anselm's beginning, altered his conclusion, ignored his argument, and used the *Cur Deus Homo* only to assist what Anselm was concerned to deny. This is a complication of evils. If the two passages are read in their context there can, I believe, be no doubt that it was Anselm who 'borrowed' the statement of the argument which he intended to destroy. This procedure is entirely consistent with the form of his argument and with the final modification of his source. If this is so—and the evidence must be left to the reader's judgment[2]—we have a distinct point of contact between the *Cur Deus Homo* and the theological teaching of the school of Laon in its prime.

In the *Cur Deus Homo* Anselm—and, we must now add, Boso—asked questions which were being asked in the contemporary schools. But the discussion follows lines which were quite different from those of the schools. In the schools the questions arose in the course of biblical commentary. They arose quite haphazardly and no single question could detain the master for long. He had to pass to other questions, unrelated to each other except by the chances of textual proximity. Even when the questions of the schools became independent of the biblical text and achieved an autonomy and system of their

---

[1] J. Rivière, 'D'un singulier emprunt à S. Anselme chez Raoul de Laon', *Revue des Sciences Religieuses*, xvi, 1936, 344-6.      [2] See Appendix I.

own, the need to pass on to the next question without too much delay remained an ineradicable characteristic of the secular schools. It is this even-paced progress which chiefly distinguishes the method of the schools from that of Anselm. He was in no hurry. He could examine the problem in all its ramifications, leaving no corner unexplored. His work has thus an organic completeness which cannot be expected in the fragmentary discussions of the schools. Moreover, despite all the sharpness and controversy of scholastic argument, Anselm had fundamentally more freedom than the secular masters. I do not think he would long have survived in the schools without being harassed by charges of heresy. It was not difficult to find statements in his works which contradicted the Fathers or were liable to be misinterpreted: even Roscelin could find the taint of heresy in the *Cur Deus Homo*.[1] Removed from the fierce light of controversy Anselm could allow himself subtleties, ambiguities and novelties which would have brought down a load of criticism on a secular master. He was fortunate in his circumstances, even as archbishop.

## (iii) *Gilbert Crispin and the Jews*

There is one last source of inspiration which cannot be ignored in our approach to the *Cur Deus Homo*: the Jews. They were the only learned, the only uncompromising opponents of the whole idea of the Incarnation within the range of Anselm's experience. Dialectic might cause Roscelin to err in relating the Incarnation to the Persons of the Trinity; tradition might mislead the masters of Laon on the rights of the Devil; but only the Jews stood out against the whole idea of divine Incarnation. Anselm spoke of the questions asked by learned and illiterate alike, and we know dimly whom he meant. But he also spoke of unbelievers. For them his work was to provide an irrefutable demonstration of the Christian doctrine. In the *Proslogion* the unbeliever was probably imaginary; but not in the *Cur Deus Homo*. He was to be seen everywhere in the Jews, already familiar in Normandy, and rapidly becoming

---

[1] *PL* CLXXVIII, 362 (letter of Roscelin to Abelard).

familiar in England also. They have been too much overlooked as a source of criticism and an incentive to inquiry.

In the course of time Christian apologists became too confident to feel any apprehension about Jewish criticisms. But this was certainly not so at the end of the eleventh century. The questions which were being asked within the fold were not unlike some of the hostile questions from without: each gave an edge to the other.

The Jewish attack was twofold. On the one hand it traversed the old ground of Old Testament exegesis. Was the Old Testament to be interpreted literally or allegorically? If literally, how could Christ satisfy the Messianic requirements? If allegorically, what grounds were there for this extension of the plain meaning of words? All this was a commonplace dispute on which nothing new could be said and nothing old could convince. But in addition to this there was a new line of attack which affected very deeply both the Jewish and the Christian conscience. It concerned the dignity of God. How could the Incarnation with all its indignity of human contact, insult, injury and shameful death be reconciled with the supreme dignity and stability of God? To the Jew, this issue of God's transcendent majesty was of immense importance. And not less to the Christian who saw in royal splendour the earthly image of God. Anselm had special reasons for feeling the force of an argument which urged the indecorum of the Christian treatment of God. He is outstanding among theologians for the emphasis he laid on the honour of God. This is a word of complex meaning as we shall see, but it certainly included the preservation of God's dignity against affront.[1] It was essential therefore that the accusation of dishonouring God should be met. This need was all the more urgent at a time when art and piety, with Anselm in the lead, combined to emphasize and elaborate the indignities and sufferings of Christ.[2] The Jewish criticism could not have been made at a more impressionable time.

[1] See below, pp. 106, 111.
[2] The emphasis on Christ's sufferings in Christian art was stressed by the Jew in Gilbert's dialogue (*PL* CLIX, 1034). For Anselm's treatment of the theme in his Prayers, see Or. II (Schmitt, iii, 6–9).

It is not surprising, therefore, that the first enunciation of this criticism should coincide with the writing of the *Cur Deus Homo*: it was one of the impulses, and perhaps the main external impulse, in its composition. The unbelievers of whom he speaks at the beginning of his work could only be the Jews:

The unbelievers deride our simplicity, objecting that we do God an injury, and disgrace him, when we assert that he descended to a woman's womb, was born of a woman, was nourished with milk and human food, and—not to mention many other things unbecoming to God—suffered weariness, hunger, thirst, scourging and death on the Cross among thieves.[1]

At the time when Anselm came to England, or very shortly afterwards, his friend Gilbert Crispin was attempting to answer this same criticism formulated in similar terms.[2] Gilbert's opponent was a Jew of Mainz, lately settled in London in the Jewish colony. It is quite certain that some kind of collaboration took place between Anselm and Gilbert in preparing the answer to the Jew's attack, for Gilbert's reply shows clear traces of the ideas which Anselm developed in the *Cur Deus Homo*. But it is also reasonably certain that Gilbert's treatise was finished before the *Cur Deus Homo*, for he shows no knowledge of Anselm's refutation of the traditional view of the Devil's rights over Man: Gilbert, on the contrary, made these rights a basic presumption in his argument. It is of course possible that he knew Anselm's refutation and rejected it without comment, but his theological views were so strongly Anselmian that this is highly unlikely. It is much more likely that Gilbert's account of his dispute with the Jew was written at a time when he was able to draw on Anselm's ideas while they were being formed and before the *Cur Deus Homo* was finished.

I have argued elsewhere that Gilbert's argument was being prepared while Anselm stayed with him in the winter of 1092–3,

---

[1] *CDH* i, 3.

[2] 'Ad haec, si Deus est quo nihil maius sive sufficientius cogitari potest, qua necessitate coactus humanae calamitatis particeps et tantorum factus est consors et patiens malorum?'—and more to the same effect. (*PL* CLIX, 1018).

and that the London Jew from Mainz was therefore one of the seminal influences on the *Cur Deus Homo*.[1] It would appear, however, that the textual evidence for the date of Gilbert's treatise is too slight to give this hypothesis anything more than a shaky foundation. But whether or not the Jewish criticism was the starting point of Anselm's treatise in point of time, he makes it in fact the starting point of his argument. It must therefore be given a high place among the influences which helped to formulate the problems discussed in the *Cur Deus Homo*.[2]

Anselm was often blamed by his later critics for attempting to show that the Incarnation was *necessary*—that it was the only possible means of Man's Redemption. The sensible and traditional view was that God could have chosen many other means but that this was the most suitable. Leaving aside for the moment the question whether by 'necessary' Anselm meant anything else than 'most suitable', this criticism does not show sufficient appreciation of the task which Anselm set himself. The Jew required one or other of two proofs: either a proof drawn from the Old Testament, and over the centuries this argument had conspicuously failed to carry conviction; or a logical proof from which there could be no appeal. This was what Anselm attempted to give.

The limits within which he was successful must now be examined.

---

[1] *MARS* iii, 1954, 78–115. The latest editor of Gilbert's dialogue (B. Blumenkranz, *Gisleberti Crispini Disputatio Iudei et Christiani*, 1956, pp. 11–12) does not accept my conclusion, and prefers to leave the date of the work uncertain, with the single proviso that the discussion on which it was based probably took place before 1096. While agreeing that the arguments for a precise date are not at all conclusive, I think he does not give sufficient weight to the manuscripts (there are now four) in which Anselm is addressed as abbot and not as archbishop of Canterbury. How are these to be explained except on the hypothesis of an early date?

[2] For further evidence of the importance of Jewish criticism in stimulating discussion about the necessity of the Incarnation, see Odo, bishop of Cambrai, *Disputatio contra Judaeum, Leonem nomine, de adventu Christi Filii Dei* (*PL* CLX, 1105–'12): this dialogue, which makes use of *CDH* reports a dispute with a Jew at Senlis in 1106. Also A. Landgraf, *Écrits théologiques de l'école d'Abélard* (Spicilegium Sacrum Lovaniense, xiv, 1934) p. 158: in this work (the *Ysagoge in Theologiam*) the *Rationes Incarnationis*, mainly derived from *CDH* are formulated in reply to the objections of a Jew.

## 2. THE ARGUMENT[1]

### (i) *Synopsis*

The main line of Anselm's argument, like that of the *Proslogion*, can be simply stated, and no special knowledge is required to understand it. Leaving aside digressions, the essential stages may be set out in two complementary sequences:

A.1. Man was created by God for eternal blessedness.
  2. This blessedness requires the perfect and voluntary submission of Man's will to God.
  3. But the whole human race is guilty of disobedience.
  4. Any deviation of Man's will must either be punished by deprivation of blessedness or rectified[2] by an offering greater than the act of disobedience: there can be no free remission.
  5. No member of the human race can offer anything to God beyond his due obedience: there is no human capital with which to redeem the past, not to speak of the present and future.
  6. Therefore the whole human race must forfeit the blessedness for which it was created.

B.1. On this argument, God's purpose in the creation of man has been frustrated.
  2. But this is impossible.
  3. Therefore a means of redemption must exist.
  4. But the offering necessary for redemption ought to be made by Man.

---

[1] It is not my intention in what follows to go over once more the ground which has recently been covered in the excellent book by J. McIntyre, *St. Anselm and his Critics: a re-interpretation of the Cur Deus Homo* (Edinburgh, 1954), but I should like here to acknowledge the help I have had from this stimulating and judicious work. Perhaps I should add that the critics with whom Professor McIntyre deals are all modern, and that there is room for a study of the medieval critics of the *Cur Deus Homo*.

[2] It is impossible to give a really satisfactory translation of the phrase 'pro peccato satisfacere'. In the chapter (i, 11) where Anselm deals with it in detail it has some feudal associations which we shall later examine. Leaving these aside—though it is impossible to give an explanation without the use of some image—it may be thought of as an adjustment of a balance, which requires an equal distortion in the opposite direction if it is to regain its lost equilibrium.

92

5. And since Man has nothing to offer, it cannot be made by Man.
6. The offering required is greater than the whole existing Creation.
7. Nothing is greater than the whole Creation except God.
8. Therefore only God can make this offering.
9. Since only God can, and only Man ought to make this offering, it must be made by a God-Man.
10. Therefore a God-Man is necessary.
11. Therefore the Incarnation is necessary.

This bare sketch can give no idea of the subtlety and power of Anselm's argument, but it may suffice to give some idea of its intense rigour. It is also a necessary foundation for some remarks about the preconceptions and personal characteristics disclosed in Anselm's argument. As in the previous chapter we are not primarily concerned with the truth or falsity of this argument, but with the fundamental ideas without which it can have no claim to plausibility. Even a cursory reading of the argument presented above will show that it cannot claim the *a priori* certainty claimed for the argument of the *Proslogion*. Each stage presupposes a wealth of established truth which Anselm, for all his determination to pursue every objection and answer every doubt, only partially elucidates. The purpose of the following pages is to provide the elucidation necessary for placing the work in its personal and historical setting.

(ii) *The Rights of the Devil*

The first point at which Anselm's account of the Atonement differs from previous accounts is in its omission of the rights of the Devil over mankind.[1] We have already noticed his vigorous language in rejecting the current ideas on this subject. This rejection is all the more striking in that it sets him in clear

---

[1] For the general background, see J. Rivière, *Le Dogme de la Rédemption au début du Moyen Age*, 1934; D. E. de Clerck, 'Questions de sotériologie médiévale,' *RTAM*, xiii, 1946, 150–84; J. Rivière, 'Le dogme de la rédemption au xii siècle d'après les dernières publications', *Revue du Moyen Age latin*, ii, 1946, 100–12, 219–30; D. E. de Clerck, 'Droits du démon et nécessité de la Rédemption dans les écoles d'Abélard et de Pierre Lombard', *RTAM* xiv, 1947, 32–64.

opposition, not only to traditional and contemporary opinion but to the authority of St. Augustine. It is one of the ironies of Anselm's career that, having by his own account started as a modern mouthpiece for Augustine's views, he should have ended much further from Augustine than the contemporary secular masters; and the neglect of the *Cur Deus Homo* in the Schools of the twelfth century was partly caused by this deviation.

The masters of the Schools had strong reasons for conservatism at this point. The traditional view of the Devil's rights was not only recommended by authority but also by logic and experience. It was recommended by logic because it provided a straightforward explanation for the Incarnation. Man had voluntarily submitted himself to the Devil and to his empire of Death. This voluntary submission established a certain order and justice in the Devil's empire, not to be broken by an arbitrary exercise of God's omnipotence. If God seized Man by force from the Devil's rule, this would be a breach of the order and justice of the universe. Similarly, if the Devil extended his kingdom beyond the range of his voluntary subjects, this too would destroy the order and justice of his empire, breaking down his claim to a just and universal rule over mankind. In subjecting the sinless Man Christ to his empire of Death, the Devil overstepped the bounds of the rule and forfeited his claim to justice. In this way the breach by which Man could escape was made, and this was the justification for the Incarnation.

Besides its rational claims, this view of the economy of the Incarnation was reinforced by the experience of the early Middle Ages. The empire of the Devil in nature and supernature was a matter of daily experience: the Devil's empire and the daily breaches made in it by Christ provided the framework of history. The contemplation of God's triumphant strategy satisfied imagination and piety alike. And if in this world-view there was a strong element of dualism, this was no disrecommendation in an age which saw the forces of God and Devil locked in continual struggle. The dualism of experience and logic did not often rise to the level of the explicit heresy of the Manichees—it needed an unusual combination of circumstances and interests to give it this edge—but it had an orthodox expression in the recognition of the Devil's rights. Thought and instinct alike recommended the old view; and they alike persuaded Anselm to reject it. He had too uncompromising and too unitary a view of God's dominion over the whole Creation to accept any view which allowed the Devil, or any other rebel, a claim to justice against God. Rebellion deserved nothing but punishment; and to have seduced mankind into rebellion only increased the punishment: it did not create an Empire.

Brave words and difficult to deny, but immensely puzzling in their consequences. Anselm's elimination of the Devil from his logical structure—though not of course from the actual history of the Fall of Man—satisfies every moral instinct. His direct confrontation of God and Man in the work of Redemption makes an appeal to humanism as well as to logic. But Anselm drew back from the humanism, and found that he had created a logical problem of formidable dimensions. The three-cornered drama of God, Man and Devil corresponds to a readily intelligible situation in human affairs: one (Man) owes a service to another (the Devil) from which he cannot free himself; and a third person greater than either (God) steps in and effects his discharge. All kinds of dimensions of love and worship and gratitude can be added to this simple story, but it remains a situation which commonsense and experience both pronounce to be possible. But if the Devil is eliminated, and if Man owes only to God the service which he cannot pay, what scope is there for a Mediator? Where there is only a debtor who cannot pay, and no third person to acquit the debt, commonsense and experience suggest that the creditor must for ever forego his debt. He may punish or he may forgive, but he cannot be paid; and there is an air of subterfuge and unreality in any attempt to show that he can.

However successfully Anselm may deal with the problem which he created, his whole attempt is dogged by this suspicion of logical legerdemain, which Abelard at once detected. Anselm must have had great confidence in his logical powers at once to aggravate his problem by removing the third party to the transaction, and to insist more stringently than ever on the necessity and possibility of payment by a bankrupt who cannot pay to a creditor who cannot receive. It may at once be said that the verdict of Anselm's immediate successors was against him. Even those—they were chiefly monks—who most appreciated the rest of his argument, were unwilling to abandon the rights of the Devil.[1] And in the Schools the tendency was to ignore Anselm's argument altogether, insisting without his help on those elements in the case which were made familiar by the school of Laon. The only school of thought which wholeheartedly accepted the refutation of the traditional account of the Devil's rights was that of Abelard. But he and his followers drew from this refutation a conclusion which was the opposite of that which Anselm intended: since Man could make no payment to God, and God need make no payment to the Devil, the purpose of the Incarnation could not be that of making a payment at all. As Abelard said,

We are justified in the blood of Christ and reconciled to God because, by . . . receiving our nature and persisting in it until death, and teaching us by word and example, He bound us to Him more firmly by love; because of this—being inflamed by so great a benefit of the Divine grace—true charity bears all suffering without fear.[2]

This complicated sentence (I have simplified it), whether right or wrong, contains one of the great new ideas of the twelfth century: the significance of the Incarnation lay not in satisfying the claims of God or Devil, but in the teaching and example of the life of Jesus, and in renewing the love of Man for God. In what it leaves out, this view is divided by an impassable gulf from the position of Anselm, and—like

---

[1] The chief adherents of Anselm's views in the generation after the completion of the *Cur Deus Homo*, besides those mentioned above, p. 91 n. 2, were Honorius Augustodunensis and Rodulfus (see below pp. 206–17), and the anonymous authors of the following abridgements of Anselm's works: *Libellus Cur Deus Homo*, ed. E. Druwé with the misleading title *Libri Sancti Anselmi 'Cur Deus Homo' prima forma inedita* (Rome, 1933); *Disputatio Anselmi inter Christianum et Gentilem* found in a number of MSS. listed by A. Wilmart in *Archives d'histoire religieuse et doctrinale du Moyen Age*, ii, 1927, p. 11; and an abridgement in the form of Questions and Answers in British Museum MS. Egerton, 3323.

[2] Abelard, *Expositio in Rom. iii*, 23–6 (*PL* CLXXVIII, 833–6).

Anselm's view but more slowly—it was excluded from the main tradition of the Schools. Abelard's view stands against all the elements in Anselm's thought that we are now to examine. If Anselm's reply is monastic and feudal in inspiration, Abelard's is secular, and humanistic. But, since Abelard's opinion comes by the shortest possible route from the rejection of the Devil's rights, it too may claim Anselm as its parent.

### (iii) *The New Problem*

By removing the Devil from the picture, Anselm concentrated the widely scattered tensions of the old world-view into a simple relationship between God and Man. In the old three-cornered conflict of God, Devil and Man, Man had played a very subordinate rôle; in the new order the rôle of Man was necessarily greater, and that of God less easily defined. As soon as the complication of the Devil's rights was removed, it might seem that there was nothing to prevent God's free forgiveness of Man's sin, and that this was the only alternative to Man's damnation. Forgiveness no longer presented an affront to justice, and it would appropriately express the divine quality of mercy. But if sin were freely forgiven, the sacrifice of Christ would lose its point, and the Jewish criticism that Christianity irrationally and unnecessarily exposed God to the pain and indignities of human life would have to be answered (if it could be answered at all) in a way quite different from that of traditional doctrine. This was the problem to which Anselm's treatise was primarily directed.

The first question to which an answer was required was this: why should God not freely forgive Man's sin?[1] To this Anselm has two answers. In the first place, such forgiveness would place the disobedient will on the same level as the obedient one. Indeed (and this is a characteristic touch), it would make the disobedient will more Godlike than the obedient one, for disobedience (like God in this respect) is subject to no law; if in addition it were to be blessed, sinners would be—as Satan promised Eve—truly Godlike, whilst the sinless (if such existed) would remain human in their dependence on law. Secondly, such forgiveness would do

[1] *CDH* i, 12, 15.

nothing to correct the disturbance of the order and beauty of the universe caused by sin. On the contrary, it would lead to an ever-widening area of disorder and anarchy in God's kingdom. But in this kingdom, the slightest uncorrected disorder argues a deficiency either in justice or in power—a conclusion totally contrary to the divine nature. Hence the rational order of the universe requires that sin shall not be freely forgiven.

The intensity of Anselm's insistence on this point is one of the most remarkable features of the *Cur Deus Homo*.

God cannot freely forgive sin as a mere act of mercy, and Man has nothing with which he can merit forgiveness. Forgiveness therefore can only come from God's mercy: but mercy cannot work against justice. How then are justice and mercy to be reconciled? The commonsense view is that they cannot be reconciled: to be just is to render to each, and exact from each, his due;[1] to be merciful is to render more, and to exact less, than is due.[2] Formulas can of course be found to rub away the sharp antithesis, to make justice mild and mercy rational, until the two are indistinguishable. In a sense this is what Anselm does; but there is a difference between glossing over a contradiction by verbal ambiguities and discovering behind the contradictory appearances the unitary law which governs them. It must be left to others to judge whether his success is of the first or second kind, but at least his formulas are a result of a long and painful struggle with what he takes to be 'reality'. They are the fruit of an experience at once devotional and philosophic. Already in the *Proslogion* he had passionately sought the source of the identity of justice and mercy:

Certainly, if thou art merciful because thou art supremely good, and supremely good because thou art supremely just, then it follows that thou art merciful because thou art supremely just. Help me, oh just and merciful God, whose light I seek, help me to understand what I say: thou art merciful because thou art just.[3]

[1] Justitia est habitus secundum quem aliquis constanti et perpetua voluntate ius suum unicuique tribuit (Thomas Aquinas, *Summa Theologica*, 2, 2, q. 58, 1).
[2] Deus semper miseretur, puniendo citra condignum et premiendo ultra condignum (*ibid.* 1, q. 21, 4 ad 1).     [3] *Proslogion*, 7.

It was in such experiences as these that the solution to the main problem of the *Proslogion* was prepared. In the *Proslogion*, he had asserted that justice and mercy were indistinguishable; but in the *Cur Deus Homo* he had to give a convincing proof and illustration of this improbable conclusion. He did it in this way. The rational order of the universe requires that sinful man shall be everlastingly unblest. This is the way of justice. But the rational order of the universe also requires that man shall be everlastingly blessed: it was for this end that he was created. This is the way of mercy. Therefore within the created order there are these two strands, both deriving from God's rational plan of creation, and both therefore just.[1] In being merciful, God is also just—not in the sense of rendering to each his due (this is not Anselm's idea of justice), but in the *Proslogion* sense of doing that which befits the supreme goodness of God.[2] And the blessedness of Man, which is his true end, is prior to his damnation, which is the result of sin. In this sense mercy is more just than justice, and must prevail.

But here Anselm meets an apparently inescapable conclusion which is the opposite of that which lately confronted him. It now appears that we have gone from one extreme to another. From being impossible that sin should be forgiven, it now appears impossible that it should not be forgiven. We seem to be falling back into the free forgiveness for all men which the opponents of Christianity had urged at the beginning. And since the offering made by Christ is greater than all the sins of the world, past, present or to come, and capable moreover so far as 'value' is concerned of saving the fallen Angels as well as Man, there is no logical objection to this universal forgiveness for all.[3]

---

[1] Cf. *CDH* i, 19 and ii, 4–5.

[2] Ita justus es, non quia nobis reddas debitum, sed quia facis quod decet te, summe bonum (*Proslogion*, 10).

[3] Anselm had special reasons for rejecting the possibility of the redemption of the fallen Angels, but these did not affect the possibility of the universal redemption of Mankind or the capacity of Christ's satisfaction for effecting this. Cf. *CDH* ii, 21 where after arguing against the possibility of the Devil's redemption, he adds: 'Quod non dico, quasi pretium mortis eius (Christi) omnibus hominum et angelorum peccatis sua magnitudine non prevaleat, sed quoniam perditorum angelorum relevationi immutabilis ratio repugnat.'

Anselm was here in a considerable difficulty. God's plan required that Man should be saved. By this we may mean either 'the species Man' or 'all men'. In the first case God's plan would be fulfilled by the salvation of a single representative of the race—that is, the Saviour himself; in the second case, the damnation of a single individual no less than that of the whole race would frustrate the intention of the creator. Of these two possible meanings Anselm seems logically to be committed only to the first, and this agrees with his general tendency to think of the species as more real than its individual components.[1] But though the salvation of the Saviour himself may be said to satisfy the *logical* requirements of his system, the benefits of the Saviour's offering are by an act of grace extended to those whom he chooses. In default of logic Anselm falls back, as he often does, on a feudal image. He likened the work of Redemption to the action of a king whose people had all, except one, been guilty of a crime worthy of death. But the one innocent man, besides his innocence, offered to perform a service greater than the offence of all his fellow-subjects put together. The king accepted this service and agreed that it should effect the pardon of all who wished for it, on condition that they presented themselves on the day the service was performed. Moreover, even if they could not come on this day, provided they came on another day, they would receive their pardon.[2]

In this image it is noteworthy that Anselm attempts no logical explanation of the condition of attendance which the king imposes. Such acts of renewal of homage and fealty, either by whole communities or by men guilty of rebellion, were a familiar part of his world. They were not capable of a strictly logical justification, but he accepted such acts in practice, and he used them here to bridge the gap in his logic that would have restricted salvation to one or enlarged it unacceptably to all.

With the help of his feudal illustration Anselm retreated from the prospect of a universal salvation, but even this illustration left the door to salvation very wide open. It opened on

---

[1] Cf. *CDH* ii, 4: 'valde alienum est ab eo (*scil.* Deo) ut ullam rationalem naturam penitus perire sinat. . . . Necesse est ergo ut de humana natura quod inoopit perficiat.'      [2] *CDH* ii, 16.

to a new phase of religious history. The old view of the Incarnation was associated logically, and even more emphatically emotionally, with a harshly limited prospect of salvation for the few. The warlike and resourceful God who had outwitted Satan was not easily to be bent to the milder ways of mercy. Although by his strategem God had wrenched Man from the hold of the Devil, it was not at all clear that he had given him any means of escaping the renewed assertion of the Devil's rights arising from actual sins: these could only be atoned for by immense penances and abundant alms. And this is what we find. The recompenses which men were struggling to pay for their sins in the early Middle Ages were great, and for many quite hopeless.

In many ways Anselm's own religious outlook is of this stern, unbending type. He sees very little hope for men in the world. Few will be saved, and most of these will be monks. It is they alone who have achieved a complete baptismal renewal by the surrender of themselves in their monastic vows; and they alone have the means of renewing this renewal daily by fasts and penances and masses. Anselm accepted wholeheartedly the unique virtue of this monastic system of redemption, and of the practices which were based upon it. Among these practices was that which magnates frequently adopted of taking monastic vows shortly before death. To this Anselm also attached great importance:

This counsel I presume to give you that if you feel the danger of death to be imminent, give yourself wholly up to God before you depart from this life; and for this purpose always keep a veil prepared secretly beside you.[1]

So he wrote to the saintly Matilda of Tuscany, who had already given everything to the Church. If this advice was necessary for her, how much more necessary was it for Hugh of Chester, or Roger of Montgomery, or any other Norman baron? Anselm's letters are impressively full of warnings about the great difficulty of salvation in the world, and the urgent need for recourse to the monastery before it was too late; and if he spoke thus to men in the world, his words to his own monks are even more explicit. Few would be saved. How few no man

[1] Ep. 325 [iv, 37].

knew; but unless a monk lived as the few, he could be sure of damnation; and even if he lived as the few, this few might be too many.[1]

Yet, despite all his severity of outlook, his doctrine of Redemption—and not only this—opened up a quite different line of thought. An offering had been made, capable of obtaining remission, had it been permissible, 'of all the sins of men and angels'. Why then should anyone be damned? Anselm did not answer, or even explicitly ask, this question, but he did not contradict Boso when he expressed his reaction to the whole argument: 'it seems to me that God will reject no man coming to him under this name (of Christ)'.[2]

If Redemption is necessary, it will never seem to serious men easy. But undeniably it seemed much easier from this time onwards. This was not a result of the *Cur Deus Homo*. Anselm simply caught in his own fashion something of the hopefulness that others experienced in their various ways. It is not an accident, for example, that Indulgences began to be common almost at this very moment of time.[3] These much abused documents— abused in their time by their beneficiaries and donors, and later by their critics—at least express the sense of the rich, untapped, treasures of forgiveness within the grasp of ordinary men, hitherto undreamt of. It is this which the *Cur Deus Homo*, despite Anselm's own deep pessimism, also expresses.

### (iv) *Freedom, Obedience, and Punishment*

In the *Cur Deus Homo* then, despite Anselm, we see an opening to the genial and relaxed religious aspirations of the later Middle Ages, which confounded monastic institutions, and sometimes sought to extend the operation of divine mercy even to unbelievers. It is hard to know which of these characteristics would have appeared more damnable to the religious con-

---

[1] The fullest exposition of these ideas is in Ep. 2 [i, 2]. Anselm himself seems to have regarded this as his most complete exposition of a programme of spiritual development, for he sent its main sections bit by bit to a young monk at Canterbury in the following divisions: Ep. 8 [i, 8] 'the frauds of the world'; Ep. 35 [i, 27] 'the shortness of life'; Ep. 51 [i, 43] 'the fewness of the elect'. For other statements of these themes, see Epp. 81 [i, 72], 101 [ii, 12], 117 [ii, 19], 120 [ii, 28], 121 [ii, 29], 167 [iii, 18], and 184.

[2] *CDH* ii, 19.

[3] See N. Paulus, *Geschichte des Ablasses in Mittelalter*, 1922–3.

science of the eleventh century. And Anselm, though he opened the door, had no intention of entering into *that* inheritance. The moral force behind the *Cur Deus Homo* is provided by Anselm's utter abhorrence of sin even down to the smallest detail. He did not reject the rights of the Devil in order to make man's yoke lighter, nor to give man a wider scope for self-expression. For that whole range of thought which appeals to man's creative instincts and sees the fulfilment of the divine purpose in the development of human knowledge or experience, Anselm had no use at all. There is much of this outlook in Abelard, and it makes him a man of a new age compared with that of Anselm. By contrast Anselm is resolutely monastic and conservative.

The foundation of the monastic life is obedience, and Anselm embraced obedience with passionate intensity, as his reported conversations make clear. This obedience, in the words of the Rule, is to be 'neither fearful nor slothful nor languid nor murmuring nor partial'.[1] In a word, it was to be total, and in this it reflected the obedience owned by Man to God. This aspect of Anselm's thought is fundamental to the understanding of his practical life as well as his theology. In both it led to difficulties. Anselm was more successful in resolving the theological than the practical difficulties; but, whether successful or not, his starting point was a passionate instinct for obedience.

Unless this is appreciated, a good deal of the *Cur Deus Homo* will appear to be the expression of a somewhat glacial legalism. It is saved from this by two qualities, the one intellectual and the other moral. The moral quality arises from the intensity of Anselm's rejection of disobedience: 'Were it not better that the whole world, and whatever exists except God, should perish and be reduced to nothingness, than that you should do anything however small against the will of God?'[2]

The expression here is wholly Anselmian, and it must surely be the inspiration of a more famous passage in which Newman expressed the same idea:

It were better for sun and moon to drop from heaven, for the earth to fail, and for all the many millions who are upon it to die of

[1] *Regula S. Benedicti*, 5.          [2] *CDH* i, 21.

starvation in extremest agony, as far as temporal affliction goes, than
that one soul, I will not say, should be lost, but should commit one
single venial sin, should tell one wilful untruth, though it harmed
no one, or steal one poor farthing without excuse.[1]

Newman's words have a rhetorical exaggeration which is
foreign to Anselm, and the contrast between these two passages
may help to illustrate a characteristic of Anselm which is easily
overlooked; what he says is often extreme, but he never says
more than he means, and he never means more than his
argument requires. It was essential to his argument that the
slightest sin—even, in his striking phase, a single glance of the
eye against the will of God—should be (negatively) 'greater
than' the whole positive value of the universe apart from God.
But though this is the necessary logical foundation for his
argument, its power would be negligible apart from Anselm's
persuasion that the unwavering, perfect, eternal submission of
the will to God is a consuming interest and everlasting possibility. To many it will appear neither possible nor tolerable,
but Anselm has written in vain if it is easy to feel this while
reading him.

It might, however, be objected that Anselm's insistence on
obedience as the fundamental rule of life destroys the higher
privilege of freedom. Anselm's answer to this objection is
similar to his resolution of the problem of justice and mercy.
The problem of freedom is one which occupied his mind at
widely different periods of his career, but his opinion never
altered. For him, freedom is not the power of choice between
good and evil, but the power of not acting contrary to the will
of God. Here, as so often, he departs from the commonsense
view—and from at least one view of St. Augustine—that the
essential quality of freedom is an unfettered power of choice.
For his own definition he turns from the freedom of commonsense and experience to the more remote and ethereal freedom
of the sanctified will—freedom from the power of erroneous
choice. The first of these freedoms is the freedom of the everyday world; the second is that of the saints in Heaven; and we
know enough about Anselm's predilections to feel no surprise

[1] Cardinal Newman, *Certain Difficulties felt by Anglicans in Catholic
Teaching*, Lecture VIII, 1908 ed., p. 240.

that only the second engages his interest. In this blessed state freedom is the power of not being free to sin. It is therefore indistinguishable from obedience.

In his habitual way Anselm expressed this conclusion in two ways: by definitions and by a parable. The definitions were these. Of obedience: 'Simple and true obedience exists when a rational nature freely and without necessity preserves the will which it has received from God.'[1] And of freedom: 'Freedom of the will is the power of preserving the rectitude of the will for its own sake.'[2] Now since the 'will received from God' in the first definition is indistinguishable from the 'rectitude of the will' in the second, it follows that true obedience is indistinguishable from freedom. Moreover, since justice is the 'rectitude of the will preserved for its own sake',[3] and freedom is the power of preserving this rectitude, it follows that freedom is the power of acting justly, and obedience is the free exercise of this power. Obedience is therefore the practical exercise of freedom in the preservation of justice.

Anselm's parable expressed the same view dramatically. A woman had several daughters and servants. She placed them all under a mistress, who gave them a single comprehensive command: they were not to leave the house. The daughters (the free) obeyed without cavil; the servants (the unfree) sought pretexts for gaining exemption from the rule, and took the refusal of permission with varying degrees of ill-will but with an equal lack of power to disobey.[4] This was a situation frequently met with in monastic life and Anselm often returned to the theme: those who sought freedom were the unfree; those who willingly submitted were free. Obedience and freedom are willing submission; disobedience and servitude are unwilling submission. Freedom lay in *desiring* to stay at home. Hence the cloister was the home of true freedom.

Anselm has thus attempted to satisfy the claims of both freedom and obedience, and to express the heinousness of the slightest deviation from the will of God. This heinousness,

---

[1] *CDH* i, 10.     [2] *De Libertate Arbitrii*, 3 (Schmitt, i, 212).
[3] *De Veritate*, 12 (Schmitt, i, 194).
[4] *De Similitudinibus*, lxxxv–lxxxviii. The authority to be attached to this work is discussed below, p. 221–6.

which Anselm demonstrates in argument and parable, is expressed eternally by God in the act of punishment. In Anselm's argument God cannot treat the disobedient will in the same way as the obedient will. To do so would be to raise injustice above justice, and to destroy the order and beauty of the universe. But this order and beauty have already been disturbed by sin; and though it is fairly clear how Redemption or 'payment' for sin restores the broken harmony, it is much more difficult to see how punishment can achieve the same object. Boso pointed out this difficulty, and Anselm attempted to meet it in a chapter which has probably done more harm to his reputation than any other part of his works: here if anywhere is to be found the God whom some of his critics have thought they detected in the *Cur Deus Homo*—a royal tyrant jealous for His honour and finding in punishment a substitute for service.[1] Little though this accords with the general tenor of Anselm's works it must be admitted that at this point there is room for misunderstanding. If Anselm had been content with his demonstration that the disobedient will cannot be admitted to blessedness, criticism would have been silenced. But this alone did not satisfy his demand for an exquisite harmony of the universe. The mere exclusion of the sinner was not enough; even his replacement by another in order to complete the perfect number of souls—a concept dear to Anselm's sense of the numerical harmony of all things[2]—was not enough. There still remained a shadow to be erased from the brightness of the whole. The shadow is faint but perceptible. Anselm has explained that the preservation of God's honour is an essential function of the divine justice;[3] and he adds that it is incapable of diminution by sin.[4] Nevertheless this is what the sinner has attempted, and this, though unsuccessful, is the shadow to be erased. Anselm erases it by what one may call a congruity of

[1] *CDH* i, 14.
[2] It is a curious fact that the longest chapter in the whole work is the discussion of the 'perfectus numerus quo civitas illa superna perficietur' and the way in which it must be made up (*CDH* i, 18).
[3] Si Deo nihil maius aut melius, nihil justius quam honorem illius servat in rerum dispositione summa justitia, quae non est aliud quam ipse Deus (*CDH* i, 13).
[4] Deum impossibile est honorem suum perdere (*CDH* i, 14).

opposites, reverting for once, in a way unusual at this stage in his career, to the verbal antitheses which had been a favourite mode of expression in earlier days. The sinner has refused his due and willing subjection: God exacts his unwilling subjection. The sinner has taken what is God's: God takes what is Man's —his blessedness.[1] God has no use for what He has taken from Man, but the fact of taking it shows it is His, not Man's, and this fact God uses for His honour.[2]

I do not think it is possible entirely to obliterate the disagreeable impression of these last words, but there are two or three considerations which will help to soften it. In the first place, we must do justice to the motive behind this argument: Anselm was not concerned with a pettifogging game of tit-for-tat, but with the task of reconciling the present sinful state of Man with the incorruptibility of the divine glory, and with the perfect relationship of God and his Creation. This perfection was Anselm's only interest: the human point of view with its excuses and tenderness for rebels against just authority interested him not at all. Secondly, when he spoke of 'honour', he meant something different from the word in modern usage. He spoke not of that personal thing associated with a man's good opinion of himself and the good opinion of others, but of something objective, social in its nature, and the guarantee of social stability. To understand this we must turn to a feature of Anselm's thought, more conspicuous in his informal than in his formal teaching, that here comes abruptly to the surface: his feudal imagery.

### (v) *The Feudal Imagery*

Anselm's feudal imagery is not likely at first sight to commend his thought to modern readers; and nothing in this much criticized work has offered an easier target for indignation and ridicule than his use of feudal concepts. But before following this line of attack, we must be clear what we are criticizing. There are two problems. In the first place, how important is

[1] Sicut homo peccando rapit quod Dei est, ita Deus puniendo aufert quod hominis est. (*CDH* i, 14).

[2] Licet Deus hoc ad usum sui commodi non transferat quod aufert, . . . hoc tamen quod aufert utitur ad suum honorem, per hoc quia aufert (*ibid.*).

the feudal imagery in Anselm's thought; and secondly, if it is important, what does it mean? On the first question, Professor McIntyre has effectively answered the criticism that the *Cur Deus Homo* is irretrievably feudal in temper. Everything of importance in Anselm's argument can survive the removal of every trace of feudal imagery and the supposed contamination by elements of Germanic law. The power of the *Cur Deus Homo* does not come from its feudal imagery, but from its combination of religious insight and logical force. This is entirely true; and for the theologian it suffices to save the argument from the disrepute to which the mere mention of feudalism has sometimes been thought to relegate it. But for the historian, this answer does not go far enough. Even if the argument can be stated without any feudal imagery, it is nevertheless also true that Anselm's thoughts about God and the universe were very much coloured by the social arrangements with which he was familiar. The formal argument can survive, but its temper is quite different if the contemporary imagery is removed; equally it is quite different if the monastic fervour is brushed aside.

The *Cur Deus Homo* was the product of a feudal and monastic world on the eve of a great transformation. With all its originality and personal intensity of vision it bears the marks of this rigorous and—if the word can be used without blame—repressive régime. Anselm's favourite image of the relations between God and Man was that of a lord and his vassals. The status of these dependants varies. Sometimes they are knights, sometimes freemen, sometimes serfs, but the emphasis is always on their subordination to the lord's will.[1] It is characteristic of all these classes that they must render a full service to their lord or lose their inheritance. This is the state of mankind. It had happened once at the very beginning of history that the great diffidation had taken place which condemned all the successors of Adam to the loss of their inheritance. At great cost the lord had paid the service in full. He had not only paid the original service; he had made it possible for future deficiencies to be paid—but only under certain conditions, in appearance simple, but in practice so arduous that only a few would in fact fulfil them. The simplicity of the

[1] *CDH* ii, 16; *VA* ii, 21; *De Similitudinibus*, passim.

conditions lay in the demand for no more than faith, submission and repentance; the difficulty lay chiefly in the need for a rigorous submission of flesh to spirit, of spirit to law, and of law to God. Hence, despite all the resources thrown into the scale of salvation, few would be saved because few really willed to be saved. The superiority of monks over other men lay in their more complete submission. The laity had kept something back, even if that 'something' were no more than the promise of total obedience. In one of the striking similes which we owe to the reports of Anselm's conversation, the difference was expressed in the story of two tenants who each had a precious fruit tree; one of them took his lord an offering from the fruit, the other gave him the whole crop for his own use, so far as he needed it, for ever. The first represented the incomplete offering of the layman, the second the surrender of the monk.[1]

Anselm expressed the same idea in another simile in which he compared the various states of life to a countryside strongly reminiscent of the feudal scenery of the eleventh century. At the centre there is a castle, and within the castle a keep; around the castle there is a town, and outside this the open country. Those who live in the open country are Jews and unbelievers: the enemy destroys them without difficulty. The faithful laity are the dwellers in the town: here the enemy breaks in without much difficulty and they will be fortunate if they escape. The monks are those in the castle: they have many alarms, but they are safe so long as they remain inside and keep out of sight. When they hear that their relatives are being killed and wounded, they must not so much as look through the window for fear of the enemy's arrows. Within the keep, which is inside the castle, are the angels: they are immune alike from danger and alarm.[2]

These were the themes which Anselm reiterated again and again in his spoken words. They appear scarcely at all in his writings, but they contain the practical application of his grand concepts and were reported by his pupils. Even in the

[1] De Similitudinibus, lxxxiv, and cf. lxxx–lxxxiii. For the same idea in his letters of exhortation to the monastic life, see Ep. 121 [ii, 29]: 'Plus namque placet Deo, etiam post grave peccatum, cuius propositum est et ante et post quo maius habere non potest, quam ille, qui nec ante nec post simile peccatum vult proponere quo melius non potest.'
[2] De Similitudinibus, lxxvi.

imperfect form in which they have been preserved their force is not lost. It is unlikely that many now will find this aspect of his thought attractive, and if we knew nothing else there would be something repellent in the ideal picture of a well-ordered world of disciplined tenantry so assiduously ingratiating themselves with their lord. But no one could deny that even the greyer aspects of Anselm's thought have the stamp of all serious religious reflection in the stern, proud and uncompromising refusal of easy comforts and consolations, and the rejection of facile excuses for human frailty. If Anselm paints the human scene in drab colours, it is not that he hates colour, but that all colours are drab beside the true glory.

Anselm took the social institutions of his time as he found them. It would be idle to look for social criticism in his works. We may regret that God should appear in the guise of a lord castigating disobedient serfs, but nothing can be gained by denying that he did so appear to Anselm. At the centre of his thought about the relations of God and Man was the idea of a *servitium debitum* on which Man had defaulted and which had to be made good. In one of his feudal illustrations of the relative positions of angels, monks and laymen he likened God to a king with three kinds of tenants: those who held fiefs in return for a fixed service; those who served in the hope of regaining a lost inheritance forfeited by their parents; and those who served for wages with no hope of a permanent establishment. The first class was that of the angels, established for ever in a position of due service and reward; the second were the monks, enduring hardships and buffetings in the hope of a fixed inheritance; the last class consisted of secular men serving only for the present with no hope in the future.[1]

This illustration was addressed to the monks of Canterbury in October 1097 when the *Cur Deus Homo* was almost finished. It was a critical moment in Anselm's life, when he spoke to his monks for the last time for several years, and perhaps for ever. He spoke of the things which moved him most: the due service of man to God and the essential hopelessness of those who broke this bond. Such men stood outside the law. For those who were prepared to suffer, the Incarnation provided an

[1] *V.A.* II, 21; cf. *De Similitudinibus*, xxxix, lxxx.

extension of the limits of the original covenant. But it was an extension with very strict limits.

These feudal and monastic illustrations come from Anselm's sermons and conversation. Naturally there was little room for them in his formal treatises, but in the light of these illustrations we can now examine the conception of God's honour which (as we have seen) has an important place in the *Cur Deus Homo*. It is the attempted violation of God's honour that constitutes the essential sin of disobedience: 'He who does not render to God this due honour, takes from God what is His, and dishonours (exhonorat) God: and this is sin.'[1] Due honour is equated with *servitium debitum*: it is capable of being paid, withdrawn, restored; the satisfaction required from Man is the payment of the honour withheld from God, with an additional payment *secundum exhonorationis factam molestiam*; the Supreme Justice, which is God, is nowhere seen more justly than in the preservation of God's honour; Christ offers His life *ad honorem Dei*; and God uses the punishment of the sinner *ad honorem suum*.

It is possible to understand these phrases in the context of the ordinary language of worship. Yet something more seems to be required if Anselm's language at this point is to be intelligible.[2] The solidity of his concept of honour, with its minute gradations and equivalents, and the way the idea

---

[1] *CDH* i, 11.

[2] It may be convenient to list the main passages in which the concept of God's honour plays an important part in the argument: i, 11 ('Qui honorem alicuius violat non sufficit honorem reddere, si non secundum exhonorationis factam molestiam aliquid, quod placeat illi quem exhonoravit, restituit.' In this chapter *honorem solvere* is equated with *satisfactio*.); i, 12 (On the impossibility of forgiveness 'sine omni solutione ablati sibi honoris'); i, 13 ('Nihil minus tolerandum in rerum ordine quam ut creatura creatori debitum honorem auferat.' 'Necesse est ergo ut aut ablatus honor solvatur aut poena sequatur.'); i, 14 ('Deum impossibile est honorem suum perdere.' 'Hoc tamen quod aufert utitur ad suum honorem, per hoc quia aufert.'); i, 22 (Man was made to overcome the Devil 'ad excusationem et honorem Dei et ad confusionem diaboli', but he permitted himself to be overcome 'contra voluntatem et honorem Dei'; it is therefore 'contra honorem Dei', that he should be reconciled to God 'nisi prius honoraverit Deum vincendo diabolum, sicut illum inhonoravit victus a diabolo.'); ii, 11 (Christus 'ponit se ad honorem Dei', 'tradit se ipsum morti ad honorem Dei', 'vincit diabolum ad honorem Dei'.); ii, 18 ('Filius Dei ad honorem suum se ipsum sibi sicut patri et spiritui sancto obtulit').

reappears at the most important moments in his argument suggests a background quite different from our own or from that, for instance, of St. Augustine or St. Thomas Aquinas. This background, which sets Anselm as far apart from Patristic as from modern thought, is the complex of feudal relationships. In the language of feudal tenure a man's honour was his estate. Normally this was a unit of land, but the term honour also embraced his title and status. The fundamental crime against a lord, and against the social order, was to attempt to diminish the lord's honour. The seriousness of the crime was quite independent of the rebel's power to give effect to his evil intentions: it was his disloyalty, the loosening of the social bond, which outlawed him. At the time when Anselm was writing, the word 'honour' was at the height of its development as a term of social importance. It was the maintenance of a king's 'honour' which preserved his kingdom, of a baron's 'honour' which preserved his barony, and so on down the scale. Slowly honour dissolved into something private, incommunicable and socially unimportant, but that dissolution lay far in the future in Anselm's day.[1] The fate of this term kept

[1] For the social significance of the word *honor* at this time, see F. M. Stenton, *The First Century of English Feudalism*, 1066–1166, pp. 54–8; D. C. Douglas, *Feudal Documents from the Abbey of Bury St. Edmund's*, cxlvi–cxlix; P. Vinogradoff, *English Society in the Eleventh Century*, 348–50. In feudal usage, the term *honor* was used, not for land in itself, but for lands and rights with a permanent, organic individuality; men could therefore be said, on inheriting their rights, to come 'ad honorem', and to hold their rights 'cum honore comitis' or 'de honore comitis'. This sense of the word *honor* is perfectly expressed in a letter from Odo Count of Champagne to King Robert of France. It belongs to a slightly older generation than Anselm but to the same set of social conventions as those with which he was familiar. The *honor* to which the letter refers consisted of the counties of Troyes and Meaux which the king had seized:

> At postquam tuam gratiam avertisti a me, et honorem quem dederas mihi tollere nisus es, si me et honorem meum defendendo aliqua tibi ingrata commisi, feci hoc lacessitus injuriis et necessitate coactus. Quomodo enim dimittere possum ut non defendam honorem meum? Deum et animam meam testor quod magis eligerem honoratus mori quam vivere dishonoratus. At si me dishonorare velle desistas, nihil in mundo est quod magis quam gratiam tuam vel habere vel promereri desiderem.

This letter was written on behalf of Count Odo by Bishop Fulbert of Chartres and is preserved in his correspondence (*PL* cxli, 938–40. For the circumstances in which the letter was written, see Ch. Pfister, *Études sur le règne de Robert le Pieux*, 1885, pp. 237–42.)

pace with that of a parallel term, famous in Magna Carta as an expression of a man's status and position in society—his *contenementum*. Slowly this term also went down the same road towards social insignificance, the road which ended in keeping a man 'in countenance' and saving his face. The descent in either case was from a term of concrete social significance to a matter of private feeling and reputation.

Anselm's references to God's honour are to be interpreted in the light of contemporary usage. God's honour is the whole complex of service and worship which the whole creation, animate and inanimate, in heaven and earth, owes to the Creator. Regarded in this way God's honour is simply another word for the universe in its due relationship of service: in withholding his service Man is guilty of attempting to withdraw some part of God's 'honour'. He fails; but he puts himself outside the law and excludes himself from the order and beauty of the universe. This is his punishment. But his disobedience also requires a counter assertion of God's real possession of his honour; he takes seisin once more of that part of His honour forfeited by the sinner and hands it to another. And so, in the end, the whole *servitium debitum* of the universe will be established throughout eternity, and God's 'honour' in its full extent will be displayed in the order and beauty of the whole.

All this of course is capable of expression in entirely non-feudal language. But Anselm found the language of feudalism convenient for various reasons. It expressed the strict idea of hierarchy and subordination, which both philosophically and morally he found most satisfying; and—contrary to what is often thought—it enforced in a pictorial way the rule of reason. Those critics who have imagined Anselm's God as a jealous tyrant, greedy for recognition and honour, have failed to recognize that the feudal image, however unsatisfactory in some of its implications, stood for rational order prevailing against the inroads of self-will and chaos. The rationality of Anselm's theology is based on the principle that there is nothing arbitrary in God. God's nature and works alike express the perfect harmony of reason. From this all else flows; if it were not so, all theology would become guesswork. The *Cur Deus Homo* contains Anselm's logical deduction from the principle of the rationality of the divine action: the impossibility of an unconditional forgiveness of sin and the necessity for the Incarnation. The feudal and monastic illustrations, which are closely related in his spoken words and hinted at in the *Cur Deus Homo* illustrate this principle from the facts of everyday life. They are complementary expressions of Anselm's argument. But, we must finally ask, how rational *is* Anselm's argument?

### (vi) *The Logic of the Deus-Homo*

The argument which demonstrates the necessity of the Deus-Homo runs thus:

Only Man *ought* to make the offering for sin (*but he cannot*);
Only God *can* make the offering for sin (*but He ought not*);
Therefore only a God-Man both *can* and *ought* to make the offering for sin.

This seems simple enough and Boso accepted the argument with joy.[1] But very little consideration of the argument shows that it bristles with ambiguities, and these must be examined in order to discover the limits within which the argument can claim logical completeness.

It is certain that Anselm intended in this argument to say something very uncompromising about the necessity for the Incarnation. Put bluntly the argument is that God can but ought not, and Man ought but cannot, pay; therefore the only Being who both can and ought is a God-Man. Leaving aside the problem of the manner in which this combination is effected, and concentrating simply on the type of argument that Anselm uses to prove its necessity, it is clear that he envisages a situation in which each party contributes something which the other lacks, thus:

Only A has x
Only B has y
Therefore only AB has xy.

---

[1] *CDH* II, 6. The words in brackets are not in Anselm's text at this point, but they are implied in the preceding argument. As I shall try to show, it is only by leaving them out that Anselm can make his argument acceptable; but only by including them can the argument be given the logical force which he seems to claim for it.

Anselm's argument is only effective if it belongs to this general type: but it can only do this if the initial statement is modified in a way which greatly lessens its strength. It is clearly impossible to join together 'ought (but cannot)' and 'can (but ought not)' to get 'ought and can', in the same way that two partners can join together to combine their assets. If one of the partners *ought not* to pay, that is the end of the matter. No amount of argument can bring him into a combination in which he both can and *ought*. The reason for this is that 'ought not' does not express a mere absence of the quality of obligation but an absolute moral disability which can in no circumstances be overcome. And this is what Anselm requires, or at least seems to require. For if he is not asserting on God's side an absolute moral disability to pay Man's debt, then the whole force of his dilemma is lost, and the Incarnation is not necessary or not necessary in the way that he tries to show that it is. To state the argument in a way that avoids this destructive criticism it must be put something like this:

Man has an obligation but cannot pay,
God has no obligation but can pay,
Therefore a God-Man is conceivable having both obligation and
power to pay.

Now, whatever other weaknesses the argument may have in this form, they are not the same as those in the previous case. To take an illustration from ordinary life, a wealthy man with no obligation may combine with a poor man, who has an obligation he cannot meet, to pay the poor man's debt. Power without obligation combines with obligation without power to produce a definite result. In this form the argument contains no internal contradiction. But it is now so weak that it cannot bear the weight which Anselm puts upon it. The force of 'Man ought but cannot; God can but ought not' has disappeared: the perfect congruity promised in the combination turns out to be only verbal. If Anselm is saying no more than that God has no obligation (but can if He pleases), he is saying nothing to his purpose. For, from the mere absence of an obligation no prohibition can be inferred; and if God could at any time pay the debt if He pleased, there would be no necessity for its payment by Man: hence no *necessity* for the God-Man. The argument in this form would not answer the critics who asserted that God could remit the debt incurred by Man as a mere act of mercy without the Incarnation. Free forgiveness would be possible, and it is precisely this that Anselm asserted was impossible.

We seem therefore to discover in the initial ambiguity a defect that destroys the argument whichever way it is taken: if it is taken in one way it is destroyed by defect of logic; if in the other, it is destroyed by lack of force. Anselm did not attempt to clear up this ambiguity, and before going farther we must ask how he could leave in his argument an obscurity on so fundamental a point.

The immediate reason was probably a linguistic one. In his use of the word *debeo* Anselm did not make a clear distinction between 'I owe' and 'I ought'. The confusion was one that was specially easy for him to make. For one thing, *debeo* both etymologically and practically suggested the sense of debt. Also, Anselm's basic conception of duty, in keeping with the general feudal framework of his practical thinking, was that of a debt owed by an inferior to a superior. So he had a tendency to interpret all 'ought' in terms of 'owe', and likewise 'ought not' in terms of 'does not owe'. And this is precisely the ambiguity with which we are confronted in this argument. To be compelling, the word must be understood in the absolute sense; but to be consistent, it must be understood in the other, weaker, sense.

At first sight it might seem strange that this ambiguity at a central point should have been left by a writer who grasped more clearly than any of his contemporaries the need for clear definitions of words. He was a pioneer in this field and his early works are strewn with discussions of words which can be used in contradictory senses. In the *Cur Deus Homo* he was still insisting on the need for a special treatise on this subject:

There is another reason apart from my own weakness, why I see that I cannot perfectly or fully treat of this matter, for it requires an understanding of such words as 'power', 'necessity' and 'will' and some others which are so related that none of them can be dealt with without the others. Their treatment requires a separate work, not an easy one I think nor useless, for ignorance of these matters creates many difficulties which their understanding makes easy.[1]

The work which Anselm here desiderates was never written. Unfinished fragments, which may have been intended as a preliminary draft of a future work, have been found in recent years.[2] They do not however suggest that further linguistic analysis would have cleared up the obscurities in his central argument. There are several reasons for this. In the first place, Anselm's investigations into the use of words were not concerned with the different meanings of words in themselves. He was not a lexicographer, and it is unlikely that he envisaged any relationship other than that of one word—one thing—one meaning. His concern as a logician in analysing words was to examine the thing for which a word stood, and to discuss the different syntactical and logical contexts in which it could be used. This attitude is exactly illustrated in his discussions of the word *debeo* and nowhere more so than at the point in the *Cur Deus Homo* where he senses a difference of meaning which might affect his argument. He is discussing the different senses in which Christ both ought and ought not to die for Man's sins. In fact (although he does not say so) the difficulty is precisely the same as that with which we are concerned: it was inevitable from the way in which the problem was stated that the same dilemma should reappear at every stage in the argument. Since Christ clearly does not 'owe' His death as a debt, and yet 'ought' to die, Anselm has to recognize that there are some 'oughts' which do not imply a debt. He tries to get over the difficulty by analysing the apparent exceptions so that the element of debt is introduced. 'If' (he says to Boso)

you are disturbed because *debere* cannot be understood without some debt, you are to know that as in some other cases (like *posse*, *non posse*, *necessitas*) the quality is not in the subject of the sentence but in something else. For instance, when we say that the poor ought to receive alms from the rich, this only means that the rich ought to relieve the poor. For this is not a debt to be exacted from the poor, but from the rich. Similarly it is said that God ought to

---

[1] *CDH* I, I.
[2] F. S. Schmitt, *Ein neues unvollendetes Werk des hl. Anselm von Canterbury*, *BGPTM*, xxxiii, 1936.

rule all things, not because he is a debtor, but because all things ought to be subject to him, and ought to do what he wishes because what he wishes ought to be.[1]

In the same way (he continues), Jesus ought to die, not because he owes this *ex debito* but because what he wishes ought to be.

This part of Anselm's discussion is unusually confused and yet illuminating. It is confused because he slips without warning from a linguistic discussion, which was leading him to distinguish between the various meanings of the word *debeo*, to a theological assertion about God's over-ruling will, which on an extreme view would have destroyed the whole structure of his thought. Yet the passage is illuminating because it illustrates the two levels at which Anselm's thought habitually moved—the level of linguistic analysis, and that of metaphysical speculation. In his mind they were not far apart.

The problem of the sense in which words of obligation like *debet* could be used about God at all was one to which Anselm frequently returned—and rightly, for the answer he gives to this question will determine the scope and status of his theological arguments. In fact Anselm at this point speaks with two voices. As a practical philosopher he uses distinct phrases *Deus non potest, impossibile est, Deus non debet, Deo non decet*, and so on. These phrases give his thought a harsh clarity which has the merit of showing what he thought in the heat of argument. But, when he speculated about his thought as a whole, he drew back from the possible implications of these phrases:

God is improperly said to be unable to do something or under the necessity of doing something, for all necessity and impossibility are subject to his will, and his will is subject to no necessity or impossibility. Nothing is necessary or impossible except because he wishes it, and it is contrary to truth to say that he will or does not will something because of any necessity or impossibility.[2]

Or, more briefly, 'God ought to do what He wishes, because what He wishes ought to be'.

This might seem pure voluntarism if we did not remember a

[1] *CDH* II, 18.     [2] *CDH* II, 17.

passage in an earlier chapter, almost at the beginning of the whole discussion: 'The will of God, when He does something, ought to satisfy us as a reason, even though we do not see why He did it. For the will of God is never irrational.'[1]
It is the second of these sentences that commands attention. At first sight it seems obvious that if we know that God did something, but do not know the reason, we have no option but to be satisfied: 'what God wills ought to be'. This was the cry of the first Crusaders no less than Anselm's—'Deus le volt'. But Anselm says more than this. He says we ought to be satisfied with this 'as a reason', because God's will is never irrational. God's will is itself therefore a reason. But it is only a reason because God is the source of our knowledge, and it is ideally possible for further reasons to be discovered by the faithful inquirer. The fact, so to speak, comes to us with the stamp of reason on it, and both it and its reason become clarified by the same process of contemplative inquiry. It is this which makes it possible for Anselm to use such voluntarist expressions about God as that 'what God wills ought to be' without drawing from them the voluntarist conclusion that further inquiry is useless.

But if, in this inquiry about what God 'ought' or 'must' do, we must start by first knowing what God *has* done, the status of Anselm's argument from necessity is quite different from what it at first seemed to be. It is also much more clearly in line with his general programme enunciated twenty years earlier in the *Proslogion*: *Fides quaerens intellectum.* In this context Anselm's proofs always require a previous acceptance of that which is to be proved: they are demonstrations of logical consistency within a given framework. How does this affect their claim to convince unbelievers? And, lastly, how does it affect our judgment on the ambiguity from which we began?

As for the unbeliever, the main force of the argument must disappear when it is admitted that its cogency depends on a previous admission of the conclusion still to be proved. There still, however, remains a certain force arising from the *reductio ad absurdum* of all other possible alternatives. Since we can never be sure that the possible alternatives have all been

[1] *CDH* I, 8.

thought of, the proof must always be incomplete; but (in so far as it is logically consistent) it can claim to be a complete answer to alternatives actually put forward, such as free forgiveness or salvation by man or angel, and to objections actually raised, such as the alleged incompatibility between the Incarnation and God's dignity or rationality.

These still remain very great claims, and we must finally ask how far these claims are affected by the ambiguity which we have detected within the argument itself. The answer to this is twofold. As a logically compelling answer to the unbeliever the argument is quite destroyed by the internal ambiguity, though it may still carry conviction because of other qualities, such as moral force or religious fervour, which are not affected by logical defects. But for the believer—for Anselm, and Boso, and those for whom he chiefly wrote—the force of the argument within its more restricted scope is less affected by its ambiguity than we might have expected. For, within the limits Anselm set himself, even if his argument contained no ambiguity and was as conclusive as logic could make it, it would still remain only one possible argument 'to be received with no greater certitude than that this is how it appears to me until God shall show me something better'.[1] And on the other hand, however far short of demonstration the argument falls, so long as it contains no contradiction, it remains a possible explanation to be accepted until something better is revealed. But further: in the general context of Anselm's theological programme and in the sense in which words of obligation can be applied to God, the difference between 'God does not owe' and 'God ought not to pay' becomes minimal, however distinct these concepts are in their human context. It is a fundamental principle with Anselm that no incongruity however slight is possible in God. We have seen the lengths to which this principle 'quamlibet parvum inconveniens in Deo est impossible' can take him in dealing with the reconciliation of Justice with Mercy, and in his treatment of punishment. If the same principle is applied here, it is clear that if God does not owe, there is some *inconveniens* in His paying. And in this

---

[1] *Ep. de Incarn. verbi* x (Schmitt ii, 26), *CDH* I, 10 (Schmitt ii, 67).

sense we can say 'since God does not owe, God ought not to pay', and even 'it is impossible for God to pay'. The argument, therefore, at this point—whatever other weaknesses it may have—fulfils all the requirements of the faithful inquirer as Anselm pictured him. This inquirer is not in search of demonstrations of the unknown (though Anselm often speaks as though he were), but of explanations of truths already perceived. Between the mind of the believer and the fixed truths of the Faith there is a wide and ill-lit stretch of country. Some tracts are better lit than others, and where all else is dark the slightest glimmer affords a clue which others perhaps will be able to follow. But even the brightest patches are no more than hints which may guide the seeker to 'better reasons than those we have been allowed to see'.[1]

In the end Anselm's proofs, whether of God's existence or of the nature of God's activity, are, and must be, logically inconclusive. His immediate successors were to find this mixture of argumentative subtlety and logical inconclusiveness unsatisfying. His thought never appears to less advantage than when it is stripped of its ambiguities and classified in the academic catalogue of arguments as the Ontological Proof or the Satisfaction Theory of Atonement. He wrote for a monastic, and not for a sceptical or an academic audience, and his arguments cannot be taken from their context and quoted as definitive. In the Schools this was a hindrance to the growth of his influence; and even in the monasteries of the twelfth century Anselm's influence was soon overtaken by the growing strength of School theology. But on a long view, the very ambiguities of his arguments, their provisional status, and their power to stimulate without satisfying, have allowed them to survive all changes of intellectual climate, and even the laborious demonstration of their errors.

---

[1] The method to be followed in the discussion is described in the following passage:
'. . . volo tecum pacisci, ut nullum vel minimum inconveniens in Deo a nobis accipiatur, et nulla vel minima ratio, si maior non repugnat, reiciatur. Sicut enim in Deo quamlibet parvum inconveniens sequitur impossibilitas, ita quamlibet parvam rationem, si maiori non vincitur, comitatur necessitas'. (*CDH* i, 10).

# CHAPTER IV

# ANSELM AS ARCHBISHOP

## I. PRINCIPLES OF CONDUCT

As we have seen, obedience was the one thing necessary in Man's dealings with God, and it was this that Man had lost. In abandoning obedience, Man lost his freedom, and with his freedom his blessedness. The results were to be seen everywhere in the world. It is at this point that Anselm's theological speculations touch the plane of practical affairs.

All theological systems have their appropriate political expression, or at least a certain range of political ideas that is appropriate to them. We approach Anselm's political career with the strong expectation that obedience will prove to be the main theme of his archiepiscopate. Nor is this expectation disappointed, but the manner in which it is fulfilled contains many surprises. The theme is more complicated, and events impose a more chaotic pattern on Anselm's actions than we might expect. There are many reasons for this, not least Anselm's own lack of interest in the subject. He was no politician and he had no political views of a systematic kind. As a monk he had turned his back on the world:

If the world smiles on you with its favours, do not smile in return. It does not smile that you may smile in the end; but it mocks you with its Prince, that you with its Prince may mourn. Therefore, however it smiles on you, turn from its smile that you may rejoice when the Mocker mourns.[1]

So far as we can judge, this general attitude of abhorrence overpowered all other thoughts about practical questions, even questions like the defence of the eastern Empire, the Crusade, or the reduction of freemen to servitude, which have obvious spiritual implications. Anselm turned from all this with a

---

[1] Ep. 2 [i, 2].

gesture of indifference.[1] He saw the world as an accumulation of filth which men irrationally desired. Probably he had not always seen it so, but this is how it appeared from the time of his earliest writings, and if he had once thought differently he never looked back.

Anselm therefore was not only unpractised in the ways of the world; he dissociated himself from them on principle. Although he sometimes had an unexpected clarity of vision which surprised his opponents, he did not in general see through the details of practical affairs, as he saw through the details of theology, to a few simple and luminous truths. The world remained an enigma to him, and the race of trained men had not yet arisen to guide the hands of rulers and prelates in accordance with the principles which they understood. Anselm's practical problems were cruder and more disjointed than those of a later day, and his systematic genius deserted him in the face of casually emergent crises. Obedience might be a sufficient guide to monastic duties, or to the ordering of Man's life in his immediate relations with God; but in the world of change and decay it left many questions unanswered. Everything in Anselm's earlier life had predisposed him to obedience as a rule of conduct for himself and others. But to whom and in what respects? In the stormy sea of English affairs this was not an easy question to answer.

There was obedience to the pope in the first place. But the pope was far away, difficult of access, and when interrogated he often spoke with an uncertain voice. Anselm sought papal advice with the ardour of one who desired to obey a father, but his knowledge of papal decisions and the development of papal policy could scarcely have been more meagre. Contemporaries in the midst of great events (we are apt to forget) often knew much less about their world than we do, and Anselm's ignorance

---

[1] See Ep. 117 [ii, 19]: 'Moneo, consulo, precor, obsecro, praecipio ut dilectissimo, ut dimittas illam Ierusalem, quae nunc non est visio pacis sed tribulationis, et thesauros Constantinopolitanos et Babylonios cruentatis manibus diripiendos; et incipe viam ad caelestem Ierusalem, quae est visio pacis, ubi invenies thesauros non nisi istos contemnentibus suscipiendos.' And Ep. 17 [i, 15]: 'Quid enim, dilectissime, monachorum interest et eorum qui se profitentur velle fugere mundum, quibus vel quo nomine serviant in mundo?'

of the major decision of papal Councils in his own lifetime would be thought disgraceful in a modern candidate for historical honours. Even the decrees of the Council of Clermont in 1095, to which he sent an envoy, remained unknown to him and were unheeded in practice for several years.[1] To a modern mind trained to expect decisions to be made and to be effectively communicated to those whom they concern, such a lack of business-like habits is almost incredible. But in this case it must be attributed not only to Anselm's personal indifference to business, but to the unsystematic habits of the most advanced chancery in Europe, which had no regular means of communicating decisions to those who were most affected by them.

If Anselm did not know about contemporary papal decisions he was scarcely better equipped with the decisions of the past. Thanks to the work of Z. N. Brooke, everybody knows that Lanfranc brought to England a collection of canon law.[2] There are many indications that Lanfranc studied this collection: he quoted it in his letters and it was certainly owing to his influence that it became widely disseminated throughout England. There are only the faintest signs in Anselm's letters of any similar study. A medieval compiler who put together a small collection of Anselm's letters of juridical interest found very little indeed to put in his collection, and his few texts have scarcely been extended by modern scholarship.[3] Twice in successive letters shortly after he came to England, Anselm quoted texts which are to be found in Lanfranc's collection, but there is good reason to think that he borrowed these from his friend Gilbert Crispin.[4] At a much earlier date, while he was still prior of Bec he had written a letter containing references to

---

[1] Anselm's envoy was Boso (*Vita Bosonis*, ed. Giles, *Opera Lanfranci*, i, 329).

[2] For the manuscripts of 'Lanfranc's Collection', see Z. N. Brooke, *The English Church and the Papacy from the Conquest to the reign of John*, pp. 231–5.

[3] See A. Wilmart in *R. Bén.*, xl, 1928, 319–32, for the small collection of Anselm's letters in MS Bodl. Laud misc. 344, f. 36ʳ–40ʳ, by a 'compilateur qui a voulu réunir plusieurs réponses interessant la jurisprudence ecclésiastique'. The collection includes Epp. 468 [iii, 154], 65 [i, 56], 169, 281 [iii, 74], and (perhaps by accident) 240 [iii, 161].

[4] Epp. 161, 162 [iii, 12, 13]. On the question of borrowing from Gilbert Crispin, see *MARS* iii, 1954, 90–1.

texts in this collection.[1] Since Lanfranc brought his collection from Normandy to England it is not surprising that it should have been at Bec, and Anselm's quotation may be taken as a proof that he knew the collection and had some acquaintance with its contents. It could scarcely be otherwise. But Anselm's treatment of his authorities in this early letter is very characteristic. He had been asked whether an unchaste priest could be allowed to resume his office after confession of his sin. He replied that this was permissible, and gave his reasons. But for the benefit of those 'who would not be persuaded by any other argument than authority' he mentioned two texts of Popes Calixtus I and Gregory I, where this opinion could be found. He then proceeded to the more congenial task of elaborating his argument, bringing forward considerations of individual psychology, the effect of various judgments on the penitent, and the necessity for prudence in the actions of confessors. Anselm's reply belongs in spirit to the confessional manuals of the thirteenth century rather than to the legal compilations of of his own time. It differs widely from the normal contemporary treatment of legal problems, in which texts and authorities were more highly prized than the finer points of moral theology.

Somewhat similar reflections are suggested by the only letter which Anselm wrote after his consecration as archbishop on a topic requiring a knowledge of general canon law. It is significant that it never found a place in the main collection of his letters; he evidently made no attempt to preserve it and it is only by chance, and generally in a mutilated form, that it has survived.[2] Yet it deserves some consideration, because it shows Anselm in an unusual light, making an independent attempt to

---

[1] Ep. 65 [i, 56]: The passages in the letters of Popes Calixtus and Gregory, to which Anselm refers, are both in *Pseudo-Isidore*, ed. P. Hinschius, pp. 142, 737.

[2] Ep. iii, 159. The manuscript used by the first editor of this letter (J. Picard, *Anselmi Opera omnia*, Cologne 1612, and thence reproduced in all subsequent editions with the exception of Dom Schmitt's) appears to be lost. But the greater part of the text, without the address, is found in two twelfth-century manuscripts, Hereford Cathedral, O. 1, vi, f. 43, from Cirencester, and Oxford, Bodleian, Digby 158, f. 91, from Reading, with the title *Sententia Anselmi archiepiscopi de motione altaris*, 'Quod de altari et de ecclesia . . . simpliciter cum processione aspergatur.'

assemble authorities and opinions on a point of canon law. Also, it illustrates the difficulties experienced at this time in getting an answer to questions which were a part of the routine of ecclesiastical administration.

Anselm's letter was written to an Abbot William, probably the abbot of Fécamp, who was engaged in rebuilding his abbey church at this time.[1] It answers a question which must often have arisen in this period of extensive rebuilding and enlarging of churches: Did an altar require to be reconsecrated after it had been moved? It was not easy to find an answer to this simple question. The only authoritative pronouncement available at the time would appear to have been a text ascribed to the second century Pope Hyginus, which Burchard of Worms had included in his collection of canon law, and which thus made its way with the works of Ivo of Chartres and Gratian, and so became part of the law of the Church.[2] But this was unknown to Anselm. Nevertheless he tried to answer the question. He knew of no authoritative text, but he had been told (wrongly however) that a letter of Pope Eugenius had settled the question. However, when he was in Rome he spoke to Urban II on the subject, and the pope's opinion was that an altar once moved should never again be used as an altar; others who were present held that the altar could be used again without any reconsecration, by simple reconciliation. Faced with this conflict of views, Anselm was driven to express his own opinion, which is in favour of reconsecration. This was contrary to the opinion of the pope and the others at the papal court. He put this argument forward as his own: 'others certainly may have thought of it, but I received it from no one'; so it was only an interim argument until better advice could be had.

Better advice, as it happened, was to be had without difficulty. The abbot of Fécamp put the same question to Ivo of Chartres, the greatest canonist of the day, and he was able to produce the text quoted by Burchard of Worms.[3] Apart from this, Ivo's

---

[1] The letter may be dated 1098–9. For the rebuilding of Fécamp, see Ordericus Vitalis, iv, 270.

[2] Burchard, iii, 11, 12; Ivo, *Decretum*, iii, 13, 4; *Panormia*, ii, 20, 21; Gratian, De cons., Dist. i, c. 19.

[3] Ivo of Chartres, Epp. 72, 80 (*PL* CLXII, 92, 101).

126

argument is very similar to that of Anselm. So, after travelling round half Christendom this small problem finally had an acceptable solution.

The difficulties experienced by the abbot of Fécamp in getting a decision on this small point illuminate the conditions in which Anselm had to work. They show that a mere simple acknowledgment of papal authority could raise as many problems as it solved: the pope was wrong; the Curia was wrong; Anselm's argument had no authority; Ivo's authority was almost certainly spurious; but it produced an acceptable result. A papal judgment on this point would have dispelled all doubts, but it was not easy to get.

Not only was a papal judgment difficult to get, but there were some points on which even Anselm was not prepared unreservedly to abide by a papal judgment. These were points concerning the rights and privileges of his own church. They complicated the whole problem of obedience in a quite remarkable and irrational way.


## 2. THE PRIMACY OF CANTERBURY

Anselm's general habits of thought would not lead us to expect him to be strongly influenced by local privileges. His habitual thoughts were of a monolithic type, making no allowance for exceptions and giving little room for variety. Hence we should expect the local to be swallowed up in the general, and if this did not happen we may judge with what force local considerations forced themselves upon him.

As abbot of Bec, Anselm had been little, if at all, troubled by the problems raised by the privileges of a local church. But at Canterbury the situation was quite different. He was the guardian of a rich, varied, and passionately cultivated local tradition. He felt it to the full. He was always receptive. But even had he been much less receptive than he was, the duty of handing on intact to their successors the rights, privileges and possessions of the churches they were called upon to rule was one which weighed heavily on all prelates of this period. Never had these rights weighed more heavily than at this time, when they were threatened not only by the perennial violence from without, but also by the corrosive influence of a higher ecclesiastical authority from within. Within the next few generations the struggle was largely settled and local loyalties abated some of their pretensions; but this was still a distant prospect in the eleventh century.

To speak of these loyalties as 'local' immediately gives the impression that they were rather trivial: it would be a better definition of their character to say that they were personal and sacred. A prelate was clothed in the authority, and in a real sense assumed the *persona* of the saint to whom his church was dedicated or by whom it was founded. When the pope wrote to Anselm that 'we behold in you the venerable *persona* of St. Augustine the Apostle of the English', this was more than a complimentary politeness, it was the recognition of an important truth.[1] If this truth is ignored, the squabbles about precedence, privileges and insignia which smouldered doggedly on from generation to generation—squabbles which have in our eyes no importance in the effective life of the Church—would be no more than, in Milton's expressive phrase, 'the wars of Kites or Crows fighting in the air'.

In the settlement of these quarrels, the pope's authority was with difficulty, if at all, admitted to be final. When the monks of Canterbury, in the course of a later struggle, warned the pope that if he gave a judgment diminishing the rights of their church they would appeal to the tribunal of the Supreme Judge, this might be written off as the unsubstantial threat of an aggrieved community.[2] But we must take a more serious view when Anselm, after suffering two exiles in the papal cause warned the pope that if he gave an adverse judgment in the dispute between Canterbury and York 'I would on no account remain in England; for I neither ought nor can allow the primacy of our church to be destroyed while I am alive'.[3] The motive force of such a threat requires attention.

It is in the first place important to recognize the extent to which the church of Canterbury inherited the pretensions of

[1] Ep. 452 [iii, 153].
[2] This threat was made by the monks of Canterbury in the course of their dispute with the archbishop about his proposed foundation at Hackington. *Chronicles and Memorials of the reign of Richard I*, ed. Stubbs, *RS*, ii, 63.
[3] Ep. 451 [iii, 152].

the Anglo-Saxon kings to a quasi-imperial authority over Britain and the adjacent islands. At the level of secular government, the practical good sense of the Norman conquerors abandoned these pretensions, which were only seriously revived as a secular issue in the time of Edward I. But the negligence of the secular ruler with regard to the past made the church of Canterbury all the more necessarily the guardian of tradition. Many influences combined to place Canterbury in this position. There was the influence of the geographical lore handed down from the ancient world, which imagined the British Isles to form a separate world, an *alter orbis*, from the main complex of lands centred on the Mediterranean and surrounded by the ocean.[1] If we may trust Eadmer on this point, Urban II paid homage to this point of view when he introduced Anselm to the Curia as 'one who is almost our equal, being as it were Pope and Patriarch of the *alter orbis*'.[2] Then there was the influence of the charters of pre-Conquest kings, of which Canterbury had a substantial share, in which they called themselves with varying degrees of circumlocution Emperors of this British world. These imperial expressions preserved the sense of unity expressed all too long ago in the papal correspondence preserved by Bede, granting Canterbury an ecclesiastical authority over the wide territories of the English and the surrounding nations.[3] Lanfranc had seized upon these traditions as an opportunity for building up a patriarchal authority at Canterbury similar to that claimed by the archbishops of Hamburg, Lyons and Milan. It was a great design, with deep though uncertain historical roots; but above all it came to express the corporate image of a great church.

The Canterbury claim to primacy has come almost exclusively to be associated with a barren and unedifying wrangle with York which continued at intervals throughout the Middle Ages. But this was only a by-product of the great design. In its essential nature it called for a return to the wide authority

---

[1] On this, see C. Erdmann, *Forschungen zur politischen Ideenwelt des Frühmittelalters*, 1951, pp. 8–11, 38–43.  [2] *VA* ii, xxix and n.
[3] *Historia Ecclesiastica*, ii, viii, xviii. For the interpretation of this evidence in the time of Lanfranc, see R. W. Southern, 'The Canterbury Forgeries', *EHR*, lxxiii, 1958, 193–226.

which the first archbishop, St. Augustine, had exercised over the whole British Church including its Celtic elements, and the recognition of his exceptional position as a special envoy of the pope. The aim was not independence of the pope, but the mediation of his authority through a local representative at Canterbury. The design only came to look anti-papal with the development of, and resistance to, the more direct exercise of papal authority in the ordinary affairs of the Church during the twelfth century. The resistance to the expansion of papal authority is often looked on as primarily a matter of royal policy: but in the early years of the century it was quite as much an interest of the archbishop of Canterbury as of the king. At the same time the larger purpose was not simply the maintenance of ceremonial precedence, as it later came to be, but the spread of discipline, especially of monastic discipline, and the bringing of ecclesiastical order to distant parts of Britain.

The foundations of this design are very complicated, and turn out on inspection to be very shaky, but the structure was taken over by Anselm in its entirety. His most consistent aim as archbishop was to preserve this structure intact, and indeed to complete it at those points where Lanfranc had left it incomplete or weak. When Anselm adopted a position he was apt to take it up with a logical stubbornness which contrasts with the more pliable spirit of Lanfranc. So it was here.

For the sake of clarity it is well to distinguish two main aspects of the Canterbury claims which Anselm vigorously pressed forward, though the foundations of both are the same. These are, firstly, claims with regard to the limitation of papal action; and, secondly, claims with regard to the extent of Canterbury's territorial authority. Anselm was concerned with both from the very beginning to the end of his pontificate.

(i) *The Legatine Authority*

With regard to papal action, the main claim concerned the pope's right to send legates into the area of Canterbury's jurisdiction. The claim seems to be new in Anselm's time: he certainly went further than Lanfranc and was stiffer than Rufus and Henry I on this point. The first hint of trouble was in 1095 when the papal legate, Walter, cardinal-bishop of Albano, brought the archbishop's pallium and suggested that the two of them should together hold a Council. Anselm's reply is exceedingly curious:

I see as well as you the things which need to be corrected, and no man could have more desire than I have to correct them, by God's help, with the assent and aid of my lord king and other suitable persons, when the occasion and opportunity shall arise.[1]

He could not (he said) even meet the legate to discuss the question, because the king had entrusted to him the defence of the south coast during his own absence in Scotland, 'and therefore I dare not leave Canterbury, except to go in the direction from which the enemy is expected'. The picture of Anselm as a man of war is an unusual one, but it shows that he took his obligations step by step as they arose. For the moment he was closer to the king than to the legate. The reason for this was partly his instinctive regard for established authority, including that of the king; but chiefly no doubt, his concern for the rights of Canterbury. This comes out clearly three years later: when he was in Rome, he put his objection to the sending of legates on the basis of general principle:

I spoke to the pope (he wrote) about the Roman legation over the kingdom of England, which the men of this realm say has been held from ancient times until our own time by the church of Canterbury; and I showed him that it ought necessarily so to be, and could not be otherwise without damage to the Roman and English Church.[2]

In speaking of something being *necessarily* so and not otherwise, Anselm was using the language of his theological speculations; and much ink has been spent in discussing just what such words mean in their theological context. In their practical context, there can be no doubt what they mean. They did not commend themselves to the pope. Three years later, in 1101, Paschal II appointed Guy, archbishop of Vienne, papal legate for England, but Anselm refused to receive him.[3] In answer to Anselm's protest, the pope promised to send no legate with authority over Canterbury during Anselm's life-

---

[1] Ep. 192 [iii, 36].    [2] Ep. 214 [iv, 2].    [3] *HN* 126.

time; but it is clear that he did not, and could not, accept the Canterbury claim, voiced by Anselm, that he should never appoint a legate in England other than the archbishop himself.[1] Indeed the basis of this claim is very obscure, and it is interesting that Anselm should have taken up with such vigour a position which even Lanfranc had not adopted, and which depended only on hearsay. In judging Lanfranc's statement of his primatial claims, and indeed in all these controversies about ecclesiastical rights, it is well to remember how little evidence was sufficient to convince Anselm where the rights of his Church were concerned. We are accustomed to hear of the 'barrier' between England and Rome established by the Norman kings, but it is surprising to find Anselm taking the lead in repelling papal legates from England.

### (ii) *Primatial Authority*

It was not only on the question of legatine authority that Anselm went further than Lanfranc. In extending the territorial limits of Canterbury's jurisdiction, he also made a notable advance. This was partly accidental. He became archbishop at a time when the expansive energies of the Norman conquerors were beginning to make an impression in Scotland, Wales, and—as yet very tentatively—Ireland. The way for ecclesiastical expansion was prepared by conquest or marriage, but we must admire the energy with which, despite his other distractions, Anselm took advantage of the situation to press forward the authority of Canterbury.

*Wales.*

His most lasting success was in Wales. When Anselm became archbishop, his friend, Hugh earl of Chester,—on whose account he had first come to England—had recently completed the conquest of the northern coastal area as far as Anglesey, and a bishopric was established at Bangor in 1092 to give ecclesiastical expression to this conquest.[2] The bishop,

---

[1] Ep. 222 [iii, 44].
[2] For the relations between Canterbury and the Church in Wales, see J. Conway Davies, *Episcopal Acts relating to Welsh Dioceses, 1066–1272*, (Historical Society of the Church in Wales) i, 1946.

Hervey, a Breton, was the first of a long series of members of the English royal court to be provided with Welsh sees. Since Canterbury was vacant, he had been consecrated by the archbishop of York; and this also marked an epoch, for there is no certain case before this of a Welsh bishop receiving consecration in England. There were two other bishops in Wales at this time, at Llandaff and St. David's, both Welshmen and both following the customs of the Celtic Church. One of Anselm's first actions, during his first year as archbishop, was to suspend them both.[1] This was the first time an archbishop of Canterbury had taken disciplinary action against a Welsh bishop. The grounds for Anselm's action are uncertain. Probably they lay in the uncertainty of their ecclesiastical obedience and orders, to which Anselm could find plenty of grounds for objection. The bishop of St. David's quickly made peace with Anselm and was restored. Thereafter Anselm lent him such aid as he could against the despoilers of his see among the Norman barons who had recently penetrated, as far as Pembroke. Chief of these was Arnulf of Montgomery, a friend of Anselm, and one of his earliest devotees after his death. Here, as elsewhere, Anselm's familiarity with important members of the baronage made his task easier.[2] The bishop of Llandaff seems never to have submitted, and it was not until 1107 that Anselm was able to consecrate a bishop thoroughly devoted to the interests of Canterbury. By the time of Anselm's death, therefore, the whole Church of Wales, which had never before been subject to Canterbury, was completely subordinated to the English primate. This was the most lasting expansion of the authority of Canterbury before the seventeenth century. Essentially, the position which Anselm established lasted till 1920, despite the heroic struggle of Gerald of Wales in the early thirteenth century to establish an archbishopric at St. David's.

*Ireland.*

In Ireland, the success of Canterbury was much more short-lived, but the tide flowed strongly in favour of Canterbury in Anselm's lifetime. Lanfranc had already consecrated a monk

---

[1] Ep. 175 [iii, 23]; *HN* 72.
[2] *VA*, II, lxix, and n.

from Worcester as bishop of Dublin in 1074, and he seems to have envisaged a dependent archbishopric in Dublin on the model of what he hoped to achieve in York.[1] Things turned out very differently, but what is remarkable about Ireland is the enthusiasm with which the authority of Canterbury was at this time received, and Anselm was able without controversy to extend the area within which the authority of Canterbury was effective. He was no less prompt here than he had been in Wales. Lanfranc's authority over the Irish Church had been confined to the well-established Canterbury connexion with Dublin, but shortly after his consecration Anselm wrote generally to the bishops in Ireland urging them to establish canonical discipline; 'and if any question arises among you which you cannot determine canonically, we urge you in the bonds of charity to bring it to our notice, so that you may receive counsel and comfort from us'.[2]

This is the gentlest of expressions of authority, but authority it undoubtedly supposes; and the Irish Church was for a time willing to help to bind itself more closely to Canterbury. Anselm had powerful friends in Ireland and during his lifetime the ecclesiastical future of the country seemed to lie in his hands. In 1096, when everything else was going badly, he consecrated two bishops for Dublin and Waterford. The latter was the first Irish bishop outside Dublin to make a profession of obedience to Canterbury. Murchertach, the High King, whose daughter married Anselm's friend Arnulf of Montgomery, promoted the extension of Canterbury's authority; and Anselm, in his correspondence with him and with the bishops of Dublin and Waterford, and later of Limerick, spoke as a superior who might in due course enforce his authority with discipline.[3] The whole situation, however, was full of

---

[1] For the relations between Canterbury and the Irish Church in the late eleventh and early twelfth centuries, see the series of articles by Fr. Aubrey Gwynn S. J. in the *Irish Ecclesiastical Record*, 1941–2, vols. lvii–lix: 'The Origins of the See of Dublin', lvii, 40–55; 'Lanfranc and the Irish Church,' lvii, 481–500, lvii, 1–15; 'St. Anselm and the Irish Church,' lix, 1–14; 'The Origins of the Diocese of Waterford,' lix, 289–96. Fr. Gwynn, however, does not seem to me to attach sufficient weight to the consistency of the Canterbury claims under Lanfranc and Anselm.

[2] Ep. 198 [iv, 116].

[3] Epp. 277 [iii, 27], 278 [iii, 72], 427 [iii, 142], 429 [iii, 143], 435 [iii, 147].

instability. Norse, Irish and Norman elements were all competing for an advantage, and the future of the Canterbury
claims, which seemed so bright in Anselm's lifetime, depended
too much on obscure cross-currents of political ambition to be
assured. Within half a century of Anselm's death the only
traces of the once active policy were to be found in the strong
Canterbury complexion of the ecclesiastical calendar of the
church of Dublin: the primacy had vanished with the setting
up of four archbishoprics directly dependent on the papacy.
This was a development, however, which Anselm would probably have felt himself obliged to resist with all his power.

*Scotland.*

From direct authority in Scotland, the church of Canterbury
was cut off by the massive barrier of the province of York. The
Scottish bishops of this period were normally consecrated by
the archbishop of York, and there was no protest against this
practice until Anselm's disciple Eadmer himself attempted
to assert the rights of Canterbury in his own consecration as
bishop of St. Andrews. That this was an ill-advised step is
very clear to us, but Eadmer was only pressing a claim which
was felt to be inherent in the original jurisdiction of Canterbury.
Indeed, if the Canterbury claims meant anything, they could
not stop short of a general authority over the whole British
Isles: anything less would have done a violence to the early
history of the see as it was understood at Canterbury, and to the
large geographical and historical conceptions which lay behind
these claims.

*York.*

In order to exercise this authority, however, it was first
necessary to settle the dispute with York, and it was on his
handling of this issue that Anselm's reputation with the monks
of Canterbury chiefly depended. They compared him, to his
disadvantage, with Lanfranc. The conventional view, then as
now, was that Lanfranc had carried all before him in asserting
the rights of Canterbury, above all in 1072 when he had publicly
defeated the archbishop of York and obliged him to make a

profession of obedience to Canterbury.[1] By contrast Anselm appeared to have achieved nothing. This judgment was mistaken. It exaggerated the extent of Lanfranc's victory, and attributed to Anselm a failure inherent in the situation which he inherited. Lanfranc's permanent failure was for the moment concealed by his personal success, but it was fatal. In the first place he had failed to get an oath of obedience from the archbishop of York except during his own lifetime; and secondly he had failed to get a papal confirmation of the position established in 1072.[2] The result of these failures was apparent as soon as Anselm became archbishop. On the day of his consecration, Thomas of York, on being required to consecrate Anselm as primate of all Britain, retired to the vestry, unrobed and refused to move until the offending words of primacy had been deleted. We cannot tell whether Anselm yet understood the significance of this objection; it is not recorded that he took any part in the wrangle, and he did in any case submit to the deletion without protest.[3] From this moment the position of Canterbury was very weak; but it was not until 1108 that it became critical. Archbishop Thomas had died in 1100, and his successor Gerard required no archiepiscopal consecration, since he had already held the bishopric of Hereford. It was therefore possible to allow matters to slide: one side assumed that the obedience Gerard had promised to Canterbury as bishop of Hereford still bound him as archbishop of York, and the other side assumed the exact opposite. While Gerard lived, the quarrel got no nearer a solution, but it was not for lack of trying on Anselm's side. He was not idle. In the early years of Henry I's reign Anselm's messengers never went to Rome without pressing forward the claims of Canterbury. If the main business was investitures, a subsidiary theme was the primacy; and since the pope was in process of letting Anselm down on the major issue, the least he could do was to satisfy him as far as possible in minor matters. Indeed, in making this distinction between major and minor issues we

---

[1] *HN* 252–3; for the terms of the profession of obedience, see H. Boehmer, *Die Fälschungen Erzbischof Lanfranks*, p. 167.

[2] *EHR* lxxiii, 1958, pp. 201–3.

[3] On the evidence for this day's events, see below p. 303.

are probably conceding too much to the modern point of view. The issues appeared in different proportions at Rome and at Canterbury, but no one was inclinded to minimize the importance of the Canterbury theme—and rightly, for the establishment of a primacy such as Lanfranc and Anselm desired would have altered the shape of the medieval Church in England more than any concessions in the matter of investitures. With every inducement to satisfy Anselm—and Anselm did not hesitate to urge his sufferings on behalf of the papacy as a reason for conceding the claims of Canterbury—Paschal II, however, was careful to concede nothing of lasting importance.

In the summer of 1102, the messengers who brought conflicting reports of the pope's attitude on investitures, brought also a confirmation of the primacy to Anselm personally as his predecessors had held it.[1] In March 1103, the messengers who brought the papal letter which caused Anselm to leave England, brought also a letter from Paschal II ordering Gerard to promise obedience to Anselm.[2] When Anselm arrived at Rome later in the same year, the unsatisfactory outcome of his mission was sweetened by a privilege extending the primacy to Anselm's successors.[3] Anselm at once sent it to Canterbury to be copied and diligently preserved.[4] It marks the only advance made for over thirty years. This, rather than the decision of 1072, was the high-water mark in the Canterbury case, for no other genuine document exists which granted the primacy to the whole succession of archbishops. But when it came to the final crisis even this was valueless. It confirmed only 'such primacy as had been enjoyed by Anselm's predecessors', and it still remained for the church of Canterbury to prove just what, if any, primacy they had enjoyed. This was precisely what could never be done; at least, not without resort to forgery.

The privilege of 1103 is the last—and, in the sense desired in Canterbury, almost the first—papal intervention in favour of the Canterbury claims. From this moment the current of informed opinion began to run ever more strongly against Lanfranc's conception of a British patriarchate. Anselm, how-

[1] Ep. 222 [iii, 44].    [2] Ep. 283 [iii, 131].
[3] Ep. 303 [iii, 169].    [4] Ep. 307 [iv, 40].

ever, expressed himself in word and deed increasingly strongly in favour of this conception. He had failed to obtain an express concession of the legatine position claimed by Canterbury, but he had a promise for his lifetime that no legate should come to England. He now did all he could to ensure the supremacy over York. During his exile he could do nothing, but he raised the question on his return and, according to Eadmer, in the general settlement of 1107 Archbishop Gerard promised to show him the same obedience as he had owed as bishop of Hereford. This promise, however, was expressed in no document; it had the character of an informal arrangement which had no binding force on the future.

The real test in Anselm's lifetime came with Gerard's death, and the appointment of Thomas II as archbishop in 1108. Anselm was now 75 years old and in failing health, but he put out all his powers to bring Thomas to submission. The correspondence of his last year is filled with the subject, and no one can mistake the exaggerated intensity of Anselm's feeling on the subject. He wrote to the pope begging him not to send Thomas his pallium until he had sworn obedience to Canterbury; for if he once possessed his pallium he would never make his submission, 'and, if this should happen' (Anselm wrote),

you may know that the Church of England would be torn asunder and brought to desolation—according to the word of the Lord that every kingdom divided against itself will be made desolate—and the vigour of the apostolic discipline would in no small measure be weakened. As for myself I could on no account remain in England, for I neither ought nor can suffer the primacy of our Church to be destroyed in my lifetime.[1]

This is strong language; it shows that Anselm was quite as ready to face exile for the primacy as he had been for his obedience to the pope. He maintained this attitude to the end. His last letter before his death, written with the full dignity of the primacy of all Britain, speaking on behalf of God himself (*loquens ex parte ipsius Dei*), suspended Thomas from his priestly office until he renounced his rebellion against

[1] Ep. 451 [iii, 152].

138

the church of Canterbury. A copy of this was sent to every bishop in England.[1]

Anselm died before Thomas's obedience was secured. It was in the end secured by the traditional combination of king and bishops which Anselm had so often fought against.[2] No one, however, could accuse Anselm of indifference to the claims of Canterbury, and we may therefore ask why he left this impression on the monastic community. The answer can be found in the circumstances of Thomas's submission after Anselm's death. It must have been clear to everyone that the claims of Canterbury could only be successfully urged if they had the support of the king and the English bishops. This combination had been irresistible in 1072; it again proved its value in 1109 after Anselm's death. While Anselm lived, this combination was broken and the papal letters proved a very half-hearted substitute for the king's support. As the York writer noted, the king did not love Anselm after he had thwarted him in the matter of investitures.[3] Henceforth he supported York until Anselm's death brought him back to his father's policy of supporting the unity of the Church under the southern see. By this time, however, it was too late to alter the general swing away from such over-lordship as that claimed by Canterbury. If anything permanent were to be achieved, it should have been done under Rufus or in the early years of Henry I. Probably even by that time the whole policy was out of date; but it did not seem so to the monks of Canterbury nor to Anselm himself. On this they agreed; and it must have seemed to the monks that Anselm had wasted his opportunities by dividing, in the interests of an obscure principle, the forces of king and archbishop, which alone could have brought victory on the home front.

The vision of the church of Canterbury as it might be, which inspired Lanfranc, Anselm, and the community of Christ Church during these years came to nothing. It broke up within a few years of Anselm's death under the impact of forces which were too strong for it. It is therefore easy to

---

[1] Ep. 472 [iii, 155].
[2] HN 207–9; *Historians of the Church of York*, ii, 120–1.
[3] *ibid.* ii, 110, 114, 119, 121.

ignore. But it has an importance for the understanding of Anselm in showing that his practical policies could have the same sharp edge as his theological insights. His was not the eye of a statesman who saw a large range of affairs in due proportion: he worked on a narrow front, and he saw things clearly or not at all. The clarity of his vison took him to extravagant lengths as a man of action, and worse men showed more moderation. Shortly before writing his last letter, Anselm asked the advice of Samson, the aged bishop of Worcester, about the rights of Canterbury. Samson had seen the whole dispute from the beginning in 1072. He came of a family of royal officials who had used the Church as a means of promotion. He was a bishop of the old school, with no reputation for spirituality, but his reply contains, in not very good Latin, a just rebuke: 'If I truly knew what would be best both for you and us, I should not hesitate to tell you. But this I may say, that it seems to me unworthy that you should be too angry over this affair.'[1]

These few words of Bishop Samson introduce an element of moderation into the quarrel which is singularly lacking in the antagonists themselves at every level. Samson was the loyal suffragan of Canterbury. But he also expressed the views of the more secularly minded towards the dispute as a whole: it were well that York should submit, but it was undignified for Canterbury to urge the case with such unlimited fervour. Samson was a man of worldly tastes and habits: he was well-connected, well-educated, generous and rich; his brother had been archbishop of York, and the present archbishop was his son; another son was bishop of Bayeux; he himself had long been a royal chaplain. He was everything that the Hildebrandine Church abhorred. He was probably self-indulgent, but he had virtues which won him the warm friendship of Marbod, the talented bishop of Rennes, and Ivo of Chartres; they were not, however, the virtues of the cloister.[2] He probably had little understanding of the intensity of feeling

---

[1] Ep. 465 [iv, 97].

[2] This picture of Samson is derived from the following sources: *Gesta Pontificum*, 289–90; Ordericus Vitalis, *Historia Ecclesiastica*, ii, 249–50, iii, 266; Ivo of Chartres, *Ep.* 165 (*PL* CLXII); Marbod, *Carmina* xxi (*PL* CLXXI, 1658); *Regesta* nos. 147, 158, 182, 210, 308, 315.

about their rights and dignity which the communal life of the ancient monasteries engendered. And indeed it requires a strong effort of historical imagination to understand this intensity.

Many factors contributed to its formation. The most respectable was that stiff, unflinching regard for the full observance of God's rights which made Anselm declare that he would as soon be deprived of everything as of a little. Not far behind this came the anxious consideration that the particular saints of each church, for whom the present community was only the trustee, would demand from their trustees a full account of their stewardship down to the most minute particulars: what once had been given could never, without injustice and danger to their souls, be alienated. Anselm himself remembered from his youth, and in old age told his companions, a deplorably silly story of a Roman judge in the time of Pope Leo IX, who was condemned to eternal punishment because he had incurred the hostility of Saints Agnes and Laurence by depriving their churches in Rome of a garden and three houses respectively.[1] The judge was only saved from this predicament by the intervention of St. Praeiectus whom he had honoured in his lifetime. Anselm and his companions took the story quite literally. With all his theological subtlety and insight into human behaviour he accepted the common views of the time in attributing to the saints in Heaven the manners and morals of preparatory schoolboys. The grand vision of the position of Canterbury was reinforced by anxieties such as these; and the anxieties may have been more potent than the vision. Hence Anselm was afraid—and the memory of his fear was still preserved at Canterbury in the time of Archbishop Becket—to die and to appear in the sight of God until he had punished the archbishop of York for his infringement of the jurisdiction of Canterbury.[2]

This attitude was kept alive by a strong sense of the permanence of human arrangements in the matter of property, which seems to us of all things the least permanent: gifts to the Church were made to last till the Day of Judgment and

[1] *MARS* iv, 1958, 213–15.
[2] John of Salisbury, *Vita Anselmi*, PL CXCIX, 1035.

many of the documents in the Canterbury archives desired that, on that Day, God and all his saints would destroy those who violated their provisions. Such phrases were taken seriously. No clear distinction was made between the temporal and spiritual privileges of the Church; they all stood on the same level, enforced by the same sanctions, guaranteed by the same authority, reflecting the same divine ordering of the world. It was a world in which freedom and individuality meant little; corporate continuance came before everything else. In examining the life of the monastery at Canterbury, we shall see that everything combined to make the ancient communities, throughout every level of their being, and in their virtues as well as their vices, implacable custodians of what were imagined to be their rights. They remained so throughout their existence—the force of history and tradition was too strong to be resisted—but they gradually lost the sympathy of the world which placed a higher value on convenience and commonsense than on permanence and impossible loyalties. It is this new spirit that Samson represents, while Anselm on this matter represents the old.

## 3. CONTEMPORARY ATTITUDES

However important the rights of Canterbury appeared in his own eyes, Anselm's archiepiscopate will always be chiefly remembered for his disputes with William II and Henry I. It was in these disputes that the quarrel between Church and State, which in varying forms has continued to the present day, is first to be seen in England. It is surprising therefore that we owe our knowledge of the struggle wholly to Eadmer's account of it and to the collection of Anselm's letters made at Canterbury after his death. Without these Canterbury witnesses we should know very little more than the bare events of Anselm's exiles, with almost nothing about their purpose or circumstances. The English chronicles of the period, except in so far as they borrow from Eadmer, are almost entirely silent about the cause of the struggle. The Anglo-Saxon Chronicle, the chief contemporary source for the period, shows no comprehension or interest in the issues. Of Anselm's first exile it simply notes that he 'left the country because, in his opinion, little was done lawfully or as he directed', and after the King's death it merely mentions without explanation 'the great injustice which King William had done to him'.[1] As for the second exile, it simply says that 'Anselm went to Rome as he and the King had agreed'.[2] It says nothing about his return or the agreement which preceded it. Henry of Huntingdon, who was old enough to have known the period of Anselm's pontificate, relies on the Chronicle for his main outline, but elaborates the Chronicle's account of the first exile to make it appear a purely secular struggle, and ignores entirely the second exile; as the son of a priest, his chief interest was in Anselm's legislation against clerical marriage.[3] Hugh the Chanter of York is the most independent commentator on Anselm's activity, but he was almost wholly concerned with the struggle between Canterbury and York; his account of the causes of Anselm's struggle with William II is confused and anachronistic, and his comment on the result of the struggle under Henry I is famous for its cool and unfavourable appraisal of the resulting situation.[4] William of Malmesbury, who was a young man when Anselm died, has no important fact which does not come from

---

[1] *ASC* an. 1097, 1100.  [2] *ibid.* an. 1103.

[3] Henry of Huntingdon, *Historia Anglorum*, ed. T. Arnold, *RS*. His personal interest in Anselm appears only in the annal for 1102 on the occasion of the Council of London, 'in quo prohibuit sacerdotibus Anglorum uxores antea non prohibitas. Quod quibusdam mundissimum visum est, quibusdam periculosum; ne dum munditias viribus maiores appeterent, in immunditias horribiles ad Christiani nominis summum dedecus inciderent.' (p. 234) If, as seems likely, Henry of Huntingdon was born about 1080 or not long after, and succeeded his father as archdeacon of Huntingdon and Hertfordshire in 1110, he was in a position to speak of Anselm's pontificate from experience.

[4] Hugh the Chanter (*Historians of the Church of York, RS*, ii, 98–220) wrote his treatise on the struggle between Canterbury and York after 1127, but he had first-hand knowledge of at least some of the events of Anselm's pontificate. He confused his two exiles and wrongly thought that the dispute with Rufus was over investitures (p. 106, 110), but on Anselm's relations with the archbishop of York he is our most reliable authority: he gives the best account of the quarrel at his consecration (pp. 104–5), and he stresses the connexion between the investiture dispute and Henry I's hostility to the claims of Canterbury during Anselm's lifetime (p. 114, 119). For his comments on the result of the investiture dispute, see pp. 110–11.

Eadmer.[1] 'Florence of Worcester', whoever he was, could have supplied a contemporary view, but he has only faint and inaccurate traces of information not to be found either in the Chronicle or Eadmer.[2] So, in a period rich in chronicles written by men who were alive while Anselm was archbishop there is very little indeed to suggest that either the archbishop or his struggle with the king made any considerable impact on the country at large.

It is less surprising that foreign sources should have almost nothing to tell us about Anselm's activity. Ordericus Vitalis, as we should expect, has several details which he had not found in Eadmer, but he saw Anselm's life through a glow, in which all exact detail is blurred.[3] Even when we have independent accounts of those events which were important not only for Anselm and English history but also for Europe, there is a curious lack of corroboration or contradiction. There are, for instance, several accounts of the Vatican decrees of 1099 on which the whole of Anselm's pontificate hinges, but none of them mentions the investiture decree which gave the Council its importance. One account stresses the observance of Friday fasting, another the Greek schism, another the Crusade and the problem of clerical concubines. No one except Eadmer so much as mentioned the decree which made the Council important in the history of the relations of Church and State.[4]

[1] Leaving aside William's embroidery of Eadmer's information, his factual additions to Eadmer can be reduced to the following: a remark of Anselm that he was fit for no position of authority except that of a prior (*Gesta Pontificum*, p. 84); an account of Ranulf Flambard's visit to Canterbury on the day of Anselm's consecration (later erased: *ibid.* p. 84, n.); a story that the anti-pope had Anselm's portrait painted so that he might be recognized as he returned from Rome in 1099 (*ibid.* p. 103); some stories illustrating Eadmer's relations with Anselm (*ibid.* pp. 121–2).

[2] Most of the information about Anselm in Florence of Worcester comes from Eadmer; there is very little from *ASC*. The very few additions to these sources (an. 1093: Rufus's treatment of Anselm after his election; an. 1103: the events leading up to Anselm's departure for Rome) are inaccurate.

[3] Ordericus had read the *Vita Anselmi* at Bec before 1127 (iv, 55–6: a passage written, according to Delisle between 1125 and 1127), and he several times refers the reader to this work for further information (iv, 13, 55–6, 298). He appears to have retained only a rather inaccurate memory of its contents. He had not read the *Historia Novorum*, but he knew something about Anselm's life at Bec, no doubt from his friends there (ii, 244–6, 306; iii, 309, 431; iv, 64). [4] See *VA*, II, xxxviii, and n.

As so often happens, the witnesses seem all to have been looking in different directions. But this itself is an indication that the focal point was not as clear to them as it is to us. Indeed, it is certain that these disputes held a much less important place in the minds of Anselm's contemporaries than they do in our own. Eadmer has imposed on us his picture of Anselm's pontificate, certainly formed after the event and certainly in many details simplified. In retrospect he invested the disputes with a unity which they did not possess.[1] The thread of his narrative compelled him to pass over many months and even several years which contributed nothing to his theme. His extraordinarily vivid accounts of the debates in which Anselm took part must not blind us to the unlikelihood of some of the speeches which he reports but could not himself have heard. Biblical and hagiographical parallels came to his mind and coloured his narrative. Yet in the main he seized on the important points and gave them prominence; if he simplified his story, he did so in a way which brought out an essential truth.

We can see this very clearly in his account of the personalities of the king and bishops. Eadmer was very ready to listen to disreputable stories about William Rufus but it is hard to think that they greatly falsified his character.[2] Taking him all in all, Rufus is the most secular of all medieval English kings, the one who used the Church most consistently for his own material ends. This was a trait which grew stronger with the passage of time. His religious benefactions are very few, but such as they are, they belong to the earlier years of his reign and seem chiefly inspired by devotion to the memory of his father. He had a considerable largeness of spirit which even hostile observers were constrained to praise.[3] His life was given over to military designs, and to the raising of money to make them possible; for everything that did not minister to

---

[1] See below, p. 310.

[2] *HN* 99–102. William of Malmesbury, *Gesta Regum*, ii, 371, tells a similar story.

[3] For this side of his character, see Suger, *Vie de Louis le Gros*, ed. A. Molinier, pp. 5–7; William of Malmesbury, *Gesta Regum*, ii, 374, 396–7; Wace, *Roman de Rou*, lines 9391–2. The last witness, despite his late date, preserves a valuable record of the impression Rufus made on lay society.

these ends he showed a supreme contempt. Whether he was in any definite sense an unbeliever is a question to which our sources will allow no clear answer. In his illness in 1093 he submitted to the advice of his bishops, but this was the action of a sick man, and it was only after this date that his most secular characteristics became apparent. A later, and probably legendary, account of his death describes how

> He asked for the Sacrament,
> But there was none to give it him.
> Far from any minster was he, in a waste;
> But yet a hunter took some herbs with all their flower;
> He made the king eat a little;
> Thus he thought to communicate him.
> He is in God, and ought to be:
> He had received the *pain bénit* the Sunday before,
> Which should be a good warrant for him.[1]

None of these details can be relied on, but they are as near as we can get to the residual beliefs of one whose practice expressed contempt for religion.

With regard to the bishops, Eadmer's attitude is more open to question. It is unlikely that they ever openly avowed a preference for the king's will to that of God, as he makes them do.[2] But that they also were men with a strong secular bias can scarcely be doubted. Of Anselm's thirteen episcopal colleagues when he left England in 1097, eight at least had been royal chaplains, and three of these, as chancellors, had formerly been at the head of the royal administration.[3] These

---

[1] Geffrei Gaimar, *Lestorie des Engles*, RS, lines 6337–47. This passage contains what appears to be a clear piece of evidence for the practice of distributing *pain bénit* at the Mass to those who had not received the Sacrament.     [2] *HN* 56.

[3] The former royal chancellors were: Maurice at London, 1086–1107; Osmund at Salisbury, 1078–99; Robert Bloett at Lincoln, 1094–1123. The former royal chaplains were Thomas at York, 1070–1100; Gerard at Hereford, 1096–1101; Robert at Lichfield, 1086–1117; Walchelin at Winchester, 1070–98; Samson at Worcester, 1096–1112. According to Ordericus Vitalis, iv, 11, John at Bath and Wells, 1088–1122, and Herbert Losinga at Norwich, 1091–1119, had also been royal chaplains, but there is no independent confirmation of this assertion. Of the seven bishops appointed during Anselm's lifetime, after 1097, five had been chaplains of the king or queen: William of Warelwast at Exeter, 1107–37; Regenhelm

146

men held the most important sees. Of the remaining five, only two were monks: Anselm's friend Gundulf at Rochester, an unimportant see; and Herbert Losinga at Norwich, a man compromised by the scandal which surrounded his elevation to the bishopric, and, at least in Anselm's early years, immersed in his own affairs. These simple statistics, which did not greatly vary during Anselm's lifetime, tell us very little about the character of the episcopate. But they indicate that in any discussion, practical issues (not necessarily bad) would have more weight than any possible theoretical considerations. This made an immediate barrier between Anselm and almost everyone with whom he had to deal.

Among the bishops a single man stands out with sufficient breadth of interest and activity in ecclesiastical affairs to make him formidable, either as a friend or enemy of Anselm: William of St. Calais, bishop of Durham, the founder of the monastic community at Durham.[1] He had died before the final conflict with Rufus in 1097, but he had been Anselm's chief enemy in 1095. Scholars have found this difficult to understand. William of St. Calais had many of the qualities which should, in our eyes, have made him well disposed towards Anselm's policy. He had himself been in disgrace with the king in 1088, and according to a contemporary record he had defended himself by appealing to papal authority. How then could he oppose Anselm in 1095? It has seemed to many historians that he must have changed greatly in the intervening years; and the difficulty has appeared so grave that a recent scholar has suggested a falsification of the record of proceedings

(the queen's chancellor) at Hereford, 1107-15; Roger at Salisbury, 1107-39; William Giffard, the chancellor, at Winchester, 1100-29; Ranulf Flambard at Durham, 1099-1128. To these should be added the successive archbishops of York, Gerard (translated from Hereford) 1101-8 and Thomas II, 1109-14. The only appointments outside the royal household between 1093 and 1109 were Richard de Belmeis at London, 1108-23, and Ralph d'Escures at Rochester, 1108-14. Of these, the latter appointment was in the gift of the archbishop; and the former went to a man who had distinguished himself in secular service and loyalty, and was the founder of the greatest ecclesiastical dynasty of the twelfth century (on which see Stubbs, *Historical Works of Ralph de Diceto*, RS, i, xxi-xxix).

[1] For Bishop William's activity at Durham, see *Symeonis monachi Opera omnia*, RS, i, 119-35; R. A. B. Mynors, *Durham Cathedral Manuscripts*, 32-45.

in 1088.[1] This is a desperate remedy, and, before resorting to surgery, we must be sure that the case will not respond to gentler treatment. The trouble may be more imaginary than real.

In 1088 William of St. Calais was in a very difficult position: he had supported the abortive rebellion against William Rufus and he was faced with the certainty of confiscation and exile. According to the detailed account of the proceedings, which has long been accepted as a remarkable piece of contemporary reporting, he defended himself with great skill. The substance of his defence was a refusal to stand trial as a lay tenant unless his goods were restored to him, and, as an ecclesiastic, an appeal to the pope as the one competent tribunal for the judgment of a bishop. On this last point he quoted the Pseudo-Isidorean collection of canon law which Lanfranc had brought into England.[2] There is no difficulty in understanding both the motive and the source of his defence. But in 1091, the bishop made his peace with Rufus and returned to England. For the rest of his life he was evidently high in the king's favour, and acted as his chief spokesman at Rockingham in 1095. Eadmer gives a very unfavourable account of his behaviour; he was the *auctor et gravis incentor* of the dispute between Rufus and Anselm; it was rumoured that he hoped himself to become archbishop, if Anselm could be persuaded to resign: he promised the king that he would bring Anselm to heel.[3] Was this inconsistent with his action in 1088? Leaving aside, or even accepting, Eadmer's innuendoes and rumours, it is hard to see that the bishop of Durham showed himself in 1095 anything else than the acute debater of seven years earlier. He pressed the king's case, and he perhaps expected Anselm to submit; but he also recognized

---

[1] The proceedings are described in great detail in the treatise *De iniusta vexatione Willelmi episcopi* (Symeon of Durham, i, 170–95), which has been attacked by H. S. Offler (*EHR* lxvi, 1951, 321–41) as a tendentious work written some years after the events it purports to describe. I am not convinced by Professor Offler's arguments: the motive for falsification appears to be lacking, and the details of the trial seem to me to weigh heavily in favour of the contemporaneity of the work.

[2] William of St. Calais is known to have had a copy of this collection: Peterhouse, Cambridge, MS 74 (see Mynors, *op. cit.* 43–4).

[3] *HN* 59.

the simple point, which had formed the basis of his own earlier defence, that no tribunal except that of the pope could pass judgment on the archbishop. When Anselm resisted, William of St. Calais recognized that he had reached the end of his arguments. Eadmer reports that he counselled a final resort to violence, but he cannot have been present to hear this proposal and he may have heightened it for dramatic effect.[1] The whole conflict shows that the issues of 'papalism' and 'anti-papalism' appear much clearer to us than to those who were involved in these disputes. That William of St. Calais should on one occasion appeal to Urban II as pope, and later oppose Anselm on behalf of the king for recognizing Urban II without royal permission, need cause us no surprise. On both occasions he steered an adroit course within the limits of legality. If he had been a fool, Rufus would not have appreciated him as much as he evidently did. Probably both Rufus and the bishop expected Anselm's own attitude to be based on the same manipulation of legal concepts as their own; and they were partly nonplussed and partly contemptuous when they discovered that Anselm was as innocent as a child at this game.

The bishop of Durham, however, had his reward: he left the lands and rights of his see intact and enlarged, with the new community at Durham growing in prosperity. His work during the last few years of his life secured the fortunes of both bishopric and monastery, and it is hard to think that he looked on his support of the king as too high a price to pay for this result.[2] It was here that his chief responsibility lay. The bishop could die in peace and charity with Anselm, his work accomplished; and this he did without delay. He confessed his sins to Anselm, but we cannot assume that he reckoned his recent opposition to him among them, any more than we can assume that he imagined he was striking a blow for ecclesiastical liberty in 1088 in appealing to Rome. He used the armoury

[1] *HN* 62.
[2] For the impressive row of royal writs in favour of Durham between 1093 and 1095, see H. H. E. Craster, 'A Contemporary Record of the Pontificate of Ranulf Flambard', *Archeologia Aeliana*, 1930, 4th series, vii, 35–9 (*Regesta*, i, nos. 349, 363–5; ii, pp. 401–2, nos. 338a, 372a). For the important royal writs of 1095, see T. A. M. Bishop and P. Chaplais, *Facsimiles of English Royal Writs to A.D. 1100*. Pl. vii, ix.

God had given him in the service, he no doubt considered, of God and his see.

To speak thus may seem a superficial treatment of a problem of the deepest significance; but it is important to remember that men are not always occupied with deeply significant problems, that they have often to think of the practical effects of what they do, and that when an institution like the papacy is in the eyes of all men a very large feature of the landscape, there is room for a much greater variety of opinion about its exact size than when the main choice is between the extremes of acceptance or rejection.

## 4. RELATIONS WITH WILLIAM RUFUS[1]

Contrary to what is often thought, Anselm's disputes with Rufus have very little general interest. The points in dispute were too many and too varied, and they were discussed in too superficial a way to be important in the history of ideas. Hence the disputes are both trivial and inconclusive, and the antagonists drifted from one point to another without ever reaching an issue on which a serious argument could take place. A certain identity of view is necessary for a significant dispute, and it was this which was lacking. Anselm had seen this at once: 'You are yoking an untamed bull and a weak old sheep to the same plough'; they could neither pull together nor speak

---

[1] In the section which follows I cover ground which is in general outline very familiar, but I have attempted, in some points at least, to follow the changing scene and Anselm's reactions to it more closely than previous writers have done. I have learnt most from F. Liebermann's masterly survey in his essay 'Anselm v. Canterbury und Hugo v. Lyon' in *Historische Aufsätze dem Andenken an G. Waitz gewidmet, 1886*, 156–203, but in my view Liebermann greatly overestimates the influence of Hugh of Lyons, as also the element of political motive in Anselm's actions. There is a clear and balanced account of the dispute in A. L. Poole, *From Domesday Book to Magna Carta*, pp. 167–80, but the scale of this book precludes the treatment of the various issues in detail. Since I wrote this chapter, Mr. N. F. Cantor's study, *Church, Kingship and Lay Investiture in England, 1089–1135*, Princeton, 1958, has appeared. It is in many ways the most detailed account of the ecclesiastical issues of the period which has yet appeared. Our points of view and our interpretation of some important aspects of the subject differ so widely that I have thought it best to leave unaltered what I had written, except to register here and there a friendly agreement or disagreement.

a language which the other could understand. Perpetual disagreements necessarily sprang from this unnatural union. The
conflict took place at a level of unsophistication which would
have amazed the subtle lawyers of a later age. It is scarcely a
battle of arguments at all, but only one of wills. In some ways
this gives the quarrel its interest. When men know how to
cloak their intentions in elaborate argument, we lose sight of
their motives and personalities. They tread carefully, not
because their desires have been moderated, but because they
know that a false step may lead to destruction. But before the
language of debate has been elaborated, they state their positions
with less circumspection; and from the point of view of the
historian this has much to commend it. Thus stripped, however, of artifice and systematic justification, the rival positions
lose their intellectual interest. They lose their philosophical
dignity.

This is not to deny that one side may be right and the other
wrong, but the rightness or wrongness of the rival positions
becomes merged in the goodness or badness of the rival parties.
So it is here. When we turn from abstract speculation to
practical politics, we cannot fail to notice the contrast between
the maturity and clarity of the theological issues, and the
obscurity and inconsequence of those in the political field.
Equally striking is the contrast between the decisiveness of
Anselm's response to theological problems and the uncertainty
of his political reactions.

Anselm's most persistent and powerful impulse during these
years was to find a way of laying down the archbishopric. If
this proved impossible, he had three aims: to complete in due
order the steps necessary in becoming archbishop; to maintain
undiminished the possession and privileges of his church; and
to hold a Council for the correction of discipline in the Church.
All these aims raised a variety of difficulties which Anselm met
as best he could as they arose.

(i) *From Election to Consecration*

As to the first of these aims, the necessary steps in becoming
archbishop were election and investiture, followed by homage,

consecration and the receipt of the pallium from the pope. The first two steps were taken in the confused gathering at what was thought to be the king's death-bed on 6 March 1093. The events of this day present many points of interest, but none is more extraordinary than that the choice should have fallen so unanimously on Anselm. He had no administrative abilities; he had no close connexion with the king; yet from the time of his arrival in England six months earlier there had been rumours of his succession to the archbishopric. He was borne along on a wave of popular enthusiasm which very rarely had a chance to express itself in ecclesiastical appointments. The basis for this enthusiasm lay in Anselm's close relations with several important members of the baronage. Probably both the king and the bishops were more sceptical, but in the confusion of the king's illness no one except Anselm could stop to consider the consequences of what they were doing. The events of this day made him archbishop-elect, but he still hoped that something would happen to prevent the completion of the election.

This stage of indecision lasted for five months, from March to August 1093.[1] The possible obstacles which Anselm half invited and half avoided were: a refusal of consent from one of the interested parties—the duke of Normandy, the community at Bec, the archbishop of Rouen—or a change of mind on the king's side. Of all these obstacles, the community at Bec came nearest to presenting a real difficulty. The duke of Normandy and the archbishop of Rouen easily gave their consent; and even the king showed no inclination to change his mind. But at Bec things were not so easy. Many monks of Bec were there because of Anselm, and it seems clear that he had let drop remarks which seemed to mean that he would never leave them.[2] He had, moreover, been a very severe critic of members of the community who had accepted promotion to high office. Among these was Lanfranc, nephew of the late archbishop who

[1] Ep. 176 [iii, 24]: 'feci et dixi per sex menses quod potui sine peccato, ut dimitterer.' Although in August Anselm had ordered the monks of Bec to elect his successor, in September he still hoped that the king, would refuse to accept his homage (*HN* 40–1): hence the discrepancy of one month between my statement and that of Anselm.       [2] Ep. 156 [iii, 7].

152

was still smarting from Anselm's refusal to allow him to become abbot of St. Wandrille; and there may have been others who felt that their legitimate ambitions had been checked.[1] The community therefore was divided by the news of Anselm's promotion: some were dismayed and others angry, and their consent was not unanimous. In the end, after months of hesitation, Anselm was driven to act with that autocratic firmness, not unusual in men who in spirit are withdrawn from the world: he returned his pastoral staff, he nominated his successor, and he instructed the prior to remain in his present position.[2] With some reluctance the community carried out his instructions.

He was now ready for the remaining stages of his promotion: in September he did homage to the king, and on 4 December 1093 he was consecrated at Canterbury. As yet there was no papal decree against the homage of ecclesiastics to laymen; and since Anselm had not received investiture at the king's hands, Eadmer could rightly claim that Anselm was the first bishop, except the subordinate bishops of Rochester, who had obeyed the papal decrees against lay investiture. This, however, was not intentional. Although the investiture decrees were over twenty years old, Anselm knew nothing about them. He avoided investiture only because, in his attempt to escape election, he had kept his hand clenched so that the bishops had been obliged to press the archbishop's staff against his half-closed hand. He raised no objection against lay investiture in principle, and continued throughout Rufus's reign to consecrate bishops who had received investiture from the king and done him homage.

---

[1] Epp. 137 [ii, 42], 138 [ii, 43]. Anselm's attitude to ecclesiastical promotion is expressed in a saying of his preserved at Bec with a few other fragments of his talk, in MS. Vatican Reg. 499, f. 161 (*PL* CLIX, 1052): Quidam monachus Becci petebatur ad episcopatum ecclesiae Belvacensis, cumque S. Anselmus abbas huic electioni assensum praebere nollet, et monachum suum petentibus non concederet, dixerunt petitores: 'Domine, nos eligimus eum; non ipse se ingerit; quare non vultis concedere quod petimus?' 'Si' inquit 'ipse Deus me eligeret, adhuc timerem quia ipse per prophetam elegit Saulum et per semetipsum Judam traditorem, qui ambo reprobati sunt.'

[2] Epp. 156–7 [ii, 7–8]. His letters arrived in Bec on 15 August. (*Vita Willelmi Abbatis* in *Lanfranci Opera*, ed. Giles i, p. 317).

(ii) *The Pallium*

The final step of receiving the pallium remained. Until he received this symbolic ornament from the pope he could not perform the duties of a metropolitan, and unless it was obtained within a year of consecration the archbishop was liable to deprivation. The complicated troubles over the pallium are very well known and do not require detailed enumeration. They all arose from the fact that the kings of England had not recognized any pope since the death of Gregory VII in 1085; it was still doubtful whether England would follow Germany in recognizing Clement III, or France in recognizing Urban II.[1] Anselm, however, had already, as abbot of Bec, along with the rest of the kingdom of France, recognized Urban II, and he could not change his allegiance. He did not, however, deny the king's right to decide which of the two rival claimants the kingdom should recognize. There was a right decision and a wrong decision, but it was for the king to make it, and if the wrong one were made he would leave the kingdom.

Rufus delayed as long as possible, but there was never any chance that he would recognize Clement III. The reason for this lay in his unwavering determination to bring Normandy under his rule. It would have been a very unnecessary aggravation of his difficulties to recognize two different popes in lands which he intended once more to unite. And to drive the archbishop into exile at this moment for having recognized a pope recognized by all Normandy, would have been an act of political folly. The famous discussions at Rockingham in February 1095, when Bishop William of Durham acted as the king's spokesman was, therefore, largely a display of shadow-boxing. For various reasons the king would have preferred to keep his hands free, but as soon as he realized that Anselm

[1] The clearest evidence of this uncertainty is in the letters of the anti-pope Clement III to Lanfranc between 1085 and 1089, printed by F. Liebermann, *EHR*, lxi, 1901, 328–32: perhaps the most telling detail in these letters is the fact that the monastery of Wilton had thought it worth seeking Clement III's help in recovering some lost property, which it would scarcely have done unless the king had moved some way towards recognizing his authority. (See P. Kehr, 'Zur Geschichte Wiberts von Ravenna (Clemens III)', in *Sitzungsberichte der Preussischen Akademie der Wissenschaften*, Berlin, 1921, 359.)

would not move from his position, and especially when he threatened to leave the country, he at once decided to recognize Urban II. As soon as the decision had been taken he acted with his usual promptitude; and a papal legate had arrived in England with the pallium before Anselm even knew that the king had decided to give way on this point.[1] Not for the last time, he discovered—as some of his successors were later to discover—that in the last resort the king and pope could easily combine to ignore the archbishop.

This recognition of Urban II was Anselm's only victory in Rufus's reign. From one point of view it was a victory which he scarcely desired, for it meant that at last after two years of indecision he was fully invested with the archbishopric. His own desires still turned on the hope of escaping this burden. Strangely enough, it was the faintness of his personal desires which made him formidable. Rufus would have understood either violence or guile, but Anselm fought like a somnambulist whose blows were difficult to counter because they were impossible to predict. He slept while others argued, and when they presented their demands, the unexpectedness of his answer caused consternation. Probably he had no idea in 1095 of the nature of the difficulty in which Rufus was placed, but it was no easier on that account, and the political necessity for recognizing Urban II cannot have made the king any better disposed towards his archbishop.

### (iii) *Knights and Secular Service*

The die was now cast. Unwillingly but indisputably Anselm was now archbishop. For the past two years, however, although he lacked the full power of an archbishop, he had been fully responsible for maintaining the possessions and privileges of his church. The question of its privileges has already been discussed. Over its possessions, Anselm had already in 1093 and 1094 had two acrimonious disputes with the king; a third

---

[1] The Council at Rockingham lasted from 25 to 28 February (*HN* 53–67). The pope was at Piacenza, and if the king's messengers left without delay they would just have time to reach him, conduct their business, and return with the legate by Whitsunday, 13 May. See *VA* II, xvi, n.

problem arose in 1097, and it was this which finally made him resolve to leave England. We shall not have got the perspective of events right unless we realize that this was an issue much more likely to precipitate a final crisis than any other. The first crisis over the possessions of the church of Canterbury had occurred in August 1093. At this date the king demanded that the archbishop should confirm some military tenancies which he had created on the archbishop's lands during the vacancy.[1] Probably Anselm would have been well advised to comply. It is true that the archbishop's lands were already over-stocked with knights, in relation to the military service due from them.[2] But he had a very large estate, and in the administration of it he needed the support of the king and his courts. Anselm was to learn too late that 'a man's enemies are the men of his own house', and that a landowner had more to fear from grasping tenants beneath him than from the king above. Anselm however did not think in these terms. He had a simple, deeply rooted fear of being personally responsible by some overt decision for a diminution in the lands committed to his care. If other men deceived him and stole his lands, that was their concern; but he would not be a party to a deal. As always, his thought was simple and clear-cut:

This is my thought: the king has given me the archbishopric as Lanfranc held it till the end of his life. Now he takes away from me and the church what the archbishops and the church so long have held. The archbishopric will not be given to anyone after me, except as I hold it on the day of my death; and if another king succeeds to the kingdom in my life-time, he will not allow me to hold anything which he does not find me holding on his accession.[3]

[1] According to Eadmer, the king asked Anselm 'quatinus . . . terras ecclesiae quas ipse rex, defuncto Lanfranco, suis dederat, pro statuto servitio illis ipsis haereditario iure tenendas, causa sui amoris condonaret' (*HN* 40). Cantor, pp. 73–4, has argued that these were lands held by English knights or 'drengs' at the time of Lanfranc's death. But Anselm's letter on the subject (Ep. 176 [iii, 24]) makes it clear that the lands were held by Lanfranc in demesne, but were thought to have been held by English knights before the Conquest. The legal basis of Rufus's action was his claim that these lands should once more be held by military service.

[2] At the time of Anselm's arrival, 98¼ knight's fees appear to have been created on the lands of Christ Church, Canterbury to provide a *servitium debitum* of 60 knights (*Domesday Monachorum*, p. 105).

[3] Ep. 176 [iii, 24] to Hugh, archbishop of Lyons.

The argument was impeccable. Nothing could willingly be given up. The king had to acquiesce. He did not even, as Anselm hoped, refuse to accept the archbishop's homage.[1] His masterful power had, in practice, very severe limitations. But he did not forget.

The next crisis followed almost immediately and Anselm took a similarly personal view of his responsibilities. In 1094 the king was preparing for his attack on Normandy, and he required an aid from his tenants-in-chief. It was an unjust war if ever there was one; but it is probably true to say that there was no attempt to discriminate morally between the wars of secular lords at this period unless they affected the interests of the Church. Certainly Anselm was not troubled by doubts about the motive of Rufus's war. But he was troubled about a possible imputation of simony if, as a very recently appointed prelate, he paid money to the king. In the event, he made an offer of £500. This was enough to show that he did not object to the aid in principle; but it was not enough to satisfy the king. When the king refused his offer and demanded £1000, Anselm was glad to escape from his secular toils into a world he understood: he gave the money to the poor.[2] This was charity on a princely scale, but whether it was wise is more doubtful. Politically it further exasperated the king, who would rather have taken £500 with ill-will than nothing at all.[3]

When the king next had to raise money for the duchy of Normandy in 1096, he seems to have been satisfied with Anselm's offer: at least we hear no complaint. But this time it was the monks of Canterbury who were offended, for Anselm took their plate to help him to pay. Even the grant of an archiepiscopal estate worth £30 a year, for ten years, to pay his debt of £133 to the community did not silence all their criticisms.[4] It is impossible to please everybody, but Anselm's conduct in these affairs must be judged to have caused the

---

[1] *HN* 41: 'Unde Anselmus oppido laetatus est, sperans se hac occasione a praelationis onere per Dei gratiam exonerandum.'
[2] *HN* 45.    [3] *HN* 45–7; *VA* II, vi–vii.
[4] *HN* 75: the loan was made, Eadmer says, 'connivente majori parte conventus'; he goes on to defend Anselm against the 'ora obloquentium qui usque hodie Anselmo depraedatae ecclesiae crimen intentant.'

greatest amount of dissatisfaction to the largest number of people for the least possible result. He was guided less by either principle or prudence than by a mixture of scrupulosity and distaste for the whole business which is the worst possible basis for the active life.

Leaving aside for a moment the last conflict concerned with the estates of Canterbury we may turn to Anselm's efforts to hold a Council for the reform of morals and discipline. He had no power to hold such a Council until he received the pallium in 1095, but he had very early broached the subject to the king. Eadmer reports him in February 1094 as addressing the king in these terms: 'Order, if you please, the ancient usage in the matter of Councils to be revived. . . . Let us try together, you with your royal power and I with my pontifical authority to make some ordinance which may be published throughout the realm to the terror and discomfiture of wrongdoers.'[1]

If these words correctly represent Anselm's thought, it would seem that he was prepared to allow the king more authority in ecclesiastical affairs than would later have been thought tolerable. Fortunately we have confirmation of the general tenor of these words in Anselm's letter to the papal legate in 1095, which has already been quoted: 'It cannot escape your prudence that we two can do nothing unless it has been suggested to the king, so that by his assent and aid our decrees can be put into effect.'[2]

We have seen that this letter was chiefly inspired by a jealous regard for the rights of the church of Canterbury; but taken together with Eadmer's report of Anselm's words in the previous year, it also expresses a submissiveness towards royal authority which is unexpected. Anselm had not yet given up hope of working amicably with the king. He was prepared to wait a long time to gain the king's ear and meanwhile to support the king in his enterprises. We have seen that he personally undertook the defences of the south coast when the king went north in 1095. At the same time he wrote in warm praise of his energy and practical wisdom, and ordered prayers for his protection against the malice of evil men who hated the king's

[1] *HN* 48–9.  [2] Ep. 191 [iii, 35]. See above, p. 131.

good qualities.[1] It would be quite wrong to think that Anselm was a determined opponent of royal authority or of secular policies and the virtues these policies required.

The next two years, from 1095 to 1097, were passed in peace and frustration. We know almost nothing of Anselm's activity during this period except that he consecrated two Irish and two English bishops. Only a handful of his letters for these years have been preserved; fewer than for any similar period of his pontificate. The vacant abbacies remained vacant and he could do nothing about it. He could hold no Council. The reason given was the disturbed state of the king's affairs which prevented his attending to ecclesiastical business. Anselm acquiesced in this explanation and waited for peace.

According to Eadmer, it was a small incident which opened his eyes to the true state of affairs and to the realization that, whatever the circumstances, he was not to be allowed to do anything apart from the routine of episcopal duty. The king's complaint about the quality of the knights he had sent on the Welsh expedition of 1097—perhaps an aftermath of the old dispute about the enfeoffment of knights on the Canterbury lands—gave him the hint that it was not peace the king was waiting for.[2] Peace had, it was wrongly believed, at last been

[1] Ep. 190 to Osmund, Bishop of Salisbury, asking him to institute prayers throughout his diocese for the king's safety. Of the king Anselm says: 'Est enim nunc in illa terra in qua habet inimicos (havent vicmos *edit.*) plures, qui eius prudentiae et strenuitati—sicut solent mali bonis— invident, quamvis hoc dissimulent.'

[2] *HN* 78. Sir Frank Stenton (*The First Century of English Feudalism*, 1932, pp. 145–8) has suggested that the basis for William II's complaint was the inadequate training and equipment of the Anglo-Saxon drengs whom Lanfranc had converted into knights. This suggestion is based on a letter of 1188, in which the community of Canterbury gave an account of what they believed had happened after the Norman Conquest. (*Epistolae Cantuarienses*, ed. Stubbs, *RS*, p. 225). As Stenton noticed, however, this story receives no support from Domesday Book; and it has even less support from the list of predominantly Norman knights in the *Domesday Monachorum*. It is very hard to think that any drengs of pre-Conquest days were still serving as knights in 1097, whatever may have been the case twenty years earlier, or that their inadequacies would have passed muster under two such masters of feudal government as William I and II for thirty years. Cantor, p. 73, has found confirmation of Stenton's hypothesis in Ep. 176 [iii, 24]; but the passages he quotes will not bear the construction he puts on them. See above, p. 156, n. 1.

achieved, but with it came fresh occasion for complaint. Anselm's inference that the king would never allow him to exercise his archiepiscopal functions as he wished, though arrived at on slender grounds in the immediate circumstances, was correct. Eadmer noticed Anselm's habit of trusting men long after others had seen their deceptions: but then at last he would recognize them for what they were. So it was now in his dealings with Rufus. Later he experienced a similar disillusionment with Henry I. Anselm's reaction was to ask permission to visit the pope to consult him about his troubles. The unexpectedness of this request seems to have taken the king by surprise.[1] There was some reason for his bewilderment, for Anselm does not seem to have desired or expected any practical result from this consultation except a possible release from his archbishopric. Once more, his lack of desire, his lack of policy in any ordinary sense of the word, threw the king's counsels into confusion. As a matter of course, he refused permission; Anselm temporarily acquiesced, but decided to go on asking: 'He has the power: he says what he pleases. But if he refuses now, perhaps he will agree at another time. I shall keep on asking.'[2]

## (iv) *Exile*

Simply to keep asking is not a very refined form of political action, but it is very wearing. Rufus was never to see Anselm again without the question being raised. In the end the reiteration became intolerable, and in October 1097 he let him go. He could, he thought, safely do so. Anselm was not an active enemy, and even if he had been, he could scarcely harm him now. Normandy was safely under his control until Duke Robert's return, if he were ever to return, from the Crusade. Anselm's departure contributed nothing to the solution of his own problems; it only benefited the royal treasury to which the archiepiscopal revenues were added. To Anselm it meant freedom from an intolerable position, dangerous to his soul and to his monastic vows: it held out little else—certainly no immediate prospect of practical effectiveness: 'I go indeed willingly, trusting in God's mercy that my journey will do

[1] *HN* 79–80.    [2] *HN* 80.

160

something for the liberty of the Church in future times.'[1] Just how it was to contribute to this end it was hard to see. In going into exile Anselm must have had before his eyes the example of St. Wilfrid, whose life Eadmer had recently written, but the differences are very striking. Wilfrid went to Rome to appeal against a judgment, to make a petition, and bring back a formal privilege. Anselm brought a petition of a different kind:

This is the sum of my supplication (he wrote to the pope) for which I wished to come to you, that you will free my soul from the bonds of so great a servitude and restore its liberty of serving God in tranquillity . . . ; and then that you will apply your wisdom and apostolic authority in taking counsel for the good of the English Church.[2]

What Anselm desired above everything was freedom for his soul's health. But this the pope would not give him. Moreover the pope could do nothing for the state of the English Church. He would, according to Eadmer, have excommunicated the king at the Council of Bari in October 1098 but Anselm pleaded for him.[3] This little incident raises certain difficulties of procedure and it is probable that either Anselm, or his biographer, or both, misunderstood what the pope was about to do. In any case nothing was done. After this, time was on the king's side: the papal Curia offered seemingly endless opportunities for delay, and the king made full use of them in the hope that nothing would happen. Nothing did happen. Eadmer was disillusioned by this inaction;[4] but what Anselm thought we have no way of telling. He simply returned to Lyons, in his native Burgundy, to await events. Quite unwittingly he was making a contribution to the armoury of later archbishops by presenting them with the idea and example of exile.

During his long stay at Lyons from May 1099 till August 1100, Anselm was in frequent contact with Hugh, the archbishop of the city. It has been claimed that his political ideas underwent a great change under the influence of this active and influential man. This is not easy to prove, and I do not believe that the contact with Hugh had any perceptible influence on Anselm's later conduct. He was not, as has been suggested,

[1] *VA* II, xxi.    [2] Ep. 206 [iii, 166].    [3] *HN* 107.    [4] *HN* 111, 114

more truculent or more thorough-going, or even more consistent, in the future than in the past. Yet, in thinking about the
past, his ideas about the issues crystallized. This is seen in the
letter which he wrote to the new pope, Paschal II, about the
end of 1099, explaining his position. It shows a remarkable
advance on the letter he had written to Urban II on his way
to Rome two years earlier. He no longer asked to be relieved
of his onerous position, and if he still shrank from returning to
England, it was not because he feared to lose his cherished
tranquillity:

I do not write as if desiring to return to England, but because I
fear that you will be angry if I fail to notify you of my state. I pray
and implore you, therefore, not to order me to return to England
unless I can put the law and will of God and the papal decrees before
the will of men, and unless the king restores to me the lands of the
church, and whatever he has taken from the archbishopric because
of my coming to the apostolic see.[1]

In his statement of his position there is a new note, and for
the first time something like an attack on the customs of the
Conqueror in a general way:

The king required in the name of justice my assent to his arbitrary
demands, which are against the law and will of God. For he did
not wish the pope to be recognized in England or appealed to, or
that I should send him a letter, or receive one from him, or obey
his decrees, except by his command.[2]

These words exactly describe the situation which Rufus had
taken over from his father, and in which Lanfranc and at first
Anselm had acquiesced. They sum up his experiences as archbishop in the last seven years; but the distinctness with which
the issues are stated makes the letter look forward to the days
of Henry II rather than back to the confused and erratic
events of Rufus's reign. Perhaps this new clarity came from
discussions with Hugh of Lyons, though it may equally be the
product of leisure to think over the affairs of the last few years.
For the first time since he became archbishop he had no important theological work on his hands. He no longer had a
distracting array of retainers at his back; he was responsible

---

[1] Ep. 210 [iii, 40].       [2] *Ibid.*

for no estates, no rights or privileges. He could see events in their European setting.

There must of course have been much discussion in Lyons about the right course to pursue. One of the chief suggestions was that Anselm himself should excommunicate the king, but to this he replied that 'the wiser and better counsellors advise me that it is not for me to act both as plaintiff and judge. Besides, my friends in his kingdom tell me that my excommunication would be held in contempt and derision'.[1] He was later, in the case of Henry I, to change his mind on the question of acting both as plaintiff and judge; but for the present nothing was done, and the situation was soon altered by the death of William II.

## 5. RELATIONS WITH HENRY I

### (i) *The Initial Crisis*

Anselm was still in exile in 1100 when the news of Rufus's death reached him. The news was soon followed by a pressing invitation from the new king to return to England. Anselm came without delay. Rufus had been killed on 2 August; Anselm reached Dover on 23 September and met Henry I at Salisbury a few days later.

The scene to which he returned was very different from the one he had left. In the first place, the personality of the new king made it quite certain that any dispute would be conducted in a new way. Despite the more favourable opinion of his contemporaries, Henry's personality makes a more unpleasing impression than that of Rufus. He was equally licentious, and avaricious; and in his early years at least, until he developed a pronounced strain of piety, his aims were equally secular. But he had more craft and policy; more capacity to wait, to present a good face to the world, and to advance step by step towards his goal. He was a man of great political sagacity and formidable resolution. As a younger son he had learned to be content with small advantages when greater ones were not to be had; but he had not lost the capacity for large designs or for rapid action when need arose. He was

[1] *Ibid.*

too much of a politician ever to outrage religious feelings as Rufus did, but his smooth words concealed a purpose very little different from that of Rufus.

At Rome, too, there was a new pope under whose indecisive leadership the temper of papal government changed. We are only at the beginning of a change which became more conspicuous later, but already by the time of Anselm's death it is evident. The change is one inseparable from the growth of bureaucracy: the importance of the permanent officials grows; violent pronouncements become rarer, negotiation becomes more frequent, and compromise sometimes prevails over principle.

Anselm was to experience the effects of these changes; but at the moment of his arrival in England, his position could scarcely have been stronger. It was very uncertain whether Henry would be able to retain the crown he had seized. Except for a small number of families, the baronage was either wavering or hostile. At the best, it looked as if a period of baronial bargaining between two rival candidates would develop, such as we find in Stephen's reign. But it was more likely that Henry would disappear in the coming struggle. His elder brother Robert returned from the Crusade almost at the same time as Anselm reached England: he was newly married and for the moment therefore rich; with a European reputation, military experience, and the means for commanding the service of knights. He alone could at once restore the union of England and Normandy, which was important for many great families. It was recognized at the time that it was Anselm's support which turned the scale in Henry's favour—this and the practical fecklessness of Robert.

Why did Anselm not support Robert? One can only suppose that Anselm, like most men of his time, preferred an effective ruler, however unpleasant, to an ineffective one, however recommended by his personal qualities. Why then did Anselm not make his support of Henry conditional on concessions which he could scarcely have failed to obtain? This is a question more difficult to answer, especially when we consider the other important novelty which distinguished the years after 1100 from those before the death of Rufus. This novelty was the papal decree on investiture and homage, which at last gave Anselm a clear and simple objective for which to fight.

## The Papal Decree

Since Eadmer is the only witness for the making of this decree, his words require careful consideration. He has left a detailed description of the Easter Council of 1099 in St. Peter's, at which he and Anselm were present.[1] It is a characteristic observation of his that the proceedings were a good deal disturbed by the passage of pilgrims to the tomb of the Apostle. The truth of this remark may be vividly appreciated when it is remembered that the Council was arranged round the tomb of St. Peter, with the pope and cardinals (among whom Anselm had been placed in a seat of honour) in the apse behind the altar, and the remainder of the Council spread out in front of them. The noise and disturbance had prevented many from hearing what had been said, and the pope therefore asked the bishop of Lucca to read aloud the decrees of the Council. This he did, but in the middle he broke out into an angry protest at the Council's acquiescence in secular tyrannies in general, and at the lack of any provision for the case of Anselm in particular. He was called to order, and the reading of the decrees continued. Then the pope rose to pronounce his final excommunications, and whether or not moved to action by the bishop of Lucca's protest, he included among them the anathemas which were to play so large a part in English affairs in the next few years.[2] These anathemas embraced:

1. all laymen who gave, and all clergy who received from laymen, the investiture of churches; and all bishops who consecrated those who had been thus invested;
2. all clergy who did homage to laymen for ecclesiastical honours.

On the second point the pope dwelt with special and dramatic emphasis, saying that it was intolerable that hands, by whose

[1] *HN* 112–14.
[2] For further discussion on this point, see *VA* II, xxxviii, n. Eadmer's account (*HN* 114) suggests that the excommunication of those doing and receiving homage was not part of the formal acts of the Council as read by the bishop of Lucca.

ministry God the Creator was Himself created, should suffer the indignity of contamination and subordination to hands made bloody with daily violence and shedding of blood. Anselm took him at his word. It is worth noting that Anselm nowhere expresses an opinion about the substance of the decree; he never discusses the principle behind it. Before it came to his knowledge he had made no difficulty about acting in a contrary sense, but now he treated it as an absolute command, leaving no room for discussion or negotiation. He embarrassed his friends, and even to some extent the pope by the stiffness of his obedience. When the pope finally retreated, Anselm saw a possible injustice in forcing others to a similar retreat, and for a moment he hesitated. The situation illustrates Anselm's indifference to the compromises of practical affairs. He did not understand the secular mind, which was quite as common among the clergy as the laity. When the word was spoken, he obeyed; he saw no grounds for strife or withdrawal or discussion; he took pleasure in obedience.

Yet, others had some reason for making distinctions. The two halves of the decree were not as homogeneous as they appeared to be. The first half, the investiture decree, was already more than twenty years old. It dealt with symbols which were part of the liturgical dress of the bishop, conferred in the service of consecration. Whether or not it was important that the lay ruler should already have given them to the bishop before consecration was a question on which opinions might reasonably differ, but that the symbols were intimately connected with the spiritual functions and powers of the bishop could not be doubted. But the case was quite different with regard to homage. The intolerable indignity of it had not been mentioned by any pope before Urban II, for the first time in 1095 and later, as we have seen, in 1099. In itself, homage had no spiritual significance; but it was the main legal nexus of secular society, the most solemn bond between lord and vassal. From a secular point of view nothing could be more important: as Maitland wrote, 'the ceremony of homage is as solemn as ceremony can be'. To touch it was to touch the secular world on a tender place.

The difference between the two halves of the decree is

very clear to us: the first half deals with something which is 'spiritual', the second half with something which is 'secular'. But we must beware of thinking that the difference was equally clear at the time of the decree. To old-fashioned men a bishopric was a single indivisible whole, comprising lands and authority, sacramental power and territorial rights. Of course lands and sacraments are conceptually quite distinct things. But the lands of the bishopric, or of any church, were set apart from other lands, just as the materials for sacramental use were set apart from ordinary wine and water, oil or salt: they came under another law, an eternal ordinance. And if the ecclesiastical land was thus given a sacramental quality, the power of committing spiritual authority to the pastor was in some degree lodged in the secular ruler. Ivo of Chartres might argue that in conferring the ring and staff upon the newly appointed bishop, the ruler was doing nothing of any importance. By the early twelfth century this was true, but Edward the Confessor or William the Conqueror would not have agreed. They looked on themselves as conferring a general right to undertake the work, and exercise the authority, spiritual as well as temporal, of a bishop; they bestowed on the bishop that portion of God's authority on earth of which the secular ruler was the trustee and the bishop the effective instrument.

The years which followed Anselm's return to England in 1100 saw the final cutting of these antiquated threads. Despite the long tradition of unity, they came apart very easily. But if Urban II had had his way the separation would have taken place along different lines. In withdrawing homage as well as investiture from lay hands, he would have retained the unity of the episcopal office by excluding the secular ruler from a claim on the services and ultimately on the loyalty of the bishop. Many people, however, and not least in the papal Curia, who were willing to co-operate in paring away the archaic spiritual pretensions of the lay ruler, shrank from the practical consequences of so abrupt a division between the Church and the world as that envisaged by Urban II. They preferred the elaborate compromise, which more than anything else became the mark of the medieval Church. Not so Anselm. It is symptomatic of his lack of interest in political affairs, and especially in elaborate practical compromises, that he had in principle as little objection to lay investiture as he had to clerical homage. But when they were both forbidden he treated them both alike. His only interest in the matter was in obedience.

When Anselm arrived in England in September 1100 Henry immediately required him to renew the homage which he had done to Rufus, and to consecrate his chancellor William Giffard to the bishopric of Winchester, which he had given him on his coronation day. Henry can have expected no difficulty. He had also invested two new abbots, both sons of important magnates who, as it happened, were friends of Anselm: to Robert, son of Hugh earl of Chester, he had given the abbey of Bury St. Edmund's; and to Richard, son of Richard of Clare, the abbey of Ely.[1] These were mere fragments of the complex arrangements which he had made to secure his position.[2] But Anselm objected to all these measures and revealed the content of the papal decree of 1099. This put Henry in a difficulty. He could not afford to antagonize Anselm, but—with motives very similar to those of Anselm with regard to *his* predecessors —he had no intention of abandoning any rights enjoyed by his father and brother. His only plan at this moment was to play for time. Now and always his treatment of Anselm was disingenuous, but it showed him a master of the ruses of statecraft. He did not at once press for the renewal of Anselm's homage, and William Giffard stopped calling himself bishop of Win-

---

[1] See, for Ely, *Liber Eliensis*, ed. D. J. Stewart, 1848, p. 284; for Bury St. Edmund's, F. Liebermann, *Ungedruckte Anglo-Normannische Geschichtsquellen*, p. 130–1, *and Memorials of St. Edmund's, RS*, i, 353; and for Winchester, *ASC* ann. 1100, *HN* 145, *Annales Monastici, RS*, ii, 40–1. From these sources an illuminating story can be pieced together. For Anselm's relations with the families of these magnates see *VA* i, xviii n., ii, i.

[2] Among these measures must probably be reckoned the creation of Walter Giffard as earl of Buckingham. Walter Giffard's earliest appearance as earl is in the coronation charter of Henry I, and it seems likely that the creation was one of Henry's measures to enlist support at this dangerous time. Ordericus Vitalis (ii, 221) says that he received the earldom from William I, but this is generally recognized to be inaccurate; it is not, however, generally recognized that the evidence for a creation under William II is no stronger, for Walter Giffard never appears in the genuine charters of the first two Norman kings with the title of earl.

chester. It was agreed to send messengers to Rome to discover whether the pope was inflexible. Meanwhile Anselm was restored to his lands. In the summer of 1101, faced with Robert's landing in England and the immediate prospect of widespread desertion, Henry promised a general obedience to the papal decrees, and it is possible that Anselm's activity following this promise turned the tide in his favour.[1] But Henry's general promises made in times of need meant nothing.

The messengers sent to Rome in 1100 were due to return by Easter 1101, but they were conveniently delayed, and it was not until September that the result of their mission became known. The papal letter which they brought was uncompromising, though noticeably vague in its terms. By this time, however, the military crisis was over; peace with his brother had temporarily solved his problems, and Henry abruptly demanded that Anselm should either comply with his wishes or leave the country.[2] Ironically, it was his brother Robert—angered by Anselm's hostility to himself—who counselled this truculent attitude. But to get rid of Anselm was not now quite so easy: he refused either to comply or to leave the country, and for the next few weeks lived quietly in his manors. The archbishop of 1101 with a clear principle to maintain was a different man from the Anselm of 1097 who asked for nothing better than an opportunity for escape.

In speaking, however, of a principle we must not mistake the

---

[1] *HN* 127. For the importance of Anselm's intervention on Henry's side see W. H. Stevenson, 'An inedited charter of King Henry I, June–July 1101,' *EHR* xxi, 1906, 515–19. On political grounds it is very difficult to account for Anselm's support of Henry: Robert would certainly have been more favourable to papal claims; his claim to the crown was at least as good as Henry's; and as a Crusader who had been absent on Crusade when Henry seized the throne he deserved ecclesiastical support. Anselm may have been influenced by the fact that the families with which he was most closely associated provided some of Henry's strongest supporters. But from the point of view of papal policy it was an error of the first magnitude.

[2] *HN* 131. The result of Anselm's actions in the previous months had been to unite against him both the supporters of Henry and those of Robert; as Eadmer remarks, 'rex, usus consilio fratris sui et amicorum illius qui acerbo contra Anselmum pro regni amissione odio erant inflammati, exegit ab eo ut aut homo suus fieret, et eos quibus episcopatus vel abbatias se daturum dicebat pro more antecessorum suorum consecraret, aut terram suam sine retractatione et festinanter exiret.'

nature of the obligation by which Anselm conceived himself to be bound. So far as the terms of the papal decree were concerned Anselm in these two years had lost a golden opportunity for enforcing them. Until September 1101, if he had insisted on an explicit agreement to renounce homage and investiture, Henry would have had to give way. Whether Henry would have kept any such agreement is another question, but his capacity for resistance would have been much reduced. It may be said that Anselm never knew how to press home a political advantage, and this would be true. But there is another factor which may help to explain his conduct. He always understood that the papal decrees imposed on him personally an absolute obligation, but he does not seem to have felt himself responsible for ensuring the obedience of others. In this struggle, so long as his own hands were clean, he was content. This will appear as the story unfolds.

(ii) *The Period of Negotiation*

The initial crisis of the reign was succeeded by a period of prolonged negotiations. Despite their complexity, the main development can easily be summarized. It is clear that until April 1102 the pope was still insisting on the full observance of his predecessor's decree. Paschal II's letters of this date, which reached England in August, contain an exact and uncompromising restatement of the papal position, forbidding both homage and investiture; to this statement Paschal added a series of directions to Anselm showing in detail how the decrees were to be applied to parochial churches and the lands of churches held by lay service.[1] These letters represent the high point in the campaign for a Church both spiritually and

---

[1] Epp. 222 [iii, 44], 223 [iii, 45]. The king's messengers however reported a verbal relaxation, which the pope later denied (*HN* 140–1). Ep. 222 describes the decrees of the Council in these words: '. . . sancientes et interdicentes, ne quisquam omnino clericus (hominium faciat laico aut) de manu laici ecclesias vel ecclesiastica dona suscipiat.' It may be significant of the growing confusion after this time that the text given by Eadmer in *HN* 135 omits the words enclosed in brackets, which were certainly part of the original text.

temporally independent of the secular state. The papal position was never again in Anselm's lifetime to be stated so clearly and uncompromisingly. From this moment the idea of compromise began to gain ground, not with Anselm but with those around him on all sides. This admission of the possibility of compromise is the first sign that the period of Hildebrandine reform is coming to an end and is being replaced by the age of lawyers and administrators, differing in their briefs, but in their methods understanding each other very well.

In April 1102 the pope still spoke of homage and investiture in equally uncompromising terms. By the end of the year a change of emphasis is observable. In December his reply to a new mission from the king and archbishop contained no mention of homage, while lay investiture was condemned in the most violent terms:

What are the bishops doing in the Church if lay hands confer the staff, the symbol of the pastor's office, and the ring, the symbol of faith? The honour of the Church is torn in pieces, the bonds of discipline are broken, the whole Christian religion is besmirched, if we suffer lay arrogance to usurp that which we know to belong to priests alone. It is not for laymen to betray the Church, or for sons to defile their mother with adultery.[1]

This is the sort of language which Urban II had used three years earlier about clerical homage to laymen; Paschal II uses this language about lay investiture, and the absence of any mention of homage is significant. The change of emphasis which is implied in this silence is confirmed by the negotiations of the next few years.

In the event, the letter containing the passage which has just been quoted had no effect on the subsequent negotiations. It was addressed to Anselm, but he had a premonition that if he opened it he would find himself committed to an ever-widening circle of excommunications. He adopted the simple expedient of not opening it, and agreed to go himself to Rome to obtain if possible an acceptable solution. Eadmer gives a curiously confused account of Anselm's motives at this time, but one thing stands out clearly: Anselm could not face the chaotic

---

[1] Ep. 281 [iii, 74].

personal relationships and the conflict of obligations which seemed to be imminent. He left England on 27 April 1103; and, when the opportunity for practical action had passed, he opened the papal letter.[1] There was now no need to hurry. He passed the summer at Bec and reached Rome in October to find that messengers from the king had recently arrived. He found the pope as determined as ever about lay investiture, but Eadmer says nothing about his attitude to homage. The seeds of compromise were beginning to take root. There were some able hands to tend them.

The king's business was in the hands of a servant who may with good reason be regarded as the first of that long line of men who did more than any others to make and destroy the medieval Church—the professional civil servant, equipped to forward the interests of government not by main force but by negotiation amidst the intricate issues of law and theology; men of international standing, retaining the respect of their opponents, and not too hatefully or too personally involved in the cause which they were required to maintain. There is no earlier example in England of this type of official—the more famous Ranulf Flambard being only too conspicuously *not* of this type—than William of Warelwast, the king's messenger. He stayed in Rome after Anselm's departure and procured letters of a different tenor from those entrusted to Anselm. To Eadmer, and to William of Malmesbury who enlarged and exaggerated Eadmer's words, the secret of his success was simple bribery, the common charge of disappointed litigants. But we can see that he had something more to work on than the Roman thirst for gold. It was by now becoming clear that the papal Curia was not solidly behind the more extreme form of papal policy inaugurated by Urban II and pursued so far by Paschal II. Eadmer reports that there were in the Curia those who now openly supported the royal cause,[2] and it is possible that the influence of this trend of thought is to be seen in the letter which Paschal II now addressed to the king. In it he argued temperately against lay investitures but minimized their importance, denying that he sought for himself any

---

[1] *HN* 149.      [2] *HN* 153.

increase of authority or any diminution of the king's due power. The violent metaphors which formerly had been freely used were absent, and the letter ended with a suggestion of compromise: 'If anyone has behaved harshly towards you, which we do not believe, we shall be guided by your will, so far as we can and God allows, provided that you put aside investitures.'[1] The word homage was not mentioned. The letter's main practical purpose was to urge the recall of Anselm. This suggests that the king's messengers had made known to the pope, before Anselm was aware of it, the king's intention of excluding Anselm from the kingdom until an agreement was reached. Anselm had thought he could return to England at the conclusion of his mission, but at Lyons he was overtaken by William of Warelwast, who told him that he must stay in exile until the king's demands were satisfied. Anselm was shown the letter carried by the royal messenger. After reading it, he quietly suppressed the papal letters to the king and queen with which he had been entrusted; for, as he told the pope, after the arrival of the later letter brought by William of Warelwast, they would either not be read or be read with derision.[2] Thereupon he reconciled himself without a struggle to another period of exile and peace. His hands were clean.[3]

Unlike the situation in the earlier exile he kept up a regular correspondence with England, and it was very generally thought by his friends that he reconciled himself too easily to his position. They felt that he had developed a taste for exile as an escape from business. There was probably some truth in this. He would gladly have died or suffered hardship or privation for the truth; but business made him ill and distracted him from the ends to which he had dedicated himself. To all complaints about his conduct he made the same answer: he was bound by the decrees he had heard in 1099. These obliged him to withdraw from the communion of clerks, who did homage or received investiture from laymen, and of laymen

---

[1] Ep. 305 (*HN* 155–7) of 23 November 1103.
[2] Anselm to Paschal II: 'Epistolas quas mihi praecepistis regi et reginae ex vestra parte mittere . . . per me dirigi congruum non aestimavi. Certus sum quia, si per me dirigerentur, aut omnino non viderentur, aut contemptui et dirisui haberentur'. (Ep. 315 [iv, 46]).       [3] Ep. 308 [iii, 88].

who took part in these ceremonies.[1] Hence he could not return to England, where the exigencies of his position, the need for attending the royal court, for saying Mass and crowning the king at the great festivals, would force him into communion with those whose company he was forbidden to frequent: 'Certainly I cannot expel them; to pray with them I do not dare. I ought not to withdraw from the king my accustomed duty, for the lord pope has granted him this and has ordered me to perform it if I am present.'[2]

It was a strangely anomalous position. The pope himself had put it out of his power to enforce the decree of 1099. In some ways the royal and papal courts understood each other better than Anselm understood them, or they him. For Anselm it was a position from which it was not easy to move in any direction.

Yet move, in the end, he did, on somewhat obscure provocation. When it came, his action is not easy to interpret. From December 1103 to April 1105 Anselm contented himself with justifying his exile in the face of criticisms from his English friends: his position remained unaltered, and his intermittent correspondence with the king and pope led to no result. The king continued to send messengers and letters to Rome, with the purpose, as Anselm soon perceived, of ensuring still further delay.[3] The king's letters to the pope during this period are all missing, but we have two from the pope to him. They are conspicuous for their conciliatory terms and for the fact that, though they insist as firmly as ever on the prohibition of lay investiture, they make no mention of homage.[4] Then in the spring of 1105 Anselm received a letter from the pope telling him that sentence of excommunication had been passed on Robert of Meulan and other royal counsellors, but that sentence

---

[1] Anselm to Ordwy, monk of Canterbury: 'Non enim ego prohibeo per me a rege dari investituras ecclesiarum, sed quia audivi apostolicum in magno concilio excommunicare laicos dantes illas investituras et accipientes et qui accipientes sacrabunt, nolo communicare excommunicatis nec fieri excommunicatus'. (Ep. 327 [iii, 100]).    [2] Ep. 311 [iii, 90].

[3] Anselm to Henry I, 1104: 'In responso vestro quod mihi iam bis fecistis, nihil intelligo nisi quandam, si audeo dicere, quae nec animae vestrae nec ecclesiae Dei expedit, dilationem'. (Ep. 319 [iii, 95].)

[4] Epp. 348, 351.

on the king was delayed because fresh messengers were expected in Rome.[1] To one who had waited so long, this letter might have suggested that matters were moving at last towards a solution, and that the end in some form could not now be long delayed. Anselm however understood the letter in the opposite sense and concluded that fresh delays were now all that he could expect. Despite the appearance of determination in the papal letter he may well have been right; he was in a better position to read between the lines than we are. It is nevertheless surprising that he should have chosen this moment to take decisive and even violent action in a sense scarcely compatible with that suggested in the papal letter. Eadmer says that he acted on the advice of Hugh of Lyons, and this we may well believe. According to Eadmer, Anselm now concluded that he could expect no help from Rome. He had thrice warned the king to restore his lands to him, without result; now he determined to take action on his own behalf and to excommunicate the king.

Anselm thus, at last, abandoned his earlier determination not to act as accuser and judge in his own cause. Yet the reason which prompted him to do this had, on the surface at least, nothing to do with the main causes of the quarrel with Henry I. Anselm based his action simply on the king's seizure of his lands.

To a modern reader, who is conscious of the large issues involved in the struggle, this intrusion of the local and material interests of the church of Canterbury at a critical moment may seem incomprehensible, and the suggestion has been made that the real reason behind Anselm's action was that he, and still

---

[1] Ep. 353 [iii, 171]. The letter is dated *vii Kal. Aprilis* (26 March). After recording the excommunication of the king's advisers, the letter concludes: 'Regis vero sententia ea ex causa dilata est, quia suos ad nos nuntios in praeteriti Paschae tempore debuit destinare.' This is puzzling. If Easter was past and the messengers had not arrived, why was the sentence delayed? But Easter was not until 9 April in this year. Unless the date on the letter is wrong, the word *praeteriti* would therefore seem to be a slip. But if it was less than a fortnight to Easter, it is then puzzling that the pope should have been in such a hurry to send this letter instead of waiting for the arrival of the king's messengers. It may have been this that gave Anselm the hint that Paschal intended to do nothing, and was glad to forestall the need for action by sending this letter.

more Hugh of Lyons, were dissatisfied with the spirit of compromise which was gaining ground at Rome, and were anxious to cut short the waverings of the Curia by independent action. In support of this view it has been pointed out that this would not be the first time that Hugh had shown himself more papal than the pope and had taken an independent line at variance with that of the papacy.[1] Such a view, however, is the product of a generation taught to extract from political situations what are regarded as essential interests and to subordinate everything to these interests; Anselm and even Hugh were not so politically minded as this view implies. Anselm acted with more aggressiveness than was usual with him. This may have been a result of Hugh's advice. But the object of his action was one for which he felt a personal responsibility which no one else could share. On the question of investitures and homage he acted not on his own behalf, but as an instrument of the pope to whom he owed his obedience. But where the lands and rights of Canterbury were concerned, his actions followed an independent logic of their own, and he seems now to have decided that his thrice repeated and unheeded warnings on this subject needed to be followed by excommunication even if this cut across the lines of papal policy.

(iii) *The Compromise*

Anselm left Lyons in May 1105 in order to put himself in a position from which he could effectively excommunicate King Henry. So much is clear. Henry, on his side, was once more, as in 1100–1, in no position to add excommunication to his other problems. His plans for wresting the duchy of Normandy from his brother Robert had reached a critical stage, and he was beginning to prepare for the final blow: at this

---

[1] He had been excommunicated by Victor III in 1087 (Jaffé—Wattenbach no. 5346), suspended by Urban II in 1095 for not appearing at the Council of Piacenza (Bernoldi *Chronicon*, *MGH*, *SS*, v, 462), and he had opposed the papal legates sent to southern France in 1100 (Hefele-Leclercq, *Histoire des Conciles*, v, 468). But the cause of these disagreements was not over-eager papalism, but chagrin at the loss of his legateship and a tender regard for his rights as metropolitan. Like many others, he was a strong supporter of papal rights when he was papal legate, and a strong defender of metropolitan rights when he was simply an archbishop.

juncture, as he and his enemies realized, excommunication would be disastrous. On his way north Anselm met the king's sister, Adela countess of Blois, and confided to her his intention of excommunicating the king. She was alarmed, and hastily arranged a meeting between the king and archbishop in July at Laigle on the borders of Normandy.[1] If Anselm had had large plans for forcing a final settlement, he could now no doubt have obtained a notable success. But he concentrated on the single question of the Canterbury lands, and withdrew his threat of excommunication when they were restored to him. Henry, on the other hand, was content to ward off the immediate danger while keeping his hands free for the future. He restored Anselm's lands, but he refused to give any undertaking on the general points in dispute. Anselm had thus once more no choice but to remain abroad or enter into communion with those from whose communion he believed himself excluded by the decrees of 1099. He therefore settled down in Normandy for a further period of waiting. His abrupt adventure into independent action had gained his immediate ends, but left the general issues very much where they were. For Henry the balance-sheet was more favourable. He was now able to complete his conquest of Normandy without interruption and to imprison for the rest of his life the only member of the Conqueror's family who deserved the protection of the Church.

Part of the understanding with the king at Laigle in July 1105 was that a new joint mission should be sent to Rome to effect a settlement by Christmas. Henry however was in no hurry. His hands were very full with the arrangements for his attack

---

[1] *HN* 165–6. The suggestion frequently made (for example by A. L. Poole, *From Domesday Book to Magna Carta*, p. 179), that the settlement which followed these negotiations was a triumph for the views of Ivo of Chartres, and that there is a significant connexion between the intervention of Adela, in whose country Chartres lay, and the views of Ivo, has no foundation. In the first place the settlement did not follow the general line of thought of Ivo, who was inclined rather to give an ecclesiastically satisfying explanation of the existing procedure of investiture than to attach great importance to changing it; secondly, there is no evidence that Ivo was present at any of these negotiations. (For an extensive treatment of this question see now Cantor, pp. 202–16, with whose judgment on this point I am in complete agreement.)

on Normandy, and there must also have been many discussions about the terms on which he would be willing to make peace with the papacy. Meanwhile he made every possible excuse for delay until Anselm's patience was almost exhausted. It was not until early in 1106 that the messengers finally left for Rome. By this time the king had decided that he would be prepared to abandon investiture if he could keep the homage of prelates for their lay fees.[1] He lost little or nothing by the concession and, as we have seen, the papal letters had for some time indicated the likelihood of such a solution being acceptable at Rome. Once the decision was taken there was no further need for delay. On 23 March 1106 Paschal II wrote to Anselm to announce in veiled words that a compromise has been reached: 'God, in whose hands are the hearts of kings, has turned the king's heart to the obedience of the apostolic see; wherefore the pope has condescended to raise him up. . . . No one can raise another unless he himself bends; yet even if he who bends seems to come near to falling over, he does not lose his state of rectitude.'[2] Such words as these prepare the reader for a retreat. It is nowhere stated that ground which had been occupied was to be abandoned, but that was the effect. Anselm was made to appear to have been too rigid in his interpretation of the decree of 1099: 'We absolve you, venerable and dearest brother in Christ, from that prohibition, or as you believe excommunication, which you understand to have been pronounced by our predecessor of blessed memory Pope Urban against investitures and homages.' Then the pope proceeded to the practical consequences of the new state of affairs: those who had received lay investiture, or done homage, or consecrated others who had received lay investiture, were absolved; for the future, those who received ecclesiastical preferment and did homage to the king could be consecrated provided that they had not received investiture at his hands; and this was to continue until the heart of the king was softened by the rain of Anselm's preaching. This last consequence never followed, so

---

[1] Anselm to Hugh of Lyons, c. December 1105: 'Tota difficultas causae inter regem et me iam in hoc maxime videtur consistere, quia rex quamvis de investituris ecclesiarum apostolicis decretis se vinci, ut spero, permittat, hominia tamen praelatorum nondum vult, ait, dimittere'. (Ep. 389 [iii, 123]).

[2] Ep. 397 [iv, 77].

homage succeeded by consecration continued to be the rule; and, as the York writer noted, the practical diminution of royal control over the episcopate was negligible.[1]

Anselm found this retreat difficult to accept; it must have left him with a certain sense of betrayal; but Hugh of Lyons counselled acceptance, and indeed there was little else to be done. The decision brought a more clear-cut distinction between the spiritual and temporal aspects of ecclesiastical office than ever before and there can be little doubt that it was the conclusion which best corresponded to the practical realities of the day.

Nothing remained but to tie up the loose ends of the dispute. The pope's letter reached Anselm late in April 1106. All obstacles in the way of his return to England were now removed and he set out in May. Illness overtook him and delayed him till August; but he was in England in September. The king's continued absence in Normandy prevented the public pro-mulgation of the settlement for another year, till August 1107. The final settlement contained no surprise, and followed the terms of the papal letter of fifteen months earlier.[2] Anselm was now, for the first time since his election as archbishop in 1093, free from any cause of dispute with the king and the last year and a half of his life was spent in the peaceful routine of episcopal duties, disturbed only by the growing problem of the relations of Canterbury with York.

It is natural that this side of Anselm's activities should have received most attention from historians; it concerns public events of the highest importance and the materials are com-paratively abundant. Despite their gaps, they allow a more complete picture to be drawn than for any other ecclesiastical statesman of the period except Gregory VII. Yet it was the least characteristic and least congenial part of Anselm's work. In the world of politics he had not the same clear vision of the whole question which he brought to the problems of theology and the life of the spirit. On these subjects he may or may not be right in what he says, but he speaks with the simple and clear authority of direct vision. But to politics he brought virtues and principles fashioned for other ends; in all his

[1] *Historians of the Church of York*, ii, 110–11.      [2] *HN* 186.

179

letters it is remarkable how little illumination, how few ideas, he brings to the practical problems of the time. This is not to minimize his practical achievement. He brought about in a few years a state of affairs which might otherwise have taken a generation to develop. It was not a state of affairs which he particularly wanted; his main aim was to preserve the integrity of his soul, and events formed themselves round him with little conscious direction on his part. His scale of values was that of few men, and it is hard to point to any successors in the episcopate who carried on his work.

To modern historians Anselm's period as archbishop has appeared as a turning-point in the relations between England and the papacy. It is very doubtful how far this view is justified: it would be easier to make a case for archbishop Theobald as the founder of the later medieval Church-State relationship. But whatever the justification for the modern view, it is certain that contemporaries did not see things in this way. To the community at Canterbury Anselm was a saintly but somewhat disappointing archbishop. Probably Anselm shared their disappointment. The tasks for which he felt the full weight of personal responsibility were very harassing, and his success in performing them was open to serious doubt. In the first place it was his duty to preserve intact the lands and rights entrusted to his care. As to this, Eadmer gives strong hints that he failed to prevent the encroachments of powerful tenants, but the details of these aggressions are lost, and they seem to have had no important effect on the general prosperity of the Church of Canterbury. His second task was to preserve and exercise the metropolitan authority of his see. In this he was, as we have seen, more active and more successful than is often realized.

### 6. TWO CASES OF CONSCIENCE

In dealing with the main public events of Anselm's pontificate, we have seen him in the midst of complex issues. If he achieved only a very limited success, it was not from lack of activity, nor from lack of determination to maintain the rights of his see. It was chiefly because practical success requires compromise on some points to obtain a full success elsewhere. A gradation of objectives is required and an understanding of the means to be used in attaining them. Anselm's whole philosophy, as well as his inclinations, were opposed to this careful adjustment of ends and means. The world which he understood was one in which there was an entire congruity of means and ends in the will of God. It was in this spirit that he described sin, in however slight a form, as a dishonouring of God in intention eternally; and in the same spirit that he wrote 'I would as soon be deprived of everything as of a little and I say this not from love of money but from love of the justice of God'.[1] He was writing here of the king's seizure of some of his property. He lacked the pliable spirit to assess relative advantages. Hence from the point of view of almost all men he seemed sometimes too weak and sometimes too strong for what the occasion required. He had no talent for manipulating the forces of the world. He was constantly foiled by the unexpected and the arbitrary in human affairs. Even Eadmer had to acknowledge that his successes were diluted in practice by the operation of ordinary instincts of compromise, and more worldly critics could see from the beginning that his plans would not work. This was notably true of Anselm's legislation. William of Malmesbury remarked that it was all obsolete by 1125 and he only gave the text of the decrees of the Council of 1102 for the scholarly purpose of not depriving students of the truth.[2] These decrees covered a wide field. On some points, the prohibitions they contained—for instance against abbots creating knights or monks holding manors at farm—must have been a dead letter from the beginning. But Anselm's chief concern was with the celibacy of clerks from the rank of sub-deacon upwards. To this end he applied himself with a vigour which contrasts with the temporizing attitude of Lanfranc. But here as elsewhere it was discovered that the vigour of the archbishop could achieve nothing without the activity of the king. The decree of 1102 on celibacy seems to have had little effect until the king became active on its behalf in the last year of Anselm's life; and it was only after Anselm's death that the royal authority began to achieve results which, in the eyes of contemporary commen-

---

[1] Ep. 321 [iii, 97].    [2] *Gesta Pontificum*, 117–18, 121n.

tators, were of doubtful moral value but undoubted efficacy.[1] Anselm, however, cannot be blamed for his ineffectiveness as a legislator. It was the common lot of ecclesiastical laws to be broken, and to judge correctly we must look to the long-term effects of constant effort rather than to the effectiveness of isolated decrees. Yet when all is said it is nevertheless true that Anselm was only at home either in the world of abstract speculation or in his dealings with individuals. With his great speculative achievements we are not here concerned. In his dealings with individuals, his elevation to the archbishopric brought, as we have already seen, a great change. The letters of ardent friendship ceased abruptly; the characteristic personal note of the earlier years disappeared for ever. His new way of life assisted this change. He could no longer gather his pupils round him and he could no longer write in the old way to those who had shared with him the monastic life. In some ways, however, his range of influence was extended. Several of the bishops—Gerard at York, William of St. Calais at Durham, William Giffard at Winchester, Herbert Losinga at Thetford and Norwich—came under his personal influence, and to some extent showed this in their actions. Most of all he spread himself in his dealings with the communities of women who came under his general protection.

It would not be in place here to give an account of Anselm's letters of encouragement and advice to various individuals and communities, although these are more characteristic of the man than his political activity. But there are two cases which deserve a more detailed examination. They have a certain interest for political events, and one of them had a lasting effect on Anselm's reputation. They show, moreover, more intimately than any of the larger issues, the intricate web of politics and personal relationships in which Anselm as archbishop was required to work.

Within a month or two of his consecration Anselm's attention was called to some strange happenings, not to say 'goings-on', in the noble monastic foundation at Wilton. This was the most famous refuge of English noblewomen after the Conquest and it must have been one of the greatest repositories of English

[1] *HN*, 193, 212.

182

tradition in the country. The almost total destruction of its manuscripts has deprived us of a great deal that we would gladly know, and it is therefore all the more welcome that Anselm's letters illuminate it for an instant.

Anselm's earliest letter about Wilton was written shortly after the king had parted from him in anger in February 1094.[1] It was addressed to the bishop of Salisbury and it referred to events which must, as we shall see, have been common knowledge at the royal court. Its subject was the perdition of the daughter of the king of Scotland who had been tempted by the devil to lay aside her religious habit and return to the world. Anselm said that he had delayed his open condemnation of this sin for fear that it had been prompted or condoned by King William's aid or favour. But he had talked to the king while they were together at Hastings, and had found him right-minded on the subject 'as a good king should be'. The king would be glad to see her back in the cloister, and the archbishop asked the bishop of Salisbury to exert his authority to compel her to return.

Behind this brief letter was a situation full of complications and consequences for the future. By piecing together a number of disjointed fragments of information we can obtain an unusually vivid picture of the situation. The daughter of the king of Scotland in question was Matilda, who later in very different circumstances became the wife of Henry I and queen of England. In 1094 however this was a future which no one foresaw; so far as Anselm was concerned, she was simply a runaway nun in grave danger of damnation. We do not know at what date she had gone to Wilton, but probably she had come to England with her aunt Christina in 1086 and they were certainly together at Wilton in 1093. Matilda was by this time of marriageable age. It is clear, moreover, from facts which later became public, that her father King Malcolm had never intended her for a life-long vocation in the cloister. In 1093 he was working for a general settlement of his relations with the English king, and the marriage of his daughter had an important place in his plans. The marriage which he contemplated for her was with one of the most powerful of the English

[1] Ep. 177.

183

barons, Count Alan Rufus, lord of Richmond, founder of St. Mary's York, for twenty-five years one of the most constant witnesses of royal charters, the greatest man in the north of England.[1] In point of age, he and Matilda could scarcely have been more unsuited—he a man probably in his middle fifties, she a girl of about thirteen. But in the circumstances of the time this need cause no surprise. The match, which opened up vistas of political opportunity and perhaps even greater danger, was one which might well give Rufus considerable food for thought, and it is unlikely that either Matilda's age or her monastic upbringing seriously entered into his or her father's calculations.

We cannot be sure why this marriage plan broke down, but it had already broken down by August 1093. This was the date fixed for the final settlement of differences between the kings of England and Scotland. A meeting between the two kings had been arranged at Gloucester and elaborate preparations were made for the meeting. King Malcolm was there at the appointed time, but for reasons which have never been explained Rufus refused to see him and the two parted, in the Chronicler's words, 'in great enmity'.[2] Matilda's place in all this is obscure, but the curious fact later emerged from the gossiping of Anselm's man of business, Baldwin, that Rufus had gone to visit her at Wilton on his way to Gloucester. If Baldwin is to be trusted, this visit had serious consequences, for it was on this occasion that the abbess placed a monastic veil on Matilda's head, and when Rufus saw the veil he went away.[3]

The details of Baldwin's story are confused and we cannot tell what conclusions Rufus drew from his visit to Wilton. Whatever they were, he arrived at Gloucester determined to make no treaty with Malcolm. That Matilda was a central

---

[1] To the evidence for this match adduced below may be added the testimony of Ordericus Vitalis, iii, 400, who says that Count Alan Rufus sought Matilda's hand from King William II but was prevented by death from obtaining it. [2] *ASC* 1093.

[3] Hermann of Tournai recorded his recollections of Baldwin's talk during a visit to his old monastery, probably in 1101-2, in his *De Restauratione S. Martini Tornacensis, MGH, SS*, xiv, 278-81. The treatise was written long after the conversation it describes, and this sufficiently accounts for the confusions in Hermann's details, but the substance of what he relates may be accepted.

piece in these negotiations may be inferred from Malcolm's immediate reaction to Rufus's insulting behaviour at Gloucester: he went straight to Wilton, tore the veil off his daughter's head, and took her back to Scotland. His remark as he tore off the veil has been variously interpreted. In Matilda's own words 'my father swore that he had destined me as a wife for Count Alan rather than for a community of nuns'.[1] There is no need to imagine that they were anything but a simple statement of fact. This plan however was now dead and within a few months Malcolm had been killed in a border skirmish.

In all probability the marriage plan foundered on two elementary difficulties. In the first place, Count Alan Rufus saw a young woman whom he liked better than Matilda. She too wore the monastic habit at Wilton and we may suppose that he first saw her when he visited the monastery to see his projected bride. The result was a strange and passionate romance which must once have shaken English society but is now known only from two letters of Anselm.[2] The object of the passion of this great feudal lord was Gunhilda, the last known descendent of the last Anglo-Saxon king. The union gives an unexpected twist to the history of the Norman Conquest. Harold's daughter was, like many others, a monastic refugee from Norman violence. In 1093 she must have been a woman of about thirty years of age. She had never made her profession before a bishop, but she had worn the veil for several years and seems to have been regarded as a nun.

This was certainly the light in which Anselm regarded her. He wrote two letters to her, and though the exact dates of these

---

[1] *HN* 122. Dom Wilmart, *Annales de Bretagne*, xxxviii, 1929, supposed that these words were ironical and had the sense that 'anything (even marriage to such a scoundrel as Count Alan) would be better than to see you as a nun.' But this is a very far-fetched interpretation, and the words are intelligible in their natural sense when the chronology of events in 1093 has been clarified.

[2] Ep. 168 [iii, 157] and Ep. 169, from Anselm to Gunhilda. The second of these letters was discovered and first printed in 1928 by Dom Wilmart (*R. Bén.*, xl, 319–32). Dom Wilmart also wrote a detailed interpretation of these letters in *Annales de Bretagne*, xxxviii, 1929, but the false dating of the deaths of the two Counts Alan led him to confuse the political background of these events.

letters cannot be established there are several indications that they are among his earliest letters as archbishop.[1] His interest in the nuns of Wilton and Shaftesbury is shown in several letters in the early months of his pontificate, and he probably heard of Gunhilda's abduction at the same time as he heard of Matilda's removal from Wilton by her father.[2] The event stirred him to write in a vein more reminiscent of his earliest letters than anything else he wrote as archbishop. These letters are full of his early mannerisms of style and the eloquent fervour of personal attachment. It appears that he had already met Gunhilda on some earlier visit, perhaps in 1086, and that she had been captivated by his talk:

Receive [he wrote], dearest and most longed for daughter, receive these words to the honour of God and to your own great benefit as an admonition of your true lover. You once spoke to me and said that you wished to be ever with me so that you could enjoy an uninterrupted talk. You said you found it sweet; and you afterwards wrote me a letter full of sweetness in which I could see that you would not renounce the holy profession of which you then wore the habit. I hoped you would fulfil what you promised in God's name.[3]

Gunhilda was the last person to whom he wrote in such terms of intimacy. Necessarily the letter makes painful reading. In its imagery it recalls the *Deploratio virginitatis male amissae* of long ago:

You loved Count Alan Rufus, and he you. Where is he now? What has become of the lover whom you loved? Go now and lie with him in the bed where he now lies; gather his worms into your bosom; embrace his corpse; kiss his bare teeth from which the flesh has fallen. He does not now care for your love in which he delighted while he lived; and the flesh which you desired now rots.

Whatever may be thought of this—I have softened it in

[1] For instance, in Ep. 169 Anselm used the formula 'servus servorum Christi Jesu, vocatus archiepiscopus' in the address. This is used in only five of his letters, all of them probably written after 4 Dec. 1093 and before the end of 1094.
[2] The following letters, all of about the same time (1094), relate to the affairs of Shaftesbury and Wilton: Epp. 177, 183 [iv, 105], 184, 185 [iii, 30], 168 [iii, 157], 169.    [3] Ep. 169.

translation—there can be no denying its intense urgency and power. Anselm was here on ground which he understood. He brushed aside all arguments of law, and concentrated on the central issue. Whether or not Gunhilda had ever made her profession, she had worn the habit. To turn back from the monastic life, however it had been approached, was to turn back to a world of uncertainty and to face a future in which only damnation was assured. Every step away from the cloister was a step further from salvation, bad enough in any case, worst of all when it meant a turning from the spiritual embrace of Christ to an impure love. Anselm never felt as strongly on any political question as he did on this issue.

The relation between Anselm's two letters to Gunhilda is not easy to determine and their effect is uncertain. The first letter seems to have been written when he had first heard of the case and before he knew many details; in the second the details are ample but hard to disentangle. The clearest fact is that Count Alan Rufus had died after his abduction of Gunhilda and before their marriage.[1] The date of the death of this great magnate is of some interest in feudal history and the evidence is con- flicting. It must suffice here to say that he probably died on 4 August 1093.[2] If this is so, his death may have helped to bring the negotiations between the kings of England and Scotland to an end. But a difficulty remains. If Count Alan Rufus was dead, why did Gunhilda not return to her monas-

[1] This appears from Anselm's words about Count Alan's death: 'Quis negabit Deum illi in hoc fecisse misericordiam et iudicium—misericordiam, quia morte prohibuit eum facere malum quod male volebat; iudicium, quia eadem morte punivit sacrilegam voluntatem quam gerebat?'

[2] There has been much confusion about the date of Count Alan Rufus's death. The date given by the late and inaccurate Margam annalist—1089— has generally been followed (*Annales Monastici, RS*, i, 4; even C. T. Clay, *Early Yorkshire Charters*, iv, 86n., accepts this date). But a much better source, the early twelfth century Bury St. Edmunds annotator of Marianus Scotus in Bodley MS. 297, p. 395 (*Memorials of St. Edmunds, RS*, i, 350) gives the date of his death as *circa* 1093. Count Alan was a benefactor of St. Edmund's and was buried there, so the authority for this statement is very good. Anselm's letters to Gunhilda make it clear that Alan Rufus had not long been dead, and it is hard to see how any year earlier than 1093 would be compatible with the evidence about the marriage plans for Matilda. Both Alan Rufus and his brother Alan Niger were commemorated at York on 4 August, and C. T. Clay, *loc. cit.* has suggested that this was the day on which the elder and more important of the two brothers died.

tery? The answer which emerges from Anselm's letter is that Count Alan's brother succeeded not only to his estates but to his matrimonial plans. Why these important barons, in the face of ecclesiastical censure and as an alternative to the important political alliance proposed by King Malcolm, should have preferred the daughter of Harold is a question we shall never answer. Gunhilda must have been a remarkable woman to cause Anselm to write and two great magnates to act as they did. But the secret of her power died with her. Probably she returned to her monastery, for she was later remembered there with honour.[1] But whether she returned as a result of Anselm's letters cannot be known. The brother of Count Alan Rufus, confusingly known as Alan Niger, was dead by 1098.[2] By the time that Anselm returned from exile in 1100, the whole scandal had fallen into almost complete oblivion.

Almost, but not quite. Henry I had been crowned on 5 August 1100, and one of his earliest acts was to take up again on his own account the proposal of marriage with Matilda that Count Alan Rufus had thrown away in 1093. The news of the king's proposal faced Anselm as soon as he reached England in September. The king was very determined and we may guess his reasons. This was no romantic project but, like everything else King Henry did, a calculated political move. It was not, as is sometimes thought, a grand plan of national appeasement that led Henry to seek a marriage with Matilda. In his early policy he was markedly hostile to the English and an alliance with a princess of the old stock would not in itself have appealed to him. The English could not harm him, but the Norman baronage presented difficulties of alarming proportions. In these circumstances a marriage with the sister of the king of Scotland probably offered the best means of protecting his rear.

For this marriage he required the archbishop's consent. This was something that Anselm would greatly have preferred to withhold. The popular picture of the archbishop forwarding the happy project with a glad heart is quite false. It is false

---

[1] She appears in William of Malmesbury's *Vita Wulfstani* as the subject of a miracle performed at Wilton by Bishop Wulfstan (ed. R. R. Darlington, Camden Society, 3rd Series, xl, 1928, p. 34).

[2] C. T. Clay, *op. cit.* iv, 7.

both as to Henry's intentions and Anselm's reaction to them. We have seen how he had reacted to two similar situations seven years earlier. Matilda had been withdrawn from the monastery by her father without any immediate prospect of marriage: Anselm did all he could to bring about the return of this lost daughter. Gunhilda had left the monastery to marry Count Alan: Anselm had used all the force of his eloquence to induce her to return. The two cases were not quite parallel, for Gunhilda had worn the religious habit longer than Matilda, but they were both examples of the situation for which Lanfranc had made his well-known concession. Speaking in a characteristically statesmanlike and practical way, Lanfranc had laid down that if nuns could prove by suitable testimony that they had entered a monastery not for love of the religious life but from fear of the invaders, they were to be free to leave; equally, if they had neither made their profession nor been offered at the altar, they were to be free to decide whether to stay or not.[1] According to this ruling both Matilda and Gunhilda would have been free to leave.

The legal issue was a complicated one, and at the time when these problems arose Anselm showed no knowledge either of Lanfranc's ruling or of the relevant texts in canon law. The clearest legal statement of the position could have been found in many canonical collections quoting the sixth Council of Toledo: 'Whoever, whether man or woman, having once voluntarily worn the religious habit or been given to a monastery, abandons it, shall be forced to return, though unwilling.'[2] This expressed Anselm's own view. But in 1100 his practical position was very difficult. His first meeting with the king had raised an issue which threatened to develop into a prolonged struggle. Anselm must have felt his incompetence to settle the new problem unexpectedly thrust upon him. He had said what

---

[1] Lanfranc, Ep. 35, to the royal justiciar, Geoffrey Bishop of Coutances: note the phrase 'Et hoc est consilium regis et nostrum', which shows Lanfranc's attitude towards a question of canon law.

[2] 'Quamobrem quisquis virorum vel mulierum habitum semel induerit spontanee religiosum, aut si vir deditus ecclesiae, vel femina fuerit delegata puellarum monasterio, in utroque sexu prevaricator, invitus reverti cogatur, ut vir detondeatur et puella ad monasterium regrediatur.' For the early collections in which this text was quoted, see *Corpus Iuris Canonici*, ed. E. Friedberg, i, 849.

he thought seven years earlier. Now he retired into the background and left the decision to the bishops and abbots of the kingdom. Eadmer gives a curious account of his solitary withdrawal from the discussion, awaiting their decision. Inevitably they decided for the king, supporting their conclusion with Lanfranc's authority. Anselm accepted their judgment without enthusiasm: 'I do not reject your judgment, and I accept it the more readily because it is supported by the authority of so great a Father'.[1] So Eadmer reported his words. Baldwin reported this approval in even more qualified terms. He told his friends at Tournai that Anselm accepted the judgment but advised the king not to marry someone who, for whatever reason, had worn the veil. On being pressed, he prophesied that England would not long enjoy the fruit of this marriage.[2] It may be that this prophecy was imagined after the disaster of the White Ship, but it seems clear that Anselm, who was already faced with one dispute with the king, was persuaded with reluctance not to begin another. In monastic circles his reputation for strictness suffered as a result of this decision.[3]

Seen without passion these personal relationships have an appearance of burlesque, which is misleading. The projected marriages of Matilda with Count Alan Rufus, and of Counts Alan Rufus and Alan Niger with King Harold's daughter Gunhilda, and the actual marriage of Matilda with Henry I, formed part of an intricate web of political and personal designs, to which the clues are now largely lost beyond recovery. Anselm's aims alone emerge with clarity; the rest are shadows.

[1] HN 124–5.
[2] Hermann of Tournai, op. cit. MGH, SS xiv, 281: according to Baldwin, Anselm said that while he did not dissent from the judgment of the bishops he advised the king not to marry, 'quoniam, quemadmodumque contigerit, tamen velum super caput portavit'; and when the king persisted, Anselm replied: 'Vos quidem, domine rex, consilio praetermisso, facietis quod vobis placuerit, sed qui diutius vixerit, puto, quod videbit, non diu Angliam gavisurum de prole quae de ea nata fuerit.' To this Hermann adds, 'Haec ego adolescens eum dixisse audivi; nunc vero ex magne parte video iam contigisse.' See above, p. 184, n. 3.
[3] For the criticisms of Anselm's action, see HN 121: 'Anselmum in hoc a rectitudine deviasse nonnulla pars hominum, ut ipsi audivimus, blasphemavit.'

Anselm spoke, rightly or wrongly, with a single mind and with the authority of conviction. But here, as elsewhere, he was ill at ease among the troublesome details of conflicting claims. In 1094 he wrote as absolutely against Matilda's desertion of the cloister as he did against that of Gunhilda. But whereas with Gunhilda, either his persuasion, or the fatality of events, appears to have produced the desired result, with Matilda he brought himself to acquiesce without conviction in the less rigid views of the other prelates. Canonically it is probable that good reasons could be found for distinguishing between the two cases, but Anselm took only a passive part in making the distinction. His personal feelings and reasoning pointed in the opposite direction.

With Matilda, his relations henceforth became those of a spiritual father and daughter. At the height of his difficulties in 1103, when he was on the point of leaving England for his second exile, Matilda signalized her fidelity by witnessing one of her husband's charters as *filia Anselmi archiepiscopi*.[1] This fidelity seems to have been unfeigned, though her letters to Anselm are difficult to judge. They are full of sophistication and political wariness, which can be seen in the first words of her first letter to Anselm written within a year or two of her marriage. She addressed him as 'archbishop of the first English see and primate of Ireland and the Orkneys.[2] This peculiar address conceded all Anselm's claims except those in the province of York and the kingdom of Scotland, which were likely to be resisted. This alone would be sufficient to show that Matilda tempered her enthusiasm with a strong mixture of prudence. The letter itself—a dissuasion from overmuch fasting—reads as if it had been copied from a book with all its quotations and literary allusions.

To this effusion Anselm replied with a brief exhortation, and the correspondence continued with a good deal of reserve on Anselm's part and many expressions of devotion on the side of Matilda:

Thou art my joy, my hope, my refuge. My soul thirsteth after

[1] *Regesta* no. 636, where Matilda's description of herself has been corrupted to read 'Queen Matilda *et filiae*' (for the correct reading, see *Textus Roffensis*, ed. T. Hearne, p. 227).     [2] Ep. 242 [iii, 55].

thee as a thirsty land; wherefore I have stretched out my hands unto thee, that thou mayest sprinkle its dryness with the oil of gladness. But if neither my prayers nor the public necessity recall thee, I will put aside my royal dignity, abandon the royal insignia, lay down the *fasces*, despise my crown, tread under foot my purple and fine linen, and come to thee consumed with sorrow. I shall embrace thy footsteps and kiss thy feet and no one, no not Gehazi himself, shall thrust me away until my desire is fulfilled.[1]

This appeal to Anselm in exile, with its curious mixture of biblical reminiscence and rhetoric, called forth no similar strains from Anselm. To the queen's assurance that he would in future receive more of his revenues than hitherto, he sent the chilly reply that he would as soon be deprived of all as of a little.[2] Matilda overflowed in praise of Anselm's letters, combining, she said, the gravity of Fronto, the copiousness of Cicero, the acuteness of Quintilian, the teaching of Paul, the diligence of Jerome, the elaboration of Gregory, the perspicacity of Augustine. Anselm, on his side, rebuked Matilda for her treatment of the churches in her patronage, and stiffly repelled her nominee to the abbacy of Malmesbury, despite her regard for the archbishop's rights, because the unfortunate man had sent him a present. The news of Anselm's sickness in Normandy in 1106 brought from Matilda a passionate demand to hear news of his recovery, 'for I shall either, and without delay, rejoice in your health, which is mine also, or—which God in his mercy forbid—suffer with indifference the common fate of mortality'.[3] All this seems to have left Anselm unmoved, and in his last letter to the queen, he who had interceded so easily for others in earlier days, refused her request to intercede with the king for one who had been deprived of his goods, because 'you know it is not my job to testify about things which I have neither seen nor heard'.[4]

He seems in this correspondence to have been singularly difficult to please. Perhaps he never forgot that his earliest reference to Matilda had been to a 'lost daughter' and that she

---

[1] Ep. 317 [iii, 93]. The reference in the last sentence is to Gehazi attempting to thrust away the Shunammite who approached Elisha to embrace his feet (II Kings, IV, 27).     [2] Epp. 320 [iii, 96], 321 [iii, 97].
[3] Ep. 400 [iv, 76].     [4] Ep. 406 [iii, 128].

had never returned. Perhaps too, and with reason, he was sceptical about Matilda's inexhaustible professions of devotion. Anselm came reluctantly to the conclusion that Henry I was not a man he could trust, and he may well have thought that Matilda's professions too had more policy in them than sincerity. For whatever reason, he did not respond to the rather artificial eloquence of her letters with any degree of warmth. He never addressed her with the tenderness and eloquence that he had lavished, for the last time in his life, on the mysterious and tragic daughter of King Harold.

CHAPTER V

# ANSELM'S COMPANIONS AND CONVERSATION

## I. ANSELM'S HOUSEHOLD

I T is possible to read everything that Eadmer wrote about Anselm without realizing that the move to Canterbury turned the abbot of a poor Norman monastery into a great baron. If Eadmer had been writing at the end of the Middle Ages we should have heard a great deal about the splendour of the archbishops's entourage: as it is, he leaves us with the impression that Anselm travelled round England with a few humble companions. No doubt this is how they saw themselves, *nudi nudum Christum sequentes*; but their poverty must be understood in a rather special sense. Outsiders, including the king, did not see the matter in this light. Anselm as archbishop, apart from the revenues of the monks, had an annual income from land alone assessed in Domesday Book at almost exactly £1500, and his lay vassals had in addition £350 a year.[1] Besides this he had, like the monks, his spiritualities and other unspecified payments from his tenants. But even the Domesday revenue is sufficient to put him in the very highest class of barons, and to make him the head of a very large-scale business enterprise. This enterprise could not be carried on without a large staff.

When Anselm arrived in England on the visit which brought him to the archbishopric, he had with him two monks of Bec on whom he chiefly relied in his business affairs. These were Baldwin and Eustace. The latter reappears only occasionally

---

[1] There is a very slight discrepancy between the figures for the farm of the archbishop's lands in *Domesday Book* and the *Domesday Monachorum*: DB, £1295; *Dom. Mon.*, £1304. Of this total about £883 came from lands in Kent; and £412 from lands in Oxfordshire, Buckinghamshire, Hertfordshire, Middlesex, Surrey and Sussex. To these sums must be added £173 from *Gablum* and £38 from *Constumes* (*Dom. Mon.* pp. 98–9).

194

in later years, but the former has an important place in the story of Anselm's life.

In 1093 Baldwin was a man of about fifty, and he had had a distinguished career as a layman before he became a monk of Bec. As a young man he had been the advocate, the man of affairs and chief agent, of the bishop of Tournai in Flanders, and he took part as early as 1072 in an embassy from the Count of Flanders to the Emperor Henry IV.[1] Instead of sending him back to Bec, Anselm kept him in England and made him head of his household. As a man he was practical, decisive, domineering, not given to doubt. These characteristics come out in many details supplied by Eadmer. When Anselm was staying in a house next door to one that caught fire, it was Baldwin who came to him and urged him to do something. Anselm asked what he could do. 'Go out and make the sign of the Cross in the face of the fire: perhaps God will ward it off,' said Baldwin. 'These are idle words,' replied Anselm. But he went out and was constrained to raise his hand in the sign of the Cross, with the result predicted by Baldwin. Then, when they were travelling incognito through the Alps for fear of ambush, and the abbot of Aspres-sur-Buech told a doleful story of the archbishop of Canterbury having been forced to turn back to Lyons, it was Baldwin who promptly replied: 'He has done well; but we, alas, are forced by the service of God and the command of our spiritual superior to go on.' And, a few days later, when the abbot of Susa heard that they were monks of Bec and began asking about Abbot Anselm, it was Baldwin who answered: 'He has been carried off to an archbishopric in another kingdom.' 'So I have heard; but now tell me, how is he? Is he well?' 'Honestly I haven't seen him at Bec since he became archbishop,' said the ever-ready Baldwin, 'but they say that he is very well where he is.' It was Baldwin too, and not Eadmer, who saw the hole in the boat which had brought them from England, and who later gave an account of it to Eadmer.[2] Baldwin was a great recounter of wonders, as we know not only from this incident but also from the fact that a monk of Tournai, many years later, recorded some stories

[1] For the source of our information on Baldwin's early life, see above p. 184 n. 3.　　　　[2] *VA* ii, xxiv.

which he had heard from Baldwin when he stayed with the monks during one of his journeys from England.[1] Both William II and Henry I recognized his importance: the first by sending him into exile in order to embarrass Anselm, the second by asking that Baldwin should accompany his messengers to Rome in 1105. In all the affairs of the archbishop —whether it was a fire which needed to be extinguished, or a miracle to be testified to, or an embassy to be conducted— Baldwin spoke with authority and acted with decision. He was an active, blunt and credulous man, who liked to take his ease at his old home in Tournai talking about his master and the great events with which he had been concerned.

In order to understand Baldwin's position as head of Anselm's household, it is necessary to understand its organization so far as may be done with our inadequate materials. It is not until the time of Archbishop Theobald that a satisfactory picture of an archbishop's household can be formed, but something can be said about the earlier period from analogy and fragmentary evidence.[2] In the first place, every considerable household of this period was divided into two main branches, lay and clerical. We hear almost nothing about the lay side of Anselm's household, but it certainly existed, and its main components must have been those of other households. At its head there would be a steward or dapifer and under him a number of officials—butler, dispenser, chamberlain, seneschal, cook, usher, porter and marshal, each with a distinct province in hall, chamber, kitchen or stable. The archbishop must have been constantly attended by his lay officials or their deputies and an indefinite number of assistants. Domesday book gives the titles dapifer, constable, dispenser and chamberlain to four of the archbishop's tenants:[3] some of these were men too important to have been constantly in attendance on the archbishop, but the archbishop could not have moved unless they had provided someone to perform their functions. When he

[1] See above, p. 190.
[2] For Theobald's household, see A. Saltman, *Theobald Archbishop of Canterbury*, 1956, 165–77.
[3] *DB*, i, pp. 82, 85, 87, 93, where the names are given as follows: Godefridus dapifer, Richard constable, William dispensator, Radulfus camerarius. For further details, see *Domesday Monachorum*.

went into exile, the more important officials were left behind in England to look after their own and the archbishop's interests, but Anselm took with him a staff of household officials. Since Eadmer dismissed them from his mind when he wrote of the journeys, they are almost unknown to us. We know that the permanent monastic element consisted of Baldwin and Eadmer, supplemented at various times by Eustace of Bec and Alexander of Canterbury. But in addition there were lay members like Adam, who appears by chance in Eadmer's narrative because he had a vision while he lay sleeping in the archbishop's chamber.[1] There were other members of the party, but their names were a matter of indifference to the biographer. Apart from the monks, Eadmer only mentions those members of the household who were the object of miraculous occurrences, such as Lambert, a little man who worked in the chamber and was saved from blindness by St. Dunstan; Norman, a chaplain whose horse was miraculously cured; and an unnamed young man whose house was preserved from fire long after Anselm's death by the invocation of his name.[2] Without a miracle, the chances that their memory would be preserved were negligible.

It was on the clerical side that Anselm's household differed most markedly from those of later archbishops from the time of Theobald onwards. In Theobald's household the clerical work was heavy and there was a fairly constant stream of ecclesiastical business which required expert handling. To deal with this Theobald had a chancellor assisted by scribes and clerks; some of these were men trained as lawyers and theologians, men of distinction and even of international fame. The most famous list of such men is the list of the twenty *eruditi* of Thomas Becket, who were the expert advisers of the archbishop: not one of them was a monk.[3] Of all this, in Anselm's household there is scarcely a trace. Baldwin was the only man in it of wide practical experience, and it is notable that his experience had been gained not in the schools or in ecclesiastical affairs but in the lay world. His authority

[1] *VA* II, xlvii.
[2] *Memorials of St. Dunstan*, p. 246; *VA*, p. 169
[3] *Materials for the History of Archbishop Thomas Becket, RS*, iii, 523–9.

197

extended into every sphere, even those which in later days would have been kept distinct. Eadmer calls him the *provisor ac dispensator rerum Anselmi*, and elsewhere Anselm's *provisor et ordinator rerum*.[1] At first sight it might appear from these words that Baldwin held the position of dispenser, but it is characteristic of the lack of definition in these matters that Eadmer intends something much more general. He means simply that Baldwin had a general oversight over all matters, both those which belonged to the province of lay officials and those which later would have been regarded as the province of expert legists and theologians. He was in the most literal sense Anselm's factotum.

If Baldwin's province was thus large, the rest of Anselm's clerical household was probably organized less with an eye to the efficient conduct of ecclesiastical business than the adequate observance of a liturgical and ceremonial routine. This was Eadmer's province. Anselm must quickly have chosen him as a member of his household, for they were already together at Hastings in February 1094, and Eadmer shared all Anselm's travels until the end of his life.[2] Officially he was the keeper of Anselm's chapel and its relics.[3] With this he combined the more indefinite office of being at the archbishop's side and acting, as Anselm himself says, as 'the staff of his old age'.[4] How far he acted in any definite way as the archbishop's secretary is not clear. He was an expert scribe, and it is likely that he sometimes wrote the archbishop's letters, just as he copied the *Cur Deus Homo* as a present for the monastery of Bec.[5] But it does not seem that he was responsible for keeping copies of the archbishop's letters: it is not until 1101, when Eadmer had already been Anselm's constant companion for seven years, that any consistent attempt was made to preserve for future reference the letters which Anselm wrote as archbishop—a striking omission when we consider that for over twenty years Anselm had been preserving personal letters which

---

[1] *HN* 386, 417; *VA* II, xxiv, lxvii.
[2] *HN* p. 52 is the earliest clear reference to Eadmer's presence in the archbishop's household.
[3] *HN* 181: 'capellae illius custos eram atque dispositor.'
[4] Ep. 209 [iii, 25].
[5] Epp. 208–9 [iv, 117; iii, 25].

he wrote as prior and abbot of Bec.[1] Eadmer's usefulness was of a different kind. He sat at the archbishop's feet, and besides keeping a private record of events, he made notes of some at least of Anselm's sermons and speeches.[2] When Anselm's nerves were jangled with business, he provided the sedative of spiritual conversation.[3] William of Malmesbury tells us that when Anselm became archbishop he asked the pope to provide him with someone by whose commands he could regulate his life, and Pope Urban nominated Eadmer. Thereupon, he adds, Anselm attached so much importance to Eadmer's commands that he would not turn over in his bed, much less get up, unless Eadmer told him to do so.[4] This is a typical piece of embroidery, but the general fact may well be true, as also may the example of Eadmer's authority which William gives: Anselm, who was most fearful of committing any sin, one day ate pickled eel, then recollecting himself he bitterly lamented that he had eaten raw flesh contrary to the Law. Eadmer, who was sitting beside him said, 'The salt has removed the rawness of the flesh' and Anselm replied, 'You have saved me from being tortured by the memory of sin.' In a picturesque way this may well give us our best insight into the relations between the archbishop and his biographer.

There is reason to think that the relations between Anselm and Eadmer changed in some way during the last nine years of Anselm's life. Probably nothing very dramatic took place but circumstances may have made their relationship less close.[5]

---

[1] Anselm's correspondence from 1093 to 1100 was evidently in a complete muddle and defied the efforts of the Canterbury collector of his letters, whose work is preserved in Lambeth MS. 59, to make much of it. The correspondence of 1093 which led up to Anselm's final acceptance of the archbishopric was carefully preserved, probably by the monks of Bec to whom most of the letters were addressed: these letters originally formed a separate collection of fifteen letters (Epp. 148–52, 155–64 [iii, 1–15]) of which only five were accessible to the Canterbury compiler. For the following seven years the Canterbury compiler could only find seventeen letters of Anselm, though the researches of later editors, notably Dom Wilmart and Dom Schmitt, have now brought the number up to forty-three.
[2] See below, p. 219 and App. II. [3] VA II, xiii. [4] Gesta Pontificum, p. 122.
[5] There is a marked difference between Anselm's reference to Eadmer in 1099 when he is 'domnus Edmerus, carissimus filius meus et baculus senectutis meae' (Ep. 209 [iii, 25]) and in 1103 when, in writing to his nephew, Anselm refers to him as 'dominus Edmerus, qui vere, in quantum

Anselm's discovery that Eadmer was writing his life probably led to a change on both sides. Whether Anselm became less confiding we cannot be certain. Certain it is that after 1100 the biography loses all its characteristic freshness and fullness, and another monk of Christ Church is found performing some of the functions which we should expect to find in Eadmer's hands. This was the monk Alexander. He had not accompanied Anselm in his first exile, but he was one of his companions during the second. On one occasion we find him taking Eadmer's place in the chapel, and it is chiefly to him that we owe for these later years such record of Anselm's sayings and sermons as we have. He accompanied Baldwin to Rome on behalf of the archbishop in 1102, and he acted as Anselm's messenger again in 1104.[1] It is not impossible that the better order in which Anselm's correspondence was kept after 1101 was due to his introduction into the household. In any case it is clear that Eadmer's position became more limited, while Alexander came to occupy a position second only to that of Baldwin. As a man he is obscure and as a writer he is less polished than Eadmer; he shows none of Eadmer's perception of significant detail. Nevertheless, his collection of Anselm's sayings formed the basis of one of the most popular of the works which went under the name of Anselm in the later Middle Ages.[2] Alexander's own name is mentioned only casually, and it is only by chance that we can be sure that he was the author of this collection, but there can be no doubt that he was an important man in Anselm's household in his later years.

This exhausts the list of the regular members of Anselm's household whose names are known to us. One cannot record them without reflecting on the lack of experienced and able men available for the archbishop's service. Baldwin was an active man, but he was not qualified to give advice on ecclesiastical affairs; about Alexander we know too little to give a confident judgment, but nothing he has left suggests abilities

_____

intelligo, sincero amore diligit te' (Ep. 309 [iv, 52]). The change in tone may here be insignificant, but it is supported by too many other indications to be ignored.

[1] *HN* 132; Ep. 325 [iv, 37].　　　　　　[2] See below, p. 220.

or accomplishments out of the ordinary; Eadmer had great qualities as a man of feeling and observation and as the transmitter of a complex tradition, but he had neither the width of experience nor the judgment to fit him for the conduct of business. Anselm himself hated business. He was at home with pupils and with those with whom he could discuss problems of philosophy and of the spiritual life. At Bec he had been the centre of a group of young monks, many of whom had entered the monastery to be near him. At Canterbury he had no opportunity to build up a similar group, for even when he was in England he was seldom at Canterbury. His influence therefore was concentrated on those who travelled around with him, or was scattered in a more diffused way among those with whom he corresponded. Of those in his immediate company Eadmer was the only one who can justly be called a pupil. He responded with enthusiasm to one side of Anselm's teaching, but he absorbed only that part which was compatible with, and could enrich, his English tradition. Although he was capable of giving a correct summary of Anselm's philosophical arguments, he was no philosopher. For one who for years enjoyed the company of one of the greatest of theologians, he remains remarkably, even obstinately, unspeculative in his habits of thought. Anselm was as unlucky here as he was in the supply of practical advisers. He found it easier to make disciples who revered him, than pupils who could carry on his work.

There are many reasons for this failure of intellectual communication. Anselm's methods demanded gifts of logical precision which are rare, and produced results which, luminous though they are, are too unsubstantial for common clay. He left nothing to be completed by the patient work of many hands. Moreover the church of Canterbury, even with its Norman infusion, was still markedly deficient in scholastic training and interests. Circumstances still combined with habit to impel the community to a backward gaze. Anselm needed the stimulus of philosophical discussion. The structure of his works, their origin and growth, all demonstrate how much he needed the stimulus of inquiring minds around him. To find them at a philosophical level he had to continue to look to Bec; Canterbury could not provide what he needed. In the early years of his archiepiscopate, when he was finishing his *De Incarnatione Verbi* and beginning his *Cur Deus Homo*, he sent to Bec for the monk Boso. He was one of those young men who had come to Bec during the later years of Anselm's abbacy, mainly, as his biographer says, to discuss his theological perplexities; and after the departure of the earlier generation of pupils, Anselm seems to have found in him a philosophical companion to whom he could turn for help.[1] With one interval, when he went as the archbishop's representative to the Council of Clermont and caught a disease which kept him abroad for some time, he stayed with Anselm in England until the time of the first exile. Anselm paid tribute to his help by making him his interlocutor in the *Cur Deus Homo*; and years later at the end of his second exile when his last phase of philosophical activity was beginning, he paid an even more striking tribute to the importance of his help, and his lack of philosophical resources in England, by asking for him once more 'because he would prefer to live with him in a desert than without him in great abundance'.[2] Thus Boso was with him once more when he wrote his last treatise on predestination, grace and free will.

These were the men with whom Anselm was most constantly associated during his years as archbishop. Among them only Eadmer and Alexander were monks of Canterbury, and it is to them that we owe our chief biographical records of Anselm's life and conversation. The contribution of Canterbury monks to that range of experience and achievement which finds its centre in Anselm is fairly well defined. In the main it is limited to the written works of Eadmer and Alexander. Outside these definite limits the penumbra is both faint and small. Dr. Pächt has pointed out the possibility of an important influence of Anselm and his companions on the Canterbury school of manuscript illumination,[3] and as we shall see, Anselm's visit to Cluny left its mark in the plan for the enlarged choir at Canterbury. Among the younger monks, Elmer, who became

---

[1] *VA* I, xxxiv; *Vita Bosonis* (Giles, *Opera Lanfranci*, i, 327-9).
[2] *Vita Bosonis*, p. 329.
[3] 'The illustrations of St. Anselm's Prayers and Meditations', *Journal of the Warburg and Courtauld Institutes*, xix, 1956, 68-83.

prior in 1128, caught something of Anselm's style in his letters and meditations. But Anselm's influence never informed the whole community at Canterbury as it had at Bec. To most of the monks he must have remained a distant and shadowy figure to be judged rather by the results of his work than experienced as a power in their lives.

## 2. ANSELM'S THEOLOGICAL HEIRS

If this were the whole story, the record of Anselm's personal influence in England would appear somewhat barren. But there is more to be said. Anselm's influence was pervasive; it worked with many of the instinctive impulses of his time, and reached far beyond the circle of his immediate acquaintance. His English friends were especially important, not for what they achieved but for what they transmitted. Among the great teachers of the Middle Ages it is not easy to name one whose circle of pupils was as narrow as that of Anselm, or whose influence crept forward by such slow and imperceptible advances. His monastic profession and his own inclinations made the society of a small group of pupils, linked together in a common life, more congenial than the shifting population of students in the schools. But even in the Benedictine Order, and in houses no more famous or influential than Bec or Canterbury, there were teachers with a far wider range of immediate influence. Contemporaries remarked on the slow growth of a reputation which shone so brightly in his immediate vicinity: 'why', he was asked when he was forty 'does the reputation of Lanfranc and Guitmund fly round the world more than yours?' 'Perhaps,' he replied, with the elusiveness which characterized his early literary style, 'because any flower may imitate the colour of the rose without possessing its scent.'[1] Twenty years later, when he became archbishop of Canterbury, his reputation had grown. His Prayers were becoming widely known in northern France and had reached Auvergne, England, and northern Italy; the *Proslogion* and *Monologion* were known in Lyons; and his name and good repute had reached Rome. But this does not amount to an intellectual influence such as Alcuin and

---

[1] Ep. 20 [i, 16].

Gerbert had exercised in their generation. During the next sixteen years as archbishop his name became known far and wide, but the number of his immediate pupils and his means of influencing them shrank rather than expanded. In France especially, more energetic methods of teaching and disputation were replacing the colloquies on which Anselm's pupils had been nourished. Textual commentary, the compilation and arrangement of extracts, and the discussion of their points of difference made no appeal to him. The nearest Anselm ever came to writing a commentary on an ancient text was in his *De grammatico*, and it is of all his works the most difficult and least important. Anselm did not inaugurate or advance a method of study suitable for the schools and capable of being developed methodically by those who came after him. He stood aside from the intellectual fashions of his time.

The result was that his immediate disciples were a small body of personal followers with diverse interests and talents, joined together only by a common influence. He had no intellectual heir before Duns Scotus. His pupils blossomed in his presence, learnt his tricks of phrase, and applied some of his characteristic arguments to new subjects. But their additions to the fabric, though interesting and sometimes important, are not large. To re-think Anselm's thoughts as he had re-thought those of St. Augustine, and to put them in a new and brilliant light, was beyond them. They could only reproduce, and in places develop, his ideas at a lower level of competence.

Among Anselm's pupils Eadmer has an exceptional place. His long years of close association with Anselm, the use he made of his opportunities, and his productivity as a monastic writer in fields untouched by Anselm, entitle him to a separate treatment. But the general nature of Anselm's influence may be illustrated by the works of three pupils of widely different character, and by the fragmentary evidences of the power of Anselm's spoken words. The three pupils whom we are to consider were Anselm's chief theological heirs among his immediate followers.

## (i) *Gilbert Crispin*

Of these pupils, the most clearly visible to us is Gilbert Crispin, abbot of Westminster from about 1085 to 1117.[1] He had become a monk of Bec some time before Anselm, but he was still a boy when Anselm entered the monastery at the age of twenty-seven. During the next twenty-five years he was one of Anselm's closest friends, and Anselm's expressions of his sense of loss on Gilbert's departure from England have an intensity which even for him is remarkable. Nevertheless they seem to have had no correspondence between 1085 and the winter of 1092, when their friendship was renewed by Anselm's presence at Westminster. This visit, and the years of friendship which followed, had important consequences for Gilbert, and possibly also for Anselm. Anselm was introduced to Gilbert's Jewish controversy and found in it an incentive to the writing of the *Cur Deus Homo*; Gilbert was inspired by Anselm's theological speculations to devote himself to the fundamental problems of the Christian faith, especially those of the Trinity and the Incarnation. His attempts to formulate and explain these problems are contained in a number of treatises, mostly preserved in a single manuscript. Of these, much the most important are two dialogues between a Christian and a Jew, and between a Christian and a pagan philosopher. The first of these had a considerable circulation, and it is far superior to the generality of such treatises in the cogency of its argument and the humanity with which it treats the opponent of the Christian faith. The second is less successful and shows that although Anselm imparted some of his philosophical conceptions to his friend, Gilbert was really more at home in Biblical exegesis and common-sense argument than in the refinements of metaphysics and logic. He was an able writer, and at times he

---

[1] For Gilbert Crispin's career, see J. Armitage Robinson, *Gilbert Crispin, Abbot of Westminster, Notes and Documents relating to Westminster Abbey*, No. 3, 1911; for his *Dispute of a Christian with a Heathen*, see the edition by C. C. J. Webb, *MARS*, iii, 1954, 55–77. There is a new edition of his *Dispute of a Christian with a Jew*, by B. Blumenkranz, 1956. For his relations with Anselm after 1092, see R. W. Southern, 'St. Anselm and Gilbert Crispin, Abbot of Westminster', *MARS*, iii, 1954, 78–115.

reproduced the flow of Anselmian argument with great clarity and vigour, but the final impression he leaves is of a man of sober judgment and solid learning rather than of any more brilliant gifts of intellect.

Gilbert Crispin was the most complete adherent of Anselm's theological views, and his theological treatises were mainly an attempt to expound them briefly and simply. As a writer on biblical and practical questions, whether monastic or controversial, he made a contribution of his own; but as a dogmatic theologian he lived entirely in the light of Anselm's ideas. He perhaps regarded himself as Anselm's theological executor, for in his *De Anima* he completed Anselm's work by writing on the subject which the archbishop had been thinking about at the time of his death. His own reputation as a theologian only lasted for about a generation, and then his works and name disappeared from view until modern times.[1]

## (ii) *Ralph*

The second of these theological followers of Anselm had an even more restricted frame. He is known to us by the single name of Rodulfus or Ralph, and to his contemporaries he was scarcely known even to this extent.[2] All that we know about him beyond this is that he was closely connected with, and probably a monk of, Rochester, for the library of this monastery possessed a copy of his work with the author's corrections and a special preface which alone gives us his name. At one time I thought it likely that he was Anselm's successor as archbishop, Ralph d'Escures, who was bishop of Rochester from 1108 to 1114 and had probably been in England for some years before this time. But a more likely candidate now seems to be a monk of Caen who came to England with Lanfranc and was

---

[1] For the quotation of his opinion on a theological question at the Council of Rheims in 1148, see John of Salisbury, *Historia Pontificalis*, ed. R. L. Poole, p. 20. This is a striking, but solitary, testimony to his posthumous fame as a theologian.

[2] I have put together some facts about him and his works in 'St. Anselm and his English Pupils', *MARS*, i, 1941, 14–19, 24–9. In this article I failed to notice that Ralph, third abbot of Battle (1107–24) and previously a monk of Caen who came to England with Lanfranc and became prior of Rochester, had many of the qualifications required by the author of these treatises.

made prior of Rochester by Bishop Gundulf. He became abbot of Battle in 1107 and died in 1124 at the age of eighty-four, leaving a reputation as a scholar and author and as a capable administrator.[1]

Whoever he was, his works had an uneven fortune. For some, a single manuscript is the sole authority; others are known in only two manuscripts; another, a treatise on the monastic life, had a modest anonymous success; but one group had a great success, though under the name, and among the works, of Anselm.[2] This last group was a collection of prayers and meditations, which were attached from an early date to those of Anselm and finally made their way into the printed editions of Anselm's works.[3] It is a great tribute to the force of the printed word that they succeeded in holding their place among Anselm's works for centuries; it is only in recent years that their true status has been detected. Once the discovery has been made it is very clear how different they are in style from the genuine works. Both intellectually and emotionally they are flatter, more ordinary and closer to the tradition of conventional devotion than Anselm's prayers and meditations. But in their general style of private, self-abasing, complex meditation, they belong to the type of exercise which Anselm had popularized, and no doubt they were a welcome foil and relief to readers of his more highly-wrought and exhausting effusions.

The same general judgment may be passed on Ralph's other works. In subject matter and literary form they show the influence of Anselm's dialogues. Ralph's longest and most important works were a sequence of discussions between Reason and Ignorance under various names. Two of these discussions, between *Nesciens* and *Sciens* and between *Inquirens*

[1] For the writings of Abbot Ralph, see *Chronicon Monasterii de Bello*, p. 59; and cf. Knowles, *Monastic Order in England*, 177–8.

[2] Dom Hugh Farmer is preparing an edition of the short treatise on monastic observance, *De octo quae observari debent a monachis*, of which the beginning is printed among the works of Lanfranc, ed. Giles, ii, 299–300.

[3] The following prayers and meditations printed under the name of St. Anselm are the work of Rodulfus: Med. iv–vi, xix; Or. iii–iv, vi, xv, xxv–xxviii (*PL* CLVIII; see *MARS*, i, 1941, 25–8). Their spuriousness was first detected by Dom Wilmart, but their authorship escaped him (*Auteurs Spirituels*, 158–61).

and *Respondens*, cover a very wide field. They start with a sceptic who refuses to believe anything for which he has not the evidence of his eyes. The discussion gradually leads him to accept the evidence of his other senses, to acknowledge the existence of an invisible intelligence, and thence of a supreme Intelligence and First Cause, and so to an acceptance of the whole range of Christian doctrine. This discussion is in some ways similar to Gilbert Crispin's dialogue between the Christian and the pagan: they both illustrate the growing sense of a need for a rational justification of the Christian faith. Ralph's treatment of the problem is both fuller and more fundamental: whereas Gilbert Crispin started with a pagan who was willing to admit the existence of God and of a future life, Ralph, started with a very complete, though very naïve, sceptic. Ralph's treatise is about ten times as long as that of Gilbert and extends the scope of the argument until it covers a wide field of Christian doctrine. This development was of course entirely consistent with the tendency of the time, but it was a move away from the deep and penetrating analysis of major problems for which Anselm stood. Indeed, although several of the arguments about the nothingness of sin, the true powerlessness implicit in the power to sin, the congruity of faith and reason, and the necessity of the Incarnation, show the influence of Anselm's works, Ralph is less a pupil of Anselm than a monastic student of St. Augustine, whom he takes as his chief guide and for whom he expresses his deepest veneration. Like Gilbert Crispin, and unlike Anselm, he took as his main interlocutor in his dialogues one who professed to stand outside the Christian faith; but this fiction was not very successful. While appearing to take the discussion to a deeper level, it required that the opponent should be satisfied by arguments with ridiculous ease and should soon overwhelm the Christian with his desire to hear further delightful truths. The day for discussions at this level of antagonism had not yet arrived, and Ralph is more impressive in his shorter works of exposition, which are rather meditations than arguments: it was in this pattern that his somewhat colourless thought and personality find its best expression.

Both Gilbert Crispin and Ralph are examples of the Benedictine scholars and administrators who transformed the religious life of England in the half century after the Conquest. They were men who in general have left no memorial outside the jejune and formal eulogies of local annalists. There is almost nothing now to tell us that they once were powers in the land, and the little collection of treatises of Ralph and Gilbert Crispin, scarcely read even in their own day and largely still unprinted, have a value in disclosing the thoughts and standards of judgment of two men among a large number. That it was Anselm's influence which made them authors we cannot say; but that Anselm helped to give a more precise formulation to their thoughts, that his writings were often their models, and that they consciously echoed his theories is certain. Yet, though they were more articulate than others, they had the limitations which their circumstances imposed upon them. They were men fully occupied in a round of religious and secular duties; they had themselves no problems of faith, but had to invent problems in order to answer them; they had no audience for their thoughts. To expect such men to be philosophers and metaphysicians or the creators of new literary forms, is to expect something which only the strong force of native genius or the impact of deeply disturbing events could effect.

### (iii) *Honorius Augustodunensis*

If it was the fate, or more probably the choice, of Anselm's pupils to keep their personalities obscure, they showed their originality in the means by which they chose to remain anonymous. No one in the Middle Ages showed a greater talent for this particular art than the last of Anselm's pupils who must here be mentioned, the ablest and most productive of them all—Honorius Augustodunensis.[1] The enigma surrounding

---

[1] The fullest study of Honorius is still J. A. Endres, *Honorius Augustodunensis: Beitrag zur Gesch. des Geistigen Lebens im xii Jahrhundert*, 1906; but a great number of detailed studies have appeared, which by no means exhaust the subject. Of these it is sufficient here to mention the series of studies by J. Keller in *SB*, Vienna, 1901, 1903, 1904, 1905, 1906; F. Baeumker, *Das Inevitabile des Honorius Augustodunensis* (Beiträge z. Gesch. d. Philos. des Mittelalters, xiii, 1914); E. M. Sanford, 'Honorius, Presbyter and

this prolific and popular writer is proverbial, and largely of his own making. He chose, like Rodulfus, to write many of his works anonymously, but he left a clear scent by giving his name and the titles of his works in the last entry of his biographical dictionary of Christian writers, the *De Luminaribus Ecclesiae*. It was certainly not because of any underestimate of his own works that he chose anonymity. But why, when he revealed his name, he should have chosen the epithet *Augustodunensis* is more than anyone has ever been able to explain satisfactorily, for we know nothing to connect him with the church of Autun, which would be the normal meaning of this word. All we know of him is that his works were written in the first half of the twelfth century, that he had already produced a long list of works by 1125, and that by this date he was probably attached to the Irish community of St. James at Regensburg, where he presumably stayed till the end of his life. But however obscure his personal history may be, the chronology of his mental development and literary activity is known, or can be known, with a considerable degree of accuracy. This is especially true of his earlier works, and particularly of his first three works. It is with these that we are concerned, for there can be no doubt that they were the fruit of a period of study in Canterbury when he came under the influence of Anselm.

The influence of Anselm is clearly apparent in his earliest work, the *Elucidarium*.[1] This is a sort of primitive theological *Summa*, in the form of a dialogue between a Master and his Pupil, divided into three books. This work has long been

Scholasticus' *Speculum*, 1948, 397–425; E. Rooth, 'Kleine Beiträge z. Kenntnis des sog. Honorius Augustodunensis', *Studia Neophilologica*, xii, 1939–40, 120–35. The last writer, while supporting—without, to my mind, any real evidence—the theory that Honorius was of English origin, has the merit of seeing that the late date (1151–8) generally given for his Commentaries on the Psalter and the Song of Songs will simply not do. The greater part of Honorius's literary activity is certainly, on his own authority, to be placed in the first quarter of the twelfth century, and he may well have been born as early as 1075.

[1] The latest edition is Y. Lefèvre, *L'Elucidarium et les Lucidaires* (Bibl. des écoles françaises d'Athènes et de Rome, clxxx, 1954). As a critical edition, this work has the defect that it pays no attention to the important series of English manuscripts, and does not mention the authorities quoted in the margin of many manuscripts, which certainly go back to the author.

famous for its precocious survey of Christian doctrine down to the most minute and curious details. It shows evidence of wide reading in a library well-stocked with the works of the Latin Fathers and displays an unusual predilection for the works of the Irish scholar John Scot Erigena. Several of the manuscripts have the authorities named in the margin, evidently from the hand of the author himself, and among them the name of Anselm makes a frequent appearance.[1] These references show that the author was acquainted with the *Cur Deus Homo*, which was not finished till 1098, and some remarks which cannot be traced to Anselm's written works may derive from oral teaching. The marginal references, however, do not reveal the full extent of Anselm's influence, which is clear in many of the questions asked and the formulation of the answers.

Yet though the close connexion with Anselm cannot be doubted, in spirit the work is very far removed from him. The Pupil sometimes challenges the Master to prove what he has stated, but for the most part he is content to accept what he is told without demur. The work shows a further development of the tendency already noticed in Ralph's dialogues to travel rapidly over the whole field of theology. Honorius poses a more rapid succession of questions than Ralph, and gives clearer, brisker answers: consequently his book was read throughout Europe, while Ralph lay unnoticed on the shelves of one or two English monasteries.

Although Honorius struck out a new line for himself, the Canterbury associations of his early work are certainly very striking. He made an extensive use of Anselm's ideas, and some of these ideas must have been picked up either from Anselm himself or from those who could report his sayings. In the third book of the *Elucidarium*, for instance, he used Anselm's sermon on the Joys of Heaven. Both Eadmer and Alexander have left reports of this sermon, but these were not widely circulated

---

[1] Quite apart from the presumption suggested by the manuscript tradition in favour of Honorius's responsibility for the marginal references, there is the mark of his hand in the references to John Scot Erigena as Johannes Crisostomus—a peculiarity of Honorius. (For references to Erigena in Honorius's other writings see M. Cappuyns, *Jean Scot Érigène: sa vie, son oeuvre, sa pensée*, 1933, p. 184).

until much later. Honorius may have had one of these reports or he may have heard the sermon from Anselm's own lips. In either case Canterbury is the most likely place for him to have got his information. Within a very few years the *Elucidarium*, or part of it, was translated into Anglo-Saxon, and once more the associations of the work are with Canterbury or its sister monastery at Rochester.[1]

Honorius's other early works show the same influence and local connexions as the *Elucidarium*. The *Sigillum Sanctae Mariae*, his second work, drew heavily on a sermon of Anselm's friend and successor Ralph d'Escures. His third work, a treatise on free will called the *Inevitabile*, was extensively revised in the light of Anselm's last work, the *De Concordia praescientiae et praedestinationis et gratiae Dei cum libero arbitrio*. His next work—a collection of sermons for the Christian year which he called the *Speculum Ecclesiae*—was written at the request of the community at Canterbury.[2] The preface to the *Speculum Ecclesiae*, however, makes it clear that Honorius had by this time left Canterbury; and it is equally clear that he was no longer at Canterbury when he wrote the *Inevitabile*, for he was in ignorance of Anselm's last work until it was sent to him probably by the monks of Canterbury. We therefore reach the position that the *Elucidarium* and the *Sigillum Sanctae Mariae* were written when Honorius was under the immediate influence of Anselm and his friends; that his next two works were written while he was still in touch with this group, but no longer in their company; and that he then lost touch with Canterbury and with England. His fifth work, the *Offendiculum Sacerdotum*, a contribution to the controversy about clerical celibacy, was certainly known in England from an early date, and it may have been written with an eye

---

[1] British Museum, MS. Cotton Vespasian D. xiv, f. 159–63*v*: see M. Förster in *An English Miscellany presented to Dr F. J. Furnivall*, 1901, 88–101; and *Archiv f. das Studium der neueren Sprachen*, 1902, cxvi, 312–14.

[2] The prologue to the *Speculum ecclesiae* contains two letters. The first is from the 'fratres Cantuariensis ecclesiae' to Honorius; the second is his reply, sending the collection of sermons (*PL* CLXXII, 807, and see Endres, *op. cit.* p. 29–31). It is quite possible that these letters are a mere literary device of Honorius, but they sufficiently demonstrate his connexion with Canterbury.

on the storm provoked by the vigorous measures taken by King Henry after Anselm's death.[1] But Honorius was essentially a rolling stone. Soon after writing the *Offendiculum Sacerdotum* he came under the influence of a new master, Rupert of Deutz; his ties with England were finally broken, and the German phase of his career began.

Honorius is not only one of the most obscure, but also one of the most influential writers of the first half of the twelfth century. His career, moreover, admirably illustrates the difficulties under which Anselm laboured in forming disciples during his time at Canterbury. He required a long period of common life and discussion to make his full influence felt. In the circumstances of his life as archbishop, broken by long periods of exile, this was impossible. Nor did Honorius offer the kind of dedication that Anselm required. He belonged to the new generation of scholars who sought masters wherever they could be found; he was not content with the old stability of Benedictine studies. He certainly had a lively instinct for seeking out the men who mattered. But even when he was most fully a pupil of Anselm, he was only a cursory student of the master's works and thoughts. He was a magpie, not a philosopher. This will be clear to anyone who reads the *Elucidarium*. The astonishing assurance with which he answers questions of every possible kind is of course not unusual, but it gives no evidence of a philosophic temper. He takes information from all sides and presses it into service:

D. How are the damned situated?

M. They are hung head downwards, back to back, feet in the air, stretched in torment in all directions.

D. Do not the just lament when they see them thus punished?

---

[1] There are only two medieval manuscripts of this work known to exist and one of them is English: C. C. C. C. MS. 34, p. 427–40. It is associated with an extract from Anselm's letter 65 [i, 56] in which he deals with the same subject. Honorius's conclusion supports that of Anselm, but his arguments are wildly extravagant as the following extract will show: 'Concludere igitur licet presbiteri uxorati vel simoniaci cum canes sint, porci, Christi adversarii, publice hostes Dei, fures, latrones, lupi, sunt excommunicati, et omnes qui eis communicant damnati.' (J. Kelle, 'Untersuchungen über das Offendiculum des Honorius,' *Sitzungsberichte der k. Akad. der Wissenschaften zu Wien*, cxlviii, 1904, p. 29).

M.  No.  Even though a father sees his own son in torment, or a son his father, or a mother her daughter, or a daughter her mother, or a husband his wife, or a wife her husband, they will not only not lament, but will find pleasure in the sight, as when we see fishes in a whirlpool.

D.  Now I should like to hear about Antichrist.

M.  Antichrist will be born in Babylon of a prostitute of the tribe of Dan.  He will be filled with the devil in his mother's womb, and brought up by malefactors in Khorassan.[1]

There is no need to protract the evidences of Honorius's absurd and relentless certainty, but a single instance may be given of his treatment of a philosophical idea.  In the course of the *Elucidarium* he deals, in a sentence, with free will:

D.  What is free will?

M.  It is the liberty of choosing good or evil.[2]

As his authority for this definition he quotes St. Augustine, as he was perfectly entitled to do.  Anselm, as we have seen, took a quite different view.  For him the 'power' to do evil was not freedom but the negation of freedom.  We might think therefore that Honorius, writing in the close proximity of Anselm's friends, had considered the alternative view and rejected it.  But we happen to know that this was not so: he was simply ignorant of Anselm's early work in which the rival view was developed.  This appears from Honorius's later work, the *Inevitabile*.  This work dealt with the problem of free will at length, but still in the same sense as the brief statement of the *Elucidarium*.  But after Honorius had written the *Inevitabile* Anselm's opinion was brought to his notice, and he hastened to make a second recension incorporating this quite contradictory position.[3]  He even seems to have revised his earlier definition of free will in the *Elucidarium* in an attempt to make it fit his new position.  The later recensions of this work read:

---

[1] *Elucidarium* III, 16, 20, 33 (ed. Lefèvre, pp. 449–53).
[2] *Ibid.* II, 7 (Lefèvre, p. 407).
[3] The relation between the two recensions and the significance of the changes was first pointed out by F. Baeumker, *op. cit.*

D. What is free will?

M. It is the power of men to be and to will and to do good or evil.[1]

But though this is more elaborate than the earlier definition it really comes to the same thing in the end. The two views were irreconcilable and Honorius was quite incapable of making a philosophical choice. Honorius cuts a poor figure under examination. But this should not obscure the fact that he performed a service of popular and vigorous exposition, which gave him a very wide audience throughout the Middle Ages. He was a man of indefatigable energy, who could state clearly, judge confidently and arrange systematically his very widely scattered materials.

I have said that he was a man of a new generation of wandering scholars. But it should be added—and in reading some of his wilder flights of speculation the impression is reinforced— that he was perhaps among the last of an ancient and honourable line of wanderers, the wandering scholar-monks of Ireland. Of all the mysteries that surround him his birthplace is the most mysterious, and he seems purposely to have deepened the mystery by the choice of the epithet *Augustodunensis*.[2] It is not Autun. It might be Regensburg; but there is really no evidence to suggest that it is. There is not a scrap of evidence to support the view now sometimes held that *Augustodunensis* refers to Canterbury: this hypothesis suffers from all the faults of the earlier suggestions and some others as well.[3] The meaning of the curious epithet remains unknown. But one of the few certain facts about Honorius is that he finished his life

---

[1] Lefèvre, p. 407, where what I take to be the earliest form of the text is printed in a footnote.

[2] In the *De Luminaribus Ecclesiae* he calls himself 'Augustodunensis ecclesiae presbiter et scholasticus'. Endres (*op. cit.* p. 11–13) saw in this a reference to Regensburg, but no confirmation of this usage has ever been found.

[3] The latest exponent of this view is R. Bauerreiss 'Honorius von Canterbury (Augustodunensis) und Kuno I, der Raitenbucher, Bischof v. Regensburg (1126–36)', *Studien u. Mitteilungen z. Geschichte des Benedictiner Ordens*, lxvii, 1956, 306–13. In addition to the objection that the identification of Canterbury as 'Augustine's town' is unsupported by other evidence, there is the insuperable difficulty that *Augustodunensis* does not mean 'Augustine's town' but 'the Hill of the Emperor(s)'. Canterbury is not on a hill and Augustine is not Augustus.

in an Irish community. The arrival of Irishmen in this community in Regensburg can be traced until a time contemporary with Honorius, and the natural inference would be that he too belonged to Ireland.[1] It would not be surprising to find a young Irish scholar at Canterbury in Anselm's time. The authority of Canterbury in Ireland had never stood so high, and it was never to be so high again. Irish visitors, either for the purposes of consecration or for monastic instruction, were not unusual in the years around 1100. Among them the restless omnivorous Honorius picking up the crumbs from Anselm's table before moving to a more distant exile would be a colourful but not an unintelligible object. The meaning of his title *Augustodunensis* must remain, and perhaps was meant to remain, doubtful. But it is at least plausible that Honorius should choose to perpetuate in this proud and obscure fashion the memory of the distant church and country from which he came, whose merits were too little recognized, as Irishmen are apt to think, by the world at large. Perhaps it was Cashel, literally the 'hill of the Kings'; it gives the Latin form we require. But Honorius certainly did not intend us to see too far into his mystery, and it must be left with only a tentative solution.[2]

[1] Many details about the influx of Irish scholars to Regensburg at this time are found in the *Vita S. Mariani Scoti* in *AA, SS*, Feb. ii, 361–72, where Regensburg is described as the *mater peregrinatorum praecipueque Scotorum* to which the Irish exiles came *de dulcibus Hiberniae solis*: 'pro remedio animarum de finibus Occidentis nudum Christum nudi sequentes, patriam, carosque propinquos, amore ac desiderio vitae caelestis derelinquentes, ne videamur aborigines, sicut vultur et ardea, quorum ortus et exitus soli Deo cognitus est' (p. 365).

[2] Professor Aubrey Gwynn, S. J., informs me that he had already, independently and on grounds rather different from mine, arrived at the conclusion that Honorius was probably an Irishman. He has stated his belief, without giving his reasons, in *Herbipolis Jubilans: Festschrift zur Säkularfeier der Erhebung der Kiliansreliquien*, Würzburg, 1952, p. 67. He has drawn my attention to the similarity between Honorius's extreme form of predestinarianism in his *Inevitabile* and the strange entry in the Annals of Inisfallen (ed. Séan Mac Airt, 1951) for the year 1121, in which God is represented as punishing sinners for a sin which they had not yet committed. Honorius's works would perhaps repay study for other examples of Irishisms: for example, in his *Elucidarium*, ii, 46–50, he takes an extraordinarily lenient view of 'incestuous' marriages, which were one of the recurring charges brought against Irishmen. But the whole subject requires full and expert treatment.

Of these three men, only Honorius achieved a European reputation, and he was less a disciple of Anselm than an adventurer using other men's thoughts for his own large designs. Gilbert Crispin and Ralph were much nearer to Anselm in spirit. In favourable circumstances, both of these had the ability necessary for making a substantial contribution to a theological movement. But the circumstances of their lives, and even the nature of Anselm's influence on them, precluded this possibility.

## 3. ANSELM'S CONVERSATION

It was in talk that Anselm made his most powerful impression on his contemporaries. All his utterances, whether in Chapter or at table, in formal sermons or in remarks casually elicited, have a quality which reflects the meeting of the Benedictine and scholastic ages. They are a combination of old and new: of old, in the monastic setting and range of monastic topics; of new, in the penetrating analysis, the striking definitions and the unfamiliar illustrations.

It was Anselm's talk which first excited the interest of the young Eadmer. When he visited Canterbury in 1079, he talked about the monastic life 'in a way which had not been heard of before this time'; he defended their martyr Elphege with arguments which would have seemed to them very far-fetched if their conclusion had not been so welcome; he drew aside some of the cleverer men and engaged them in discussion.[1] This was Anselm's introduction to Canterbury, and there is plenty of evidence in Eadmer and elsewhere that wherever Anselm went his talk left memories which were not easily effaced. John of Salisbury, writing over fifty years after Anselm's death, was able to report one of his sayings still remembered by the monks at Canterbury, and otherwise unknown to us.[2] Vincent of Beauvais in the thirteenth century is

[1] *VA* I, xxix.
[2] Ep. 211 (*PL* CXCIX, 235): 'Anselmus, ut a suis accepi, dicere consuevit se nihil magis habere suspectum quam quod eum Deus in tota vita nulla corripuerat adversitate.' For another example of Anselm's talk with his friends, see *Vita Gundulfi, PL* CLIX, 817, 827.

the first reporter of a story from St. Bertin's, which must have been told by Anselm when he returned from exile in 1100 and spoke of his experiences in Italy.[1] The author of the life of Lambert, abbot of St. Bertin's, gives several details of the discussions between Anselm and Lambert, and he increases Lambert's stature by attributing all the ideas—which have a strong Anselmian flavour—to his hero.[2] When Guibert of Nogent first awoke to intellectual life, he found his chief inspiration in Anselm, who sometimes visited his monastery and talked to him 'as if I were the sole cause of his coming'.[3] The author of the *Life* of Abbot Hugh of Cluny breaks his rather monotonous recital to exclaim on the sweet discourse which passed between the abbot and archbishop when Anselm and his party visited Cluny during their exile;[4] and during the same exile, Anselm's talk at Vienne or in its neighbourhood has left its mark on the canon of the Miracles of St. James of Compostella.[5]

These chance records disclose the wide extent of Anselm's reputation as a talker, and no account of Anselm as archbishop would be complete without some attempt to display the range and effect of his talk, whether in conversation or in more formal discourse. Nothing, it need scarcely be said, is more difficult. Of all the great forces which have formed the past, none has disappeared more effectively from the historian's view than the power of the spoken word. Only the most broken fragments remain. Yet no one in the early Middle Ages has had so much of his talk preserved as Anselm. We owe this chiefly to the combined efforts of Eadmer, Alexander, and some third hand; and before going further it is necessary to explain what these efforts have produced.

[1] Vincent of Beauvais, *Speculum* vii, 116b, quoted by Mussafia, *Studien zu den mittelalterlichen Marienlegenden, Sitzungsberichte der K. Akademie der Wissenschaften zu Wien*, cxv, 1887, p. 56.
[2] *MGH, SS*, xv, 949.     [3] *De vita sua*, I, xvii (*PL* CLVI, 874).
[4] Gilo, *Vita Sancti Hugonis*, ed. A. L'Huillier, *Vie de S. Hughues, Abbé de Cluny*, 1888, p. 588–9 (cf. *VA* II, xlvi, n).
[5] R. W. Southern, 'The English Origins of the "Miracles of the Virgin",' *MARS*, iv, 1958, pp. 188–90, 205–11.

## (i) *Eadmer*

Anyone who turns to the *Vita Anselmi* will at once be struck by the amount of natural and vivid talk which it contains. It is Eadmer's chief claim to fame as a biographer that he understood the importance of Anselm's talk and had the skill to reproduce it in a convincing and memorable way. Eadmer not only gives us words which seem to be those of Anselm, but he shows how they arose from the needs of the moment: how the hunted hare and the captive bird suggested parables of human life; how the parting speech to the monks of Canterbury provided the occasion for an allegory of the three classes of knights and the conditions of men in relation to God; how the troubles of the over-busy monk suggested the simile of the mill as an image of human life, and prompted the subtle distinction between acquiescence and obedience.[1] Anselm's favourite time for such talk was at meals. In this he was unusual. The Rule of St. Benedict laid down, and common practice required, that a book should be read at mealtimes. The office of reader seems, at the archbishop's table, to have been performed by his cross-bearer.[2] But St. Benedict allowed the superior to speak briefly for edification if he wished, and Anselm seems to have made a generous use of this provision.[3] If Eadmer is to be trusted—and he is not the only witness—it was only when no subject for edification presented itself that Anselm sat back and listened to the reading. Thus it arose, as Eadmer says, that he heard almost daily Anselm's reflections on humility, patience, meekness, obedience and other virtues, which would require another work to set down. What he gives is sufficient to make the reader regret the other work which might have been written. No one else was so well

---

[1] *VA* ii, xi, xviii, xix, xxi.

[2] Herbert Bosham, *Vita S. Thomae* iii, xv: '. . . lectio quae quotidie in mensa pontificis ab initio usque ad finem discubitus personabat, bajulo crucis ea hora legente, cuius in domo archipraesulum Cantuariensium ab olim id officii est.' (*Materials for the History of Archbishop Thomas Becket, RS*, iii, 226.)

[3] *Regula* xxxviii: 'Et summum fiat silentium, ut nullius musitatio vel vox, nisi solius legentis, ibi audiatur . . . nisi forte prior pro aedificatione voluerit aliquid breviter dicere.' For Anselm's practice, see *VA* ii, x.

equipped as Eadmer to write this work, but it seems that he did not do so; and when in the last years of Anselm's life Eadmer's reports of his talks dry up, the life goes out of his work. There were others, however, who in some measure filled his place, and of these the chief appears to have been Alexander.

### (ii) *Alexander*

Alexander's contribution to the body of Anselm's talk is a collection of twenty-one sermons or fragments of sermons preached on various unspecified occasions, which he took down as best he could to preserve their memory.[1] He says that he had reported other sermons which had been borrowed and never returned, but what remains is a most valuable addition to our knowledge of Anselm's method. These reports lack the intimacy of Eadmer and preserve much less of the characteristic turns of phrase with which Eadmer enlivened his work, but they supplement our knowledge in a variety of ways. They show that the similes and parables reported by Eadmer were used on more than one occasion and in various contexts. They strengthen the impression that the words attributed to Anselm by Eadmer were really used by him; though it also seems certain that Eadmer sometimes lumped together on a single occasion material which he had gathered over a longer period. A comparison with Alexander shows that there is more art in Eadmer than appears on the surface. This is clear when we compare a report of the same sermon by Eadmer and Alexander: Eadmer has preserved the repetitions and ejaculations of the spoken word which Alexander lost; Eadmer is sometimes less clear in doctrine, but more lively in detail; and he has not scrupled to add to the end of his report words that no

---

[1] This collection of sayings is anonymous and generally goes under the title *Anselmus de monte humilitatis*, being so named after the first item in the collection. The main manuscript is Corpus Christi College, Cambridge, MS. 457 from Christ Church, Canterbury, but there are several others in varying states of confusion. For further details see *MARS*, i, 1941, p. 8–10, iv, 1958, pp. 189–90, 208–16; and F. S. Schmitt, *Neue und alte Hildebrand-Anekdoten aus den Dicta Anselmi*, Studi Gregoriani, v, 1956, 1–18. An edition of this material, and of similar material referred to below, is in course of preparation by Dom F. S. Schmitt and myself; but I must accept sole responsibility for any opinions about the material which I express here.

doubt came from Anselm's lips but could not possibly have belonged to the original sermon.[1]

Alexander's reports are important because they preserve a great deal of material which seems to have had little interest for Eadmer. Eadmer found his satisfaction in the similes and parables with which Anselm's talk abounded; he says nothing about an equally ubiquitous form of Anselmian discourse—the endless divisions and subdivisions of a subject, to which Alexander's reports no less than Anselm's written works bear witness. The whole range of Anselm's writings testifies again and again to Anselm's interest in verbal analysis, and from Alexander we know that it was a feature of his conversation as well as of his more formal speculations.

### (iii) *The Anonymous Compiler*

Eadmer and Alexander were not the only collectors to whom we owe our reports of Anselm's talk, but they are the only ones we can name. The most influential of all was one whose name and circumstances are extraordinarily elusive. From a time, which cannot have been very long after Anselm's death, there circulated in England and possibly also in Normandy, a large collection of his sayings. To this collection, Anselm's name was attached, but there was nothing to explain who was responsible for it or what materials he used. Even the title was uncertain, but it gradually became fixed, from the nature of a large part of the contents, as the *Liber de Similitudinibus*. Under this title it had in the later Middle Ages an immense success. Although twelfth century manuscripts are very scarce, they begin to be common in the thirteenth, and in the fourteenth the treatise is almost always included among Anselm's works.

This popularity in the late Middle Ages reflects the increasing interest in Anselm's thought among scholastic theologians. We do not know how the work was first, at some time in the thirteenth century, introduced into University circles. It was already established academically in the mid-thirteenth century, and Thomas Aquinas cites it among the works of

[1] For a detailed description of the growth of this report, see Appendix II, below p. 362.

Anselm almost as often as the *Cur Deus Homo*. Once established it kept its place in the canon of Anselm's writings. Like Eadmer's treatise on the Conception of the Virgin, which had a similar history, it owed its success partly to the widespread desire for complete copies of the works (or supposed works) of important authors, and partly to the relevance of the subject-matter to the controversies of the fourteenth and fifteenth centuries. For a variety of reasons, therefore, this compilation, after an unpromising start, reached a wide audience and is commonly quoted from the thirteenth century onwards among Anselm's own writings.

If, however, we look back to its origins, the trail gets fainter and fainter and finally disappears. Every other work of Anselm has an excellent textual tradition going back in its most important branch to Canterbury manuscripts, prepared under the direction of his immediate pupils. By contrast, the *De Similitudinibus* is unknown among Canterbury manuscripts before the thirteenth century.[1] Nor is there any sign that they come from that other obvious source of Anselmian material, Bec. Yet it is impossible to read these sayings without being convinced that their collector disposed of genuine records of Anselm's sayings. Everywhere there are the marks of Anselm's habits of thought and speech. We know, moreover, that fragments of Anselm's works, either incomplete or in earlier recensions, were to be found in some abundance at Canterbury after his death and became dispersed soon afterwards. We have the evidence of Alexander's preface for this dispersal of his collections; and Ordericus Vitalis noted that Anselm's pupils kept not only his letters but his figurative sayings (*typicos sermones*) 'with which they not only inebriated themselves but edified others not a little'.[2]

The twelfth century manuscripts of the *De Similitudinibus* in some form or other—for their textual form varies greatly in

---

[1] The medieval catalogues of Christ Church manuscripts show a striking difference between the large number of volumes containing Alexander's *Dicta Anselmi* (nos. 38, 113, 114, 115, 121, 146, 940, 1542) and the small number of manuscripts, of late date, of the *De Similitudinibus* (nos. 545, 726). See M. R. James, *The Ancient Libraries of Canterbury and Dover*, 1903, pp. 18–129.
[2] *Historia Ecclesiastica*, ed. Le Prévost, ii, 245.

the earliest copies—come from a wide variety of libraries mainly in the west of England, from Hereford, Lanthony, Abbey Dore, Reading; but not apparently from Canterbury. This suggests that, although the compiler must have had access to the literary remains of Anselm and his pupils at Canterbury, he was not himself a member of that house. We must imagine a compiler, not himself of the inner circle of Anselm's pupils, but having access to the reports of Anselm's talk made by both Eadmer and Alexander, permitted to make use of and even to remove, some of this material. He must have been a distinguished outsider, who could thus turn over the haphazard literary remains of Anselm very soon after his death; and he must have had the habits of an author, who could turn these materials into a work preserving, not the record of Anselm's personal characteristics as Eadmer had done, but the essential matter of his talk.

The manuscript tradition, except that it points away from Canterbury, gives us no help in determining the question of authorship, and we must be content to say that, whoever the author was, he knew his own mind as well as that of Anselm.[1] He treated his material with freedom. He extracted from it the similitudes, which finally gave their name to the whole collection, and the minute analysis of concepts, which sprang from a quite different side of Anselm's genius. The rest he ignored. The result was a treatise with the name, and part at least of the nature, of Anselm upon it; at first without title, but coming gradually after many vicissitudes to be widely read and known as the *De Similitudinibus*. When Alexander was quite forgotten, and Eadmer was remembered, if at all, only

---

[1] It is perhaps worth mentioning as a possible author the name of William of Malmesbury. He certainly visited Canterbury not long after Anselm's death; he knew the works of Eadmer and he used the *Dicta Anselmi* of Alexander in his *Historia Regum*, ii, 322–5; he collected Anselm's works and had access to recensions that have not otherwise come down to us. William's manuscript of Anselm's works is Lambeth MS. 224. Among other notable things, it contains an early draft of the *De Incarnatione Verbi* (Schmitt, i, 281–90); and there are many peculiarities in the text of the letters which show that he had access to a primitive collection or drafts, no doubt at Canterbury. In his own writings, he made use of Anselm in his Prologue to his collection of Miracles of the Virgin (Salisbury Cathedral MS. 97, f. 91: see *MARS*, iv, 201).

as the writer of a not very widely read biography, the work of this anonymous compiler conveyed to a later age most of what it knew of Anselm's talk.

Late medieval scholars were not interested in the circumstances or graces of this talk. They had no interest in Anselm's pupils. They wished only to have what was useful for their purposes. The *De Similitudinibus* could never have the importance of the great treatises which were generally bound up with it in the manuscripts, but in its hundred and ninety-two succinct chapters it contained crumbs which were sometimes worth picking up. To live a posthumous life in this fossilized form was a curious fate for talk which had once been so exciting and new; and to have their records conveyed to an alien audience in this form was a strange fate for Anselm's Canterbury pupils. But anything which links Anselm's great treatises with his table-talk and daily discourses is valuable. The materials from which the *De Similitudinibus* was formed are now largely accessible to us; from them we can make a fair conjecture about the nature of the remainder; and we can see that the compiler did his work well.

These three men, Eadmer, Alexander and the anonymous compiler, were the agents who transmitted the record of Anselm's talk, and their record cannot be left without an illustration of its subject matter. We may take as our point of departure Anselm's speculations about the soul. This was something to which he often returned, and about which he said things which never got into his formal treatises:

In the soul there are three natures: reason, will and appetite. By reason it is allied to the angels, by appetite to the beasts, by will to both. Will holds a middle place between reason and appetite, inclining now to reason, now to appetite. When it turns to reason, it is imbued with those things which are rational and spiritual; when it turns to appetite, it is imbued with things carnal and irrational. So a man is either rational and spiritual or carnal and animal.[1]

Thus begins one of the sections of the *De Similitudinibus*. It

[1] *De Sim.* clxx (*PL* CLIX, 693). This chapter and the three following reproduce more or less verbatim the beginning of chapter xvii of the *Dicta Anselmi* in MS. C.C.C.C. 457.

comes from Alexander's record of Anselm's talk: necessarily therefore it belongs to a period near the end of Anselm's life. But Anselm had been saying almost exactly the same thing twenty years earlier when he was still at Bec, and his words then made a deep impression on the young Guibert of Nogent: He taught me (Guibert wrote in his Autobiography), that

that there was a three-fold or four-fold division of the spirit, and he treated the operation of the whole interior mystery under these heads: desire, will, reason, intellect. What many, including myself, regarded as a unity he resolved into distinct parts and showed that the first two parts were not identical unless jointed to the third or fourth.[1]

Here then in his talk with a young monk, whose first steps in philosophy he was guiding, he demonstrated his analytical approach not only to theology but also to psychology. That the soul was composed of parts, and that, being made in the likeness of God, these parts should be three in number, was an ancient doctrine., But Anselm departed from the form in which this division was most commonly found in the authors of the early Middle Ages from the time of St. Augustine to St. Bernard. These authors followed a Platonic tradition in making the three parts of the soul memory, reason and will. In giving an independent status to appetite or desire, Anselm seems to foreshadow a less intellectualist approach to the problem of the soul. It is no more than a hint: Anselm's thought on this question was too little developed to have an important influence on later speculations. It marks a deviation from an accepted mode of thought rather than the beginning of a new path, but it was a deviation which contemporaries evidently found exciting.

If we may judge from other fragments of his talk, the faculty of the soul to which he devoted the most minute attention was the will. On this subject he was remarkably copious in disentangling the complexities of the impulses leading to action, and he elaborated a primitive analytical psychology which perhaps helped to give the *De Similitudinibus* its popularity in the later Middle Ages. The first forty chapters of the *De*

[1] *PL* CLVI, 874.

*Similitudinibus* are entirely occupied with this analysis, and its minuteness may be judged from its classification of ninety modes of self-will under the three main divisions of *delectatio* (thirty-one modes), *exaltatio* (fifteen modes) and *curiositas* (forty-four modes). It cannot be said that this line of thought had any immediate philosophical future, but it must have contributed to the growing interest in the human faculties which characterized the twelfth century. One of those who listened to Anselm discoursing on this subject as he passed through Flanders on his way to Rome in 1103 was sufficiently stimulated to write and ask him to write down what he had said. Anselm replied:

You ask me to recall to you by letter the three modes of pride of which I spoke to you, because you have forgotten two of them. I said there are three modes: one in judging, as when a man thinks of himself more highly than he ought to think; one in willing, as when a man wishes to be treated otherwise then he ought to be; and one in action, as when a man treats himself better than he ought to do. Of these modes, the last (in action alone) is the least blameworthy because it is in ignorance; the second (in willing) is worse; but the first (in judging) is worst of all because then a man wrongly thinks he is right. These are the simple modes of pride, but they can be combined into three double modes, or into one triple mode. Thus there are seven modes: three single, three double, and one triple.[1]

Evidently, everywhere this kind of talk struck men as something new, and they were indeed witnessing the stirring of a new spirit of philosophical inquiry; yet it is characteristic of Eadmer that he preserved nothing of all this elaborate analysis, but only the similes in which Anselm expressed his reflections on the human will and the activity of the soul. Certainly he preserved the better part. The similes still live, while the analysis has died with the outgrowing of its psychological concepts. The poetry has outlived the science; the voice has become more important than what it said; and (reversing the judgment of the Middle Ages) the biography will be read when the *De Similitudinibus* is forgotten.

[1] Ep. 285 [iii, 75].

# PART II

# CHAPTER VI

# EADMER

EADMER is known to historians as the author of the *Historia novorum in Anglia*, the first piece of large-scale contemporary historical writing in England after Bede, and as the biographer of his friend and master St. Anselm. He is known to theologians as the author of the first treatise in defence of the Feast of the Conception of the Blessed Virgin Mary. The two sides of his literary achievement, are not often considered together, but they are very closely related. They are related not only to each other, but also to the life and circumstances of the monastic community of Christ Church, Canterbury, of which he was a member during almost the whole of his life, and to his friendship with Anselm, which was the most important influence in his intellectual development.

With the exception of the *Life of St. Anselm*, none of Eadmer's writings enjoyed any considerable circulation during his lifetime or for two centuries after his death; only a few had readers outside his own community, and in many cases his own copy was probably the only one which ever existed. Such popularity as he came to possess he owed entirely to his association with Anselm, and in large part to a confusion between his work and that of his master. Yet he was a man of unusual talent and power of perception, the only considerable English writer who survived into the twelfth century with memories of the Conquest, the most articulate spokesman for the interests, prejudices, and spiritual concerns of one of the greatest English monastic communities in their first bloom after the revival under Lanfranc. He and the community in which he lived deserve to be better known, and it is one purpose of the following pages to trace their complex history during the two generations after the Conquest in such detail as the evidence will permit.

Anselm was archbishop for only sixteen of these sixty years, and six of these years were spent in exile: he was in England for no more than ten years. He did not impress his mind and personality upon the community as Lanfranc had done; and, except to the devoted few, his work did not appear to the monks of Canterbury worthy to stand beside that of his great predecessor. But Anselm's work as archbishop was more deeply influenced by the community of which he was head than is generally realized. He was important in so many fields of European endeavour that the humble local origin of some of his actions is easily overlooked. We have already had occasion to notice this in considering his aims and activity as archbishop of Canterbury.

In forming our picture of the community at Canterbury which Anselm ruled, the first person whom it is necessary to know is Eadmer. This is not easy. No one wrote a biography of Eadmer as he wrote one of Anselm. We must rely almost exclusively on what he casually let drop about himself in the course of writings devoted to other subjects. Fortunately he was much given to reminiscence, and it is this which makes the task of a modern biographer possible. Inevitably many facts remain unknown, even the dates of his birth and death, and the names of his parents.

The first certain fact which we know from his writings is that he did not normally call himself Eadmer but Edmer. This is not what we should expect. He was a passionate lover of old English ways, and there can be no doubt that the old form of his name—and the form which several of his contemporaries used when they wrote his name—was Eadmer. But he was sufficiently part of the new cosmopolitan post-Conquest world to drop this insular peculiarity, and to use a form more easily accommodated to foreign tongues. Edmer was the name by which he was generally known by those who had occasion to mention him in the Middle Ages. The modern use of the more primitive form goes back to John Selden, the first editor of the *Historia Novorum*, and himself—though in a different spirit than his author—an enthusiast for the old English past.[1] It would only cause confusion to change it now, but in speaking of Eadmer we are falling into an archaism which even he avoided.

---

[1] *Eadmeri monachi Cantuariensis Historiae Novorum sive sui saeculi Libri VI*, London, 1623.

He was born a few years before the Norman Conquest. Since he tells us that he was a small boy in 1070–1 and adolescent in 1079, and since he was old enough in 1067 to remember well the arrangement of the old church of Canterbury which was burnt that year, we cannot be far wrong in placing the date of his birth about 1060.[1] Of his family our only certain knowledge is that he had a nephew, a sister's son, with the Norman name of Haimo, who was a monk at Christ Church Canterbury about 1115; and that in about 1130 another relative called Henry, a man of some substance, was probably living near Canterbury as a tenant of the monastery.[2] It seems also very likely that his mother was the poor woman to whom Lanfranc paid the considerable pension of thirty shillings a year, about which Eadmer tells a touching story.[3] Eadmer himself was brought up from infancy in the monastic community at Christ Church. These scanty facts about his family background suggest that he came from a family of English gentry, probably impoverished by the Conquest, closely associated with the church of Canterbury. This background never ceased to dominate his thought and feeling. To the end of his life he remained wholeheartedly an Englishman devoted to the interests of his monastery.

During his lifetime, several writers attempted to revive the memory of pre-Conquest days, but none expressed their English feelings so unreservedly as Eadmer, and of all of them he had the best title to his feelings. He had been brought up from childhood in the cradle of English Christianity; he was of native stock; he remembered the old days. William of Malmesbury, who was not behind him in zeal and activity and outshone him

---

[1] He was *puerulus* when Lanfranc ordered the bones of St. Dunstan to be raised from the ruins of the old church; this must have been shortly after Lanfranc's arrival at Canterbury in 1070 (see *Memorials of St. Dunstan*, pp. 232, 413). For his age in 1079 see *VA* I, xxix; and for his description of the church which was burned in 1067, see Wilmart, *Opuscula*, p. 365–6.

[2] For Haimo, see *VA, Miracula* p. 159. For Henry, *Analecta Bollandiana*, li, 1933, p. 288: 'quidam mihi cognitus et cognatus Henricus nomine.' For the piece in which this phrase occurs, see below pp. 370–1.

[3] *HN* 13–14. Knowles, *The Monastic Order in England*, p. 109, has made the suggestion that the widow of this story might well be Eadmer's mother, and this is very likely for it is hard to see how he could otherwise have known the details which he gives.

in learning, was only half an Englishman and was born at least a quarter of a century after the Conquest. The scholarly monks of Worcester who grew up under the protection of Bishop Wulfstan were as English as Eadmer in their birth and traditions, but their conservative and unassuming scholarship allowed no scope for the expression of their feelings. The Anglo-Saxon Chronicler, who wrote at Canterbury in the unquiet atmosphere of St. Augustine's, expressed more poignantly than Eadmer the pains and sufferings of foreign conquest, but he made no attempt to revive the past: at St. Augustine's that task was left to an itinerant foreigner, Goscelin. With Eadmer, pride of race, the grievances of the conquered, and the love of Canterbury combined to produce a sense of indignation and nostalgia in writing of the present and the past. If he had possessed more gift for epigram, he would have been a satirist; but, lacking this, he nursed his memories and cherished a secret sense of superiority while he watched the downfall of his nation. 'Their nationality', he wrote of the Englishmen whom Henry I passed over for preferment in favour of foreigners, 'was their downfall. If they were English, no virtue was enough for them to be considered worthy of promotion; if they were foreigners, the mere appearance of virtue, vouched for by their friends, was sufficient for them to be judged worthy of the highest honour'.[1] Nearly sixty years after the Conquest, he wrote to the monks of Glastonbury, who claimed that they had filched the body of St. Dunstan from Canterbury: 'I was not a little confounded to hear such a foolish and even laughable story, especially as it is said to have been invented by Englishmen. Alas, why did you not consult some foreigner—one of those experienced and knowledgeable men from beyond the sea, who would have invented some likely lie on such an important matter, which you could have bought?'[2]

These are the feelings of the oppressed, and though they had no frequent expression, in Eadmer they never died. The long friendship with Anselm did not extinguish the enduring influence of Canterbury and all that it stood for as a symbol of the English past. It simply gave a new content to an insular tradition.

[1] *HN* 224.    [2] *PL* CLIX, 803 B.

232

A feeling of resentment is in itself of no great interest and of no creative power. It was the additional sense of community, concentrated in the well-being of a monastic house, which gave a direction and driving force to what might have been no more than a cherished and barren grievance. The lands of the monastery had everywhere been threatened or diminished, and the task of regaining and keeping them called for more anti-quarian research in archive material than in any previous generation. The rights of Canterbury, especially with regard to York, required much turning over of chronicles, papal privileges and records of episcopal professions, to extract from them what was believed, indeed eagerly *known*, but scarcely to be demonstrated, to be the truth. The upsetting of liturgical observances and devotional habits called for an intense effort to recall and set down in writing their credentials in saints' lives and records of miracles, which had scarcely needed to be examined before. In all these ways the Conquest presented a challenge to which Eadmer, like many others whose names are now forgotten, rose according to their abilities.

The Conquest had happened when Eadmer was scarcely of an age to understand it, but he was evidently a precocious child, as children brought up in a male and adult community with interests above their years must frequently have been. He remembered vividly the arrangement of the church which was burnt when he was about seven years old, a feat of memory which might appear incredible if it had not been exactly matched almost in our own day by William Morris.[1] From an early age he was (as he himself says) deeply interested in all that passed under his eyes, especially in all that concerned ecclesiastical usage, and he was an eager listener to the traditions of the community which the memory of the older monks could carry back at first hand to the days of Cnut, and at second hand to those of King Edgar. For these tales he had an astonishingly retentive memory. The recollection of them remained with him undimmed until old age, and the fragments which came casually from his pen give us our best—almost our only— insight into the life of the community during the hundred years before the Conquest. To this subject we shall return.

[1] A. Clutton Brock, *William Morris*, 1914, p. 28.

Until 1093 Eadmer lived the life of a monk in the community. By this time he had already begun to be an author, following the tradition of local history and hagiography founded by his older contemporary at Canterbury, Osbern. The even tenor of his life was broken by the consecration of Anselm as archbishop in December 1093. It is probable that Eadmer formed part of the new archbishop's household from the beginning, and he shared the itinerant life of the archbishop until Anselm's death in 1109. This connexion brought him sixteen years of journeyings more extensive and protracted than any which had been undertaken by an English bishop since St. Wilfrid. In England the archbishop's need to maintain a large household, rather than any strictly episcopal functions, made necessary a regular itinerary through the south-eastern counties where his manors lay, with numerous diversions to the royal court wherever it might be. Abroad, there were two journeys to Rome, with lengthy stops at Lyons and two months at Cluny, a visit to southern Italy with a sight of the Normans in action at the siege of Capua, and an insight into the relations of Greeks and Latins at the Council of Bari. In these travels he made a fleeting acquaintance with all the chief ecclesiastical personalities in Europe: Urban II, Paschal II, Hugh abbot of Cluny, Hugh archbishop of Lyons, Guy archbishop of Vienne (Calixtus II), to mention only the most outstanding. All this meant a notable extension of view for a Canterbury monk whose mind had hitherto dwelt exclusively on subjects of special concern to his own house. Yet even in the midst of these scenes it was to Canterbury that Eadmer's mind instinctively reverted. The Council of Bari, for instance, was one of the great ecclesiastical occasions of Urban II's pontificate and Eadmer describes the scene with his customary vividness. He sat at Anselm's feet and took in his surroundings:

and since it was always my custom from infancy to give diligent attention and to commit to memory whatever novelty presented itself, especially in ecclesiastical affairs, I looked discreetly round the Council spread out before me, noticing the seating arrangements and the method of conducting business, perhaps with more curiosity than wisdom, as one who had never seen anything like it before. And while I looked, I saw the archbishop of Benevento, whom I already knew well, wearing a cope more precious than the garment of anyone else present; for the pope was presiding not in a cope but in a chasuble with a pallium on top of it. As I looked at the archbishop's cope and saw that it outshone all others, I remembered some words which as a boy I had heard from the older members of our church, the worthy Edwy, Blackman, Farman and others. They had been accustomed to say that, when they were scarcely more than boys, Queen Emma had enriched the church with an arm of the blessed apostle Bartholomew.

The story they had told him was that Queen Emma had bought the arm of St. Bartholomew from the archbishop of Benevento and given it to Canterbury. To the purchase price archbishop Aethelnoth had added a precious cope richly embroidered with gold, which had been taken back to Benevento. Eadmer tells the tale at great length and concludes:

I, then, when I saw the archbishop of Benevento thus adorned with a cope outshining all others, felt quite sure that it was the one about which I had formerly heard, and was not a little pleased. I pointed it out to Anselm and told him what I had heard as a boy. When the Council was finished I approached the archbishop of Benevento and in the midst of other friendly talk I began to speak about his cope and asked him where he got it from as if I knew nothing about it. He told me the whole story and related how his church had obtained it from Canterbury, just as I have described.[1]

Eadmer found himself called upon to write on many more important subjects than this, but it was on such matters that he by preference dwelt. He cannot, I imagine, have been very helpful to Anselm on matters where far-sighted judgment and decision were required.

The death of Anselm meant that Eadmer could once more settle at Canterbury for a considerable length of time. The see was vacant from 1109 till 1114. Eadmer had no duties outside the monastery and it was during these years and the two following years of quiet that most of his writing was done. Then in August 1116 he set out once more on his travels, this time as a companion of Archbishop Ralph. Neither in the importance of its cause or results could this journey compare

[1] *HN* 107–10.

235

with those undertaken in company with Anselm. The cause was the tedious quarrel with York over the primacy, and the results, so far as Canterbury was concerned, were disastrous. Eadmer was abroad for rather more than three years helping to defend a falling cause. Early in 1119 ill-health forced him to leave the archbishop in Normandy and return to Canterbury.

He seems to have had a chilly reception. A new generation of monks was growing up which looked back with admiration to the strong and successful administration of Lanfranc and deplored the weaknesses of Anselm and his successor in asserting the rights of Canterbury.[1] In self-defence, Eadmer took up his literary work again, bringing his *History* up to date, and revising his life of Anselm. Then, in 1120, came his great chance of striking an independent blow for the church of Canterbury when all hope of a successful issue in the main controversy with York seemed to be dying. Alexander I of Scotland, continuing a friendship with Canterbury established by Margaret his mother and Edgar his elder brother, invited Eadmer to become bishop of St. Andrews. Eadmer set out for Scotland determined to play on a small stage the part Anselm had played on a great one. The obedience which Anselm had insisted on showing to the pope, Eadmer demanded to be allowed to pay to Canterbury; the advice which Anselm had insisted on going to Rome to obtain, Eadmer required that he should be allowed to seek at Canterbury. It was a short struggle. Within six months he had relinquished his ring and staff without ever having obtained episcopal consecration. He was back in Canterbury early in 1121.[2]

At this moment he had been a monk of Christ Church for nearly sixty years, but so far as we know he had held no office in the community. Since 1093, he had been the friend of two archbishops and their companion in a nomadic life; consequently, with the exception of the interregnum of 1109 to 1114, he can have spent only short periods within the monastic walls. In recent years he had been concerned chiefly with

---

[1] *HN* 251, 215. Both these passages were written in 1119.
[2] *HN* 286; cf. *Symeon of Durham*, ed. H. Hinde, Surtees Society li, 1867, p. 114, for the date of his return.

external relations, and he had become increasingly immersed in the dispute with York. How great a danger of mental and spiritual stagnation there was in this absorption may be seen in the last two books of the *Historia Novorum*, which descend from high questions of principle to the bickerings of bodies of men with too little to occupy their minds, and contract from the wide circle of European society to the narrow bounds of a humdrum province.[1] Eadmer had succeeded in establishing himself as a fighter for the rights of Canterbury beyond all reason, and he had adopted the gestures of St. Anselm in the pursuit of trifles. This was a sad state of affairs, for which the leadership of the weak and amiable Archbishop Ralph was partly responsible.

When Eadmer returned to Canterbury, the archbishop was already ill, and all effective control of affairs had slipped from his hands, never to return. Archbishop Ralph died on 20 October 1122, and Eadmer played no further part in public events. The new archbishop had other and probably more up-to-date counsellors. One by one the causes for which Eadmer had worked and fought were being lost. With the death of the old archbishop who, with all his faults, had been a monk of the school of Anselm, the *Historia Novorum* comes to an abrupt end. Eadmer turned to other themes and other works.

These works show a softening of the mood which had gripped him in recent years, and a return to the things with which he had been familiar in the days of Anselm and earlier. It was probably now that he became precentor of the monastery, and this office would give him the duty of supervising the writing of new books, and the provision of necessary texts for the divine office. These were tasks for which he was well fitted, and he turned to them with new energy. During these last years he wrote a number of works to commemorate the relics of the church, for use at the appropriate times in the liturgical year. His mind turned more and more to the past. His description of the old church and many details about former members of the community come from this period of his life. Incidents of his life with Anselm came back to his mind; and, contrary to

[1] See below, pp. 307–9.

his earlier intentions, he added to his biography of Anselm a collection of miracles which brought the work formally into line with the biographies of St. Dunstan and St. Wilfrid. He composed meditative prayers in the style of Anselm and in his work on the Conception of St. Mary he broke new ground in the theological interpretation of an old English devotion. As precentor he may have been responsible for the preparation of the superb manuscript of Anselm's collected works which was made at Canterbury at this time;[1] and he may likewise have planned one of the most impressive products of the Canterbury scriptorium—a great collection of saints' lives, including that of Anselm, in six volumes, of which now only fragments remain.[2] These manuscripts, in appearance and accuracy, bear the marks of the finest period of Canterbury book-production; they embrace the main objects of Eadmer's devotion, and their completion would form a fitting end to his career.

He did not at once, nor possibly ever while his strength

---

[1] The chief manuscript of Anselm's collected works is MS. Bodley 271, from Christ Church, Canterbury. Dom Schmitt has attempted to prove that this MS. and the manuscript of Anselm's letters, Lambeth MS. 59, were written by the same scribe, Thidricus, during the last years of Anselm's life (*Scriptorium*, ix, 1955, 64–75). Unfortunately he had to work from photographs, and his argument cannot survive a comparison of the two manuscripts: they are not in the same hand, nor is either of them the work of a single scribe. As for their date, Bodley 271 cannot be linked with Anselm's letter to Thidricus (Ep. 334 [iv, 42], as Dom Schmitt, on the basis of an erasure in the *De Conceptu Virginali*, supposed. The erasure is due to a scribal error, probably caused by the similarity of the words *sentientem* . . . *consentientem* in successive lines Schmitt, ii, 144, 11, 7–8), and has no textual significance. Hence the date of the manuscript can only be determined on palæographic grounds. C. R. Dodwell, *The Canterbury School of Illumination*, 1066–1200, p. 39, dates it between 1110 and 1140, and probably about 1130. Until a thorough study of the script of the Canterbury manuscripts has been made, it would be unwise to attempt a close dating; but a comparison with other Canterbury manuscripts suggests to me the decade after 1120 as much the most likely.

[2] Fragments of this lectionary have been identified by Mr. N. R. Ker in British Museum MSS., Cotton Nero C vii, Harleian 315 and 624, and Canterbury Cathedral MS. E. 42. Of these fragments, Harl. 315 contains a text of the *VA* which must have been written very soon after 1123. The lectionary also contained Eadmer's treatise on the miracles performed by the relics of St. Ouen, with a continuation written after 1128 (see below p. 240 n.). But the continuation is in a different hand from the main text, and this confirms the date *c.* 1125 for the planning and execution of the lectionary as a whole.

lasted, give up all hope of getting back his bishopric on his own terms and in a manner consistent with what he believed to be the just rights of Canterbury. But he could confess that his zeal for the claims of Canterbury had in some ways at least been indiscreet. It is noteworthy that in one of his last works he no longer referred to Anselm as *primas totius Britanniae*—the proud title which justified his attempt to subject the see of St. Andrew's to Canterbury—but simply as *primas totius regni Anglorum*.[1] Perhaps this was a slip, but it was a significant one, and it is not the only evidence of a change of disposition. As early as 1121, shortly after his return from Scotland, he wrote to the monks of Glastonbury, in a letter which has already been quoted, bidding them

restrain the forwardness and insolence of those young men who open their mouths solely that they may appear to know, and who give free rein to whatever their loquacity may suggest, thinking themselves great when others in their simplicity will listen to them. I know there have been people like this—perhaps I was one of them—so I can easily believe that now also there are men such as I formerly was. But now I am an old man with white hair, and many things which in my youth I thought important, I now hold of no account.[2]

The purpose of this letter was polemical, but in these words humanity breaks through, and does so increasingly as the polemic dies.

The date of Eadmer's death is a subject on which no certainty can be attained. He was commemorated at Canterbury on 13 January, but as to the year we are very much in the dark.[3] It has been argued that he lived until about 1144, but this suggestion is based on a series of improbable conjectures about the composition of the *Historia Novorum* and cannot be maintained.[4] The discovery of a continuation to Eadmer's treatise on the miracles of St. Ouen, however, has given a more trust-

---

[1] *Consideratio de beatissimo Gabriele archangelo*, ed. Wilmart, *Opuscula*, p. 377; see below, p. 296.

[2] *Memorials of St. Dunstan*, p. 421.

[3] For the day, see *Anglia Sacra*, ii, xii; J. Dart, *History and Antiquities of the Cathedral Church of Canterbury*, 1726, App. xxxii–xlii.

[4] Rule, pp. lviii–lix, civ: the facts mentioned in support of this date turn out on inspection to be deductions from hypotheses which are themselves based on the slenderest foundations. See below, p. 298–9.

worthy *terminus post quem* for the date of his death. Since this continuation refers to Prior Elmer it cannot be earlier than 1128. Yet if Eadmer was responsible for this addition to his earlier work—and although not quite certain it is probable that he was—he had ceased to supervise his writings with his customary care.[1] He may have lived for some years after 1128, but he was no longer active. His own manuscript of his works, which testifies to the activity of half a life-time, had been brought to a close. His claim to the bishopric of St. Andrew's, maintained for some years after his return to Canterbury, had been relinquished; peace had been restored between Canterbury and the king of Scotland; Eadmer's successor had at last been consecrated.[2] Over much of the field of conflict in which Eadmer had been engaged, the last years of Henry I's reign were a period of peace. Superficially Eadmer had failed in his practical policies, but in a wider way than he could have understood, the links with the Anglo-Saxon past which he had worked to maintain had been strengthened beyond all expectation. Meanwhile those who were themselves part of pre-Conquest England were sliding quietly from the scene. Among them Eadmer passed away almost without remark.

[1] *Analecta Bollandiana*, li, 1933, p. 288. This continuation to Eadmer's treatise *De reliquiis sancti Audoeni* was discovered and printed by Dom Wilmart. Although it seems to come from Eadmer, it was never included in his personal manuscript, which contains all his later works so far as we know; and it was added to the Canterbury Lectionary in a later and more careless hand than that of the main body.

[2] *The Chronicle of John of Worcester, 1118–40*, ed. J. R. H. Weaver, 1908, p. 25–6, 28. Prof. G. W. S. Barrow has printed (*Scottish Historical Review*, xxxi, 1952, pp. 18–20) the letter which King David of Scotland wrote to Archbishop William and the community at Canterbury in 1128 recognizing the debt which the Scottish Church owed to Canterbury in the past and asking them to choose a suitable abbot for the monastery of Dunfermline. The tone of the letter is one of fulsome gratitude and friendship towards the archbishop and his 'odoriferus conventus', and it seems designed to close an unhappy incident in the relations between Canterbury and the Scottish Church.

# CHAPTER VII

# THE COMMUNITY AT CANTERBURY

## 1. THE PRE-CONQUEST COMMUNITY

THE recollections of the pre-Conquest community which Eadmer heard from the older monks went back at their furthest limit for two or even three generations. Sometimes they had passed through several mouths before reaching Eadmer, but the inspiration was always the same. The stories moved in a narrow circle of subjects dear to the ecclesiastically minded Englishman of the eleventh century. They told of the bringing of the relics of St. Ouen to the court of King Edgar, of the king's gift of them to Christ Church, of Queen Emma's gift of the arm of St. Bartholomew, of the translation of the body of St. Elphege, and so on. Such stories as these must have been common in all religious communities, but the constant recurrence of these themes leaves the impression that the life of the Canterbury monks was centred in a more than ordinary degree on its relics, and on the stories of the gifts, purchases, translations and miracles associated with them. This interest was probably strengthened in the years before the Conquest by the failure of more strenuous intellectual activities. The atmosphere was that of the famous treatise on the resting places of the English saints and of the days when, in Eadmer's words, 'it was the custom of the English to prefer the patronage of the saints to every worldly aid'.[1]

At the extreme limit of his own experience, Eadmer could just recall in fragments, but with the unimpaired clarity of a distant view after a storm, details of the community as it existed at the time of the Conquest. Most vividly of all, he remembered the old church, and from the description which he wrote down in old age it is possible to form a more complete picture of its internal arrangements than of any other pre-Conquest church. He remembered where the saints had lain and where the altars

[1] *HN* 109.

had stood; he remembered the old confusion of secular and ecclesiastical affairs, and the use of the south porch as the place where pleas were settled which could get no solution in hundred or shire or royal court. He recalled the ancient baptistery, which stood at the east end of the church: here the bodies of the archbishops lay, and here the trials by ordeal took place. It was not until fifty years after the great fire which had swept it all away, that Eadmer wrote this description of what he had seen as a small boy of about seven. In appearance everything had been altered since then, and much for the better, but nearly everything that he cared most about was enshrined in these earliest recollections.

Of the community before the fire it is difficult to form any picture. One anecdote told by Eadmer shows that it must have been numerous, though the number of monks in it remains obscure. It was, he tells us, the custom for the boys in the monastery to be beaten on the fifth day before Christmas; and in the year of which he is speaking (probably 1066) the masters had, as usual on this day, posted themselves with knotted thongs and leather whips at a convenient place, waiting for the boys to pass on their way into church for Lauds at daybreak.[1] Eadmer does not tell us how many masters there were, but his older contemporary Osbern speaks of as many as four groups of masters lying in wait to perform their grisly task.[2] The point of the story for Eadmer and Osbern was that St. Dunstan caused the masters to fall asleep, and they were only awakened by the sound of the boys' singing in church. St. Dunstan, in return for this favour, demanded the removal of the body of an unbaptized son of King Harold which lay beside his own tomb in the choir; the monks refused to listen to a command conveyed in this irregular way by one of the boys, and the fire of 1067 was generally believed to have been the result of their refusal. Apart however from the miracle, the existence of so many masters argues a considerable number of boys and a considerable community.

The intellectual and spiritual life of this community is reflected in a fragmentary way in the surviving pre-Conquest manuscripts. The labours of successive scholars, of whom Mr.

[1] *Memorials of St. Dunstan*, p. 229.     [2] *Ibid.* p. 140.

N. R. Ker is chief, have succeeded in identifying some thirty-seven volumes, or fragments of volumes, which belonged to Christ Church before the Conquest.[1] The story which they tell is a curious one. With one possible exception, there is not a single volume of the basic works of patristic theology; there is not the slightest sign of interest in the scholastic disciplines which were stimulating the activity of scholars in northern France and Lorraine at this time. Some of the gaps must be due to chance, but there is no mistaking the general character of the interests which these volumes display. The most significant thing about them is the extent to which they are written in the vernacular: sixteen of the thirty-seven volumes are either in Old English or have Old English glosses to a Latin text. This vernacular wealth is as much a result of the low standard of Latin scholarship as of a marked insularity of taste and feeling, for the Latin texts are often deplorably inaccurate. A high proportion of the books, ten in all, are Gospel books or Psalters; several of them are ancient volumes which came to the church through the generosity of benefactors like King Athelstan. The hand of the past lies heavily on the collection as a whole.

---

[1] The list is as follows:
CANTERBURY CATHEDRAL, Box CCC no. xixa (Bilingual Rule of Chrodegang), Add. 25 (Waerferth's translation of St. Gregory's Dialogues), Add. 32 (St. Gregory's Dialogues with OE glosses); CAMBRIDGE, University Library, Ff. 4.43 (Smaragdus, *Diadema monachorum*); Corpus Christi College, 173 (*ASC*, AS laws, Sedulius with OE glosses), 192 (Amalarius), 260 (Tractatus musici), 272 (Psalter), 304 (Juvencus), 326 (Aldhelm with OE and Latin glosses), 411 (Psalter); Trinity College, B. 3.25 (Augustine, *Confessions* and *De diversis heresibus*), B. 4.27 (Isidore, *Quaestiones in vet. Test.*), B. 14.3 (Arator), B. 15.34 (OE Homilies), o.2.31 (Prosper *Epigrammata* and *Disticha Catonis* with OE glosses), o.2.51 (Prudentius, *Psychomachia*); BRITISH MUSEUM, Arundel 155 (Psalter), Tiberius A ii, Claudius A iii, Faustina B vi, Part I (Psalter with documents), Tiberius A iii (Rule of St. Benedict, *Regularis Concordia*, etc., with OE glosses), Tiberius A iii and vi (*ASC* 'B'), Claudius A iii (Benedictional), Vitellius C iii (OE Herbal), Faustina B iii and Tiberius A iii (*Regularis Concordia* in Latin and OE), Harleian 2892 (Benedictional). Royal I D ix (Gospels), Royal I B vii (Gospels), Royal I E vii, viii (Bible), Royal 2 B v (Psalter with OE gloss, and prayers), Royal 7 C iv (Defensor, *Liber scintillarum* with OE gloss); DURHAM CATHEDRAL B iii 32 (Hymns and Canticles with OE gloss; Aelfric's Grammar); LAMBETH PALACE 771 with BM. Tiberius B iv: (Gospels); OXFORD, Bodleian, Bodl. 97 (Aldhelm, *De Laude Virginitatis* with OE glosses), Junius II (?) (OE version of Genesis, etc.); St. John's College 194 (Gospels); PARIS Bibl. Nat. lat. 987 (Benedictional); STOCKHOLM Kungl. Bibliotek (Gospels).

Except for glosses, and perhaps some of the prayers, there is no sign of original composition by any member of the community in the generation before the Conquest. Yet it would be a mistake to paint too black a picture. These books have the appearance of use, which is more than can be said of many of the stately patristic volumes which were soon to fill the library; and though they would not support an inquiring mind they have a certain intellectual coherence, however unpromising for the future. When we have subtracted the service books and monastic Rules and chronicles, we are left with a little library, which intellectually belonged to a much earlier age, earlier even than the disasters of the ninth century, scarcely touched by Carolingian and post-Carolingian learning—redolent of the age of Bede rather than that of Lanfranc and Berengar.

Conspicuous among the books are anthologies of moral and religious teaching—the *Diadema monachorum* of Smaragdus, the *Liber scintillarum* of Defensor, the *Epigrammata* of Prosper; a few poems on biblical subjects by Juvencus and Arator; some old favourites like the *Psychomachia* of Prudentius, and— each in two copies—the *Dialogues* of St. Gregory, and Aldhelm's *De Virginitate*. The emphasis is biblical and ethical; and Canterbury seems in this respect not greatly different from other contemporary English communities. The numerous glosses, and the signs of much handling, testify to the use of these volumes as school books; but it must be added that more perplexing volumes for this purpose would be hard to find. If Englishmen did not write much in Latin in the generations before the Conquest, it may largely have been because the initial stages of learning were made so difficult. And beyond the early stages they found themselves far from every living spring of thought, confined to the puzzles of chronology and divination, and the annotation of outworn themes.

Intellectually these books belong to the pre-Carolingian age; but in monastic discipline they preserve without embellishment the ideals of the tenth century. There is no sign of movement, but it cannot be at all confidently said that there are many signs of decadence. Even in the tenth century it does not appear that monastic reform in England had stimulated an intellectual

244

revival. The literary and intellectual revival associated with the names of Aelfric, Wulfstan and Byrhtferth was a brief episode of the early eleventh century, and even these writers were content to popularize learning with which Bede would have been familiar. There was no continuous development: the intellectual interests of 1060 seem little removed from those of 960. The monastic reform had, however, stimulated an artistic revival which has left its chief memorials in manuscript illumination. To this, the manuscripts of Christ Church bear witness. At Canterbury, as elsewhere, nothing is more surprising than the gap between the level of intellectual and of artistic achievement. This was a universal phenomenon of the mid-eleventh century English religious houses, and one that the Conquest only slowly obliterated. The contents of books, which puzzled the mind to discover their sense, seem often to have excited the imagination and opened up a world of visual beauty.

When little or no new writing was attempted the evidence of monastic observance must be slight. It must not, on this account, be concluded that it did not exist. The evidence is somewhat better for Christ Church than for most houses. The tenth century code of discipline contained in the *Regularis Concordia* was intended to apply to all Benedictine houses in the kingdom, but no complete copy has been preserved except from Christ Church, whence two copies come.[1] These are characteristic productions: one of them has a double text in Latin and English, the other has a Latin text with English glosses; and both are full of textual errors. Nevertheless, traces of the regular discipline peculiar to this code survived every disaster, even the disasters of the Conquest and the fire in the following year.

The fire of 1067 was blamed for many things for which it was not responsible, yet it marked the end of an epoch in Canterbury history. It brought the old way of life to a violent end. Everything was made unusable except the refectory, the dormitory and so much of the cloister as allowed the monks to

---

[1] British Museum, MSS. Cotton Faustina B iii and Tiberius A iii: the latter may be post-Conquest. See T. Symons, *Regularis Concordia*, 1953, pp. liii–lix.

go from the one building to the other without getting wet in the rain.[1] The community survived, but extensive rebuilding was beyond its means. It erected a small building over the altars in common use, and here the monks gathered round the remains of St. Dunstan for their daily offices. These must have been performed with some elaboration, for they included a dramatic representation of the finding of the empty tomb on Easter morning, which is a liturgical feature found only in the *Regularis Concordia*. This small detail, casually introduced into Eadmer's account of the miracles of St. Dunstan, is precious for it seems to be the only scrap of evidence anywhere for the actual observance of the *Regularis Concordia* on the eve of Lanfranc's arrival in England.[2]

## 2. THE COMMUNITY UNDER LANFRANC AND ANSELM

### (i) *Lanfranc*

Lanfranc became archbishop in 1070 and brought with him a few monks from Bec and Caen. It would be a mistake to over-emphasize the immediate influence of this small group. They were probably fewer in number than is often supposed, and there is no reason to think that they were intended to colonize the monastery at Canterbury. They were a small addition to a predominantly English community. It seems more likely that Lanfranc brought men whom he marked out for future pro-motion and who could meanwhile be useful to him. In addition to these, we hear of a few temporary exchanges between Canter-bury and Bec. That is all. The names of the new arrivals are best known from Anselm's correspondence: Henry, Arnost and Gundulf among the earliest, of whom the first became prior of Canterbury and the other two successive bishops of Rochester; Maurice and Herlwin, from Bec; Vitalis, Roger and Samuel from Caen; and, at a later date, Gilbert Crispin, who became

---

[1] *Memorials of St. Dunstan*, pp. 142, 231.

[2] *Memorials of St. Dunstan*, p. 231. The passage describes a miracle which took place in the temporary church built after the fire but before Lanfranc's arrival; it was on Easter eve, 'dum sub specie trium mulierum in sepulcro quaereretur corpus Domini Salvatoris'. For this observance in the *Regularis Concordia* see the edition of T. Symons, p. 49–50.

abbot of Westminster. Until new recruits began to arrive, it is unlikely that there were as many as a dozen foreigners among perhaps thirty or forty Englishmen.

The two parts of the community did not readily blend. The English element seems for some years to have resisted the discipline of Lanfranc. Eadmer has in one sentence described the state of the community in Lanfranc's early years. Those, he says, who know the state to which the monastic order had come, know that the brethren lived the lives of earls rather than monks, 'in all worldly glory, with gold and silver, with changes of fine clothes and delicate food, not to speak of the various kinds of musical instruments in which they delighted, nor of the horses, dogs and hawks with which they sometimes took exercise'.[1] This seems a very crushing indictment of a monastic house, but it is also a puzzling one, for it is hard to reconcile with the loss of lands and buildings. It is even harder at first sight to reconcile with the fact that it relates to a time when Lanfranc had already been archbishop for some years. Some allowance must be made for the exaggerated notions of a boy of fifteen recollected many years later, but we may follow Eadmer to this extent in believing that, whatever may have been the state of discipline before the Conquest, there was a time when Lanfranc with his handful of monks from Bec and Caen had been able to make little impression on a large and unruly body of Englishmen who formed the greater part of the community under his rule.

The two parts of the community faced each other with unconcealed hostility. This was not an uncommon state of affairs. Less than quarter of a mile away, at St. Augustine's, a similarly tense situation was working towards a violent conclusion. But at Christ Church the antipathies of the early years of Lanfranc's rule were peacefully resolved. As Eadmer

---

[1] *Memorials of St. Dunstan*, p. 237–8. William of Malmesbury's colourful account of the state of Canterbury when Lanfranc arrived (*Gesta Pontificum*, p. 70–1) appears to have been worked up from this passage and to have no independent authority. This is an important point since William's account is often used as evidence for the state of the Anglo-Saxon Church. It shows incidentally that William knew Eadmer's *Life of St. Dunstan* before he wrote his own *Life* of the saint, although he never mentions it—a point which puzzled Stubbs (*Memorials of St. Dunstan*, p. lxix).

saw it, the turning point came in 1076, when Lanfranc was pressing on with the building of the new church and had recently appointed Henry, one of his own Italian countrymen from Bec, as prior. At this moment an English member of the community went mad. The horrible sufferings and uproar which resulted are fully described by both Osbern and Eadmer, but it was Eadmer with his keen eye for significant detail and his strong historical sense who noted two points omitted by Osbern. He observed that, as the monks stood round the sufferer, some spoke French which the Englishmen could not understand, and also that the shock of this event caused a change of heart among the Englishmen, and a putting away of the irregularities which had hitherto been practised. After this things went more smoothly.[1] The new church was finished in the following year, and the completion of the conventual buildings must have brought a more stable and orderly life. But the division between the two parts of the community unable to speak each other's language cannot have been quickly healed.

*Osbern and the Canterbury Saints*

Among the Englishmen of mature age in the community, the most talented and probably one of the most recalcitrant was Osbern. Early in his episcopate Lanfranc seems to have found it necessary as a disciplinary measure to send him away to Bec. Here he came under Anselm's influence and flourished, growing, as Anselm reported, venerably fat, and increasing in knowledge and serenity of mind.[2] In return, it was perhaps from Osbern that Anselm first heard of a *Life* of St. Dunstan and the *Regularis Concordia*, for in the letter in which he described Osbern's progress he asked for copies of these works to be sent to Bec. After about two years Osbern returned to Canterbury and no more is heard of his past perversity.[3] He became an important man, not only as a writer, but still more as a symptom. He was the first Englishman to turn his mind to the task of reviving the old English past.

In doing this he was not moved by any abstract interest in

---

[1] *Memorials of St. Dunstan*, pp. 149–51, 234–8.
[2] Ep. 39 [i, 31].     [3] Epp. 66, 67 [i, 57–8].

history, but by the strong motive of local need. Like every other great and ancient English church, Christ Church Canterbury was rich in the relics of native saints, but poor in writings about them. From this state of affairs there followed a large part of the contempt in which these saints were held by the Norman conquerors. Not only did the saints have uncouth names and enjoy an apparently exaggerated local veneration, but for many of them there was nothing beyond vague tradition to testify to their activity or even existence. When Lanfranc questioned the sanctity of Archbishop Elphege, there were only the *verba Anglorum* describing events already two generations distant to set against his scepticism. Even when biographies existed they were unsatisfactory both as record and as literature. St. Dunstan was the only Canterbury saint of pre-Conquest times who had a contemporary biographer, and in writing about the materials for his life Osbern denounced the whole range of pre-Conquest Canterbury biography:

Of those whose business it was to pay attention to these matters, some wrote quite elegantly but without sufficient diligence, supplying simply what they judged necessary for instruction at Matins on the Feast day; others wrote with greater diligence and tried to set forth events as they had happened, but they lost all elegance and fell into that style of writing which the prince of Roman eloquence calls 'puffed up', a style which brings more tedium to the reader than profit to the listener. The writings of those who strove both to write with style and to arrange their material well were consumed in the fire, which some years ago is known to have brought such great loss to the church at Canterbury.[1]

What was true of St. Dunstan was true in still greater measure of every other English saint later than the time of Bede. The Canterbury case was not peculiar, but the dignity of the church and its wealth of English relics made it specially irksome that there should be either no written memorial or an unsatisfactory one.

We might well ask why the Anglo-Saxon Church, which had been so free in its acclamation of native saints and so careful

[1] *Memorials of St. Dunstan*, 69–70. The reference to the 'prince of Roman eloquence' is to Cicero (*Ad Herennium* iv, 10, 15). I owe this reference to Professor R. A. B. Mynors.

of their relics, should have been so indifferent to literary testimony. Probably it looked on the living testimony of miracles as the only essential evidence. But, whatever the cause, the conditions introduced by the Conquest made this indifference no longer supportable. Hence there arose in the great abbeys all over England a school of writers who made it their aim to repair the consequences of neglect as best they could. In this, Christ Church Canterbury was among the first, and Osbern's biography of St. Elphege, written with Lanfranc's encouragement, was the beginning of post-Conquest Canterbury hagiography.[1]

Osbern's work illustrates the difficulties with which the subject was beset. He did his best, but he was a man of the old school whose talent lay in music and not in writing or history. He wrote two works on St. Elphege. The first, which is lost, was probably nothing more than a long hymn, recounting the main facts of his life, for use at Matins on the anniversary of his death. Later, he eked out his few facts with a great deal of imaginary discourse and rhetorical elaboration and a little unwritten tradition to form a prose *Life* of the saint. The one thing which he makes clear is that almost nothing was known about Elphege at Canterbury except that he had been murdered by the Danes. Lanfranc was right in thinking that there was no historical evidence that Elphege was strictly speaking a martyr.

Lanfranc's scepticism did not extend to St. Dunstan, and he is reported by Osbern to have experienced the power of Dunstan's aid on more than one occasion. His liturgical arrangements, however, tell a rather different story. They indicate an abrupt fall in the esteem in which the saint was held.[2] It was probably late in Lanfranc's pontificate, or after his death, that Osbern wrote his *Life of St. Dunstan*. This is a

[1] *Anglia Sacra*, ii, 122; cf. *VA* i, xxx.
[2] In the Constitutions of Lanfranc for Canterbury there is no mention of the Feast of St. Dunstan, even among the Feasts of the third rank, although those of St. Elphege and St. Gregory are among the Feasts of the second rank (pp. 59–60, 67). This neglect of St. Dunstan in the time of Lanfranc, and likewise his rapid rise from the time of Anselm onwards, are borne out by the earliest post-Conquest calendars of Christ Church, MSS. British Museum, Arundel 155 and Bodleian Add. c.260. For the whole process, see E. Bishop and A. Gasquet, *The Bosworth Psalter*, 1908, pp. 32–3, 63–4. One further indication of St. Dunstan's rise in reputation at this time may

much more important and successful effort than his work on St. Elphege. He applied to Dunstan the same amplifying techniques which he had found useful with Elphege, but he had two almost contemporary biographies to draw on and a wealth of oral tradition. By uniting them Osbern made a lively and dramatic portrait, and wrote a work which was full of sentiment and warmth. In his account of Dunstan's cell at Glastonbury he showed a quality which Eadmer was later to develop still more fully: the quality of expressing his feelings naturally and vividly. He had seen the remains of the little building and he gives an estimate of its size. What Osbern saw, he saw with emotion. He marvelled at the smallness of the cell; he handled the works of Dunstan's own hands; and he wept copious tears while he did so, 'for I remembered how often he had heard me when I called upon him in danger, and how mercifully he had helped me; and therefore I neither wished to restrain my tears nor to leave the spot'.[1] Osbern was soon, by better historians, to be much criticized for his inaccuracies; but in temper his work set a fashion in remodelling old materials in a demonstrative and ornate way, and it easily out-distanced in popularity the works which set out to supersede it. His critics failed to drive him from the field.

Osbern disappears from view after 1093. By this date, he had outlived his youthful truculence and become an important member of the community. Yet he seems to have retained something of the habit of a rebel. This is shown in a small incident recounted by Eadmer, which happened between 1089 and 1093, during the vacancy in the archbishopric:

After the death of Lanfranc, while I was sitting one day in the cloister as usual, engaged on a book which I was writing, that most famous of precentors Osbern came to me, and sitting down he began to say, 'You know, brother, how father Lanfranc of happy memory

be seen in the new Choir as enlarged by Anselm and his priors Ernulf and Conrad: the altars of Dunstan and Elphege stood on either side of the high altar and the community bowed to them in turn as they entered the Choir; and over the high altar was a beam on which stood the figures of Christ in majesty, flanked by these same two saints. (See *The Historical Works of Gervase of Canterbury, RS*, i, 13; D. Knowles, *The Monastic Constitutions of Lanfranc*, p. 140.)  [1] *Memorials of St. Dunstan*, 83–4.

ordered and allowed us to look into the shrines and reliquaries of this church to find out what relics were contained in them. This we did, but only in part. For while we were carrying out his orders, we came on one reliquary bigger and apparently more precious than the rest. When we opened it, we found it entirely full, and we took fright and left it untouched. Now, in case we never find out what it contains (though I have a suspicion what it is), let us two go together and take the sacrists with us, and make a careful examination of the contents of the coffer.' I agreed, and without consulting the prior, we went together to the place.[1]

Eadmer later had some scruples about his part in this expedition, but they did not concern the clandestine nature of the proceedings. The four Englishmen who took part in the search were engaged on a work which in principle required no excuse and no authorization from the foreign prior.

*English Survivals*

The English part of the community did not finally disappear as a distinct element until the middle of the twelfth century. It expressed itself in various ways, not least in a small handful of post-Conquest manuscripts which, in contrast to the new collection of which Lanfranc was the founder, preserved the miscellaneous interests and even something of the physical appearance of the pre-Conquest books. Such a volume as the Cottonian manuscript, Caligula A. xv, with its miscellany of chronological data, charms, and annals, is entirely in the old tradition. It was being written in a characteristic mixture of English and Latin in Lanfranc's early years as archbishop. The annals in this manuscript were continued in English till the death of Anselm, when they changed to Latin. They are some of the latest Old English compositions at Christ Church, though a continuing interest in the language is proved by the existence of two twelfth century copies of the pre-Conquest translation of the Gospels.[2] Throughout the first half of the twelfth

---

[1] Eadmer, *De reliquiis sancti Audueni*, Wilmart, *Opuscula*, 367–9.

[2] To these should possibly be added two important pieces of translation from Latin into Old English: a translation of a sermon on the text 'Intravit Jesus in castellum', often ascribed to Anselm but really by Archbishop Ralph; and a translation of part of the *Elucidarium* of Honorius Augustodunensis. For these pieces see N. R. Ker, *Catalogue of Manuscripts containing Anglo-Saxon*, pp. 275–6, and the references given there.

century, the vernacular and Latin, the English and Continental streams, were converging. Before they finally merged they found one last expression in a Psalter of about 1145, the work of several hands but known by the name of its chief scribe Eadwine. Artistically, linguistically and intellectually this volume is a unique blend of old and new: its pictures are directly based on a pre-Conquest model, and they preserve, at the moment of becoming petrified into a Romanesque style, something of the life and movement of the Anglo-Saxon tradition; the Latin text is given in three versions—the Roman which had been current in England before the Conquest, the Gallican which displaced it after 1066, and the so-called *Hebraicum*—and each of them has an interlinear translation, the first in Old English, the second in Latin, and the third in French; finally, a marginal gloss contains the Continental learning of the early twelfth century. The manuscript is a monument to the balance of forces in the community half a century after the coming of Anselm.[1]

## (ii) *Anselm*

This, however, is to anticipate. When Anselm arrived at Canterbury in 1093, the division in the community showed no signs of healing. His first letter to the community as archbishop referred to these divisions, to the scandals arising from the refusal of some of its members to be subject to the prior, and to their habit of acting without his consent.[2] The incident of the search for the relics of St. Ouen shows that the letter was not uncalled for. Whether it had any effect is more open to doubt. No archbishop after Lanfranc had much chance of influencing the community directly except in the choice of a prior, and any attempt to interfere was more likely to cause resentment than a willing submission. There were many reasons for this: the archbishop's great position and normal absence was accentuated in Anselm's case by long exiles. Moreover, communities can rarely be reshaped after receiving

---

[1] The manuscript has been reproduced in facsimile by M. R. James, *The Canterbury Psalter*, 1935, and its place in the development of Canterbury illumination is discussed by C. R. Dodwell, *The Canterbury School of Illumination*, pp. 41-7.    [2] Ep. 182 [iii, 29].

their initial impulse until they have experienced a long decline. Of this there was no sign at Canterbury. The community stood, as Lanfranc had made it, firmly in the tradition of an elaborate monastic routine. With this Anselm had no wish to interfere; he never ceased to discourage all rebellion against the accumulation of customs with which the Rule was encrusted. Yet his relations with the community as a whole never became intimate. His letters lack the warmth of feeling which had filled his earliest letters to Canterbury twenty years earlier: this warmth seems now to have been reserved for humbler communities.[1] In his dealings with Canterbury he played the part of a benevolent but distant superior dealing with complaints about the negligence of monastic officials, restraining the over-suspicious severity of the sub-prior, remonstrating with monks who wished to leave the monastery for something vaguely better, defending his own absence, and dealing in a casual way with a variety of business. Anselm's absences seem to have encouraged a sense of frustration and unrest, which he did his best to assuage from a distance by counselling patience and submission.[2] There are no signs of grave disorders; the complaints are those which must arise in any community; but they were not, so far as Anselm's letters show, offset by more than respectable virtues.

In one respect Anselm influenced the community: by leaving it alone. Ten years after Anselm's death, when the tide of criticism was running strongly against Anselm at Canterbury, Eadmer thought it his best praise that he had allowed the monks to manage their own affairs. We can see the results of this in both the internal and external affairs of the house. There is a solitary entry in the English annals of the monastery

---

[1] Such as the small community of English ladies Seit, Edit, Thydit, Lwerun, Dirgit, Godit with their chaplain William (Epp. 230 [iv, 110], 414 [iii, 133]), and the nuns of Shaftesbury (Epp. 183 [iv, 105], 337 [iv, 128], 403 [iii, 125]).

[2] See especially his letter (Ep. 355 [iii, 108]) to the monks Farman, Ordwy and Benjamin. His attitude towards unrest in the monastic community had long ago been defined in a letter to Lanzo, later prior of Lewes (Ep. 37 [i, 29]), to which he referred one of his Canterbury correspondents (Ep. 335 [iii, 103]) with the injunction: 'Consuetudines nostri ordinis quem es ingressus, quasi a Deo constitutas studiose serva, quia nulla inutilis est, nulla supervacua.'

between 1100 and 1109 to the effect that in 1105 the body of St. Elphege was inspected and found to be incorrupt. The writer appears to have been about to give further details when he breaks off and leaves his annal unfinished.[1] Anselm was at this time in exile, but he had recently given the prior permission to make changes in the liturgical observances of the church as he thought best:

As for the celebration of those Feasts about which you have asked me (he wrote in 1104) I leave them to your disposition, and whatever you arrange, I confirm. Likewise with regard to the octave of the Nativity of St. Mary, the Mother of God, which many of the brethren wish to observe because it is kept in other churches, do as seems best to you.[2]

With this freedom, much could happen which would have been impossible under Lanfranc; and it is probable that we are here at the beginning of the process of restoration of old customs, and the adding of new ones, which in a brief space of time greatly altered the liturgical arrangements laid down by Lanfranc. The community increasingly took charge of its own affairs and felt its corporate identity. Anselm's struggles, like those of Archbishop Thomas Becket after him, only remotely affected it. It was borne along on a buoyant prosperity which, while it may have contributed to the dissatisfactions and distractions felt by the few, drew most of its members together in a sense of their importance and independence, and hastened the disappearance of earlier divisions. The number of monks increased. According to Eadmer there were over sixty about half way through Lanfranc's pontificate, and a high proportion of them must have been Englishmen of the old foundation. By the end of Lanfranc's life the number is given by a later domestic chronicler as a hundred, and it was still rising.[3] Probably it had reached its maximum by about 1120.

[1] F. Liebermann, *Ungedruckte Anglo-Normannische Geschichtsquellen*, 1879, p. 5.                     [2] Ep. 331 [iv, 41].
[3] The number of monks and the evidence is given in D. Knowles, *The Monastic Order in England*, 1940, p. 714.

## 3. THE GROWTH IN PROSPERITY

### (i) *Income*

There was a solid foundation for the increase in numbers. One of the results which Eadmer traced to the freedom enjoyed by the monks under Anselm was a great increase in their wealth. How this freedom and prosperity were related we cannot tell, but both Domesday Book and its local equivalent at Canterbury are eloquent witnesses to the economic opportunities of the community. They show that the community survived the Conquest with its fortune intact. It had lost one fortune in the ninth century and had built up another during the century before the Conquest. This was not lost: it remained the basis of the material prosperity of the church until the Dissolution. Lanfranc deserves some of the credit for this, but perhaps not so much as he is often given. The earliest account of the famous three-day trial on Penenden Heath, in which Lanfranc argued the rights of Canterbury against Odo of Bayeux and his tenants, makes it clear that the lands in question were only a small proportion of the whole estate.[1] The Conqueror had no intention of allowing the spoliation of the Church, and Domesday Book shows very well the extent of the pre-Conquest benefactions which survived the Conquest. It shows too that there was a system of farming which allowed the community to benefit immediately from the rising value of their land—an advantage which, once lost by landowners, was scarcely ever to be regained.

Domesday Book shows us something, but it does not indicate the full extent of the economic opportunities opening before the community. Expressed in terms of gross income Christ Church appears to come below both Glastonbury and Ely, to which annual incomes of about £830 and £770 respectively are allotted. By contrast the income of Christ Church was only

[1] See the texts printed by J. le Patourel, 'The Reports of the Trial on Penenden Heath' in *Studies in Medieval History presented to F. M. Powicke*, 1948, 21–6.

about £730.[1] But, in the case of Christ Church, this income was entirely free from any obligation to provide military service. Lanfranc had not indeed entirely spared the monastic lands when he created fiefs for the performance of military service, but the main burden of this service fell on his own estates. The total amount of land held by the military tenants was valued at £342, of which only about £115 a year had been diverted from the use of the community, and some of this was returned to it in the course of time.[2]

This was in addition to the £730 already mentioned. Moreover, not only was the community free from the burden of providing military service, it was also free from the obligation of maintaining the dignity of an abbot. In its freedom from this burden Christ Church was in the same position as other cathedral priories, but it had some further advantages. Most of its properties lay in Kent where the value of land had shown a spectacular rise since the Conquest. The lands of the monks and their tenants in Kent, which had been worth only £405 in 1066, were valued at £678 in 1086; and if we trace the process further back the upward swing is even more remarkable. For instance, Orpington, which was bought for £53 in about 1032, was worth £28 a year in 1086; and Godmersham, which cost £48 in about 1036, was worth £30 a year fifty years later.[3]

[1] In the treacherous field of Domesday statistics no one can claim immunity from error. I have made the figure for the monks of Christ Church about £50 higher than Professor Knowles, *The Monastic Order in England* p. 702, who in his turn was about £50 above W. J. Corbett, *Cambridge Medieval History*, v, 509. Unless I am mistaken, they must have omitted some lands in outlying counties which I have included in the total. My figures are: in Kent, £568; in other counties, £165.

[2] In the last year of his life Anselm (Ep. 475) gave back to the community the land at Saltwood and Hythe which Lanfranc had enfeoffed to Hugh de Montfort for the service of four knights. In Domesday Book this estate was valued at £29 6s 4d. (i, 4b; see *Domesday Monachorum*, p. 67, where the statement that the land was held for the service of two knights appears to be an error: cf. p. 105). At an earlier date (Ep. 474) Anselm had returned the estate at Stisted, in Essex, which as the monks could prove ought to belong to them *ad victum*: it was worth £15 a year in 1086. See also *HN* 219–20. In 1188 the community assessed the yearly value of the land which it had given up to the archbishop for the provision of military service at £200, but they may either have been exaggerating or speaking in terms of up-to-date valuation. (*Epistolae Cantuarienses*, RS, p. 225.)

[3] For Orpington, see A. J. Robertson, *Anglo-Saxon Charters*, 1939, p. 170 and *DB*, i, 4b; for Godmersham, Robertson, *op. cit.* p. 174, *DB*, i, 5.

The port of Sandwich, which was worth £15 a year in King
Edward's reign, was rendering £70 and 40,000 eels by 1087,
having risen by £30 a year since 1070, and by a further £10 a
year since 1086.[1] The archbishop's manor of Petham, which
Anselm made over to the community in 1096, provides another
striking example of rising values: it had been worth £17 6s. 3d.
a year before 1066; it was assessed at £20 a year in 1086; and
when the community took it over ten years later its actual
annual value was £30.[2] Most of these increases were probably
due not to increased productivity but to more exacting methods
of management. They could not therefore go on indefinitely,
and there were signs that the process was reaching its limit
about 1090. Nevertheless it must have given a great impetus
to the plans and ambitions of the community.

Nor was this all. The values which are mentioned in
Domesday Book refer only to the main 'farms' or rents. They
do not take account of miscellaneous payments which we know
from a chance survival to have been very considerable.[3] Nor
do these values take account of churches, tithes, ecclesiastical
dues, or offerings in the cathedral church itself. Taking everything into consideration, it would seem not unreasonable to
credit the community with an annual revenue of about £1,000
a year to be spent on its own purposes.[4] When it is considered

---

[1] This information comes from the *Domesday Monachorum* p. 89. As
to the date of this survey, I accept Professor Douglas's suggestion that the
information about Sandwich refers to the year 1087 (p. 23 of his edition).
To the reasons which he gives should be added the argument that elsewhere
in the survey (p. 100) Odo bishop of Bayeux, who was exiled in 1088, is
described as still in possession of Folkestone.

[2] *DB* i, 3b; *HN* 75.

[3] The *Domesday Monachorum*, p. 98–9, gives, for the archbishop's lands
alone, the income received in addition to the Farm in the form of *Gablum*
and *Constumes*. They represent an addition of about 16 per cent to the
Domesday figures.

[4] £1,000 a year was almost exactly the income of the priory at the end of
the twelfth century excluding the receipts from the tomb of St. Thomas. See
C. E. Woodruff, 'The Financial Aspect of the Cult of St. Thomas of Canterbury', *Archaeologia Cantiana*, xliv, 1932, p. 16, where the average annual
income for the years 1198–1213 is given as £1,406; of this total income
offerings were £426, of which £349 was directly attributable to St. Thomas.
The total income, however, was probably unusually low during these years,
which are the first for which we have exact figures, since it jumped to an
average of £2,604 in the decade 1213–22 (*op. cit.* p. 19). For further

that the maximum incomes from the lands of the greatest tenants outside the royal family did not exceed £1,750 a year, from which knights and castles and the whole panoply of secular power had to be supported, the prosperity of the community will be seen in its true light.

## (ii) *Expenditure*

Almost the whole of the income which can be accounted for was allocated to two purposes—food and clothing. This division was already ancient at the end of the eleventh century, but it is probable that the organization of these departments under the cellarer and chamberlain respectively was the work of Lanfranc.[1] Each of these officials managed estates and administered revenues which could have supported a considerable baronial family: the cellarer was credited with lands worth £465 a year for the provision of food and drink, and the chamberlain with £235 for the provision of garments, bedding and other necessaries. Above these officials in dignity was the sacrist, charged with the task of maintaining the ornaments and furnishings of the church, and provided with revenues for this purpose. The extent and nature of these revenues is difficult to define. The only land in Domesday Book which is credited to the sacrist was worth £2 13s. a year, and this seems to have been an innovation. Another estate for the provision of a light before the high altar was attached to the sacristy shortly after this time, and King Stephen gave an estate, also annexed to the sacristy, for a light before the tomb of St. Anselm.[2] But it is quite clear that the sacrist's functions required a substantial

figures see R. A. L. Smith, 'The Central Financial System of Christ Church, Canterbury, 1186–1512', *EHR*, lv, 1940, 353–69. Despite the admirable pioneering work of these scholars, of which R. A. L. Smith's *Canterbury Cathedral Priory*, 1943, is the chief monument, and despite the abundance of materials, the financial history of the priory still presents many at present unsolved puzzles.

[1] B. W. Kissan, 'Lanfranc's alleged division of Lands between Archbishop and Community,' *EHR*, liv, 1939, 285–93. The ancient division can be traced in many of the Christ Church documents printed in A. J. Robertson, *Anglo-Saxon Charters* (see nos. LXXXVI, LXXXVIII, LXXXIX, XCI), and can be studied in detail in Domesday Book.

[2] A. Saltman, *Theobald Archbishop of Canterbury*, 1956, p. 269. For Stephen's grant, see below p. 337.

income, and a papal document of 1179 shows that these came in the main from 'spiritualities'—from tithes and offerings—and therefore do not appear in Domesday Book: a further indication that Domesday Book tells much less than the full story of the community's revenue.

These very large revenues were spent in ways of which we have now no detailed record, and it is impossible to say whether or how far they contributed to purposes beyond the sphere to which they were primarily allocated. The two major works which have left traces to the present day stand outside the orbit of the three main offices with their independent incomes. These works are the new buildings and the library.

*Buildings*

Of the new building of Anselm's time only fragments remain, but they are enough to give a significant indication of their inspiration. By 1077 Lanfranc had completed the building of the new church at Canterbury on the model of that at St. Stephen's, Caen, with its notably short and stubby choir, which the increasing number of monks made inconveniently small. Probably, however, it was something more than inconvenience which caused the choir to be demolished in Anselm's day and replaced by a structure in proportions and plan unlike any other in England at the time. In 1099 Anselm and his companions in exile visited Cluny, where they saw the recently completed abbey church which had been dedicated by Urban II in 1095. Both in generosity of plan and decoration this building was a landmark in the development of monastic architecture in Europe. The Canterbury work, begun under Anselm and only completed in 1130, was on a smaller scale, but it was inspired by Cluny and must be reckoned one of the results of Anselm's exile.[1] The decoration of the new choir was sufficiently lavish to challenge comparison with Cluny: 'the like of it (says William of Malmesbury) was not to be seen

[1] The chief feature introduced into Canterbury from Cluny was the double transept, in the plan of which there is a remarkable similarity between the two buildings. See A. W. Clapham, *English Romanesque Architecture after the Conquest*, 1934, pp. 71, 74.

in England in the lights of its windows, the splendour of its marble pavements or the diversity of its paintings'.[1] Into this work the two priors Ernulf and Conrad, successively appointed by Anselm, threw their chief energies, and the necrology of Canterbury describes the ornaments which Conrad and his sacrists added to Ernulf's uncompleted work: they include five large bells which required the labours of 63 men to ring, and a cope woven with gold thread, with 140 little silver-gilt bells interspersed with precious stones.[2] This single vestment cost £100. However cautiously we attempt to equate this with the value of modern money we must reach a sum well over £10,000. Canterbury was certainly not moving in the direction of Cîteaux in Anselm's time, and it is difficult now to imagine the splendour which the vast incrustation of ornaments must have presented to the eye by the time the church was complete. Here, as in his support for the elaboration of monastic customs, Anselm's conservatism contrasts with the new intimacy of his own devotional writings. There is, of course, no formal contradiction here; but the difference illustrates Anselm's poise between the old and the new, between Cluny and Cîteaux. It is not the poise of compromise, but of standing where extremes meet, and of embracing both.

It would be a grave mistake to suppose that what was achieved by this large outlay in building and decoration was a mere architectural or ornamental extravagance. Architectural and artistic forms are more easily studied than the changing devotional and intellectual needs which they existed to serve; stone and parchment have survived when the will which formed them has perished. Hence external appearances and technical changes are always likely to get more than their fair share of attention. But the chroniclers at Canterbury have left us in no doubt that this was all subsidiary to the main design. Eadmer

---

[1] *Gesta Pontificum*, p. 138.
[2] *Anglia Sacra* i, 137, printed from British Museum MS. Cotton Nero C. ix. In the entry relating to Conrad, the bells are described as follows: 'quinque signa permaxima, quorum primum x, similiter secundum x, tertium xi, quartum viii, quintum vero xxiv homines ad sonandum trahunt. Veruntamen quintum signum venerabilis Prior Ernulfus primitus fecerat, sed postmodum fractum magnus Conradus refundendo magno sumptu expenso renovari fecit.'

and his successor Gervase have preserved a great deal of material for understanding the changes in the appearance of the church during the century and a quarter after the Conquest. Despite the interest of their architectural information, they were not primarily interested in external appearance: 'it was not my plan (wrote Gervase) to describe the disposition of stones: but I do so here because I cannot fully explain the arrangement of the bodies of the saints in different parts of the church, unless, with the help of Eadmer who saw and wrote of these things, I first describe the places where they lay'.[1] It was this, not architectural change, which interested the community and its historians.

Eadmer described the pre-Conquest church because he wanted to fix in the minds of his listeners the places where the saints had lain. The general layout was quite simple.[2] The main saints—Dunstan, Wilfrid, Elphege, Oda—were grouped within quite a small space at the east end of the church; and in the baptistery, which formed a separate building to the east of the church, were the bodies of the other archbishops since the eighth century, and the ancient archives of the church.[3] The baptistery was a very significant part of the whole arrangement. Architecturally it looked back to the early days of Roman influence in Christian England. It had been built in the middle years of the eighth century no doubt on the model of Italian buildings such as those which Wilfrid had followed at York. Already in the eleventh century it was a venerable piece of antiquity, and it played a vital part in the life of the community. It was here that the small boys of the community

[1] *The Historical Works of Gervase of Canterbury*, ed. W. Stubbs, RS, i, 12.
[2] In the outline of the building I have followed with a few modifications the plan given by R. Willis, *The Architectural History of Canterbury Cathedral*, 1845, p. 27. This beautiful and excellent book deserves to be better known. For the internal arrangements of the church the main authority is Eadmer *De Reliquiis sancti Audoeni et quorundam aliorum sanctorum quae Cantuariae in aecclesia domini Salvatoris habentur*, Wilmart *Opuscula*, p. 365–6; also *Vita Sancti Bregwini*, PL CLIX, 755; and for the suggested position of St. Elphege, Osbern's *Historia de Translatione corporis S. Elphegi*, in *Anglia Sacra*, ii, 143–7. Sir William St. John Hope, 'The plan and arrangement of the first cathedral church of Canterbury', *Proceedings of the Society of Antiquaries*, xxx, 1917–18, 136–58, differs widely from Willis in some particulars, but these do not affect the main points of internal arrangement with which we are concerned.          [3] *PL* CLIX, 755, 758.

found refuge from the severity of their masters; here—and especially at the tomb of Archbishop Bregwine—miracles were expected. Miraculous too, though in a rather different sense, were the judgments by ordeal, which, in the presence of the silent witnesses in the tombs, took place in this building. With its sanctified water in a receptacle capacious enough to hold the body of an accused person, it was a place ideally suited to inspire awe; and it could be converted from its sacramental to its judicial function with the minimum of disturbance.[1]

Miracles, baptisms, ordeals, burials—and finally archives. It was here that the archives were kept; and this too reflects the awe with which the ancient privileges of the church were regarded: they were a sacred deposit, not simply the by-products of a busy administration.[2] The main church also testified to a similar confusion of natural and supernatural, which was characteristic of the old order. Of the two porches, that on the north was used for the instruction of novices; on the south, as Eadmer notes, was that porch

which in ancient times and till our own day was called the *Suthdure*. It is often mentioned in the laws of the ancient kings by this name. Here, as if to the court of the Supreme King, came all the pleas of the whole kingdom, which could not be settled in one or even in many sessions of the hundred and county courts, or even in the king's court.[3]

In all this confusion there was something barbaric which Lanfranc desired to suppress. His instinct for order was the strongest of all his characteristics, and it is apparent in everything he did. We can be sure, from what we know of their architectural outline, that this instinct expressed itself in his buildings. Of the internal arrangements of his church we can

[1] Cuthbertus ... hanc ecclesiam (i.e. the baptistery) eo respectu fabricavit ut baptisteria et examinationes judiciorum pro diversis causis constitutorum, quae ad correctionem sceleratorum in ecclesia Dei fieri solent, inibi cele-brarentur, et archiepiscoporum corpora in ea sepelirentur (Eadmer, *Vita S. Bregwini*, PL CLIX, 755).

[2] *Ibid.* col. 758.

[3] Wilmart, *Opuscula* p. 366. Eadmer's remark remains somewhat mysterious since no mention of the South Door of Christ Church is to be found in any surviving laws; but there is no reason on this account to doubt his general description of its use for judicial purposes.

# I. THE PRE-CONQUEST CHURCH

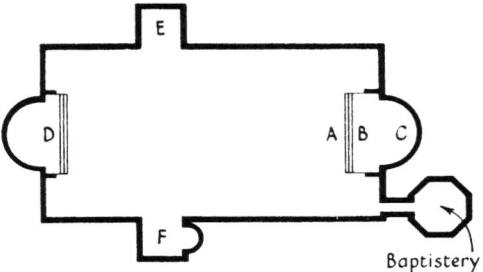

Baptistery

## ALTARS WITH THE BODIES OF SAINTS AND ARCHBISHOPS ASSOCIATED WITH THEM

| Main Church | | Crypt | |
|---|---|---|---|
| *Altars* | *Relics and tombs* | *Altars* | *Relics* |
| A. Matutinal altar | St. Dunstan | | |
| B. Altar of Christ | Head of St. Swithin and other relics; Abps. Elphege and Oda nearby. | | |
| C. High Altar | St. Wilfrid | C. Altar | Head of St. Fursius |
| D. St. Mary | St. Austroberta | | |
| E. St. Martin | | | |
| F. St. Gregory | | | |

BAPTISTERY: Here were the bodies of the Abps. from Cuthbert (740–60) onwards, with a few exceptions, of whom Oda, Elphege and Dunstan, who lay in the main church, were the chief. The precise site and shape of the building are conjectural.

# II. LANFRANC'S CHURCH

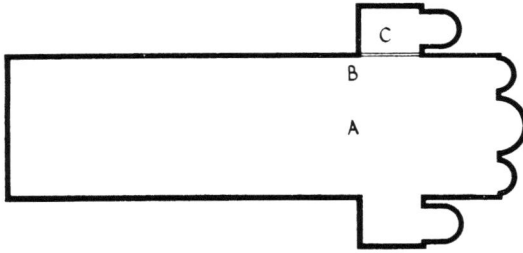

(The information about the arrangement of Lanfranc's church is very imperfect)

A. Altar of Holy Cross (over it, Lanfranc's Rood with figures of St. Mary and St. John; before it, the first burial places of Abps. Lanfranc and Anselm).
B. Altar of St. Mary.
C. Gallery with bodies of earlier archbishops.

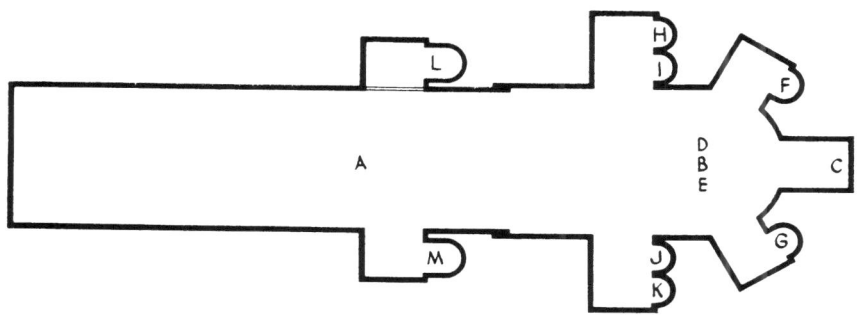

ALTARS WITH THE BODIES OF SAINTS AND ARCHBISHOPS AT THE TIME OF THE CONSECRATION IN 1130

| Main Church | | Crypt | |
|---|---|---|---|
| *Altars* | *Relics and Tombs* | *Altars* | *Relics and Tombs* |
| A. Holy Cross (Lanfranc's Rood) | | | |
| B. High Altar (over it, a beam with figures of Christ in Glory flanked by St. Dunstan and St. Elphege, and seven boxes of relics) | | B. St. Mary | |
| C. Holy Trinity | St. Wilfrid; Abps. Oda, Lanfranc[1] and Anselm[1] | C. 1. St. Augustine 2. St. John Baptist | Abp. Ethelred Abp. Eadsig |
| D. St. Elphege | St. Elphege | | |
| E. St. Dunstan | St. Dunstan | | |
| F. St. Andrew | | F. Holy Innocents | |
| G. SS. Peter and Paul (later St. Anselm) | | G. Archangel Gabriel | |
| H. St. Martin | Abps. Wilfrid and Living | H. St. Mary Magdalen | |
| I. St. Stephen | Abps. Ethelherd and Cuthbert | I. St. Nicholas | |
| J. St. John Evangelist | Abps. Ethelgar and Aelfric | J. St. Paulinus | Abp. Sigeric |
| K. St. Gregory | Abps. Bregwine[2] and Plegmund[2] | K. 1. St. Ouen 2. St. Catherine | |
| L. (*above*) St. Blaise (*below*) St. Benedict | Abps. Ethelhelm, Ethelnoth, Wulfhelm, Ceolnoth, Ralph | | |
| M. (*above*) All Saints (*below*) St. Michael | St. Siburgis and Abp. Feologild | | |

*Notes*
[1] Translated to this place before 1125.
[2] Translated to this place in 1123.

say little: nothing now remains of it, and its most important part had already been demolished when Eadmer wrote his description of the older building. He had no reason to describe it. Liturgically it probably represented no great advance on what had existed earlier. The bodies of the archbishops were cleared out of the baptistery which was swept away. Lanfranc gave a large part of their remains to his new priory of St. Gregory outside the North Gate of the city;[1] the remainder were placed in a gallery in the north transept of the new church.[2] There were many other alterations: the choir was more distinctly separated from the nave than before, though it remained small; the 'porches' were replaced by apsidal transepts; the Lady Chapel was moved from the west end to the north aisle of the nave. The changes gave the church a more modern appearance, and stripped it of much that was cherished in Eadmer's memory. Dignity, solidity, order, severity and simplicity were no doubt the marks of the new building; but they expressed no new idea, no new devotion.

The same cannot be said of the new choir begun under Anselm and his priors, and dedicated in 1130. This building, which was destroyed by fire in 1174, lives in the pages of the monk Gervase.[3] A vastly greater spaciousness and articulation replaced both the primitive confusion of the old church and the cramping simplicity of Lanfranc's design. The treasures of the church were now laid out with methodical care and a lavish use of space. In an important sense the expansion also made room for a more generous recognition of the community's past. In the completed scheme, the altars of St. Dunstan and St. Elphege were at either side of the high altar, and their effigies stood above their altars on either side of the Christ in Glory. Distributed among the surrounding chapels

---

[1] In his foundation charter Lanfranc gave to St. Gregory's 'plurimam partem de reliquiis sanctorum pontificum qui ante nos ecclesie Christi prefuere'. (*Cartulary of the Priory of St. Gregory*, ed. A. M. Woodcock, Camden Society 3rd Series, lxxxviii, 1956, p. 1.)

[2] *PL* CLIX, 758.

[3] *Historical Works of Gervase of Canterbury*, i, 9–16. Some of the details described by Gervase are later than the Dedication in 1130 (such as the Translation of St. Anselm himself to the chapel named after him), but the general arrangement must go back to the completion of the new choir. For the plan, see R. Willis, *op. cit.* p. 38, and the explanations which he gives.

were the bodies of the archbishops, which Lanfranc had huddled together in a gallery or given away. The ancient relics of the church had never been set out so advantageously, and the church had never so eloquently expressed the union of the community with its earthly past and its heavenly future. In an age of abundant symbolism it is not fanciful to see in the arrangement of the bodies of the saints, and especially in the high altar flanked by the altars and effigies of St. Dunstan and St. Elphege, the final union of the Anglo-Saxon past and the Norman present. The additions to the Canterbury Calendar which belong to the time of Anselm and his immediate successors are closely related to the arrangement of the new church: most conspicuously the Feasts of St. Dunstan and St. Elphege grew in importance until they were the equals of St. Gregory.[1] The new Feasts influenced the lay-out of the new building, and together they illustrate the most prosperous and confident phase of English Benedictine history.

*The Library*

At a humbler level, the additions to the library proved the most lasting, as they are now the most significant, of all the enlargements made at this time. Unfortunately the chronology of the manuscripts is not yet sufficiently well established to make it possible to distinguish the additions made in Lanfranc's time from those of the succeeding generation, but by the time of Eadmer's death Canterbury must have had a larger and finer library than any which had been seen in England since the Danish invasions of the ninth century. In every way the books of the new library are distinguished from those of the old: they are larger, more handsome, more stately; they are models of accuracy and careful calligraphy even down to the smallest details of punctuation; above all they are the product of a comprehensive and single-minded plan. They embody the ideal of an intellectually well-organized church consciously reproving the casual and miscellaneous interests of the pre-Conquest community: they are the best testimony to the

---

[1] Among the twelfth century additions to the calendar in MS. Arundel 155 are: May 25, Octave of St. Dunstan; June 8, Translation of St. Elphege; June 15, Octave of St. Elphege; Oct. 21, Ordination of St. Dunstan; Nov. 16, Ordination of St. Elphege.

intellectual revolution effected by the Conquest. With no other resources, it would be possible from these books alone to get a fair idea of the intellectual achievement of the Latin Church in the pre-scholastic age. The community at Canterbury was only one—though probably the most influential—of many communities which equipped themselves in this way at about the same time. A great similarity of contents and marginal annotation characterizes volumes from Exeter, Durham, Bury St. Edmunds, Rochester, St. Augustine's and Christ Church Canterbury, and it is difficult to know in any particular case from which house the original exemplar came.[1] A great deal of detailed work will be required before the connexions of most of these manuscripts can be established, but there are good reasons for thinking that in many cases the impulse came from Canterbury. These manuscripts attained a level of beauty and legibility which was never surpassed and not long maintained. Even if the community had produced no works of original scholarship—and it did not produce many—the manuscripts alone would testify to a high level, not of achievement, but of intellectual aspiration. They are the best evidence of the mind of the monastery in these years. The community was rich, prosperous and assured of its position in the world. The annoyances, injustices and setbacks from which it suffered seem small in retrospect, greatly though they preyed on the minds of its members at the time. When nearly everything else of the period has disappeared, the stately rows of manuscripts still remain to tell the story of wealth and respectability. It is true, however, that the vivid, elaborate and beautifully executed pictures with which many of the manuscripts are adorned sometimes tell another story. Here men and animals gripe at one another's throats, struggling, stabbing, biting, fighting in the midst of an entanglement of luxuriant growth and serpentine spirals; and hybrid creatures half-dog, half-serpent, swallow each other's tails and bite each other's bodies. These images of strife are not easily reconcilable with the calmness and prosperity of the outword appearances.

---

[1] There is now a fund of information available for the study of these manuscripts in N.R. Ker, *English Manuscripts in the century after the Norman Conquest*, 1960.

## 4. THE PRIORS

### (i) *Henry*

Eadmer is the only direct witness to the state of mind and feeling in the community during the first quarter of the twelfth century after Osbern's death, when the activity and prosperity of the house were at their height. The other members of the community scarcely exist, even as names, outside his pages. It does not seem that Prior Henry, whom Lanfranc brought with him from Bec and who went from Canterbury to become abbot of Battle in 1096, had the gifts to inspire a more than conventional respect. He was an Italian of the school of Lanfranc, though he appears not to have worked altogether harmoniously either with him or with the community.[1] He was one of Anselm's early friends at Canterbury, but he did not follow Anselm's advice on the one occasion when it was offered.[2] It is impossible at this distance to determine the rights and wrongs of these clashes, but the difficulties Henry experienced both at Canterbury and Battle were not offset by any counterbalancing attainments.[3]

### (ii) *Ernulf*

His successor Ernulf (1096–1107) was a man of great distinction both in learning and practical achievement. He was a Frenchman who had been a monk of Beauvais, but he had left this monastery with Anselm's approval about 1073, and had settled at Canterbury.[4] He was known, either as a pupil or a fellow-countryman, to Ivo of Chartres, whose interest in canon law he shared. This interest dominated his two surviving

---

[1] For his troubles with Lanfranc, see Anselm, Epp. 63 [i, 54], 73 [i, 64]. For his troubles with the community, Ep. 182 [iii, 29]. The date at which he became prior is not quite clear: probably 1076. (Anselm Ep. 58 [i, 49], written in 1076 or early 1077, is the first letter in which he is given this title.)

[2] Anselm advised him not to go to Italy to defend his sister who had fallen into servitude (Ep. 17 [i, 15]), but he went (Ep. 24 [iv, 123])—perhaps, however, on the business of the monastery.

[3] For his reputation at Battle, see *Chronicon monasterii de Bello*, 1846, p. 44.

[4] Anselm, Epp. 38 [i, 30], 64 [i, 55], 74 [i, 65]; cf. Ivo of Chartres, Ep. 78 (*PL*, clxxii, 100).

treatises, which are concerned with some intricate problems of marriage law and Eucharistic practice.[1] They show no trace of the influence of either Lanfranc or Anselm, though they prove that Ernulf was a travelled and well-read man whose advice was worth having. But his real talents were as an organizer and builder, and in these capacities he adorned the communities which he ruled, whether as prior at Canterbury, as abbot at Peterborough, or as bishop at Rochester. At all these places he showed a gift for introducing order into their affairs and a greater magnificence into their buildings. 'In his days we had all good things, and joy and peace, because King Henry and the magnates loved him and always called him Father', says the Peterborough chronicler.[2] Ernulf is commonly credited with antiquarian tastes and a sympathy for English traditions. Some of the evidence for this is not very satisfactory, but the devotion of the Anglo-Saxon Peterborough chronicler to his memory is striking, and suggests a man of large sympathies and generosity. He can be connected with varying degrees of probability with the continuation of Anglo-Saxon annals at Canterbury and Peterborough, with the great collection of Old English laws in the *Textus Roffensis* at Rochester, and with the beginning of the revival of English devotional practices at Canterbury.[3] Whatever his part in these various manifestations of English activity, he was a man whose arrival all these communities welcomed and whose departure they watched with reluctance.

### (iii) *Conrad*

Conrad, who was prior from 1107 to 1126, is known as a builder and as nothing else. His splendid and ponderous additions to the church have already been mentioned; they were sufficient to earn him a magnificent eulogy in the Canterbury martyrology as a man *sublimiter institutus* in divine and secular learning.[4]

[1] *PL*, CLXIII, 1457–74; D'Achery, *Spicilegium*, iii, 470–4.
[2] *The Chronicle of Hugh Candidus*, ed. W. T. Mellows, 1949, p. 90; *ASC* ann. 1114; *Gesta Pontificum* 138.
[3] See *ASC* for the year 1114 and the notes of C. Plummer, *Two of the Saxon Chronicles Parallel*, ii, liv, n. and 290–1; and F. Liebermann, 'Notes on the Textus Roffensis,' *Archeologia Cantiana*, xxiii, 1896, p. 103.
[4] J. Dart, *History and Antiquities of Canterbury*, 1726, App. p. xxvii.

Like Ernulf he evidently gave general satisfaction to the community which he ruled. At a time when its external dignity as a primatial church suffered its most serious reverse, he raised the community to its highest point of splendour and corporate growth. This was indeed balm to a wounded pride; yet in the history of English monasticism as a whole, it was an ominous sign that a great community should have been so easily dispirited by a political reverse, and so easily satisfied by such a catalogue of bells, carpets and costly vestments as that with which Conrad was credited.

## (iv) *Elmer*

It is noticeable in both Anselm's appointments to the position of prior that he chose men of outstanding practical ability and vigour rather than men of his own kind. He had the good sense to value in others the practical gifts which he himself lacked—as he showed also in his support of Henry I, when theoretical considerations might have led him to support Robert. It was not until 1128 that Canterbury had a prior who was at once an Englishman, a writer of the school of St. Anselm, and a ruler of mild and unforceful habits. This was Elmer, prior from 1128 to 1137.[1] He was remembered as a man of simplicity and peace, who deplored the growing spirit of jealous and aggressive hostility to the encroachments of the archbishops on the community's liberties, which became an endemic and deplorable feature of Canterbury life throughout the second half of the twelfth century. Elmer is a writer who could never have achieved greatness, because, though he says many good things, his flights of originality are too short to make a marked impact on the reader.[2] When he writes at length he becomes

---

[1] For his personal characteristics and the date of his death, see *The Historical Works of Gervase of Canterbury*, ed. Stubbs, *RS*, i, 98, 100.

[2] A small collection of his letters, sermons and meditations has survived. Most of them are printed by Dom J. Leclercq in *Studia Anselmiana,* xxxi, 1953, pp. 62–117. Other pieces are printed among the Meditations of St. Anselm, *PL* CLVIII, 709–22, 809–16. In Cambridge University Library, MS. Ii, 4, 19, f. 31–74, there is a primitive scholastic compilation chiefly from Augustine, Ambrose and Isidore arranged in systematic form and bearing the title *Quidam liber sententialis et sacramentalis: Compilationes Ailmeri.* It may very well be the work of Prior Elmer.

dull. He was sufficiently in touch with the movements of his day to have caught the habit of systematizing; but in doing so he showed the English poverty in theological speculation and fell into the fault of mere accumulation, the permanent temptation of monastic writers.

Yet his letters and meditations have a place in the tradition of spiritual reflection which Anselm introduced into England. When he speaks of his feelings, he speaks with energy and warmth; and he shows himself a pupil of Anselm in his hatred of external activities and distractions of mind, in his love for the pleasant paradise of the cloister, and his desire to forget all transient things; above all in his talent for the sweet communion of souls in spiritual conversation. His expressions of friendship have the same ardent quality found in the early letters of Anselm, and they are alike in expressing an ideal relationship of mutually imagined qualities rather than a personal love: 'my ignorance of your appearance, which I have never seen, does not diminish my love for you, for I believe you are such as I would wish myself to be', Elmer writes to one of his friends in a phrase which catches the remote and ethereal passion of Anselm's own expressions of friendship.[1] Elmer had known Anselm's teaching at first-hand, and he could quote at least one characteristically polished fragment of Anselm's talk which has not come down in any other form: *monachi (inquit) esse est gaudere se suum non esse propter Deum*, 'the essence of a monk is to rejoice that his being is not his own, for the sake of God'.[2] His meditations follow those of Anselm very closely in their attempt to elevate the mind to the perception of God. They lack the concentration of their model, but they sometimes reveal a strange power of imagination. Elmer was a man who desired to be quiet and to forget the passing show: 'I have such a joy in study, in meditation and in writing, that I count a day wasted in which I have not been engaged in these employments'.[3] He found his chief model in St. Gregory and the chief subject for his meditation in the mystical senses of the Bible. His most insistent theme was the need to flee from the 'deadly joys of worldly pleasures' to the wardrobe of the

---

[1] Leclercq, *op. cit.* p. 65.    [2] *Ibid.* p. 84.
[3] Leclercq, *op. cit.* p. 63.

cloister in which the soul could be clothed in the garments of eternity. In a community increasingly concerned with secular affairs, his was a small but refreshing voice, the last of its kind.[1]

By the time that Elmer died, Eadmer was almost certainly already dead, and the community was passing into a state of rigidity. With their deaths the last traces of Anselm's direct influence disappeared, and the last personal links with the pre-Conquest community were broken.

[1] I have abandoned with regret the attribution to Elmer of Meditation I in the edition of Anselm's works (PL 158, 709–22), despite the authority of Dom Wilmart and Dom Leclercq (*Auteurs Spirituels*, 193, 204, 209; Leclercq, *op. cit.* p. 47–8). The only evidence for Elmer's authorship of this remarkable piece is the statement of the sixteenth century bibliographer John Bale (*Index Britanniae Scriptorum*, ed. R. L. Poole and Mary Bateson, 1902, p. 70), who quotes the first four words of the Meditation as the beginning of a work by Elmer. But no manuscript has been found to support this attribution, nor has any manuscript been found earlier than the fourteenth century, if indeed there is any as early as this. In the absence of any manuscript evidence Bale's statement is of very little value.

# CHAPTER VIII

# EADMER'S DEVOTIONAL AND HISTORICAL WORKS

A MONG the Canterbury authors of Anselm's time, Eadmer has—apart from the archbishop himself—an easy pre-eminence. Outside Canterbury, his only possible contemporary English rival, in the range and importance of his writings, is William of Malmesbury. There are many similarities in their background and in their sources of inspiration—both members of famous old English monasteries, both enthusiastic researchers into the history of pre-Conquest monasticism, both extensive historians of their own times, both writers of theological and devotional works. As between these two, judgments will differ. To some, William's wide learning and love of ancient books, his sharp judgments expressed in crabbed and incisive phrases, his curious antiquarianism, and the astonishing precocity which made him by the age of thirty the writer of the most important and original surveys of English history since the time of Bede, will put him in the first place among English writers of the generations after the Conquest. But for those who prefer lucidity to wit, original observation to learning, and a certain naive candour to a strain of sour vindictiveness, Eadmer will appear the better man and the better historian. They are both writers with severe limitations —the limitations, largely, of the monastic environment, which also gave them their opportunities. Eadmer's chief limitation is the extent to which he was willing to suppress or distort the truth in the interests of his community. From this point of view William of Malmesbury appears to have been more of an individualist—his vision extended farther beyond his own immediate experience than did Eadmer's; and when he distorted the truth, it was rather in the interests of a good phrase or a good story, or through mere carelessness, than from any exaggerated devotion to the communal interest. But he had seen less of the world than Eadmer; he had less to communicate; he could never feel himself in the centre of great events or in touch with greatness as Eadmer did.

Eadmer's works are the most complete expression of the life of an English monastic community at this time. From them we can learn, better than from any other source, what range of experience was possible for a sensitive and talented member of a monastery which stood at the centre of affairs in the last age of the undisputed Benedictine supremacy in the religious life. It is important that the historian should bring his judgment to bear on the state of mind and spirit which these works disclose. It is easy to write in glowing terms of the monastic regeneration of this period, of the revival of discipline and learning, of the great and orderly effort of building and administration, of the wealth of literary manuscripts and charters. But of the thoughts and feelings which all this effort made possible, which it brought into existence and subserved, it is more difficult to speak; we are separated from them by a gulf which can now scarcely be bridged. Eadmer's writings provide a bridge. They show what the monks of Canterbury thought important; how they looked on English history, and what place they conceived themselves to have in it; they illustrate the connexion between local activities and some of the main movements of European religious life. Consciously or unconsciously, Eadmer was often, as we shall see, the spokesman for the whole community at Canterbury: he expressed the opinions, the ambitions, the thoughts which filled all their minds and directed their counsels.

He also spoke as a man who had more opportunities for the enlargement of his horizon than any other member of his house. His long intimacy with Anselm, if it could not turn him into a philosopher or a systematic theologian, raised his mind above the interests of his community. He learned from Anselm a new language of devotion, and he was given new objects on which to exercise his historical and biographical gifts. The results of this influence, and the ways in which it reacted on Eadmer's expression of the communal needs of the monastery, will be examined in the following pages. But it may at once be said that the judgment to be passed must often be a severe one. If Eadmer's works were the product of the monastic life in exceptionally favourable circumstances, we must conclude that the religious communities bred men who looked on the preservation of their rights and interests as a primary duty, more important in the last resort than truth; and that relics and wonders, substantiated by the flimsiest of evidence, or no evidence at all, were accorded an importance in the religious life, which is in striking contrast to the intellectual movements outside the monasteries. These were the limitations of the monastic environment, and they are to be seen to some extent in everything that Eadmer wrote. It is impossible to read his works without seeing that the intellectual and spiritual leadership of Europe had slipped from the hands of the black monks, through their devotion to their own past and the narrowness of their loyalties.

Yet there is a surprising charm about institutions and the men they foster at the moment of transition, when, at the height of their worldly fortune and good repute, they no longer have anything to give the world commensurate with their good fortune. Eadmer's works have this charm. He knew what he loved, and he had an unshakeable sense of its importance. Even when the reader feels the fallacy of his confidence, he is drawn by the strong flow of his affections. Eadmer's safety and confidence gave him, as perhaps at a much higher level they helped to give Anselm, an independence and originality of view, except where the interests of the community were involved. With all his intellectual limitations, Eadmer exhibits a refinement of feeling and power of observation, which communal jealousies never obliterated. And, almost by accident, themes which have a lasting importance become mingled with those of local and temporary interest, and Eadmer rises for a moment to greatness. He does not sustain himself long at this height; he sinks back into his more representative rôle, in which he expresses the sentiments and interests of those around him. But it should be added, if we are to do justice to Eadmer, that though Anselm's works show everywhere the evidence of a far superior mind, they also show on careful examination the same background of sympathies and prejudices and jealous regard for local privileges as do Eadmer's. In Eadmer this background is clearer because he has less of his own to add; but Anselm, for the most part silently, but also actively and vocally when necessary, acquiesced in all the themes which take up so large a place in Eadmer's works. Here, as elsewhere, Anselm's part was not to resist or denounce the religious tendencies of his day, but to explain and make them articulate. He would have found very little to take exception to in what Eadmer wrote. Only in two places can we be sure of Anselm's disapprobation, and these were both places where his own influence was most conspicuous. In the first place, in his treatise on the Conception of the Virgin Mary, Eadmer adopted Anselm's theological method but contradicted his views on the subject. Secondly, in completing the *Vita Anselmi*, Eadmer acted in disobedience to Anselm's express command. But for the most part Eadmer's treatises portray the everyday world of Anselm and his monastic friends; they display the common furniture of their minds, and quite apart from the strong influence of Anselm in these works, they have a place in the portrayal of the monastic experience which he shared and helped to form.

There are three distinct strands in Eadmer's writings. The first is made up of works of local hagiography written chiefly in response to the need of the church of Canterbury for a record of its saints and relics; the second consists of what may briefly be called, devotional works; thirdly, there are the two works of contemporary history by which he is now best known —the *Historia novorum in Anglia* and the *Vita Anselmi*. It will be convenient to deal with them separately in this order.

## I. LOCAL HAGIOGRAPHY

### (i) St. Wilfrid

Most of Eadmer's writings are deeply marked by the influence of Anselm, but it was not the association with Anselm which first made Eadmer an author. The needs of the church of Canterbury provided the earlier stimulus, and it was in hagiography that he learnt to be a fluent writer and a historian. His earliest work of any length was his *Life of St. Wilfrid*. He had no new facts about the saint's life, but it is easy to see why his

SAINT ANSELM AND HIS BIOGRAPHER

work was called for. Canterbury had, or claimed to have, the bones of St. Wilfrid, but the claim was disputed. Wilfrid had been buried at Ripon. According to the Canterbury story Archbishop Oda had visited Ripon shortly after the middle of the tenth century, and had removed the saint's body to Canterbury from a church desolated by Danish raids. This tradition was preserved in a tenth century *Life of St. Wilfrid* which was thought to give Oda's own account of this affair;[1] but the situation was complicated by the existence of another account telling how Bishop Oswald of Worcester found the body still at Ripon some thirty years later.[2] It was therefore necessary to establish the Canterbury version in a definitive way, and this was the chief reason for Eadmer's writing. There is a revealing sentence which discloses his approach to such problems: 'It is not permitted to us, who have received these bones, to be troubled by doubts about them.'[3] It would be easy to make this apparently naïve statement seem more ridiculous than it is. He does not mean that he is under orders to believe, but that the whole tradition and experience of the community for a hundred years or more demanded his allegiance. The claim was guaranteed, not indeed by startling miracles, but by strange visions; it was part of a communal inheritance of which he was only the transmitter. The same sense of the smallness of his individual freedom lies behind another remark about an incident introduced without documentary authority: 'I confess that I have nowhere read this, but so many reputable men assert that it happened, that I believe it would be great impudence not to believe it.'[4] The reputable men were doubtless members of the community and the story they told was that Wilfrid had seen a vision of the damnation of the dead King Egfrith of Northumbria. An almost identical story was told at Canterbury of St. Dunstan and King Edwy, and in the chattering atmosphere of Christ Church things doubtless often got

[1] The work was written by Frithegodus at the request of Oda, who supplied a preface which (in the absence of an author's name) gave Eadmer the idea that the whole work was written by Oda. See *Historians of the Church of York*, i, 105–59; the latest edition is by A. Campbell, in the *Bibliotheca scriptorum latinorum mediae et recentioris aetatis*, Zürich, 1950.
[2] *Historians of the Church of York*, i, 462.
[3] *Ibid.* i, 225.    [4] *Ibid.* i, 226.

278

mixed; but this chatter was accorded the status of an intimate spirtual revelation, and it does an injustice to Eadmer's sense of seriousness in reporting it to overlook the reverence with which such talk was commonly received.

It was with an equally uncritical seriousness that he received the accumulation of talk about the rights of Canterbury. The monastic forgeries of this age cannot be understood unless allowance is made for the sanctity of corporate traditions— sometimes, like 'age-old' custom itself, of recent growth— which outweighed all consideration of what we should call facts. The primatial claims of Canterbury are a case in point. In writing a *Life of St. Wilfrid*, these claims presented Eadmer with a delicate problem. He could not write favourably of Wilfrid without admitting that Archbishop Theodore had misused his authority in his arbitrary dealings with the northern dioceses; but he could not write worthily of Canterbury unless he underlined the archbishop's authority over the whole Church in Britain. He satisfied these competing claims with great discretion, though his insistence on the metropolitan rights of Canterbury required some distortion of the contemporary sources. These distortions, as they must now appear, were essential if the views of the community were to be expounded; but, so ingrained is the habit of reading history backwards, that they probably appeared to Eadmer and his contemporaries as no more than necessary explanations and expansions of obscure events. What Eadmer succeeded in producing was a readable *Life* intelligible in the terms of contemporary experience. The old *Life* by Eddius Stephanus was by comparison stiff and remote and indifferent to the claims of Canterbury; the tenth century *Life* in verse had a strong Canterbury bias, but its strange latinity made it barely intelligible. Eadmer could be understood with ease, and he omitted nothing which the most ardent lover of Canterbury could desire.

(ii) *Archbishop Oda*

The chronological succession of Eadmer's hagiographical works is uncertain, but the next *Life* in his own manuscript is that of Archbishop Oda, and it may well be next in time. Oda was a central figure in Eadmer's view of English history. He had enriched the church of Canterbury with the relics of St. Wilfrid and St. Ouen; he was the first English adherent of the new Continental monasticism of the tenth century and the first instigator of the reform movement in England; in Canterbury legend, he first acted on the view, dear to Eadmer, that the archbishop of Canterbury must be a monk; he prepared the way for St. Dunstan and prophetically designated him as his successor; he was the uncle of St. Oswald.[1] From a national as well as a local point of view, these were in Eadmer's eyes facts of the first importance. In the eyes of modern scholars Oda is a dim, though vaguely important, figure; to Eadmer, who was born only a century after Oda's death, he was the founder of his own familiar world. Moreover he was the first distinguishable figure in the old traditions of Canterbury, to which Eadmer had listened in his youth. It was probably to these traditions that he owed the story, which is otherwise unknown, that Oda miraculously repaired the sword of King Athelstan at the battle of Brunanburh, and refused to be archbishop until he had received the monastic habit. A similar tradition related that Dunstan had given him the title 'the Good', by which he was still known in Canterbury in Eadmer's day. These facts gave Oda a claim to veneration at Canterbury which was ill supported by the written evidence.

The only pre-Conquest account of Oda was found in an anonymous *Life of St. Oswald* written by a monk of Ramsey about the year 1000.[2] This and the *Lives* of St. Dunstan provided Eadmer with most of his information, and he had to make what he could of it. It is at once noticeable that, unlike Osbern in a similar situation, he did not take refuge in extensive imaginary oratory; he showed the bent of his mind in other ways, and most significantly in the care he took to construct a plausible historical background. He arranged the succession of kings under whom Oda lived, and distinguished the phases of

---

[1] For these facts and traditions about Archbishop Oda, see Eadmer's *Vita sancti Odonis*, in *Anglia Sacra* ii, 78–87 (*PL* cxxxiii, 933).

[2] *Historians of the Church of York*, i, 399–475. The points at which Eadmer diverged from this work are listed in J. A. Robinson, *St. Oswald and the Church of Worcester*, British Academy Supplemental Paper, v, 1919, pp. 45–51.

his life in relation to their reigns. Most of his conjectures and the alterations he made to his source are certainly wrong; but they are not pointless, and they sometimes do credit to his historical imagination. For instance, he says that Oda learned both Latin and Greek, and he explains this by supposing that disciples of Archbishop Theodore had kept this knowledge alive for three hundred years.[1] Both the fact and the explanation are quite false; but Eadmer probably deduced the fact from the extraordinary Greek-laden latinity of the writing ascribed to Oda, and—being ignorant that the strange words came not from a profound knowledge of Greek but from a glossary—gave them the best historical explanation he could. In this, as in other works, he took great care to make tenth century ecclesiastical procedure correct by contemporary standards: when his source said that a bishop or archbishop was appointed by the king, Eadmer reduced the king's rôle to suggestion or persuasion; he duly stressed the functions of the archbishop and made him, rather than the king, the summoner of ecclesiastical councils. All this is false history, but even his mistakes show that the history of England was for him a living reality. They help us to understand his mind and to see the importance he attached to the idealized picture of the tenth century as the anchor to which his whole view of English history was attached.

## (iii) St. Dunstan

Eadmer's next considerable work was his *Life of St. Dunstan*, the central figure in the old English tradition as seen from Canterbury.[2] If the tenth century gave shape to English history, it was St. Dunstan who gave shape to the tenth century. Moreover the fortunes of the community at Christ Church were in a special degree bound up with the veneration of the saint. Already before 999, within ten years of his death, a remarkable

---

[1] *Anglia Sacra*, ii, 79.
[2] The date of the work cannot be at all exactly determined. It was later than the death of Bishop Wulfstan of Worcester in 1095 (*Memorials of St. Dunstan*, p. 164) and probably before the death of Anselm in 1109 (*ibid.* p. 246). It is clear that Osbern was dead and that Eadmer now felt himself of sufficient authority to correct and criticize his work. A date about 1105–9 seems most likely.

document drawn up by a Canterbury monk recognized him as the chief 'of all the saints who rest at Christ Church'.[1] Nothing had happened since this date to shake his position among those who understood the traditions of the community. Even here, however, the community was involved in one of those vulgar disputes with a sister house about the possession of the saint's relics which disfigured the period: the monks of Glastonbury claimed to have got possession of St. Dunstan's body by fraud, and at a later date Eadmer was concerned to pour scorn on their assertions.[2] This quarrel seems not to have agitated him at the time when he wrote his *Life*, and it is not at first sight very clear what prompted him to embark on this task. Osbern had already collected almost everything that local tradition could tell him about Dunstan, and he had given an account of his life far superior to the earlier biographies in interest and intelligibility. Osbern's account was in fact never superseded in popular esteem in the Middle Ages, but it was sufficiently defective in the eyes of his contemporaries to stimulate both Eadmer and William of Malmesbury independently to try to replace it.[3] Their complaint was that Osbern was inaccurate, but this complaint turns out to be much less far-reaching than might at first sight seem likely. When Eadmer reproached Osbern for inaccuracy, he was not thinking of those additions to the contemporary material which have won Osbern a bad reputation with modern historians—the stories of Dunstan seizing the Devil by the nose, seeing King Edwy's soul being carried off by demons, reproving King Edgar for corrupting a nun, and so on. These were evidently the kind of tales with which the community at Christ Church abounded, and no doubt the extraordinary paucity of written sources encouraged their circulation. Eadmer was entirely at one with Osbern in accepting the gossip of his brethren as true history. The errors which offended Eadmer's critical sense were Osbern's mistakes in ascribing the dedication of Worcester Cathedral in Dunstan's day to St. Mary, in making King Edward the Martyr of illegitimate

[1] King Ethelred's confirmation of Æthelric's Will, 995–9, ed. D. Whitelock, *Anglo-Saxon Wills*, 1930, p. 45.

[2] *Epistola Eadmeri ad Glastonienses (Memorials of St. Dunstan*, 412–24).

[3] All these lives are collected in Stubb's indispensable volume *Memorials of St. Dunstan, RS*, 1874.

birth, and other details of a similar kind, which he quietly altered or suppressed. Yet his story is essentially the same as Osbern's; the greatest improvement is in the style. Eadmer set out to write in every-day speech in contrast to the rhetorical elaboration of Osbern which William of Malmesbury ridiculed, but which Eadmer, who was correcting the work of a revered master, was content to leave to the judgment of others.[1] The change of style however was symptomatic of Eadmer's attempt, already apparent in his *Life of St. Wilfrid* but here much more fully developed, to convey speech and actions with natural ease. This was a talent he developed most fully in writing about Anselm, but it was in writing about St. Dunstan that his mature powers as an author began to be apparent. One of the most attractive features of this *Life* was the way he gave a sense of vivid reality to the inner experiences of the saint: his descriptions of Dunstan being suddenly touched by the sweetness of the psalmody, of his receiving the Devil in human form with his accustomed courtesy, of his loneliness in exile, and a multitude of similar touches, have no parallel in the earlier biographies. They are quite imaginary, but they prepare the way for the genuine intimacy of the *Life of Anselm*.

(iv) *St. Oswald*

The next large work, the *Life and Miracles of St. Oswald*, was not written for the needs of the church of Canterbury but for Eadmer's friends at Worcester.[2] It met, however, a need similar to the works which have just been described, and it belongs to the same class of writings. The only earlier *Life of*

---

[1] *Ibid.* p. 162.

[2] The only certain *terminus post quem* is the death of Bishop Wulfstan in 1095 (*Historians of the Church of York*, ii, 53). But since the work was written at the request of the monks of Worcester (*ibid.* pp. 1, 59), Eadmer must by now have attained a certain degree of fame, and the writing (as also the visit to Worcester mentioned in the work, p. 50) may possibly be connected with the election of Nicholas as prior in 1113. Nicholas was a friend and correspondent of Eadmer and had close connexions with Canterbury (see Knowles, *Monastic Order in England*, p. 160; William of Malmesbury, *Vita Wulfstani*, ed. Darlington, p. xxxviii n.) One of the fires described at the end of Eadmer's work (*ibid.* p. 55–7) may well be the great fire of 19 June 1113 which destroyed the city (*Fl. Wigorn.* ii, 66). On all grounds therefore a date about 1113–15 seems probable.

*St. Oswald* was the anonymous biography which Eadmer had already used for his *Life of Archbishop Oda*. In its wealth of detail this is the most valuable of all the tenth century biographies. But Eadmer is right in saying that it is burdensome to the reader: it is diffuse, often irrelevant, and difficult to understand. Eadmer avoided these faults, and, as always, he gave to past events a contemporary gloss which must have made his narrative acceptable to his friends. The following passage is an illustration of this habit:

About this time (c. 970) St. Dunstan, archbishop of Canterbury and primate of all Britain, with the sanction and authority of Pope John, called a general council and decreed that all canons, priests, deacons and subdeacons should either live chastely or lose their churches together with everything pertaining to them. In this he had King Edgar as a faithful and constant helper and firm defender.[1]

This single sentence contains at least five anachronisms concerning the primacy of Canterbury, the celibacy of the clergy, the relations of pope and archbishop, of archbishop and king, and of king and ecclesiastical council. What it describes is not history but imagination: it is what Eadmer would have liked the present to be. He did what many others since his day have done: he read the present into the past and presented his idealized picture of the past as an object-lesson to contemporaries. The political nuances of the tenth century were quite beyond the reach of Eadmer and his contemporaries; imagination filled the gap. This is not to say that everything for which no earlier documentation can be found is quite worthless as history. At Worcester, as at Canterbury, Eadmer learnt facts about the condition of the community in the late tenth century which there is no reason to doubt, but no reliance can be placed on facts of general history which are not known from earlier sources.

### (v) *Miscellaneous Works*

The *Life of St. Oswald* was the last of Eadmer's hagiographical works of any length. From 1116 to 1121 he was, as we have seen, chiefly occupied in an uneasy struggle for the rights of

---

[1] *Historians of the Church of York*, ii, 20.

Canterbury, and it was only after this that he produced a few small works of local historical interest. His letter to the monks of Glastonbury defending the Canterbury claim to possess the bones of St. Dunstan, although its purpose is polemical, must be reckoned among them. It was not often that Eadmer in his polemics had so good a case, and the letter is a lively and convincing piece of historical argument. It is chiefly interesting for Eadmer's recollection of his own boyhood when he saw the elevation of St. Dunstan's body and the deposed abbot of Glastonbury, Aethelnoth, living at Canterbury with one or two of his monks.[1]

The next work of Eadmer was a brief account of the eighth century Archbishop Bregwine. Eadmer knew nothing of the historical events of Bregwine's pontificate, but it gave him an opportunity to talk about the old church and the burial places of the archbishops in the eighth century baptistery. All this had been destroyed by fire in 1067, and the mention of the fire stirred in the elderly Eadmer a long-standing feeling of bitterness:

A great and never to be ended sorrow presses on our church to this day, for the privileges of the Roman pontiffs, of the kings and rulers of this realm, carefully sealed and presented to this church for the perpetual protection of it and its property, were (in the fire) utterly consumed. Even if copies of them have been found in various places, the bulls and seals were burned with the church in which they were preserved, and cannot be replaced.[2]

This outburst expressed an accumulated sense of injury which had recently been given a sharper edge; for only a few months before it was written, the primatial privileges of Canterbury had been laughed out of court at Rome, and the supremacy over York, with the whole fabric of primacy which had been cherished for fifty years, had in an instant become no more than a shadow.

[1] *Memorials of St. Dunstan*, 413–14, 420.
[2] *PL* CLIX, col. 757–8. The *Life of St. Bregwine* was first printed by Wharton in *Anglia Sacra*, ii, 184 with his customary omission of several miracle stories; the work was thence reprinted in *Acta Sanctorum*, August, v, 830, with the addition of some but not all of the miracles, which still remain in part unprinted. The work was written after January 1123 for it refers to a visit to the royal court at Woodstock after the death of Archbishop Ralph, and this could only have been in January or March 1123 (*ASC*).

There is a similar note of bitterness in a letter which Eadmer wrote at this time to the monks at Worcester begging them to make sure of electing a monk as their new bishop:[1] the times were evil; wicked men were seeking to exclude the monastic order from the bishoprics; worse desecrations were to be expected unless they stood firm. This also was a cry from the heart. For Canterbury, after all its struggles, had in recent months been given an archbishop whose appointment broke a tradition of Benedictine archbishops, which, as the monks of Canterbury liked to believe, went back to St. Augustine. The Worcester election, as it turned out, was to go the same way. Henceforth the community stood alone against the world, and Eadmer returned to his memories and to more personal themes.

The more personal themes will be discussed below. The memories were most fully expressed in a little work on the relics of St. Ouen which is important only as a repository for Eadmer's recollections: 'What as a youth I received from the elders of the mother church of Canterbury, now white-haired myself I bring to the notice of others at the request of my friends.'[2] It was in this mood that he sat down to recall how the relics were brought to Canterbury in the days of King Edgar and Archbishop Oda, how the old church had looked before the fire, how Osbern with the sacrists and Eadmer himself had opened the reliquary after Lanfranc's death at the time when Archdeacon Aschitill died. Passing from one recollection to another he brings his story to the events and miracles of his own day. At this distance of time, the cures and visions, the strange prohibitions, the tears and the rumours, the monks hurrying to touch and kiss the bones, all seem very remote. But they live in the experience of a single man as he writes his last words; they were the air he breathed. As he thought of it all he ventured one of his rare classical quotations:

Quo semel est imbuta recens, servabit odorem
Testa diu.

This tiresome tag was often quoted in the Middle Ages. Eadmer was not addicted to classical quotations, but this one

---

[1] *Anglia Sacra*, ii, 238 (*PL* CLIX, 807–8). The ascription to Eadmer is not quite certain but is highly probable.   [2] Wilmart, *Opuscula*, p. 362.

expressed to perfection the temper of his life and the spirit which animated his works of local hagiography.

## 2. THE DEVOTIONAL WORKS

The division of Eadmer's works into different groups must be rather artificial, since they all shared a similar purpose and were addressed in the first place to the same audience. But there is a group of four works which differ in some ways from the others: they are neither history nor hagiography, and though they are connected with corporate worship and envisage a monastic audience, they express primarily a personal devotion. It is perhaps not an accident that in Eadmer's own manuscript they are the only treatises to which he attached his name. The personal emphasis of the titles is unmistakable, and it will be well to have their full titles in mind in considering them:

(i) '*Consideratio Edmeri peccatoris et pauperis Dei de excellentia gloriosissimae virginis matris Dei*'[1]

This is the earliest of these four works. It was in existence when Eadmer made the first collection of his works about 1115, but apart from this its date is uncertain. Its form and even its title, are remarkable as an expression of the affective piety of which Anselm was the chief initiator, and many of its phrases show distinctly the influence of the language of Anselm's prayers: 'Excitemus ergo mentem nostram, fratres mei, et enitamur, quantum possumus, ut in celsitudinem tantae Virginis attendamus.' Or again: 'Erigite, obsecro, fratres mei, erigite aciem mentis vestrae ad contemplandam tam miram divinae dignationis operationem, tam ineffabilem et stupendam omni seculo huius mulieris gratiam et exaltationem.'[2]

Sentences such as these indicate the spirit of the work. It was a meditation written in the effusive and enthusiastic manner to which Anselm had given his authority and which gained general currency in the course of the twelfth century. But in

---

[1] *PL* CLIX, 557–80.

[2] *PL* CLIX, 558 D, 564A. With these phrases compare Anselm's *Oratio ad sanctam Mariam* (Schmitt, Or. vii; *PL* CLVIII, 953): 'Enitimini, viscera animae meae, enitimini quantum potestis—si quid potestis—omnia interiora mea, ut eius merita laudetis, ut eius beatitudinem ametis, ut eius celsitudinem admiremini, ut eius benignitatem deprecemini'.

one respect there is a great difference between Anselm and his pupil. Thirty years or more before Eadmer, Anselm had given a new turn to the expression of Marian devotion in three prayers which he sent to his friend Gundulf at Canterbury, and these prayers must from an early date have been known to Eadmer.[1] In these prayers Anselm strained every resource of language to express the limitless fervour of his devotion, and in the third and longest of them especially he poured out a cascade of newly coined and daringly conceived formulas:

All nature was created by God, and God was born of Mary. God created all things and Mary brought forth God. God, who made all things, made himself from Mary, and so remade all things which he had made. He, who could make all things from nothing, would not remake them when corrupted unless he first made himself the son of Mary. God therefore is the father of all created things, and Mary is the mother of all things recreated. God is the father of all things in their constitution, and Mary is the mother of all things in their restitution. God begot him through whom all things were made, and Mary brought forth him through whom all things were saved. God begot him without whom nothing is, and Mary brought forth him without whom nothing is as it should be.[2]

There is nothing like this in Eadmer. These are the words of a man who combined the passion of a logician and a poet, who had elevated a word-game of antitheses and assonances to express the tensions of universal redemption. Eadmer's gifts were lowlier and nearer therefore to the main stream of popular devotion: he was a historian. Of historical events there is in Anselm's three Marian prayers nothing; they move on a plane of metaphysical ecstasy. By contrast Eadmer wrote in a mood of historical rhapsody. It was a mood which was to have a great future:

If anyone asks why the Evangelists do not report that the most piteous Lord first and foremost appeared to his sweetest and most beloved Mother after his resurrection I shall answer what I heard a

---

[1] For an account of the development of these prayers, see A. Wilmart, *Les propres corrections de Saint Anselme dans sa grande prière à la Vierge Marie* (*Recherches de Théologie ancienne et médiévale*, ii, 1930, 189–204.) The important letter to Gundulf, sending the prayers to Canterbury, is Ep. 28 [i, 20].

[2] *Oratio* 7 (LII in *PL* CLVIII): Schmitt iii, 22, where the variant readings first analysed by Wilmart, *op. cit.*, are of considerable interest.

certain wise man say to those who asked him this question. He said that the narrative in the Gospels is of so great authority that it contains nothing useless or superfluous or obvious. But if they had related that the Son rising from hell appeared to his mother, the mistress of the world, as he might have appeared to anyone else, to tell her of his resurrection, who would not think this superfluous? This would be to bring the Queen of heaven and of earth and of every creature down to the level of this or that man or woman to whom he appeared.[1]

The method of deducing the necessity of otherwise unknown historical events from arguments of theological propriety, which is here tentatively adopted, was a development of Anselm's method of proving the necessity of known dogmatic truths by arguments of theological propriety. Eadmer, in his next work, took a more important step in the same direction; here it is simply an aside.

The work as a whole was a meditation on the events in the life of St. Mary. It contains some anticipations of later medieval piety, of which it must here suffice to mention its treatment of the Joys of the Virgin. The contemplation of these Joys became in the course of the twelfth century one of the most popular of private devotions. In Eadmer's day it was relatively un-developed, being confined so far as we know to the daily repetition of a short anthem which is first found—the location is perhaps significant—in a Canterbury manuscript of about 1040:

> Gaude dei genitrix uirgo inmaculata.
> Gaude quae gaudium ab angelo suscepisti.
> Gaude quae genuisti aeterni luminis claritatem.
> Gaude mater.
> Gaude sancta dei genitrix uirgo.
> Tu sola mater innupta.
> Te laudat omnis factura domini.
> Pro nobis supplica.[2]

The origin of this piece is obscure, but by the end of the

[1] *PL* CLIX, 568B.
[2] Printed from Cotton MS. Tiberius A iii f. 111, by E. S. Dewick, *Facsimiles of Horae de Beata Maria Virgine* (Henry Bradshaw Society, XXI, 1902). For the early history of this anthem, see A. Wilmart, *Auteurs spirituels et Textes dévots du Moyen Age latin*, 1932, p. 330–3.

eleventh century it had obtained a European circulation by being associated with a legend of a clerk to whom the Virgin appeared on his death-bed and promised a heavenly reward for his daily devotions expressed in this anthem.[1] What is new in Eadmer's treatment of the theme is not his reference to the Joys and their contrasting Sorrows, but his imaginative elaboration of the theme. Eadmer had learned from Anselm a language of devotion which allowed him to treat his theme with an emotional abandon, which now often seems faded and enervating, but then brought new life and a more vivid sense than ever before of personal participation in the events of the Gospels. Anselm was the medieval father of this manner of speech, and Eadmer was his earliest, and one of his most effusive pupils. As the spirit of the new devotion swept over Europe, obscure monks in English monasteries found themselves in the vanguard of a great movement. Eadmer was only one of several who found themselves in this position, but he was more articulate and more gifted than most. He had many successors, but this treatise of his did not influence them, for it had no circulation until the fourteenth century. Then, together with works of other pupils, it found its way into the standard collections of Anselm's works and reached a wide audience. The same fate befell the following work which took Eadmer's Marian devotion a stage further.

(ii) '*De Conceptione sanctae Mariae editum ab Eadmero monacho magno peccatore*'[2]

Unlike the previous work, this is one of Eadmer's latest compositions. It was probably written about 1125, when his ambitions as a practical expounder of the rights of the church

[1] The text is found in a large number of manuscripts and printed books. It is conveniently printed in E. F. Dexter, *Miracula sanctae Virginis Mariae* (University of Wisconsin Studies in the Social Sciences and History, vol. 12, 1927). For further references, see R. W. Southern, 'The English origins of the "Miracles of the Virgin",' *MARS*, iv, 1958.

[2] *PL* CLIX, 301–18, where the work is printed among the spurious works of Anselm. The correct attribution to Eadmer was not established until H. Thurston and T. Slater published the work from Eadmer's manuscript, C.C.C.C. 370, in *Eadmeri monachi Cantuariensis tractatus de Conceptione sanctae Mariae*, Freiburg, 1904.

of Canterbury had collapsed. The struggle with York had ended in disaster, the papal forgeries had been exposed, the hope of bringing the see of St. Andrew's under the jurisdiction of Canterbury had faded, the jealously guarded tradition of Benedictine archbishops had been broken. Eadmer's mind turned to the past, to his days with Anselm and to the antiquities of his church. Among the latter he looked back to

those former times when the Feast of the Conception of St. Mary, the Mother of God, was more widely celebrated, particularly by those in whom a pure simplicity and humble devotion to God was strong. But afterwards greater knowledge and a more searching examination of things puffed up the minds of some, so that the simplicity of the poor was despised, and the celebration of the Feast was done away with and utterly abolished as being contrary to reason.[1]

'The men,' he said, 'who brought about this abolition were men of great authority, abounding in riches and able to give a reason for what they did.' He does not mention Lanfranc by name, but Lanfranc's name must have been in his mind when he wrote these words. Nearly fifty years had passed since, as a young man, he had first been delighted to find that the authority of Lanfranc in casting down the English saints could be successfully opposed by subtle arguments. Anselm then had shown the way. Now Eadmer himself was to break new ground in defending the simplicity of the past against the reasoning of the present. Here, as elsewhere, it was his mission to give voice and reason to the mute instincts which had formed the piety of the Anglo-Saxon Church.

Most of Eadmer's works had only a local significance, but at this point he was engaged on a more momentous adventure than he knew. He thought he was defending a local title when he was a leader in an international event. There was a greater future in store for his treatise and the cause which it advocated than could have been foreseen by one who had his eyes firmly fixed on the old English pieties which had been swept away by the Conquest. There had been many such casualties: St. Dunstan had lost some of his glory; St. Elphege had only just survived; the Ordination of St. Gregory had only recently been

[1] *PL* CLIX, 301.

restored; other celebrations, such as the Conception of John the Baptist, had gone for good. Among those which had gone, and had recently come back, was the Feast of the Conception of St. Mary on 8 December.[1] By 1129 it was being celebrated again at Bury St. Edmunds and Westminster and at Henry I's new foundation at Reading; and to these houses we may, on the evidence of Eadmer's treatise, confidently add Christ Church, Canterbury. Yet, like every other restoration, it could not come back on the old terms. It could never again have the old simplicity. It must come back either supported by a sufficient authority or a sufficient explanation. Either was difficult to discover.

Already in Eadmer's day it was quite uncertain how this celebration had arisen, where it had originated, or by whose authority it had been introduced; and we know scarcely more than he did. Eadmer seems to have thought that it was more widespread in pre-Conquest England than modern research could justify; probably all he really knew was that it had existed at Canterbury before Lanfranc, and in this he was certainly right. If we further add that it was also found at Winchester we shall have added almost all that can now certainly be discovered. At about the same time as Eadmer was writing his treatise, a legend of a revelation to Abbot Aelsi of Ramsey was being spread to give a supernatural authority to the celebration of the Feast.[2] This legend played an important part in the early propagation of the observance, and Anselm's name and authority finally became attached to it. The circulation of such stories was the easiest of all ways of winning adherents to a cause, but Eadmer did not take this way. Perhaps he was ignorant of the legend, for it was only beginning to gain currency when he was writing. Whatever the reason, it is to his credit that he based his defence of the Feast entirely on theological and devotional considerations; and in so doing he was the first of a huge host to write a defence of this most controversial of all medieval devotions.

---

[1] For the evidence, see E. W. Williamson, *The Letters of Osbert of Clare*, pp. 11–13.

[2] For this story, and some of the large literature surrounding it, see *MARS* iv, 1958, 194–8.

He who comes first will generally see things much more simply than his successors. So here. When the problem of the Immaculate Conception of the Virgin became a really serious theological issue in the early fourteenth century, it was treated with a wealth of subtle distinctions and an awareness of fundamental issues which Eadmer by no means possessed.[1] He was concerned only to give a sufficient justification for a devotional practice; to make it intellectually and practically possible. In whatever way the practice had arisen, it was certainly not a result of theological speculation. It seems quite possible that its original justification was simply the incongruity of giving to John the Baptist, whose Conception was widely celebrated in the Anglo-Saxon Church, a liturgical honour denied to the Blessed Virgin.[2] Whatever their reasons, the pious innovators of the tenth or eleventh century would have been surprised to learn that their innovation called for theological justification, or that it would become a storm-centre in the history of Christian devotion. It was characteristic of the late Anglo-Saxon Church to put piety before theology. But to Lanfranc, among others, it must have been clear that a theological problem of the first magnitude was raised by this harmless devotion. Trained theological minds saw a danger which had escaped the obscure innovators of pre-Conquest days.

The whole economy of Redemption depended on the inescapable transmission of Original Sin in the act of conception. If this link between natural conception and the taint of Original Sin could be broken in one case, then the necessity of Christ as a redeemer of the whole human race would be jeopardized. It

---

[1] The late medieval discussions on the subject are inexhaustible. Some idea of the literature may be obtained from A. di Lella, 'The Immaculate Conception in the writings of Peter Aureoli,' and I. Brady, 'The development of the doctrine of the Immaculate Conception in the fourteenth century after Aureoli' (both in *Franciscan Studies*, xv, 1955).

[2] In a subject so bristling with difficulties one must beware of thinking that anything is simple, but I am surprised that in the great literature in the origins of the Feast this simple explanation does not seem to have been discussed. For the wide observance of the Feast of the Conception of St. John the Baptist before the Conquest, and its later disappearance, see F. Wormald, *English Kalendars before A.D. 1100* and *English Benedictine Kalendars after A.D. 1100* (Henry Bradshaw Society, lxxii and lxxvii).

was this consideration which obliged Anselm to mark very clearly his conviction that even the most privileged of the human race had been born with the taint common to all mankind: 'the Virgin herself was conceived "in iniquity, and in sin did her mother conceive her", and she was born with Original Sin, for she also sinned in Adam "in whom all have sinned".'[1] These words from the *Cur Deus Homo* were put by Anselm into the mouth of his pupil Boso, but he did not reject their conclusion: the Virgin, like some other privileged persons, was cleansed from the taint of Original Sin before the birth of Christ, but not before her own birth, through faith. This also was the position which Eadmer had held in his *De Excellentia Virginis*: 'we hold that her heart was made clean from all sin, whether original or actual if any there were, by faith, so that the Spirit of God might truly rest on her . . .'[2]

It is clear that when Eadmer wrote these words, either the Feast of the Conception of the Virgin had not yet been restored at Canterbury, or that he had not yet considered its theological implications. Once these considerations were raised, the only alternatives were either to abandon the Feast, as the celebration of the Conception of John the Baptist had been abandoned, or to abandon the view of Anselm and all previous theologians on this important point. Eadmer chose the latter course, and his words deserve respect, both for the modesty of their expression and for the very far-reaching consequences of the view they express. They have the importance which must be attached to the first expression of a revolutionary idea:

If anyone shall say that she was not altogether free from the sin of our first parent, since she was conceived through the union of a man and a woman under the law, that is the catholic opinion. I do not wish by any means to dissent from the truth of the catholic and universal Church; nevertheless when I consider, so far as I can with my clouded mind, the magnificence of the workings of the divine power, I seem to see that if there was anything of Original Sin in her procreation, it belonged to the parents and not to the progeny. Consider the chestnut . . . all prickly without, but smooth and white as milk within . . . ; could not God grant that, though conceived among the spikes of sin, she likewise could be altogether free

---

[1] *Cur Deus Homo*, II, 16.      [2] *PL* CLIX, 561 C.

from their sting? Clearly he could and would; and if he would, he did. *Potuit plane, et voluit; si igitur voluit, fecit.*[1]

The argument here is balanced on a precarious tight-rope. It did not commend itself to the robust theologians of the twelfth and thirteenth centuries: St. Bernard, Peter Lombard and St. Thomas Aquinas, together with all the most influential theologians of these centuries who discussed the question, rejected it. It was one sign of the great change in the theological scene at the beginning of the fourteenth century that the argument emerged with new authority as a serious candidate for theological considerations. The development was helped by the fact that Eadmer's treatise, under the supposed authorship of Anselm, began to circulate in the universities. John Baconthorpe, who in 1320 had called the doctrine of the Immaculate Conception a 'fantastic kind of heresy' wrote of it with new respect when he found that 'Anselm' (in reality however, as we now know, Eadmer) 'in a treatise entitled *De Conceptione B.V.M.* holds that she did not contract Original Sin. I first found this book in the house of the Brothers Minor at Cambridge (this was about 1325), and afterwards I found the same book in Paris in the hands of an ordinary stationer'.[2]

By 1325, therefore, Eadmer's treatise was beginning to have a wide circulation, not under the name of an obscure monk, but under the name of a theologian whose views and methods of argument were at last beginning to arouse widespread discussion.

In 1328, a provincial Council in London under Archbishop Simon Mepham quoted the authority of Anselm in ordering the Feast of the Conception to be observed in all churches throughout the province of Canterbury.[3] A century later, in 1438, the Council of Basel decreed the obligatory observance of the Feast, and prescribed portions of Eadmer's work, under the name of Anselm, among the Lessons to be read at Matins.[4]

---

[1] *PL* CLIX, 305 B.
[2] Quoted by I. Brady, in *Franciscan Studies*, xv, 1955, p. 196n.
[3] Wilkins, *Concilia Magnae Britanniae et Hiberniae*, 1737, ii, 552.
[4] The decree was passed on 17 Sept. 1438, largely under Spanish pressure and against Dominican opposition. John of Segovia composed the Office with the passages from Eadmer's work. See *Dictionnaire de Théologie Catholique*, vii, 112-13.

The association of Anselm's name with these developments was of course misguided, since his own distinctly expressed views were contrary to those of the advocates of the Immaculate Conception. Those who quoted him in support of these views were really quoting Eadmer, and the more clear-sighted recognized that this treatise contradicted views which Anselm had expressed elsewhere. But, despite his opposition to their conclusions, Anselm was to a significant extent the founder of the type of argument used by those who mistakenly quoted his authority. Indeed, anyone who reads the chapter of the *Cur Deus Homo* which contains the clearest rejection of the doctrine, will see many openings in Anselm's discourse to support a quite different conclusion. The argument *Deo decuit: Deus potuit: ergo Deus fecit* pervades Anselm's thought, even though he never expresses it in this way. It was Eadmer who seized the significance of this type of argument as a means of establishing historical facts. Despite all later elaboration, the main outlines of the discussion remained as Eadmer, very briefly, had indicated: 'God could; it was fitting that He should; therefore He did.' Whatever the merits of the case, this application of Anselm's argument is a witness to the complexity of Eadmer's opportunities as a bridge between old and new.

## (iii) *Minor Works*

Two other works must be mentioned among Eadmer's devotional writings. The first is a meditation on the events of St. Peter's life. It may be described in Eadmer's own words as a 'devout rumination on the things which God has done for Man'.[1] It derives very clearly from Anselm's prayer to St. Peter which has already been quoted; but instead of Anselm's sharp and painful ejaculations Eadmer ruminates with peaceful loquacity. The second piece is more original and more personal. It is a meditation on his Guardian Angel, whom Eadmer believed to be the archangel Gabriel. It may be that we have here a relic of Anglo-Saxon devotion, thought its composition belongs to Eadmer's old age. The most interesting passage is that in which Eadmer describes how he came to know the name

[1] Wilmart, *Opuscula*, p. 193.

of his special angel. It had happened long ago during the time of his exile with Anselm:

I was one of the servants and companions of his journey, and being far from my native soil and from my compatriots and friends, I often sat alone and turned over in my mind many things, some of them transitory and temporal, and some—but much more rarely— eternal. At times the enormity of my sins overcame me, and I sighed with confusion and wondered at the long-suffering patience and goodness of God. It seemed to me that I saw Him depute some good guardian to defend me from the attacks of the evil demons. . . . Meditating often about this, I desired greatly to know the name of my guardian, so that I could, when possible, honour his memory with some act of devotion. One night I fell asleep with this thought and behold someone stood by me saying that my prayer was heard, and that I might know without doubt that the name I desired to know was Gabriel.[1]

The early history of prayers to Guardian Angels has been traced by the master-hand of Dom Wilmart.[2] His crop of examples from the ninth to the fifteenth centuries was not large, and the majority of his discoveries came from England. Eadmer's experience is unique in disclosing the name—and such a name—of his Guardian Angel, but our knowledge is too fragmentary to provide a substantial background to his meditation. Neither of these two minor works had any circulation at any time: they are known only from Eadmer's personal manuscript.

Judged by the highest standards, none of Eadmer's devotional writings with the possible exception of the *De Conceptione sanctae Mariae* can be counted among the great works of medieval religious literature. But, taken as a whole, they show the enlargement of expression which Anselm brought to the limited resources of English piety. There are several signs that the pre-Conquest monastic communities contained men who were groping after the means of expressing their personal devotion in new ways, but they were cramped by the limitations of their environment. It was only in the visual arts that they

---

[1] *Ibid.* p. 451.
[2] *Auteurs spirituels et textes dévots du Moyen Age latin*, pp. 537–88.

seem to have been able to express themselves as they wished; but this power of artistic expression was accompanied by an atrophy of the written word. Anselm helped to break this silence by introducing a method of discourse, both speculative and affective, which others could imitate. Eadmer was among his best imitators, and yet he was never merely an imitator. He lacked Anselm's clarity and depth of feeling and his passion for an ordered world of intellectual experience. But he made up for this to some extent by a sense of the past, by a simplicity and grace in writing, and by an interest in himself and others. Without Anselm he would have been a local hagiographer, filling some of the large gaps in the records of the old English saints, displaying perhaps a more than ordinary talent for investigation and historical reconstruction, and an unwearied curiosity in all that concerned the church of Canterbury. Anselm opened to him a world of devotional expression and, as we shall now see, the vocation of a historian.

### 3. THE 'HISTORIA NOVORUM IN ANGLIA'

#### (i) *The First Four Books*

The *Historia Novorum* in its original state consisted of four books ending in the year of Anselm's death. In this state the work was certainly finished by about 1115, though the stages in its composition cannot, except in broad outline, be distinguished. It is necessary to say this because M. Rule, the editor of the work in the Rolls Series, has given a very elaborate account of the growth of the work. His views may be summarized in a series of propositions: the work was put out by instalments, a book at a time, the first book forming originally a volume in itself; when completed the whole was contained in three, not four, books which were 'not improbably' finished by the autumn of 1111; finally, the four books were finished in or before the year 1112. Into this text some thirty-seven passages, including the greater part of the documents, were (according to Rule) inserted at widely different dates down to the very close of Eadmer's life which Rule placed in 1144.[1]

---

[1] *HN* pp. xv–lxiv.

This whole construction, however, must be rejected as a series of unsupported hypotheses. It is based on trifling hints which are often capable of other explanations, and sometimes require no explanation at all. For instance, whenever Eadmer speaks of inserting a document in the text, this is taken to mean that he is making an addition to an already finished text; similarly, if he makes a digression and then says that he is returning to his main story this is interpreted to mean that he has interpolated a passage into an already existing narrative. Rule performed a valuable service in his edition in making available the text of the best manuscript, but nearly the whole of his discussion of the text in his Preface must be set aside.

We know much less about the composition of the work than Rule thought. The most that can be said is that, having collected materials during the whole or greater part of Anselm's pontificate, Eadmer put them into shape in four books during the years 1109 to 1115, bringing his history down to the year of Anselm's death. Four years later he began a continuation of the work.[1] We have no copy of the work in its original state. Alterations and additions which cannot now be detected may have been made to the text when Eadmer wrote his continuation. Indeed, there are two or three passages which have every appearance of being additions, and it is clear that the last two pages of Book IV were added when Eadmer took up the work again in 1119.[2] But there is a strong reason for thinking that no thorough revision was carried out; for Eadmer never altered his Preface to comprehend the material he added after 1119; and the Preface itself, which was probably written when the first four Books were completed, contradicts in one important respect the narrative which follows it. This contradiction is important, for it helps to show that Eadmer did not alter his narrative to bring it into line with his later views.[3]

At what point in his friendship with Anselm Eadmer began writing about the things which came to his notice we cannot tell, but it was probably not long after 1093. The long account

---

[1] *HN* 214–15, 217.
[2] Paschal II, who died 21 January 1118, was already dead when these pages were written (*HN* 215).
[3] For a discussion of this contradiction see below, p. 310.

of the Council at Rockingham in 1095, or even of the discussions at Hastings in 1094, could scarcely have been written except from notes made at the time, and the general accuracy in his naming of places and dates confirms this impression. It is also confirmed by what we know of the composition of the *Vita Anselmi*, which was probably well advanced by 1100. On the other hand, the putting together of the material for both the *History* and the *Life* did not take place until after Anselm's death. There are several pages in the *History* which refer to a time after Anselm's death.[1] The latest of these implies that Thomas, archbishop of York, who died on 24 February 1114, was already dead, and probably the work in its earliest form was finished not long after this date.

Only two errors in date have been detected in a work which abounds in exact references to dates of obscure events. These are both in the account of 1095, where two incidents are said to take place exactly a fortnight after their real date. The first of them is the meeting at Rockingham which is assigned to 11 March instead of 20 February; the second is the date on which Anselm received his pallium at Canterbury, which is given as 10 June instead of 27 May.[2] Since the second date at least must have been well known at Canterbury, the mistake would seem to suggest an exceptional degree of carelessness on Eadmer's part. But the *Vita Anselmi* provides a clue to its origin. Here the date of the Council at Rockingham is given as the third week in Lent, which is correct. It seems very likely, therefore, that this was the way in which Eadmer dated events in his draft notes, according to the familiar ecclesiastical calendar. But, in working up his notes for the *History* and putting the dates in secular form, he miscalculated the date of Easter in 1095, and so got these two dates a fortnight out.

This small detail is of some interest because it provides a rare instance in which Eadmer can be seen at work on the composition of the first four books of the *History*. For the most part he has left very little trace of his methods of composition. A close examination, however, reveals a distinct change in the character of the work in the year 1100. This is all the more

[1] *HN* 75, 175, 211.
[2] *HN* 53, 72. The mistake was noticed by Rule, p. lxii.

significant because it corresponds to a similar, and even more drastic change in the *Vita Anselmi* at the same date. Down to the year 1100 the *History* is remarkable for its long accounts of things said at a succession of royal courts and papal councils. The discussions at the royal court at Gloucester in March 1093, at Rochester in July 1093, at Hastings in February 1094, at Rockingham in February 1095, at Winchester in October 1097, and at the Councils at Bari and Rome in 1098 and 1099 are reported in great detail and in direct speech. The last discussion which is reported at comparable length took place in November 1100, when the king's marriage was discussed. After this date the debates in which Anselm was involved take a minor place in Eadmer's narrative, and there are few and only brief reports in direct speech until after Anselm's death. Despite this change, the scale of the work was not seriously affected. The reason for this is that the large amount of space which had previously been devoted to debates was now taken up with the texts of original documents. For the eight years 1093–1100 Eadmer quotes only three documents; for the next eight years, treated at approximately the same length, he gives thirty-eight.

This change of emphasis requires an explanation which must be deferred until the similar change in the character of the *Vita Anselmi* is considered. Meanwhile it is sufficient to remark that the earlier part of the narrative, with its eye-witness accounts of discussions at royal and ecclesiastical councils, is undoubtedly the more interesting. It is here that Eadmer is seen as an eager and curious recorder of the spoken word and of all that was going on around him. After 1100, there is comparatively little in the *History* that could not be known from other sources, principally from the collected correspondence of Anselm himself. There is no compensation for the loss of the lively descriptions of the earlier years.

It was Eadmer's original intention to stop his *History* in 1109 with the death of Anselm. Eadmer's perambulating life as a member of the archbishop's household had come to an end, and he rightly considered 'that if I went on writing, I should either write about trivialities, or about things which my retired life prevented me from knowing as fully as was necessary'.[1]

---

[1] *HN* 217.

This decision and its reason showed that Eadmer understood his limitations as a historian. He was not one of those chroniclers of contemporary events who could observe with an impartial interest the events of the time and record them with whatever detail his circumstances allowed. The great service of monastic chroniclers in general, from Matthew Paris down to the annalists of obscure houses, was precisely this: having no opportunity for taking part in events in the world, they yet eagerly watched them from a distance and preserved whatever information or documents came their way. Eadmer at Canterbury was as well placed as Matthew Paris at St. Albans for knowing what was going on in the world—but he was not greatly interested in it. He mentions almost no facts about the policies of Rufus or Henry I which are not strictly related to his own experience and to the archbishop's affairs. In their secular policies and in secular events in general, he shows no interest. Even to portents and marvels he was, as a historian, almost equally indifferent: he mentioned a comet in the year of Anselm's death, and an exceptionally low-tide on 10 October 1114, which probably came to his notice because he had on that day to go from Canterbury to Rochester.[1] But of the more famous portents, which were generally considered to have a profound influence on the course of history, he says nothing. He is equally, and perhaps more reprehensibly, indifferent to the fate of great issues once his own part in them came to an end; and, though he easily digresses to report some personal experience with a relic or a cope, he had no eyes for business which did not concern him, even if transacted in his presence. He shows no interest in the Investiture dispute after Anselm's death, and he does not—as even the Worcester chronicler did —transcribe documents to illustrate, or even mention, the continuation of the dispute in Italy and Germany, though this was a subject on which the English king evidently kept a careful watch.[2]

Eadmer, in his *History* and elsewhere, only wrote about events within the orbit of his own experience or that of the community with which he was identified. This had the effect of making him a highly selective historian; but he had the

---

[1] *HN* 212, 225–6.     [2] *Fl. Wigorn*, ii, 60–6.

advantage of writing, as most monastic historians did not, from experience. It could seldom happen to them as it did to Eadmer to be at the centre of affairs, and few could have made such good use of the opportunity. William of Malmesbury, who seldom praised his contemporaries, spoke with a touch of envy of Eadmer's opportunities and gifts, which with all his superior intellectual powers he himself lacked: 'he described things so lucidly that they seem to take place under our very eyes'.[1] In the quality of vivid and natural description Eadmer excels all his contemporaries, and the early books of the *History* show his descriptive powers at their best.

Although he is candid in all that concerns himself and his own impressions, there is an early warning that when the interests of his community were involved his candour deserted him. The first evidence for this in the *History* is to be found in the account of Anselm's consecration as archbishop. Eadmer describes the wrangle which took place in the middle of the service when the archbishop of York objected to the title by which he was expected to consecrate the new archbishop. According to Eadmer the title to which he objected was 'metropolitan of all Britain', and the title to which he finally agreed and by which he consecrated Anselm was 'primate of all Britain'.[2] Now this cannot be right, for it was to the latter title that the archbishop of York consistently took exception. In his earlier oath of obedience to Lanfranc, Thomas of York, the consecrating archbishop, had expressly reserved his acknowledgment of the supremacy of Canterbury to Lanfranc's own lifetime, and what he must have objected to in the formula placed before him by the monks of Canterbury was the phrase *totius Britanniae*. It would have made no sense at all if, placated by the meaningless substitution of *primate* for *metropolitan*, he had agreed to allow the Canterbury claim to jurisdiction over all Britain. On this subject, Hugh the Chanter of York, who records that his archbishop objected to the primatial title and agreed to consecrate Anselm merely as 'metropolitan of Canterbury', has more claim to credence than Eadmer.[3]

By contrast, Eadmer's account of the disputes between

---

[1] *Gesta Pontificum*, p. 74.    [2] *HN* 42–3.
[3] *Historians of the Church of York*, ii, 104–5.

Anselm and Rufus and Henry I seems, so far as it goes, eminently trustworthy. He tells the story, of course, from the archbishop's point of view; he omits much that could be said in favour of Rufus, and he lends a ready ear to discreditable rumours. He sometimes seems to have misunderstood technical details of procedure—for instance in his report of Urban II's proposed excommunication of Rufus—but attempts which have been made to convict him of wilful distortion in this field have not been successful.[1] He showed considerable moderation in his estimate of Anselm's practical achievement; and his general lack of political sense perhaps saved him from the habit of wild mis-statement which so often afflicted contemporary writers on the Investiture contest. No dispute in the Middle Ages so muddied the streams of historical truth as this; but Eadmer, without having severer standards than his contemporaries, was not sufficiently personally involved in the subject to be led astray by passion.

Unfortunately the one subject on which passion reigned supreme became increasingly important as time went on. This was the rivalry between Canterbury and York; and when Eadmer in 1119 decided to add to his *History* he displayed this weakness to the full.

(ii) *The Continuation (Books V and VI)*

The mood in which the continuation was begun was very different from that which had accompanied the writing of the first four books. Eadmer's purpose was still to write about the things which he had himself seen in the company of the archbishop, and about events which closely—more closely than ever

---

[1] *HN* 106–7. Eadmer says that Urban II at the Council of Bari in 1098 was on the point of excommunicating Rufus, when he was with difficulty dissuaded from doing so by Anselm. It has been pointed out by Liebermann, 'Anselm u. Hugo v. Lyon' (*Historische Aufsätze dem Andenken am G. Waitz*, 1886, p. 178 n. 8) and by others that this can scarcely be correct, first because the three necessary preliminary warnings could not yet have been given, secondly because it was customary to excommunicate the king's advisers before touching the king himself, and thirdly because Urban II later had plenty of time in which to excommunicate Rufus and did not do so. The first of these arguments alone is convincing, but it is possible that Urban II himself was breaking the ordinary rules of procedure, for Eadmer was well aware of the need for a threefold warning before excommunication.

before—affected the fortunes of the church of Canterbury. But here the similarity between the original work and its continuation ended. The most obvious difference is in the personality of the archbishop. Anselm's successor Ralph was a man acceptable to the community at Canterbury and a defender of its interests; but Eadmer has very little to say about him. Probably there was very little that could be said. He seems to have been a good and pious man, but a nonentity; Eadmer's silence about any trait of personality or thought, after years of companionship, is eloquent testimony to this.[1]

But an even more important cause of the difference between the original work and its continuation lay in the situation of the community during the years from 1114 to 1122. In these years all its energies were absorbed in the dispute with York. The Canterbury community looked on itself as a beleaguered fortress and showed all the symptoms of a siege mentality—suspicious of treason, quick to sense hostility and unfairness, unwilling to face disagreeable facts. This is the state of mind to which the continuation of Eadmer's *History* bears witness. It was of course very absurd; the position of the community was not threatened in its essential interests even in a worldly sense. But so important had the dispute with York come to appear that a fixation of interest set in, which afflicted the body as a whole and Eadmer among the rest.

We have already seen that the conflict with York had been assuming an ever greater importance in Anselm's last years. After his death, as a result of the king's intervention, there was peace for five years while the long vacancy at Canterbury continued. Then in 1114, within a few months, both Canterbury and York got new archbishops: the former the undistinguished Ralph, the latter the determined, inflexible and widely respected Thurstan. It is interesting to contemplate what would have happened if the rôles had been reversed, but

---

[1] He was the author of a sermon which became famous under the name of Anselm (*PL* CLVIII, 644–9: *Hom.* IX) and was translated into Anglo-Saxon (ed. M. Förster in *Anglica: Brandl Festschrift*, 1925, ii, 8–69). At one time I thought that he was the author of other works in the style of Anselm, but this does not now seem to me very likely (see above p. 206). His character is sketched by William of Malmesbury, *Gesta Pontificum* 132.

the main course of events would probably have been unchanged. Every living force and all enlightened and objective opinion was turning against the claims of Canterbury's supremacy. Yet it is hard to think that any archbishop would willingly have abandoned, or been allowed by the community to abandon, a claim which had become an integral part of the complex personality which the archbishop assumed and took under his protection with his office. Thurstan might have acted differently but, in his rival's position, his aim would have been that of his rival.

Probably Eadmer would not have been impelled to reopen his *History* to record the melancholy story of the struggle if he had not had a strong personal as well as corporate reason for doing so. He was the companion of the new archbishop as he had been Anselm's, and was closely implicated in his failure. Together they had gone to Normandy and to Rome in 1116 to press forward the claims of Canterbury. The journey had soon become an exile—a flight from the authority of the pope whose only reply to their petition had been to order Ralph to consecrate his rival without exacting an oath of obedience.[1] Ralph carried out Anselm's threat to prefer exile to any diminution of the rights of Canterbury, and Eadmer stayed with him in Normandy till the beginning of 1119.[2] Ill-health then obliged him to abandon the archbishop and return to Canterbury. He evidently expected an unfriendly reception, for he came provided with a letter from the archbishop praising his exertions in the common cause and soliciting for him a friendly and grateful reception: but this he did not receive.[3] He found the community critical of himself for deserting the archbishop, critical of the archbishop for his lack of success, and—casting its mind around for further scapegoats—critical of Anselm for his failure to uphold the privileges of Canterbury as Lanfranc before him had done.

---

[1] *Historians of the Church of York*, ii, 148–9. In *HN* 244, Eadmer, while giving the pope's letter to Henry I as in the York account, omits the much sharper one to the archbishop of Canterbury.

[2] Eadmer (*HN* 244) says that the archbishop found it impossible to break away from the king's company. Hugh the Chanter gives the true reason: if he returned to England, he would have been obliged to carry out the pope's order to consecrate Thurstan (*Historians of the Church of York*, ii, 150). For Anselm's threat, see above, p. 138.     [3] *HN* 250–1.

It was principally to rebut these charges that Eadmer took up his *History* again. First he added a new conclusion to Book IV designed to demonstrate Anselm's activity and success in the struggle with York. Then, still occupied with the theme of Anselm's care for the interests of the community, he opened a fifth book: 'Before I begin, I have something to say to those who do not fear to criticize the holy archbishop for his lack of zeal in secular and ecclesiastical organization, to which, as they say, while he had the power, he did not give the same attention as his predecessor Lanfranc.'[1] He then gave an account of Anselm's stewardship of the corporate property and concluded: 'Let then the detractors of so great a man and so magnificent a benefactor of Christ Church hold their tongues and look to their own souls. For if God does not spare those who are secret detractors of their neighbours, I fear he will utterly destroy those who publicly and unjustly pierce their father with wicked words.'[2]

With those words he turned to give an account of what had been done under Anselm's successor. He was still engaged on this work when he was called away to the see of St. Andrews in June 1120. When he returned at the beginning of 1121 he continued his task and brought his *History* down to the death of Archbishop Ralph in October 1122. The work ends abruptly at this point. There is no conclusion; the narrative, which had become increasingly fragmentary, ends with an unfinished correspondence about his own see of St. Andrews and a brief note of the archbishop's death and burial. Perhaps the succeeding months, which saw an Austin canon elected archbishop and the ignominious defeat of the Canterbury case against York at the papal court, were too painful to record. In any case Eadmer's own part in public affairs had once more, and this time finally, come to an end.

The continuation is far below the original work in interest and quality. Despite a few lively passages of personal interest, the main theme is marred not only by its intrinsic poverty, but by Eadmer's inability to tell the truth about it. We have already seen that he is unreliable where the interests of the community were concerned; and necessarily this fault is more

[1] *HN* 217.      [2] *HN* 220.

conspicuous when the interests of the community fill the whole picture, as they did from 1114 to 1122. There is not even the genial influence of success to add generosity to the narrative. Nothing can excuse its morose deceits except the deep feelings of humiliation and Eadmer's determination to demonstrate his solidarity with the community. Everything is left in the dark which could reflect discredit on Canterbury or weaken its case: the results of the archbishop's visit to Rome, the cause of his prolonged absence in Normandy, the reasons for his unwillingness to meet the pope at the Council of Rheims or afterwards— all these essential points have to remain imperfectly explained, because the explanations were in all cases discreditable or unwelcome.[1]

It is one thing to omit explanations and to suppress inconvenient documents; it is another to insert false documents with a false account of their origin. For the first of these procedures there is abundant evidence in the continuation of the *History*; equally certainly it contains false documents and a misleading account of their origin. These are the famous forgeries of papal documents in support of the primacy of Canterbury, for the 'finding' of which in 1120 Eadmer is our sole authority. According to his account they were found in this year in ancient Gospel Books of the church. No one now believes in the genuineness of these documents, but it has often been thought that their falsity is compatible with the truth of Eadmer's account of their re-discovery in 1120 after nearly fifty years of neglect. I do not believe this can be maintained, and I have argued elsewhere that the documents were a product of the years of humiliation from 1120 to 1123.[2] Probably they were made after the archbishop of York's triumphant return to England in 1121; but in any case after his consecration in 1119. There is, however, no reason to think that, because Eadmer was responsible for putting historians on a false scent, he was himself the forger; and there are several reasons for believing that he was not. The chief of these is that, even after the

---

[1] The explanations are readily supplied by Hugh the Chanter of York, and though they are the explanations of an enemy, they are convincing. (See *Historians of the Church of York*, ii, 138, 150.)

[2] 'The Canterbury Forgeries', *EHR*, lxxiii, 1958, 193–226.

appearance of the forgeries, he continued to defend the rights of Canterbury by a historical commentary on the inconclusive documents and traditions which had held the field for fifty years between 1070 and 1120.[1] By contrast, the forgeries were a new solution concocted in the face of imminent defeat. Almost certainly they were the work of men impatient with the meagre results of years of inconclusive action under Archbishops Anselm and Ralph—the work therefore of the critics of Eadmer and his masters rather than of Eadmer himself. Yet Eadmer cannot be defended from the charge of deceit. He can scarcely have been ignorant that the documents were recent forgeries and that his account of how they were found was false. No doubt he told the story to which the community was committed, and there we must leave it. For the embarrassments and contradictions to which the story led, it is necessary to go to the York writer, who could enjoy the double luxury of triumph and truth. But we may spare some sympathy for the vanquished. They believed in their case; they believed that, among the ruins of their archives, there would have been found documents sufficient to prove that they were right. The situation was difficult to bear. It is easy now to feel the folly of it all, but a cause which won the violent allegiance of Anselm, no less than of Lanfranc and Ralph, must have appealed with irresistible force to men even more closely involved in its success, almost from birth, than they were. Such was Eadmer. Where greater men fell, who were new-comers to Canterbury, he could scarcely have continued to stand upright.

### (iii) *Eadmer's View of English History*

The *Historia Novorum* ends in disaster from every point of view. But before leaving it we may go back to the Preface, which was written in all probability after the first four books, but before the continuation. It preserves Eadmer's views about the course of English history in his lifetime, seen in the light of Anselm's completed work. After writing the first four books Eadmer thought he saw the pattern which so often

---

[1] *HN* 276-9.

eluded him, and in the Preface he tells us which of the many
novelties of his day was the chief *nova res* of the age: it was the
resistance of the archbishop of Canterbury to the royal authority
over the Church. When he wrote the Preface it seemed to him
that it was Anselm's glory and mission to have been the first
prelate in England after the Conquest (with the exception of
the subordinate bishops of Rochester) to receive his office
without either doing homage or receiving lay investiture: 'it
was because Anselm wished to abolish this custom as contrary
to God and the sacred canons, and to destroy the injustices
flowing thence, that he became hateful to the kings and was
forced into exile.'[1]

In a large sense it was true that the conflict between secular
and ecclesiastical authorities on grounds of principle was something which distinguished the age from all previous ones, and
Eadmer was the only English writer who clearly recognized
this fact. But it would be a mistake to think that this was a line
of thought which was habitual with him. He seems here, for
once, to have been carried along on the wind of continental
doctrine, and to have written, perhaps, under the influence of
the papal documents with which the third and fourth books of
his *History* were liberally scattered. In the moment of illumination he forgot that the issues of homage and investiture
could not be referred back to the reign of Rufus, that his own
*History* showed Anselm doing homage to Rufus, and having no
inclination to quarrel about lay investiture. He forgot that
Anselm only learned in 1099 that it was his duty to renounce
these practices.

In detail, therefore, the Preface is misleading. Anselm's
policy had not the simple consistency which it suggests, and
Eadmer's own historical perspective was normally much more
insular. The early pages of the *History* are a better guide to
this perspective than the Preface. In his first sentence, he
brought together the names of King Edgar and St. Dunstan,
and in the next few pages he traced the decline from this
golden age of peace and monastic revival. This decline comprised the whole period down to Eadmer's own day: it was,
rather surprisingly, not checked by the reign of Edward the

[1] *HN* 2.

310

Confessor.[1] Eadmer had none of the feeling about Edward the Confessor which became so important to Englishmen of his disposition in the reign of Henry I. For him, Edward's reign was simply a time when the destruction of the monasteries reached its climax. Similarly he had none of those hopeful premonitions about the results of the marriage of Henry I and Matilda, which were cherished by those who looked on this union as a fulfilment of the death-bed prophecy of the Confessor, and a return of the old royal stock after three generations of foreign rule. For Eadmer, as for Anselm, this marriage raised difficult problems, but it excited no national aspirations. It was not in this direction that the true continuity of English history lay.

As for the Norman Conquest, Eadmer's attitude was ambiguous. It was in itself an evil, and a judgment of God on the perjury of Harold, just as the initial disasters of Ethelred's reign had been a judgment on the treacherous murder of Edward the Martyr. It brought evil consequences: the destruction of the English, about which Eadmer could not bring himself to speak; the subjection of the Church to the arbitrary regulations of the Conqueror, which Eadmer summarized in a famous passage often quoted out of its context without the reprobation which he certainly intended to convey. The long tale of disaster under a foreign oppression was not finished, and the prospect of its continuance stretched out into an indefinite future. Eadmer was more pessimistic than those who foretold an easy lifting of the Norman yoke. The Conquest was one of the long chain of disasters foreseen by St. Dunstan, which was to last for many centuries while the land lay under a foreign domination; relief was not to come quickly. This was one of the subjects on which Eadmer's interpretation of the events of Dunstan's life differed from that of Osbern. Osbern had referred Dunstan's prophecy of disasters to the attacks of the Danes, but Eadmer took a longer view:

the misery which overwhelmed and destroyed the whole of England after his death is sufficiently evident in chronicles and in our tribulations, even if I am silent. I do not see why I should write about

[1] *HN* 5: 'Regnante autem Edwardo . . . monasteriorum quae usque id temporis destructioni supererant plurima destructio facta est.'

something which is so clear that everyone can see these real miseries. What or when the end of them will be I do not know; but this I do know, that God has done all these things to us by a just judgment because we have sinned against him and have not obeyed his commandments.[1]

But in one respect the Conquest had brought an alleviation: it had brought Lanfranc and Anselm, and with them the revival of monastic life and the fight for the rights and privileges of Canterbury. Here, as elsewhere, the strong emphasis on local privileges must strike the modern reader as unbalanced, but it would be foolish to overlook their importance in Eadmer's eyes. He cared for other things than the material grandeur of the church of Canterbury, and he could not approve Lanfranc's break with traditions which he considered an essential part of the life of the community. But the preservation of every legitimate right came first, and even Anselm found no obligation more pressing than this. Lanfranc had stood firm for the rights of Canterbury at a critical time, and this fact blunted every instinct of rebellion against the Conquest. Eadmer never said that what was good for Canterbury was good for England. He did not formulate his thoughts in this way; but this is very nearly what he felt. English well-being had followed the same curve as that of Canterbury. The great days of Oda and Dunstan had coincided with those of Athelstan and Edgar; the disasters of the time of Elphege, with those of Ethelred; the darkness of Stigand, with the Conquest. As for the post-Conquest prosperity which now seems to us so striking a feature of Canterbury history, Eadmer and his contemporaries were only grudgingly aware of their good fortune. That they had much to be thankful for they were aware; but they were even more aware of what they had lost or failed to secure. Like England, they had survived into a difficult and disappointing age, in which the new things were more conspicuous and less good than the old.

To Lanfranc's charity it is possible that Eadmer owed a heavy personal debt, and he always spoke of him with admira-

---

[1] *Memorials of St. Dunstan*, p. 222; Eadmer uses almost the same words in *HN* 3. For the parallel passage in Osbern with its much narrower application, see *Memorials*, p. 127.

tion and gratitude. But, for all this, he remained a remote and awe-inspiring figure, to whose labours rather than to his person Eadmer paid homage. It was for Anselm that he reserved his personal devotion, and it was this which made him the first copious writer of history in England since the time of Bede. Contemporary history had never before—not even by Bede— been written in England on the scale on which Eadmer wrote.

However far the *History* in the end drifted away from its original source of inspiration, it was Anselm who inspired the greater and only important part of it. Looking on the *History* as a whole, its strength and weaknesses reflect in a curious way the strength and weakness of Anglo-Saxon culture. It is the work of an impressionable and unsystematic nature, producing brilliant and original passages, but with a tendency to collapse through the absence of an adequate structure. Eadmer has the great merit of displaying himself in what he writes, and necessarily he displays his weaknesses. His *History* was concerned with the two abiding influences in his life: his friendship with Anselm and his ties with Canterbury. These influences were inextricably bound up together, but they were not identical. The corporate experience was the more deeply rooted of the two, but, as we have seen, it led into ever narrower and less defensible courses of action; the friendship, on the other hand, brought wider prospects geographically as well as spiritually. In the end, Eadmer seems to have been aware of this, as he came to dwell more on his memories of Anselm and less on his ambitions for the church of Canterbury. Of this final phase the *History* shows no trace. It ends under the strong influence of corporate ambition; but at about the same time the *Vita Anselmi* was also taking the final shape in which Anselm's place among the English saints was assured.

# CHAPTER IX

# EADMER'S 'LIFE OF ANSELM'

## I. THE WRITING OF THE 'VITA ANSELMI'

W E may start with the Preface. There is a business-like quality about it which at once commands attention. In a sense it conforms to what was expected in the preface to such a work, but with a freedom which suggests that the work is not going to conform to type. The elements of a preface consecrated by tradition were these: an expression of obedience to some higher authority in undertaking the task of writing, an acknowledgment of unworthiness and especially of stylistic inadequacy, a brief commendation of the virtues of the subject, and an assertion of the truth of what was to be said. Eadmer's Preface contains vestigial traces of these elements but they are not conspicuous. He writes at the request of his friends; his style is *incultus* and, without apology, *planus*; the more fulsome and elaborate traditional formulas are omitted. Instead, he concentrates on pointing out the relationships between the *Vita* and the *Historia Novorum*: the latter contained an account of Anselm's public acts, which any contemporary could have known about but which might be lost to posterity; the present work would speak of Anselm's private life and miracles.[1] Each work, he said, was complete in itself, but those who wished to know the full story must read both. Nothing could be more free from conventional embellishment.

At first sight this Preface might suggest that Eadmer had finished the *History* before he began to write the *Life*. But

---

[1] We may compare with this William of Malmesbury's division of St. Wulfstan's life after 1066 into two parts: i. Miracles, ii. Private life: 'Hactenus et dixi et dixisse iuvat miracula, pauca quidem sed quae sufficiant ad documentum sanctitatis Wlfstani; nunc interiorem eius vitam et mores dicere aggrediar'. (ed. R. R. Darlington, Camden Series, 1928, p. 46.) In his account of Wulfstan's 'inner life and manners', William includes whatever in his public life is not miraculous, but the distinction is only imperfectly observed.

though this may be true of the task of giving the *Life* its finished form, it is not true of the work of composition. We know this because Eadmer tells us that Anselm discovered him at work on the *Life*, and after providing some corrections, finally ordered him to destroy it. Eadmer does not mention the date of this incident or the length to which the work had progressed at this time. But he says that Anselm's order involved the destruction of several *quaterniones*, and since the whole of the *Life* in Eadmer's own manuscript occupies only five quires it would seem that the work was already well advanced. As we know, Eadmer obeyed the order in the letter but not in the spirit, for he made a new copy before destroying the old. It is to this that we owe the existence of the work; but his act of disobedience must have involved a severe struggle. Some of the strongest sayings of Anselm reported by Eadmer were on the subject of feigned obedience, and the application to himself cannot have been overlooked. He seems to have been unwilling to make public the story of Anselm's disapprobation: it forms the latest addition to the text of the work, and one manuscript from Canterbury tells us that he added it by the command of Archbishop Ralph. The appeal for the prayers of his readers which follows was probably not a formality.

Although Eadmer does not mention the date of this incident it is possible to make a plausible guess. We have seen that the *History* changed its character in some important respects in the year 1100. After this date there is very little, if anything, which suggests an immediate reporting of words spoken by the archbishop. There is an abrupt change of emphasis: reports of the spoken work disappear almost completely and documents take their place. Turning to the *Life*, an even greater change is immediately evident: the talk dries up, but it is not replaced by documents. The last eight years of Anselm's life occupy only eight pages in Eadmer's manuscript; the previous eight years required thirty-two pages. Moreover the last eight years contain nothing that could not have been written after Anselm's death; the only incident fully reported in Eadmer's accustomed style from his own experience was his personal mishap in attempting to get a relic of St. Prisca from the bishop of Paris. For the most part, the treatment of these last years

315

is not only bare but banal. As in the *History*, so here, all the important and vivid reporting of Anselm's words comes from a period not later than 1100. After this date we find the monk Alexander, instead of Eadmer, acting as the recorder of Anselm's sermons and sayings, and the conclusion seems irresistible that Eadmer was no longer free to keep a record of events and of talk as he had formerly done. It seems very likely that this change is to be associated with Anselm's order for the destruction of the biography. Eadmer could carry his disobedience to the extent of preserving what he had written, but not to the extent of continuing to write while Anselm lived. Eadmer virtually ceased to be Anselm's biographer in 1100; what follows is a mere shadow.

Eadmer would thus seem to have abandoned his biography in 1100 and not to have taken it up again until after Anselm's death. The requests of his friends then encouraged him to put his earlier notes into shape, and to complete them in a conventional way with some very commonplace miracles and a long account in traditional form of Anselm's death and burial. At this point Eadmer brought his work to a close, with the remark that various people had seen visions of Anselm in glory which he fully believed, but, since it would be impossible to record them all and invidious to select some and reject others, he preferred to pass them all over in silence and to let what he had already written suffice. We may reasonably interpret this to mean that at the time when he finished the *Life* in its earliest form he had no posthumous miracles to record.

The date at which the work had reached this state cannot be at all closely determined, but it must have been sometime before 1114, when Ralph became archbishop of Canterbury.[1] To judge from the existing manuscripts, the first demand for a *Life of Anselm* came not from England but from his friends abroad. There are nineteen manuscripts of the work in the earliest recension, which is more than for all the other recensions put together, and every one of them comes from a foreign source. The manuscripts of this recension fall into two clearly defined groups, going back in all probability to the continental

---

[1] He is still mentioned as bishop of Rochester in the earliest addition to the work: *VA* II, lxx.

monastic houses with which Anselm was most closely connected: to Bec and to some monastery in Flanders, probably
St. Bertin, where Anselm was well-known and where Canterbury associations were close. The original manuscripts sent to
these places are both lost, but the families which descend from
them show the general area in which the work was read. It is
somewhat strange that it seems to have been more popular in
Flanders than in England. In the course of the twelfth century
it found its way to Anchin, Marchiennes, Clairmarais, and
through these Cistercian houses to Clairvaux. The family
descending from Bec seems chiefly to have been confined, as
one would expect, to Normandy.

Eadmer was an indefatigable reviser of his work, and the
slow multiplication of copies allowed him to make each
exemplar slightly different from its predecessor. It was, after
all, the only work which in his own day gave him a modest
international reputation; it was the chief means by which
Anselm was likely to be known to posterity. It therefore
behoved him to make its details as faultless as possible. To this
end he altered the order of words and revised the punctuation,
and made divisions of chapters where previously there had been
a connected narrative. Only very occasionally were the alterations extensive.

There were two incidents in particular which seem to have
given Eadmer a lot of trouble. They both occurred in the last
few years of Anselm's life and concerned miracles which
Eadmer did not himself witness: one of these, at Lyons, was
reported by Alexander and was added to the *Life* only after its
completion; the other took place in Normandy in the entourage
of Ralph, abbot of Séez in 1106[1] For some reason which is
now difficult to determine Eadmer long continued to be dissatisfied with his manner of reporting these incidents, and it
was only after several efforts that they assumed their final form.
For the most part it was small matters of style which continued
to give Eadmer an inordinate amount of trouble. Eadmer had
in full measure the author's itch for revision, and many of his
improvements seem scarcely worth the work of emendation;
but some of his alterations were made in explanation of points

[1] *VA* ii, liii, lviii.

317

which had been left obscure in the first recension. Why had Anselm's companions not questioned Abbot Hugh of Cluny more closely about his prophecy concerning the death of William Rufus? How had Eadmer heard the story of the strange experiences of the innkeeper at Florence who slept in Anselm's bed? Why had Eadmer himself not been present when Alexander saw the miracle at Lyons? One can imagine that it was in reply to questions such as these that Eadmer added sentences of explanation.[1] One of the corrections reflects the growing sense of the inadequacy of the political settlement achieved by Anselm. In the first recension, Eadmer had spoken of the 'victory for the liberty of the Church' achieved by the archbishop in 1107: to this description Eadmer now added the qualifying phrase *quodam modo*, 'to a certain extent'.[2] It seems that Anselm's reputation was being somewhat shaken by criticism.

In general, however, Eadmer's reply to criticism of Anselm was not to acquiesce, but to defend him against the charges which were made and the doubts which were raised about his sanctity. In the continuation of the *History* he answered some specific charges against Anselm's administration of the estates of Canterbury; in the continuation of the *Life* he sought to comfort his friends and to confute doubters by examples of his miraculous powers. The first addition to the end of the *Life* must have been made very soon after the main stylistic alterations already mentioned. It is first found in Eadmer's own manuscript of the work described below.

Eadmer tells us that he changed his earlier resolve to conclude the work with Anselm's death at the request of those friends 'whose love for Anselm still burned brightly'. Materially however there was another reason for this change of plan. In addition to the unremarkable visions which had previously provided the only posthumous proof of Anselm's sanctity, he now had two concrete events to describe. In themselves they were very trivial, but they provided the evidence of miraculous intervention necessary for the full recognition of Anselm's status as a saint. In all probability they were added not long before Ralph became archbishop of Canterbury in 1114, and it

[1] *VA* II, xlvi, li, liii.　　　　[2] *VA* II, lxiii.

is a measure of the slow growth of Anselm's reputation for sanctity that in five years only two trifling incidents could be discovered worthy of record by the most assiduous of his friends.[1]

It was probably slightly later, and (if the note to a late Canterbury manuscript is to be trusted) after Ralph became archbishop, that Eadmer added the account of his disobeying Anselm's instructions to destroy the whole work. With this addition, the text of the *Life*, in all but small stylistic details, was finally completed. This was the state of the work when Eadmer went abroad in 1116. When he returned in 1119 he began, as we have seen, to make additions to his *History*; but it does not appear that he made any additions to the *Life* until after the death of Archbishop Ralph in October 1122. By this time several copies of the work had been made, and it seemed more suitable to begin a new book of *Miracles* than to make further additions to the original work. The addition of this appendix would moreover bring the *Life of St. Anselm* into line with those of Dunstan and Oswald. Eadmer was now entering the last phase of his life. He had no more part in practical affairs, and his ambitions for the church of Canterbury were crushed. The book of *Miracles* was his last tribute to Anselm. Though fourteen years had passed since Anselm's death he still had very few miracles to record: a few visions, some cures by means of Anselm's girdle, a final miracle of the extinction of a fire at Bury St. Edmunds, written down as it came to hand. It was not much. The doubts of the young monks at Canterbury about Anselm's spiritual powers are easily intelligible; but slowly the tide was turning in his favour. His tomb was becoming a place of resort for those who sought the counsel and aid of the latest of the Canterbury saints, though there still were detractors who thought that Eadmer had written too much and proved too little. He had done what he could; if anything more was to be added it could not be by him. He may have meant it literally when he said that his trembling fingers forced

---

[1] Although Ralph was still bishop of Rochester at the time of the incident recorded in *VA* ii, lxx, there is good reason to think that he was already archbishop when chapter lxxii was added, for MS. I (a late but authoritative Canterbury manuscript) says that this chapter was added by his order.

him to lay down his pen; in any case he could do no more. From being the record of the friendship of a saint the work had become in the fullest and traditional sense a Saint's Life, and in this form it was copied into the new Canterbury lectionary of about 1125.

## 2. THE PLACE OF THE 'VITA ANSELMI' IN MEDIEVAL BIOGRAPHY

### (i) *Traditional Patterns of Biography*

In order to understand the literary context of Eadmer's *Life of Anselm* it is necessary to give some account of the literary models at his disposal. In bulk these models formed a considerable section of the books in regular use in the monastic community. Some of them were part of the daily reading of the community, others were the preserve of the scholar. No exact classification can cover them all, but the main elements in the tradition may be distinguished under four headings.

*The Heroic Pattern*

The great models of ecclesiastical biography in Eadmer's time were the lives of the saints and martyrs from the fifth to the eighth century. These biographies were themselves dominated by a few great examples of the type to which they conformed, and of these the *Life of St. Martin of Tours* by Sulpicius Severus was probably the most influential. The main characteristic of this type may briefly be described as an overwhelming concern with the impact of supernatural power on the natural world. It was the chief task of the biographer to show this supernatural power in action. As a consequence of this he had little concern with the portrayal of individual character, though sometimes indeed a small modification or omission in words borrowed from an earlier source will, as it were accidentally, throw light on a personal idiosyncrasy on which it was no part of the biographer's duty to insist. The strength of this literature lay in the frequent scenes of awe-inspiring power, and these scenes bore little relation to the personal characteristics of the saint. Even when saints were believed to possess a special efficacy in one or other element, as

320

St. Benedict in the element of water, these preferences had no personal roots, and in freely transferring the miracles of one saint to the account of another, the authors of their lives simply recognized the unimportance of the individual in comparison with the power of which he was the channel.

The chief instrument for the display of personality is talk, and though biographers who had little interest in personality were necessarily even less interested in talk, they did not entirely exclude this element from their accounts. Above all they were interested in everything that concerned the last moments of the saint, those moments that served as a bridge between earth and heaven. The spectators bent forward to catch whatever of prophecy or vision, exhortation or farewell, fell from the dying saint's lips. The biographer made it a special duty to gather what he could learn of these dying words, and to this we owe some of the most unforgettable scenes in the whole range of the literature of this period. The last moments of St. Cuthbert, Benedict Biscop, and Bede retain a freshness that comes when literary traditions give way to immediate experience. But the words were important for their visionary character and not because the biographer was overcome by a sudden desire to display the man rather than the saint. Hence, although there is no time when talk is wholly omitted from biography, it is not used as a clue to the personality of the saint. Even in the *Life of St. Wilfrid*—who more than any man of his day waged a war of words—we have no report of the words that would best reveal the manner of man he was: we know what he thought of the Easter question, but not what he said to his kinsman Tatberht as they rode together while Wilfrid discoursed on his manner of life.[1] We may regret these omissions, but they were not accidental. They had no place in a literature in which the only essential and invariable features were portents at birth, miracles and prophecies during life, a death-bed with its attendant signs, and a continuation of miraculous intervention after death. Nothing could be allowed to break the essential harmony of this pattern.

In comparison with the Continent, England had not been rich

[1] *The Life of Bishop Wilfrid by Eddius Stephanus*, ed. B. Colgrave, 1927, p. 140.

in examples of this type of biography. The lives of Cuthbert, Wilfrid and Guthlac almost exhaust the list of English contributions to the heroic age of Christian biography. The main stream of the tradition was to be found in the lives of the Frankish saints. This body of literature was certainly well known in England in the generation after the Conquest.[1] The Canterbury lectionary, which has already been mentioned as a probable product of Eadmer's years of office as precentor, is one of the main witnesses to the inflow of these lives from the Continent at this time. It was a literature that had left its mark on the daily and public reading of the monastic community, and Eadmer, whether as author, precentor or monk, must have known it intimately. Indeed a considerable part of his literary activity sprang from the deficiencies of the English contribution to this literature.

Between the age of Bede and the age of Dunstan, England ceased to contribute towards the hagiographical literature of Europe. The biographies of Dunstan, Oswald, and Ethelwold signalized the return of English writers to this field, but they also revealed a significant change of emphasis. They are disappointing works by men fumbling to restore a lost tradition, and only dimly conscious of the new needs which biographers were being called upon to meet. The monastic reformers of the tenth century influenced the world by their thoughts and plans more clearly than by their exercise of supernatural powers. Their work involved a revolution in organization; it required the co-operation of many men, and it must have been accompanied by much discussion and argument. But of all this we learn almost nothing from the biographies of the leaders of this movement. Of the personal differences, the differences in taste, outlook and temperament of Oswald, Ethelwold and Dunstan, there is more to be learned from the exiguous evidence of charters, manuscripts, and hazy deductions from casual events, than from the men who knew them face to face.[2] As a

---

[1] For the introduction of these biographies into England after 1066, see B. Krusch and W. Levison, *Passiones Vitaeque Sanctorum Aevi Merovingici*, *MGH*, vii, 545–6, 573–4, 631–3.

[2] See J. Armitage Robinson, *St. Oswald and the Church of Worcester*, British Academy Supplemental Papers, v, 1919; *The Times of St. Dunstan*, 1923, pp. 129–30.

personal record, these biographies are a failure, without achieving success as impressive records of supernatural power. The disappointment is greatest and most complex in the case of St. Dunstan. More than any of these leaders, he called out for some new kind of biographical treatment. He was a talker. He liked to sit in a circle of friends, recounting his visions and his memories of English history, and giving instruction in the vulgar tongue. But we learn of these characteristics by chance. His earliest biographer, who had sat with him and heard him talk, shows a perverse disinclination to satisfy our curiosity about the man. The tale he tells is a strange and inconsequent mixture of visions and miracles, and to this extent no doubt true to the impression Dunstan made upon his contemporaries. But of Dunstan's thoughts and talents, his plans and aims, we learn almost nothing. So far as biography is concerned, England in the tenth century was wandering between the two worlds of heroic supernatural exploit and reforming organizational zeal:

> two worlds, one dead,
> The other powerless to be born.

Eadmer, who had been called upon to write or rewrite the lives of Dunstan, Oda and Oswald, had good reason to know the weaknesses of the English tradition at this point.

## The Commemorative Pattern

At about the time when England was failing to provide adequate biographies of the great monastic reformers, Cluny was rising to its opportunities in this respect. In its best years Cluny did not produce much original literature, but over a period of two hundred years the series of *Lives* of its abbots reflected the community's sense of its mission in the world. These are the first biographies of saints which avowedly subordinate the display of supernatural powers to the display of activity directed towards a practical end:

Let those who will, praise exorcists of demons, curers of diseases, and famous miracle-workers. I shall praise first in my Odo the virtue of patience, his contempt of the world, his zeal for souls, his restoration of monasteries, his clothing and feeding of monks, his pacifying of churches, his reconciling of kings, his perseverance in vigils and prayers, his care for the poor, his correction of the young, his honouring of the aged, his improving of morals, his encouragement to virgins and those of continent life, his rigid observance of the Rule, his practice of all virtues.[1]

This passage from the *Life of Odo*, the second abbot of Cluny, shows the spirit of the new style of monastic biography. It was a style designed to meet the need felt by communities that had risen to honour in the world, to commemorate the authors of their spiritual and temporal prosperity. In the most prosperous centuries of Benedictine monasticism this was a very widespread impulse, and the eleventh century is especially rich in biographies of this kind. We cannot, of course, tell how many of these biographies were known to Eadmer, though it is very likely that he knew some of the *Lives* of the abbots of Cluny. But the type arose so naturally from the monastic conditions of this period that it everywhere displayed similar features. As expressions of grateful and domestic piety these biographies are one of the best monuments of the period:

Although we cannot recount miracles and wonders after the manner of those who write the lives of martyrs and saints, yet we shall relate many things worthy of imitation by those who desire to live well. We do not write for those outside this monastery. We shall be content with readers within these walls, asking only this: if we sinners, now alive, have helped our benefactor before his strict Judge less than he expected or perhaps needed, let those who come after us at least not cease to plead for him. For it was by his zeal and industry that they have been gathered in this place, where they receive temporal aid and spiritual succour.[2]

These words were written between 1090 and 1100, far from England, about Bishop Benno of Osnabrück, but they may be quoted here as an example of the solid loyalty of a monastic community. If anyone of this period deserved such words it was Lanfranc who found Christ Church a ruin and left it in the full tide of rising prosperity. But it must be noticed that no monk of Canterbury wrote Lanfranc's life. The only

[1] *Vita S. Odonis, PL* cxxxiii, 49.
[2] *Vita Bennonis II episcopi Osnabrugensis auctore Nortberto abbate Iburgensi,* ed. H. Bresslau (*MGH*, 1902), p. 1–2.

literary monument they raised to his memory was a very jejune record of his Acts added to the Christ Church text of the Anglo-Saxon Chronicle.[1] Whether it was the gratitude or the literary impulse that was lacking we cannot tell, but the one great opportunity for a commemorative biography in eleventh century Canterbury was lost.

These commemorative biographies during the tenth and eleventh centuries form a remarkable record of disciplined activity and successful diligence. But even at their best they are not intimate biographies. If they are less concerned with miracles than with persons, they are nevertheless more concerned with action than with thought and speech. They expressed the gratitude of great communities for something more substantial than words.

*The Secular Pattern*

The biographies which approached nearest to the ideal of personal portraiture at this time were biographies of secular rulers. They at least had not the distraction of supernatural powers, and they followed a tradition which encouraged the blunt and ruthless disclosure of personal traits and eccentricities of character. The great mentor of the West in this field was Suetonius, whom William of Malmesbury used effectively as a model in drawing his portraits of the English kings of his day. The lesson which Suetonius taught was the use of vivid detail, however unimportant in its general context, to illustrate the habits of mind and character of the subject. In his search for significant personal detail he presented as great a contrast as could be imagined to the tradition of Christian hagiography. Hence he was only acceptable as a teacher of secular biography, and even here his influence was more often bad than good. Only Einhard in his *Life of Charlemagne* mastered the art of using the pattern of Suetonius without making his subject a pale reflection of an ancient Caesar: the figure of Charlemagne with his huge appetites and normal instincts, his health and vigour of mind

---

[1] C. Plummer, *Earle's Two Saxon Chronicles Parallel*, 1892, i, 187–92. This is partly based on Lanfranc's own account of his dealings with York (H. Boehmer, *Die Fälschungen Erzbischof Lanfranks von Canterbury*, 1906, p. 167; William of Malmesbury, *Gesta Pontificum*, p. 39–43.)

and body, powerfully stands out through all the padding of classical phrases. By contrast, William of Malmesbury used his Suetonius, as he used everything else, as one whose knowledge of books was greater than his knowledge of men: his portraits are biting without being convincing, and his details are never clearer than when they are least credible.[1]

Suetonius was a dangerous model for writers who had not learnt to observe with candour and precision the play of character in events. Eadmer had some talent for observation, but neither his subject nor his tastes were likely to lead him to learn from Suetonius. He had no gift for analysis or epigram, and he learnt little from books which were not an essential part of the monastic life.

The whole area of secular biography lay outside the range of Eadmer's vision, and for all that it could teach him this was probably no bad thing. It could only have taught him a technique he was incapable of handling. The one thing we may regret is that he did not learn from secular biographers the importance of describing the physical appearance of his subject. No biography can be complete which fails to leave an impression on the eye. Yet this formed no part of the hagiographical tradition: it was irrelevant to the description of those spiritual powers with which this literature was chiefly concerned. It was only in writing of secular rulers that biographers commonly felt the need for physical description. There were two reasons for this. In the first place, the impact of the ruler on the eye was an integral part of his majesty and royal character. Secondly, in the biographies of Suetonius, and even better in the description of the Gothic king Theodoric II by Sidonius Apollinaris, there were models which medieval authors could follow. Without a model they experienced a singular difficulty in achieving a physical description; and the

[1] For William of Malmesbury's use of Suetonius, see M. Schütt, 'The literary form of William of Malmesbury's *Gesta Regum*', *EHR*, xlvi, 1931, 255–60. The interest in Suetonius at this time is illustrated by a letter of Herbert Losinga in which he asks the abbot of Fécamp to send him a copy of Suetonius since he cannot find one in England (E. M. Goulburn and H. Symonds, *Life, Letters and Sermons of Herbert de Losinga*, i, 64). The *Lives of the Caesars* was evidently a rare book, but not as rare as Herbert imagined.

words of the model, more or less clumsily modified, are apparent in most of the attempts at this art in the twelfth century. In the same period we can observe the occasional extension of this art to hagiography.[1] These intermittent attempts underline the difficulty of the performance. It was difficult to find a place for physical description, and even more difficult to find words for it. Eadmer did not try: such an attempt required talents and interests which he did not possess.

## The Tradition of the Desert

Strangely enough, the best examples of natural and intimate biography were to be found not in the elaborate and painfully developed traditions which have been described above, but in something much more primitive, in the records of pre-Benedictine monastic life. The Lives of The Desert Fathers, and the record of their sayings as reported by Cassian, were in every monastic library. Their use in public reading was laid down in the Rule.[2] They were familiar to every monk. Their influence on literature, however, appears to have been very slight, at least in the tenth and eleventh centuries. There were various reasons for this. The great difference between the fully developed Benedictine life and the austere heremitical life of the Desert, and the existence of a strong hagiographical tradition of later growth no doubt helped to make the original records of this early stage of monasticism seem uncouth and formless. They were far removed in spirit from the dominant forms of the tenth and eleventh centuries. Yet these records preserved one

---

[1] Dom Hugh Farmer O.S.B. has pointed out to me two attempts in twelfth century hagiography to give physical descriptions of a saint. The first is in William of Malmesbury's Life of St. Wulfstan (ed. Darlington, p. 46), and the second is in the Life of St. Godric of Finchale by Reginald of Durham (Surtees Society xx, 1847, p. 212–13). The first of these descriptions is confined to generalities, but behind them may be seen the influence of Einhard's Life of Charlemagne, chapters 22–24. The second uses as its model the full and exemplary description of Theodoric II by Sidonius Apollinaris (MGH Auct. Antiquissimi, viii, 2–3). In date of composition the latter is almost exactly contemporaneous with the first full description of an English king, Henry II, by Peter of Blois using the same model (PL 207, Ep. lxvi).

[2] Regula S. Benedicti, xlii '. . . sedeant omnes in unum et legat unus Collationes seu Vitas Patrum, aut certe aliud quod aedificet audientes . . . parvo intervallo mox adcedant ad lectionem Collationum, ut diximus.'

feature which the later Latin biographies had largely omitted: they had an abundance of lively and natural conversation recorded for no other purpose than to preserve the memory of the personalities and wisdom of the founders of monasticism. The Desert literature is filled with the excitement of the spoken word. The spoken word, unpremeditated, vivid and passionate, was the normal vehicle of instruction, and it made a deep impression on the men like Cassian who had gone to the remote and secluded centres of Desert religion to see those men with their own eyes. The record of the words they heard has a natural force very different from the rhetorical elaboration of later writers. Here is an example from Cassian. He is describing his meeting with Abbot Joseph. He records the abbot's talk about spiritual friendship, and continues:

When this discourse was finished, and the silence of night had fallen, we left the holy abbot and went to a cell apart. Our hearts were so inflamed by the fire of his words that we passed the whole night without sleep. We left the cell and sat down in a retired spot about a hundred paces from it. The shades of night and the privacy of the place gave us an opportunity for talk. As we sat there, Abbot Germanus groaned heavily and said: 'What shall we do? See what a dilemma we are in and how wretched our position is: reason and the lives of these saints both teach us the road to spiritual perfection, but our promise to our superiors prevents our choosing it.'[1]

The words of the Desert Fathers convey the sense of spiritual crisis and illustrate the rôle of friendship and discussion in the formation of an ideal. These elements can never have been absent from monastic life, and they are conspicuous in the lives of Anselm and his friends. But it was in the nature of this influence that it should be difficult to detect. In Anselm a few sayings, a few principles, can be traced back to Cassian. It is a slender thread. In Eadmer the influence is even less obvious, but he may have found in this literature an inspiration for the kind of biography he wished to write. Though far removed in time and circumstance, it provided his nearest and best model.

[1] Cassian, *Collationes* xvii, 1–2 (ed. Petschenig, *CSEL*, xiii, pp. 465–6).

## (ii) *Eadmer's Art*

We must, however, ask whether, and how far, Eadmer intended his biography to conform to any of the types described above. The secular biography may be dismissed at once: it has left no recognizable mark in anything that Eadmer wrote. But each of the three other broadly distinguishable types made some contribution to the formation of Eadmer's purpose. Formally the most powerful influence is certainly the pattern of biography which I have called heroic. There is no reason to doubt that from the beginning Eadmer was aiming at writing a biography which would take its place beside those of the great Anglo-Saxon saints, in the context of a lectionary predominantly filled with the heroic lives from the sixth to the tenth century. The stages by which he could work towards the complete realization of this plan were naturally not at once clear to him. There was a long way to go from the early jottings of 1093 or 1094 to the fully articulated *Life* and *Miracles* of 1123. The collecting of miracles was especially troublesome and their very existence could only be guaranteed by future events. But already in 1092 when Anselm arrived in England he brought with him a companion who had no doubt about his miraculous powers. Probably these powers were already generally recognized at Bec, and within a few months of Anselm's consecration as archbishop the officious Baldwin was instructing him to put forth his powers to arrest the progress of a fire at Winchester.[1] As Eadmer reports the incident, Anselm reluctantly agreed to act as Baldwin required, and this gave Eadmer his first miracle to record on English soil.

From this time, therefore, he had no doubt that he was dealing with a saint of a familiar kind. In several of the incidents he describes, Eadmer must have had in mind the model of earlier saints: in striking the rock for water at Liberi Anselm was doing what St. Dunstan had done; the miraculous powers of his girdle recalled the similar use of St. Cuthbert's girdle; the miraculous supply of balsam, the enlargement of the sarcophagus, the extinguishing of fires—all these incidents had many precedents. An instructed reader like John of Salisbury

[1] *VA* II, iii.

329

could supply the parallels.[1] Yet taking the work as a whole, the parallels are slight, and the deposit of the past does not lie heavily on Eadmer's work. When the authority of his hagiographical models is considered his emancipation is very striking. The chief reason for this emancipation was probably the slowness with which the collection of miracles went forward. There was no rapid multiplication of miraculous incidents. On this point we can feel confident of two things—firstly that Eadmer regretted the infrequency of the miracles he had to record, and secondly that this paucity of material was largely a result of a peculiarity of his own temperament. Eadmer's regret at the comparatively meagre tale of miracles is evident in his account of the doubts which members of the community continued to have, long after Anselm's death, about his status as a saint. In the condition of the time, the question of sanctity was one that only a generous supply of miracles could settle decisively. The miraculous was at the height of its reputation as the explanation for any and every apparent deviation from the course of nature. Within a few decades, natural (often quite misguided) explanations for events began to challenge the solid hold of the miraculous in every walk of life. Eadmer, however, was not at all in advance of his time. In his expectation of an incessant impinging of the miraculous in everyday life he was as uncritical as his contemporaries. But between Eadmer and those who were nearest to him in the friendship of Anselm there was an important distinction. His two rivals for Anselm's regard, the monks Baldwin and Alexander, saw miracles more frequently and more clearly than Eadmer was able to do. It is not a hazardous suggestion that if either of them had been writing Anselm's life there would have been many more, and more striking, miracles than Eadmer reports. Baldwin and Alexander both told him stories which were a good deal more bluntly miraculous than anything that Eadmer himself saw. Baldwin, for instance, told him that they had crossed the Channel with a hole in the boat through which no water came: Baldwin saw the hole, not Eadmer.[2] Alexander told him that in his presence

---

[1] John of Salisbury found parallels in the Lives of SS. Benedict, Martin, Clement and Basil (*PL* cxcix, col. 1012, 1013, 1027, 1031, 1037).
[2] *VA* ii, xxiv.

Anselm had cured a blind man, completely and at once. Alexander saw this, not Eadmer.[1] Both Baldwin and Alexander claimed that they were themselves the objects of Anselm's miraculous interventions: Eadmer was less fortunate.

It is necessary to emphasize this peculiarity of Eadmer's experience and vision, because it did much to determine the kind of biography he would write. He would have been glad to see miracles, but he somehow failed to see anything very conclusive. Why was this? Probably because he was a rather exact observer. We have only to compare the account, which Alexander gave him, of the curing of the blind man at Lyons with Eadmer's own account of the curing of a mad woman on the road to Cluny, to see the difference. Alexander's account is quite crude and unsophisticated: a blind man begins making an uproar; Anselm sends to find out the reason; Alexander reports; Anselm tells the man to come forward; he makes the sign of the Cross and splashes holy water on the man's eyes; the man goes away seeing with perfect clarity. This is the kind of story which the eager credulity of the times demanded. But when Eadmer tells a story it follows a quite different pattern: while they are riding along towards Cluny a clerk approachs and asks Anselm to cure his mad sister; Anselm turns a deaf ear to his tearful entreaties and rides on; the man redoubles his plea, but Anselm repels him; then they come on a crowd holding the mad and gesticulating woman; the crowd gathers round and seizes Anselm's reins; they beg him to put his hands on her; he refuses; they revile him; at last he relents, makes the sign of the Cross and rides quickly away, drawing his cowl over his head weeping, leaving his companions. But was the woman cured? On this point Eadmer, who said so much, could only speak from hearsay. He believed what he heard, but he could not say that he had seen a cure.[2] For a work in the old tradition of hagiography it was a weakness that he should have said so much on what was so little to the purpose, and so little that was conclusive about what mattered most.

Eadmer would no doubt have liked to write a work bristling with conventional miracles, but for this he had the misfortune to see at once too much and too little. He himself deplored his

[1] *VA* ii, liii.    [2] *VA* ii, xlii.

habit of observing what was going on round him with more curiosity than wisdom. That is to say, he saw what interested him and not what his judgment told him he ought to see. This is a defect with many compensations, but it meant that Eadmer could not write a work of conventional hagiography on a contemporary subject where observation had to take the place of ancient authority. We may go back to his Preface for an indication of the way his mind worked. The external events of Anselm's archiepiscopate had been dealt with in the *Historia Novorum*. That was the commemorative side of his narrative dealing with major events of policy, though even here Eadmer often allowed his curious eye to stray from matters of high concern. But the *Vita* was to be a record of things not open to the public eye: *privata conversatio, qualitas morum*, and *exhibitio miraculorum*—in this order.[1] It was therefore a private history, below the surface of public events. This is in itself an interesting distinction. There is nothing like it in the difference between Bede's *History* and his *Life of St. Cuthbert*: both these works deal with the same kind of events. Eadmer's emphasis on the private events of Anselm's life, not necessarily miraculous, was something new. He was not alone in experiencing this change of interest. Anselm's own prayers and meditations were an example of the emergence of private sentiments to articulate expression alongside public events. But Eadmer was the first to display this change of emphasis in the writing of biography. He had the advantage of a subject ideally suited for a new kind of biographical treatment; but he deserves the credit for taking, however accidentally, his opportunity.

The phrase *privata conversatio* in the Preface is an indication of his new approach. There was nothing unusual in calling his biography the *Vita et Conversatio Anselmi*. This title had often been given to earlier English saints' lives. But the *conversatio* which these lives described was not private. In the Benedictine Rule, and generally in Benedictine writers, this word comprised the whole discipline of regular religious life. Traditionally therefore it referred to something essentially corporate and public. By the addition of the word *privata* Eadmer put it in a different context of personal and intimate dealings, which only

[1] *VA, Praefatio.*

those who had lived in the friendship of Anselm could know. 'Conversation' in this sense was not talk. But 'private conversation' was necessarily—especially with such a person as Anselm—largely a record of talk. Eadmer has recorded the impression made on him by Anselm's talk at their first meeting in 1079. It was something quite new in his experience. After 1093 he heard Anselm talk on very many occasions, and until 1100 it is Anselm's talk that gives Eadmer's biography its distinction and substance. Much of this talk must have come to him at second-hand, and it can be proved that in some of his reports Eadmer put together words which he had heard on several different occasions. But this is only to say that there is more art in Eadmer than appears on the surface. No one who reads the biography can doubt that Eadmer's chief claim to fame as a biographer lies in his rediscovery and mastery of the difficult art of recording the spoken word in a vivid and natural way. This is a difficult art at any time, but it was especially difficult in Eadmer's day when, following a long rhetorical tradition, the use of direct speech was regarded as an embellishment, not intended to convey the actual words and sentiments of the speaker, but expressing as well as possible the thoughts the speaker might be supposed to have entertained. This kind of rhetorical speech can be exemplified everywhere in the writings of Eadmer's contemporaries. The reader is not deceived. If Eadmer's contemporaries failed to convey the impression of reporting words actually spoken, it was because they were not trying to do so. They preferred rhetoric to nature. It was Eadmer's merit that he chose to be natural.

This was more than a technique of writing. It was the stirring of a new vision. We have had to record that Eadmer was not always a candid observer and reporter. When the interests of his monastic community were involved he saw what the community saw. But when he was free from this overwhelming weight of opinion he came to events with a fresh eye. He saw clearly because he only saw the things that interested him. But Anselm interested him more than anything outside the community at Canterbury; he saw and reported what perhaps no other biographer would have troubled to report. This is his chief claim to our regard.

(iii) *The Future of Intimate Biography*

The report of talk and the publication of letters must be the chief instruments in any biography that claims to be intimate. It is only in this way that we can learn more of a man than events and his published works can tell us. Anselm's early letters come nearer to our idea of private correspondence than those of any of his contemporaries—much nearer even than those of Abelard and Heloise. But strangely enough, Anselm did not look on them as private letters—he corrected and arranged them for the world to see. It was therefore chiefly in reporting his talk that his biographer could break new ground. This was Eadmer's main contribution to the art of biography. The novelty of this procedure can be judged from the aversion to mere words which contemporary biographers express. For a serious biographer talk appeared either too unimportant or too private. The secret places of the heart were not for him: the thoughts of the heart were known only to God and should be left to His judgment. The biographer trespassed at his peril. Some thought of this kind must have inspired William of Malmesbury when he wrote in his *Life of St. Wulfstan*:

I have omitted to relate the words which were spoken or may have been spoken from time to time, being anxious in all things not to jeopardize the truth. It is the mark of an idle man to dispense words when deeds may suffice—unless indeed there are some words which require a brief mention because of their special splendour.[1]

Here speaks the rhetorician and the scholar who, while maintaining the traditional preference for deeds over words, cannot yet bring himself to omit something of educational value.

A similar expression is to be found in the *Life of St. Stephen of Grandmont*, another of Anselm's contemporaries. Here the relevance to Anselm's case is reinforced by the fact that Stephen was evidently, like Anselm, an influential talker. His disciples retained the memory of his sayings, and his biographer sacrificed them unwillingly in obedience to a principle:

I pass over in silence the things that he taught his disciples when he spoke to them about the observances of religion, the formation of

---

[1] *Vita Wulfstani*, ed. Darlington, p. 2.

morals, and whatever pertains to the salvation of souls. Such things are written in his *Sententiae*. I hasten to speak of the most evident marks of his sanctity, for credit should be given to *things* rather than *words*. For who knows the thoughts of man except God who 'fashioneth all the hearts of them and understandeth all their works?'[1]

Perhaps the most remarkable thing about these passages is that the writers thought it necessary to explain their omission of the words they might have recorded. In an earlier age there would have been no need to explain. It would have been understood that mere talk was not material for the biographer. By the early twelfth century, the situation had become less clear, but Eadmer's contemporaries still hesitated. He took the plunge: 'It seems to me impossible to obtain a full understanding of Anselm's manner of life if only his actions are described and nothing is said of how he appeared in his talk.'[2]

Eadmer took an opportunity which many others in the future would have been glad to seize. The taste for psychological elaboration became very widespread in the course of the twelfth century and left a deep mark on the literature of the period. Everyone felt the need to infuse a passionate inner life into the characters of literature and to elaborate the thoughts and words of historical characters. The omissions of earlier biographers were repaired by rhetorical additions. But this impulse did not have as much effect on the art of biography as might have been expected. The need for brevity—essential in works designed for public reading—disappeared. The *Lives* of St. Bernard, St. Thomas Becket, and St. Hugh of Lincoln are vast by the standards of an earlier age, but they did not achieve the intimacy that Eadmer achieved. The reason for this lies partly in the subjects, partly in the writers. The most interesting character among these saints was probably Thomas Becket, and his best biographer knew him well. He freely displayed himself in his talk, and Herbert Bosham reported his words at length. But Bosham's record was made after Becket's death, when he remembered the martyr rather than the man. A contemporary record of talk is very rare, and a vividly remembered

[1] *Vita S. Stephani Grandimontensis*, cap. xxv (*PL* cciv, 1019).
[2] *VA* i, xxi.

record is even rarer—especially in lives written, as most medieval biographies were, for an ulterior purpose, as a basis for a process of canonization or as the authoritative picture of a saint. It is therefore not surprising that despite the new interest in the secrets of personality Eadmer had few successors in the art of intimate biography. It was an art which needed an unexpected combination of circumstances and talents.

Nothing indeed could have been more unexpected than the circumstances which produced the two most successful examples of this art in the Middle Ages—the primitive *Lives of St. Francis* and Joinville's *Life of St. Louis*. In both these cases, the recollections of unlearned men long after the events they described achieved a poignancy and intimate truth seldom attained in this branch of literature. These *Lives* were the work of old men with a unique experience to communicate. They wrote of a friendship that had been the chief event in their lives, and they wrote as naïve men who were not overshadowed by great literary models. Eadmer's achievement was less substantial than theirs. His work was cut short when only half finished, and it was preserved with an uneasy conscience. But what he accomplished was done in the face of great difficulties. He was an established hagiographer and a member of a great community. Both these facts suggested a certain routine of events and experiences in which individuality was lost. Yet to a surprising extent he shook off the weight of tradition and left a record of his friend, so far as it goes, as good as anything left by Joinville or the companions of St. Francis.

3. THE FUTURE OF THE 'VITA ANSELMI' AND THE
CANONIZATION OF ST. ANSELM

Eadmer's work seems never to have enjoyed in England even the modest popularity which it obtained abroad. The existing manuscripts, and the few notices of lost ones, suggest that it reached only a few of the larger monastic houses and gained a small circulation in their neighbourhood. Anselm's medieval reputation as a saint was even more restricted. The only English church outside Canterbury where there is unambiguous evidence for the liturgical observance of the day of his death is St. Werburgh's, Chester, which was a daughter house of Bec.[1] At Canterbury itself his reputation continued to grow slowly until it was eclipsed by the fame of St. Thomas Becket in 1170. Even at Canterbury the evidence is very scanty, but the main lines of the story can be fairly well established.

The first writer after Eadmer whose evidence is worth anything is Archbishop Theobald. When he referred to his predecessors in his letters, Theobald regularly made a distinction between Lanfranc and Anselm; Lanfranc was merely *bonae memoriae* or *piae recordationis*, while Anselm was generally *sanctae* or *sanctissimae memoriae* or *beatus*.[2] In these years King Stephen gave land to provide a light before the tomb of St. Anselm.[3] This certainly implies an established veneration, but there is no reason to think that there was any liturgical commemoration of Anselm even at Canterbury until the time of Archbishop Thomas Becket. In the calendar of Eadwine's Psalter of about 1145, Anselm's day is marked with the simple notice *ob. piae memoriae Anselmus archiepiscopus*, and this represents the liturgical state of affairs under Theobald.[4]

With the coming of Becket a great change took place. Henry II might have noted an ominous significance in his admiration for Anselm. Indeed it is very probable that the most important of all the clues for understanding the transformation in the archbishop after his elevation is his modelling of himself on Anselm. We know that he used Anselm's prayers as an aid in repressing his wandering thoughts during the Mass, and this is

---

[1] F. Wormald, *English Benedictine Kalendars after 1100 A.D.* (Henry Bradshaw Society lxxvii), i, 103: Anselm's name is a 15th century addition to the Calendar of St. Werburgh's. There are, however, traces of the observance elsewhere in England. Professor Wormald had pointed out to me the following entry in the martyrology composed for the use of the diocese of Norwich: 'xi Kl. Maii. Ipso die Cantuarie depositio sancti Anselmi episcopi et confessoris'. (MS. British Museum, Cotton Julius B. viii 15th century).

[2] A. Saltman, *Theobald, Archbishop of Canterbury*, pp. 241, 262, 271, 285, 293, 444, 446, 451. But on p. 278 (a charter of 1153–4) Anselm is simply *bonae memoriae*.

[3] For this grant and for other documents concerning Anselm's posthumous reputation at Canterbury see W. Urry, 'St. Anselm and his cult at Canterbury' in *Spicilegium Beccense*, i, 1959, 571–93.

[4] M. R. James, *The Canterbury Psalter*, 1935, f. 2.

the earliest direct testimony to the use of these prayers outside Anselm's immediate circle of friends.[1] More important, in Anselm he had an example of a saint in exile. Thomas Becket became archbishop in 1162, and he made it one of his first objects to secure Anselm's canonization. At the Council of Tours in May 1163, within a year of his election, he presented an account of Anselm's *Life* and *Miracles* to the pope with a request for canonization. It is probable that this work was not Eadmer's, but a summary of it made for the occasion by John of Salisbury.[2] This summary follows Eadmer very closely. It adds only one fact about Anselm which is not known either from the *Life* or the *Historia Novorum*: this was a remark, evidently handed down among the monks of Canterbury, that he would not dare to appear in the sight of God until he had punished the disobedience of the archbishop of York against his jurisdiction.[3] John of Salisbury's slight additions to Eadmer are sometimes interesting but apart from this saying, and another which he reports elsewhere, he adds nothing to our knowledge of Anselm.[4] Necessarily, in view of the purpose for which his summary was written, he was mainly concerned with miraculous occurrences. When he came to the posthumous miracles he rearranged them to make clear a distinction commonly observed between those performed before and after burial; and by a reference to the *grandia volumina* from which he had selected only a few examples, he tried, not quite honestly, to give the impression that there were many others of a similar kind. In fact, however, he reported all the miracles which he found in Eadmer, and only added a single item to Eadmer's collection. This addition is the only evidence that miracles continued after the period at which Eadmer wrote, and for the sake of completeness it may be given here: 'A certain Elphege (wrote John of Salisbury), as is generally known, was blind, deaf, dumb and lame from birth; and this is public knowledge. He, as his present state testifies, received a full cure at St. Anselm's tomb.'[5]

---

[1] *Materials for the History of Thomas Becket*, ed. J. C. Robertson, *RS*, iii, 210. For the manuscript tradition of Anselm's prayers, see A. Wilmart's introduction to *Méditations et Prières de Saint Anselme*, traduites par D. A. Castel (Collection Pax, 1923).     [2] *PL* cxcix, 1009–40.
[3] *Ibid.* col. 1035.     [4] Ep. 211 (*PL* cxcix, 235).     [5] *PL* cxcix, 1040.

The way in which this is worded makes it clear that the cure was a recent one, so it would appear that no incidents could be found for the period between about 1130 and 1160. From this we can only conclude that after Eadmer no record was kept of any miracles at Anselm's tomb.

At the time when this request for canonization with its summary of evidence reached Alexander III he was harassed by a number of similar demands. In a letter dated 9 June 1163, he therefore remitted the whole question to a provincial Council to be called by the archbishop of Canterbury.[1] There is no record that such a Council ever met and it has generally been assumed that nothing came of this initiative of Archbishop Becket. By October 1163 he was already quarrelling with the king and was isolated from most of the bishops; a year later he was in exile. Despite these preoccupations, however, it seems very likely that the formalities of canonization were completed before he went into exile, though the fact was forgotten in the excitement of the times and the obliteration of all lesser objects by Becket's martyrdom. The evidence for this is found in a calendar from Christ Church, Canterbury, of the mid-twelfth century. It must certainly be dated before 1171, for it omits to mention the martyrdrom of the archbishop on 29 December 1170. Liturgically it marks a considerable advance on the calendar of Eadwine's Psalter. It contains, instead of the simple *obit* of the earlier calendar, the following entries:

7 April: Translatio Sancti ANSELMI archiepiscopi et confessoris

21 April: FESTIUITAS gloriosissimi patris nostri ANSELMI archiepiscopi et confessoris.[2]

These entries certainly imply a liturgical observance of the

---

[1] J. C. Robertson, *Materials for the History of Thomas Becket*, RS, v, 35–6.

[2] Bodleian MS. Add. C. 260, fol. 2[v] The Calendar clearly belonged to Christ Church, Canterbury, but probably passed to another church since some of the distinctively Canterbury Feasts have been partially erased (e.g. the Dedication of the Church on 4 May). The Translation of St. Anselm and the words *gloriosissime patris nostri* in the entry for 21 April are marked for omission. The entries printed above are in a hand slightly later than that of the main text.

date of Anselm's death, and since Becket had taken the trouble to seek papal authority for this it seems unlikely that he would have sanctioned the observance without going through the form prescribed by the pope. In any case the archbishop must have authorized the Feast, so it would appear likely that the calendar is later than 1164, and that the entry refers to the state of affairs at Canterbury in the last years of Becket's life.

The date of the Translation on 7 April, however, raises a difficulty. A Translation would normally follow an act of canonization, and the only date between 1163 and 1171 when 7 April fell on a day suitable for such a ceremony was 1168.[1] If the Translation took place in this year there would have been time to prepare a shrine in the chapel, henceforth known as St. Anselm's chapel. It was certainly here that his body lay at the time of the fire in 1174, which destroyed a large part of the church.[2] Yet it is strange that there should be no mention of the event in the bulky correspondence between England and the exiled Archbishop Becket, and it is just possible that a Translation may, in 1163 or earlier, have preceded the process of canonization.

Although the whole affair went unnoticed in the chronicles and correspondence of the period, there is evidence that it created a considerable local stir, for a document of about this date shows that there was a guild of St. Anselm at Canterbury with a hundred and thirty-five members. Many of them can be identified as members of families who lived in the town, and they include the port-reeve, together with a large number of craftsmen, clerks and servants of the monastery.[3] It seems likely that, if the martyrdom of Thomas Becket had not intervened, St. Anselm would have become the most popular of

[1] The normal day would be a Sunday, and this would make 1163, when 7 April fell on the second Sunday after Easter, a possible year; but in all the surrounding years except 1168 the date was quite unsuitable: 1161, Friday before Palm Sunday; 1162, Easter Eve; 1164, Tuesday in Holy Week; 1165, Wednesday after Easter; 1166, Fifth Thursday in Lent; 1167, Good Friday; 1169, Monday after Passion Sunday; 1170, Tuesday after Easter.
[2] *The Historical Works of Gervase of Canterbury*, ed. W. Stubbs, RS, i, 15.
[3] For the text of this document, see W. Urry, *op. cit.* p. 585. Dr. Urry gives a valuable commentary on the names included in the list, which he is able to date, with great probability, 1166–7.

Canterbury's local saints. The martyrdom, however, was fatal to Anselm's popularity. The last entry in the list of members of the Anselm guild shows that his eclipse was already taking place, for the latest member—the only one, it would seem, of noble birth—promised an annual payment of half a mark in honour not of Anselm but of the new martyr, Thomas.

After this date, the Feast of 21 April regularly appears in calendars of Christ Church, Canterbury, though nothing more is heard of the Translation on 7 April. For another two hundred years or more, the observance of the Feast made very little progress, and even at Canterbury Anselm fell into comparative obscurity. It is not until the end of the fifteenth century that there are signs of a revival of interest. Since the beginning of the fourteenth century, Anselm's name had been becoming increasingly familiar as the author of works, many of them falsely ascribed to him and some, as we have seen, by Eadmer and other pupils, which were highly valued as expressions of the popular devotions of the later Middle Ages. On the basis of Eadmer's *De Conceptione sanctae Mariae* Anselm was especially associated with the Feast of the Immaculate Conception, which now enjoyed an almost universal popularity. This may have helped to provide the inspiration for a renewed attempt to carry through a formal canonization.

When Henry VII began to interest himself in the canonization of his predecessor Henry VI, he joined to his petition to the papal Curia a similar petition on behalf of Anselm. The first moves were made before 1492, in the time of Innocent VIII, but the earliest surviving document relating to them is a letter of Alexander VI dated 4 October 1494.[1] This ordered the archbishop of Canterbury and the bishop of Durham to investigate the life and miracles of Anselm and to report to the papal Curia. What, if anything, was done as a result of this order we cannot tell; but a few years later a Canterbury monk, Richard Stone, made a full collection of materials relating to Anselm, including Eadmer's *Life*, John of Salisbury's abbreviation of it, Alexander III's letter, and a few miscellaneous poems on Anselm which are found in earlier manuscripts. The compilation was made in 1507 'ad laudem et honorem Dei et

---

[1] Wilkins, *Concilia Magnae Britanniae*, 1737, iii, 641.

sancti patroni mei Anselmi'.[1] It may still have been hoped to bring the process of canonization to a successful conclusion. But Richard Stone was Anselm's last disciple among the monks of Canterbury. In the little that we know about him he recalls Eadmer, in his historical interests, his zeal for the Canterbury saints and the observances of his church, and the meticulous accuracy of his texts; but he lacked Eadmer's creative instincts and has left nothing of his own words except the few phrases which record the progress of his manuscript and his devotion to Anselm.

After this date, there seems never again to have been any question of formal canonization, or any new examination of the record of Anselm's life for this purpose. His name did not appear in the *Martyrologium secundum morem Romanae curiae* of 1498, nor in the revised editions of this work before 1568. But in the new edition of the Roman Martyrology made by John Molanus of Louvain in this year, there appeared among the additions printed in italics under 21 April, this entry:

*Sancti Anselmi episcopi Cantuariensis et confessoris*

A note to the entry gave a reference to Eadmer's *Life*, in the recently printed first edition of 1551 by Joannes Gravius at Antwerp. The sources of Molanus's additions were largely the calendars of Belgian churches, and Gravius's edition of the *Life* was based on a manuscript of the kind common in this area. It would appear, therefore, that Anselm owed his inclusion in the Roman Martyrology to the diffusion of his fame in Flanders, where Eadmer's biography had gained an early popularity. Anselm retained his place in the Roman Martyrology when it was officially revised under Gregory XIII, and from this time his position was never assailed.

The future Pope Benedict XIV, in his great work on canonization published in 1734, mentioned Anselm among those who were regarded as doctors of the Church, though no formal declaration of their position had been made.[2] The office of St.

---

[1] Lambeth Palace MS. 159, f. 176. The date 1507 is also found in f. 183[v] with the addition: 'Sancte Anselme ora pro nobis omnibus.'

[2] Prosperus de Lambertinis, *De Servorum Dei Beatificatione et beatorum Canonizatione*, 1734, Lib. iv, pars. ii, xii, 9.

Anselm had already been approved by the Congregation of Rites in 1703, and in 1720 Pope Clement XI, at the request of 'James III, King of Great Britain, etc.', raised the status of his Feast from semi-duplex to duplex.[1] Eadmer might have found a certain piquancy in the exiled Pretender in Rome petitioning on behalf of the archbishop whom *his* ancestors had driven into exile. But he would have thought his labours well rewarded: without them it is very unlikely that Anselm would have been remembered as a saint.

[1] Clementis XI, *Opera Omnia*, Frankfurt, 1729, col. 1215. Before the approval of the Office in 1703 it seems that a collection of testimonies to Anselm's sanctity was made, and his doctrine was examined, but there was no detailed enquiry such as that instituted in 1494. (Prosperus de Lambertinis, *op. cit.* Lib. iv, pars. ii, xi, 15.)

# CHAPTER X

# ANSELM AND EADMER

T HAT Anselm and Eadmer were men of very different levels of ability and historical significance requires no argument. Anselm made a contribution of lasting importance to a wide variety of fields of experience in philosophy, theology, politics and devotion. Eadmer made some interesting experiments in history, biography and devotional meditation, which were soon scattered and lost in the rising tide of creative activity in the century after his death. Yet if the two achievements are separated by a wide gap in scope and importance, they are linked in many subtle and interesting ways. They are linked in the bond of personal sympathy which in his best years inflamed Eadmer's imagination and extended his experience. They are linked also in the common experiences of the community at Canterbury and the problems of Church and State in a turbulent and formative time. But in a more general way they have a bond as the work of men who stood conspicuously at the parting of the ways and who felt strongly and imaginatively the force of both the old and the new. However widely they were separated in talents and equipment they both responded to the tensions of their day with a freshness which still keeps their experiences alive and still has the power, which ability alone cannot give, to make them interesting.

Eadmer had lived through a social and political revolution without parallel in English history. He had the strongest reasons for identifying himself with the past—as an individual, because his family had suffered in the change; as a patriot, because he saw his countrymen despised and rejected; as a member of a religious community, which he imagined had once been more richly endowed with lands and dignity; as a venerator of saints, whom he saw neglected or deprived of the fullness of the worship due to them. Yet, however much he deplored these changes, he was equally conscious of the benefits conferred by the restoration and enlargement of discipline, of

344

buildings, of the library, and of the dignity of worship, by the practical magnanimity of Lanfranc, and by the saintly and intellectual splendour of Anselm. With all these evidences of present good fortune, it was hard to know whether to be more attached to the present or to the past. Eadmer solved the problem by being a passionate partisan of both—not always to the same extent, but wavering from one to the other as the circumstances of his life and his friendship with Anselm led him now one way, now the other. His biographies of the Canterbury saints, his asides in the *Historia Novorum*, his defence of the rights of Canterbury, are the product of the one mood; the greater part of his *History* and the whole of his biography of Anselm, of the other. In his devotional works the two streams converged, for here, if he was defending an ancient piety against the innovations of Norman reformers, he was also moving with a tide which was soon to break the banks of Norman and Anglo-Saxon provincialism alike. It is this ambivalence which keeps Eadmer's personality historically alive, and would make him memorable even if he had not provided a mass of indispensable facts about the events of his own time and about the life of Anselm.

Anselm's personality is naturally much more substantial and vivid to the historian than that of Eadmer, but it is largely because of Eadmer that this can be said. If Anselm was necessary for Eadmer's development, Eadmer was scarcely less necessary for Anselm's survival as a distinct personality. They are complementary, both in what they did for each other and in their reactions to their own time. They were both intimately affected by the convulsion which changed England from an archaic society governed by antique rules to a comparatively sophisticated society shaped by the active agents of papacy, king and barons. Eadmer suffered and observed the change; Anselm suffered and—more from force of circumstances than intention —promoted it. It was similar in the fields of piety and speculation. Here Eadmer made one original intervention, but it was disguised as a return to the past. The originality of Anselm's interventions allowed no such disguise, but even with him we have observed a reluctance to accept change. While Eadmer thought of progress as a return to the Anglo-Saxon past,

Anselm thought of it as a return to St. Augustine. This was his starting point and he claimed it as his goal. But neither Anselm nor Eadmer could achieve the conservatism of their heart's desire.

If there is one quality which Anselm's thoughts have more than another, it is the quality of originality, at a time when originality was a doubtful virtue and laborious compilation was (with some justice) regarded as the best contribution which the moderns could make to the deposit of ancient learning. Anselm had no talent for laborious compilation—hence, in part, the spasmodic nature of his later influence. On the whole, the future lay with organized compilation and with the refinement of methods of adjusting one authority to another, rather than with the speculative methods of Anselm. He was altogether a strange mixture such as could have been seen at no other time. If he removed authority from his arguments, it was not with the intention of putting doubt in its place. Quite the contrary; the conclusions he sought to establish were those already guaranteed by authority. It was the peculiarity of his system that reason neither went beyond authority nor fell short of it: the spheres of reason and of faith were identical; faith did not cease because its tenets were established by reason, nor did reason add certainty to faith. In many respects his qualities are those of a mathematician; and if mathematics is nothing but a series of tautologies in which every conclusion is contained in the premise, the same may be said of Anselm's arguments. For example, in his argument for the existence of God, God's existence turns out to be nothing more than a condition of our very idea of a Supreme Being. Or, again, Anselm's attitude to the arguments by which he establishes the necessity for a dogmatic truth is similar to that of a mathematician who discovers the proof of a theorem which he already knows to be true. Yet at the time when Anselm wrote, the very idea of the precision of mathematical proof had vanished from men's minds. Mathematics was a dead language. It could give him no hints of the type of reasoning which would satisfy him. He was alone.

From a general point of view the time could scarcely have been less propitious for such a mind as that of Anselm. Quite apart from the distrust of reason, quite apart from the crude and primitive procedures which passed muster as satisfactory examples of the reasoning process, the monastic life as it had developed in the tenth and eleventh century, was wholly unsuited to the development of systematic theology. In the first place it allowed too little time for study; secondly, it did not normally provide a questioning, eager and ever-changing audience of fresh minds. But above all it was directed to other ends than rigorous intellectual activity. The heavy burden of repetition, the effort of attention demanded by the musical requirements of the divine office, the interruptions of study and sleep at uncomfortable hours, the responsibilities of communal discipline and complex estates—all these factors encouraged the type of intellectual labour which could be taken up or put down like a piece of knitting, and discouraged lengthy efforts of intense concentration which could not easily be discontinued or taken up again without an effort. That Anselm felt these restraints, and that he was worried by the pull of conflicting obligations, is certain. That he overcame them was due in the first place to his natural vigour of mind, but also to the mould in which his thought was cast: his independence of authorities allowed him to pursue his own meditations as opportunity arose without the need for constant reference to texts or for a large scholarly apparatus. Besides this, he left to others many secular obligations which strictly fell to him as abbot and arch- bishop, and he was fortunate in having—constantly until 1093 and intermittently after this date—a supply of young men to whom he could devote himself and whose questions served as a starting point for his inquiries.

Meditation and dialogue were the two forms in which he wrote most naturally. The exigencies of his life rather than literary fashion dictated this preference. Monastic study, if it did not mean compilation, must find its chief outlet in medi- tation; the dialogues, on the other hand, were a tribute to the essential stimulus of the young. Anselm's dicta about the young are some of the best which Eadmer preserved. His educational theories—if his genial similes can bear so pompous a description—resemble those of a much later time. On no issue is he more remote from his own age than in his opposition to the insensate brutality with which monastic authorities—no doubt imitating the rest of the world in this—treated the children under their care. His similes of the growing tree which requires freedom for growth rather than restraint, and of the goldsmith who works by gentle pressure and a discreet evocation of the desired shape rather than by hammer-blows, belong to a train of thought which only found full expression in the romantic theories of nineteenth-century educationalists. And the answer which he gave to those who asked him why he devoted more attention to adolescents than to children or adults looks as far back into the past as these similes look forward into the future. He answered that the wax of youth was alone fit to take a new impression, being neither so soft as to lose, nor so hard as to repel, the imprint of the seal.[1] This is a simile used with a rather different application by Plato in the *Theaetetus*:

*Socrates.* I would have you imagine, then, that there exists in the mind of man a block of wax, which is of different sizes in different men; harder, moister, and having more or less of purity in one than in another, and in some of an intermediate quality.

*Theaetetus.* I see.

*Socrates.* Let us say that this tablet is a gift of Memory, the mother of the Muses; and that when we wish to remember anything which we have seen, or heard, or thought in our own minds, we hold the wax to the perceptions and thoughts, and in that material receive the impression of them as from the seal of a ring; and that we remember and know what is imprinted as long as the image lasts; but when the image is effaced, or cannot be taken, then we forget and do not know.[2]

Anselm cannot have known this or any other passage in the *Theaetetus*, and no one can read the Dialogues of Plato and compare them with those of Anselm without seeing that those of Plato have a dramatic force, a width of interest and a breath of the busy world which is lacking in those of Anselm. But in his determination to leave no objection unanswered, and to answer each in his own words and in his own way, Anselm comes nearer to the great master of philosophic dialogue than any other medieval writer.

[1] *VA* i, xi.

[2] *Theaetetus*, 191 c–d (*The Dialogues of Plato*, translated by B. Jowett, 4th edition, 1953, iii, 294–5.)

Despite every handicap, the cloister provided the background for this achievement. That it could do so was a personal triumph of Anselm's genius, helped by the growing discontent with the intellectual and spiritual restraints of Benedictine monasticism. Anselm himself felt none of this discontent. He took great pains to argue against, and where necessary to repress, the discontents which broke out in his own community. He had no sympathy with those who felt the weight of accumulated customs too burdensome:

Whoever undertakes the vows of monastic life must study with the whole of his mind to root himself with the roots of love in whatever monastery he may have made his profession, unless it is such that he is there unwillingly forced to do evil. Let him refuse to pass judgment on the manners of others and on the customs of the place even if they seem useless, provided that they are not against the divine commands. Let him rejoice at finding himself at last where he can remain for the whole of his life, not unwillingly but voluntarily, driving away all thought of removal so that he may quietly give himself up to performing the exercises of a pious life. And if it seems to him that his spiritual fervour could achieve greater and more useful ends than the institutions of his present monastery allow, let him believe that he is either deceived, in thinking that those things are greater which are in fact equal or inferior, or in supposing that he could accomplish what is above his power; or at least let him believe that he does not deserve what he desires.[1]

This is as strong an argument for monastic conservatism as it would be possible to find. Yet however strongly in intention he clung to the past, in his feelings he belonged to the future. There is a striking illustration of this in the preface to his collection of prayers and meditations:

The purpose of the prayers and meditations which follow is to excite the mind of the reader to the love or fear of God, or to self-examination; hence they are not to be read in a tumult, but quietly, not cursorily or quickly but slowly and with intense and thoughtful meditation. Nor should the reader trouble about reading the whole of any of them, but only so much as (with God's help) he feels to be satisfying or useful in stirring up his spirit to pray. Nor is it necessary for him to start at the beginning, but wherever he pleases. . . .[2]

[1] Ep. 37 [i, 29].     [2] *Orationes*, Prol. (Schmitt, iii, 3).

This passage is very far indeed from the communal worship of the monastic office, which in the minds of the reformers of the tenth and eleventh centuries had filled an ever-increasing part of the horizon. It is far from the injunction in the Benedictine Rule that books were to be read *per ordinem ex integro*, from beginning to end.[1] It is addressed no less to the laity in the midst of secular cares than to monks in the midst of their religious routine. It introduces a series of religious exercises which have as their point of departure the stirring of the emotions rather than the discipline of the will. Needless to say, the emotional response is simply a beginning and not an end; but it is a new point of departure, for which indeed others before Anselm had prepared the way, but no one before him had so clearly defined.

Opinions will differ about the desirability of this new point of departure, this new *via pietatis* sprinkled with many tears; but that it is a main road through the religion of the later Middle Ages cannot be doubted. The art, the prayers, the biographies, the literature of the centuries after Anselm equally proclaim the fact: by contrast the saints and sinners before him are comparatively dry-eyed.

We have seen how the uninhibited expression of emotion coloured Anselm's friendships, and how closely thought and emotion were combined in what he wrote on that subject. But it must not escape notice how little the older monasticism encouraged friendships such as those Anselm made at Bec. They broke up the solidarity of the community on which its health and strength depended.

Yet here, as elsewhere, although Anselm gave a powerful impulse to the movement towards individuality and liberty which characterized the piety of the later Middle Ages, the general drift of his thought was in quite a different direction. In his metaphysics, and in his views on conduct, it is difficult to discover any place for individual liberty. He had the same basic difficulty as all thinkers of a Platonic tendency in separating the world from God and in separating one individual from another. This does not mean that he was anything but orthodox in his dogmatic views, but it leads to a certain blurring

[1] *Regula,* xlviii.

of his philosophic clarity at the point of separation of one individual from another and of the world from its Creator. In philosophy, Anselm was an extreme idealist attaching an unqualified existence to general concepts: 'Whoever does not understand how many men are one man in species, how can he understand in the most secret and sublime nature how several Persons, each being perfect God, are one God?'[1]

If Anselm had lived in a time of advanced philosophical controversy, even a generation later, words like these would have come under severe scrutiny. Does he mean to suggest that the unity of all men in the single species 'Man' is in any degree similar to the unity of the three Persons of the Trinity? And if so, in what measure, and in what way? Anselm did not have to answer such questions. He could evolve his philosophy in peace, using images which he thought suggestive without having them torn to pieces in debate. This situation has both merits and demerits—the former, for one of his temperament, by far predominating.

When Anselm was born, theological speculation was dead. The reasons for this were various, partly psychological and partly technical, and not all of them were bad. We must remember that the veneer of Christianity was still very thin. Beneath the surface of ecclesiastical order there was a large mass of paganism only partly suppressed. It is not until the eleventh century that we get the first convincing signs—they can scarcely be expected to be attractive—that Christianity was becoming a popular religion, engaging the passions and inclinations of the population at large. The fragile structure was held together by authority, and it might well have seemed foolishness to imperil the unity of thought by controversy, especially when it was the common view that all that could usefully be said on most topics had already been said.

The main Christian doctrines of the Trinity, the Incarnation and Redemption, Heaven and Hell, were established in a form which no doubt lacked refinement, but which stated the Christian position with a blunt force. But when problems of interpretation arose, the methods used for solving the problems were extremely crude and mechanical, lacking both historical

[1] Epistola de Incarnatione Verbi, i (Schmitt, ii, 10).

perspective and logical refinement. It is impossible to read the Eucharistic dispute between Lanfranc and Berengar, which is the highest point of eleventh century theological debate before Anselm, without a certain sense of disgust at the arguments which satisfied the protagonists on either side. It must be added that this dissatisfaction does not arise from any lack of seriousness or talent, for both Berengar and Lanfranc were men of very distinguished abilities, but from their lack of tools for dealing with the problems, and still more their unconsciousness of their lack. It was into this dreary and perplexed situation that Anselm broke with the insight of fresh vision.

His instruments of thought were very simple, much simpler than they would have been a generation later. He took words very seriously and sometimes played with them with the solemnity of a child with its bricks: they were the doorway to the kingdom of essences to which the mind had the key. Hence he pushed his analysis of words with relentless activity. But he was not very much concerned with the pattern of syllogistic reasoning, though he spoke often about the subtle pitfalls of this method of argument. He was fortunate in living before the discovery of the full range of Aristotle's logical works, which had the effect of distracting the mind from the substance to the manner of thought. This could only have been a hindrance to him. But the price he paid for his freedom was a certain philosophical naïvety. Likewise it may perhaps be claimed that a share of philosophical naïvety is as much an aid to understanding his thought as it would be a hindrance in understanding the thought of St. Augustine or St. Thomas Aquinas.

St. Augustine's writings are full of a long philosophical tradition; those of Aquinas are monuments of technical proficiency in a highly complex art. They both lived in times of high dispute and keen debate when nothing but the highest accomplishment could survive. The age of St. Anselm was by comparison an age of innocence. His thought is that of the cloister round which the raging winds of controversy are only just beginning to be heard. He could think in peace, in a peaceful assurance which was surprised to find itself called in question.

As for his place in the history of thought, the old saws about his being the 'last of the Fathers' and the 'first of the Scholastics' are, if taken together as the expression of a paradox, more suggestive than such labellings generally are. In method, he was quite different from the later scholastics, since the foundation of their method was to accumulate and dissect authorities, and to order them in a reasoned and harmonious system; the tensions of dialectic, the setting of one opinion against another, the clash of debate, were the foundation of their systems. All this was quite foreign to Anselm: he eschewed the quotation of authorities, his method was solitary and peaceful contemplation, and his thought grew by drawing out the meaning of concepts, not by the confrontation of opposites. Yet he approached the scholastics in having a single method for describing the whole of reality. The way in which his works appeared, apparently casually and without any claim to completeness, conceals the unity and system which underlay all that he wrote. In the later theological writers the system is on the surface: they work down from God to the Angels, from the Angels to Man, the Fall and the Sacraments. In Anselm the system is implicit, not visible at first sight; but it is there. His place in relation to scholasticism may be likened to that of Descartes in relation to the scientific movement from Newton to our own day. Descartes was, in the view of Newton and his successors, wrong in most of his detailed scientific concepts, but he anticipated them in seeking a single method to describe the whole of the physical universe. That is what Anselm did with the intelligible universe of the Christian Faith.

Whatever may be the judgment on Anselm's theological system, or on his recorded words and actions, they had a unique power to stimulate those whom he met; and they retain this power unimpaired to the present day. There is nothing in Anselm which is simply ordinary. Even in those fields where his response was most fully conditioned by his circumstances and by the thoughts of those around him—as, for instance, in all that concerned the primacy of Canterbury—he brought a sharper definition of the ideal to bear on practical action. This sharpness of mental images was not always fortunate for his work as an ecclesiastical statesman. But for a writer it is the one thing needful, and it made Anselm an effortless innovator.

He touched the thought, the piety and the politics of the time at every important point; and whatever he touched looked different afterwards. He founded no school, and in many ways the immediate future turned against his methods and ideas. Ironically, his influence was most conspicuous where it was least personal—in the sphere of politics. His own pupils, though stirred into activity by his large and perceptive spirit, went their various ways. They left no easily recognizable impress on the future. Yet they helped, by collecting his works, by recording his conversation, by adding their own more commonplace though not negligible appendices to the body of his writings, to keep his influence alive. In all these activities Eadmer took a leading part. But, most important of all, it is to him alone that we owe the record of Anselm's personality which joins together the many widely different branches of his work, and would suffice to keep his memory fresh even if all else had disappeared.

# APPENDICES

# THE RELATION BETWEEN *CUR DEUS HOMO*, I, 7, AND RADULFUS OF LAON

The outline of chapter i, 7 of the *Cur Deus Homo* has been described above (Ch. III). It consists of:

1. An introductory statement of the traditional doctrine of the rights of the Devil over mankind.

2. The main argument with a refutation of this doctrine.

3. A brief restatement of the traditional doctrine so far as it is acceptable.

The parallel text from the school of Laon first pointed out by J. Rivière is found in two compilations containing the theological teaching of this school, the *Liber Pancrisis* (MS. Troyes 425) and MS. Avranches 19[1] In both manuscripts, the text in question has the simple heading *Radulphus*. It begins with the question: 'Queri solet cur per humanitatem incarnati verbi Deus pater humanum genus redimi voluit, cum per aliquem prophetarum vel angelum hoc posset fieri.' The text then examines the various possibilities:

1. Redemption by a man: this is impossible because the whole human race was corrupted and the Devil 'justly possessed Man, who had voluntarily submitted to him'.

2. Redemption by an angel: this is impossible because:
   (*a*) The angelic nature had sinned once and might sin again.
   (*b*) If Man was redeemed by another creature, the dignity of Man would be impaired.

---

[1] *Revue des Sciences Religieuses*, xvi, 1936, 344–6. The text is printed in G. Lefèvre, Anselmi Laudunensis et Radulfi fratris eius Sententiae excerptae, 1895, no. 31; also in *RTAM*, xiii, 1946, 217; and finally in O. Lottin, *Psychologie et morale aux xii^e et xiii^e siècles*, v, 1959, 185–6.

3. (*a*) Redemption by Christ 'whom the Devil unjustly subjected to death, although he had no rightful power over Him'. By the unjust exercise of his power, the Devil justly lost the power which he had over sinners. If, however, Christ had unjustly deprived the Devil of his just possession of Man, this would have been an act of unjust violence against the Devil.

(*b*) The nature of the Devil's just possession is briefly indicated.

(*c*) The superiority of the Deus-Homo over the man and angel of the earlier possibilities (1 and 2) is pointed out.

4. The 'inconvenience' of the Incarnation of the Father is pointed out: it would lead to a Quaternity in place of a Trinity since the Father would be both Father (as God) and Son (as Man).

5. A similar 'inconvenience' would follow the Incarnation of the Holy Spirit.

6. Therefore the second Person of the Trinity alone was Incarnate.

It will be seen that this text contains a complete argument, covering some of the same ground as the *Cur Deus Homo*. On several points the attitude of the writer is similar to that of the *Cur Deus Homo*—on the impossibility of Redemption by a mere man or angel, and the 'inconvenience' of the Incarnation of any Person of the Trinity except the Son. At these points of agreement, however, there is no verbal similarity with the *Cur Deus Homo*, and the arguments in favour of these points are briefer and cruder than those of Anselm. It is only where Radulfus and Anselm are in disagreement that they use the same words. At this point, and only at this point, one author borrows from the other. But who borrows from whom?

The passage in Radulfus comprises the part of his argument I have numbered 3, *a* and *b*; and I have placed it beside the beginning and end of *Cur Deus Homo*, i, 7:

*Radulfus*

Nullum itaque peccatum habuit
qui per concupiscentiam natus
non fuit. Cui iniuste diabolus
mortem intulit in quo nullum ius
sue potestatis invenit. Iuste
ergo suam in hominibus perdidit
potestatem qui in Christo suam
iniuste exercuit tyrannidem *ut
cum diabolus eum in quo nulla
mortis est causa et qui Deus erat
occideret, iuste potestatem quam
super peccatores habebat amitteret. Alioquin iniustam violentiam* Christus *diabolo fecisset*
qui *iuste possidebat hominem quem
non ipse violenter* sibi *attraxerat,
sed idem homo ad illum se sponte
contulerat.*

*Diabolus dicitur iuste* POSSI-
DERE *hominem quia Deus iuste
hoc permitt*ebat *et homo iuste
pati*ebatur *quod promeruerat.
Non sua iustitia homo pati iuste
dicitur, sed quia iusto Dei iudicio*
patitur.

*Cur Deus Homo i, 7*

SED  ET  ILLUD  QUOD
DICERE  SOLEMUS—Deum
scilicet debuisse prius per iusti-
tiam contra diabolum agere, ut
liberaret hominem, quam per
fortitudinem,
*ut cum diabolus eum in quo
nulla mortis* erat *causa et qui
Deus erat occideret, iuste potestatem quam super peccatores
habebat amitteret, alioquin iniustam violentiam fecisset* illi,
quoniam *iuste possidebat hominem,
quem non ipse violenter attraxerat,
sed idem homo ad illum se sponte
contulerat* — NON  VIDEO
QUAM  UIM  HABEAT
[Anselm gives his reasons, and
concludes]  HOC  ITAQUE
MODO *diabolus dicitur iuste*
VEXARE *hominem quia Deus hoc
iuste permitt*it *et homo iuste
pati*tur. SED ET HOC QUOD
HOMO  IUSTE  DICITUR
PATI, *non sua iustitia pati iuste
dicitur, sed quia iusto iudicio
Dei* punitur.

If these parallel texts are read attentively, the small changes
in detail are readily intelligible on the assumption that Anselm is
fitting the Laon text into his own rather involved sentence: they
are much less intelligible on the assumption of a borrowing in
the opposite direction from Anselm. But apart from details,
which can be deceptive, the assumption that Radulfus borrowed
from St. Anselm in the one place where he disagreed with
him, and ignored him where he agreed; and that, when he
borrowed, he omitted the whole of Anselm's argument, and
chose passages at the beginning and end of his chapter to

support a view exactly opposed to that of Anselm—all this is to heap one improbability on another. On the opposite assumption everything is clear. St. Anselm had no need to borrow from the Laon writer where they agreed, because he had fuller and better arguments for the views they both held; but he borrowed where they disagreed, because he wanted a contemporary expression of the traditional view to hold up for examination. Finally he had to account for the strength of the traditional view, and by a judicious alteration of the Laon text he was able to concede a small part of its argument.

If this account of the matter is correct, we can go farther and admit that many of the questions discussed in the *Cur Deus Homo* were already being discussed in the school of Laon by the time Anselm was writing; they were not new. The interest in the problem of the necessity of the Incarnation was in the air, partly as a result of Jewish criticisms, partly as a result of Biblical study, partly as a result of the growth of critical interest in the Christian faith. The Laon masters discussed the problem especially in connexion with the verse ii, 10 in the Epistle to the Hebrews; and several of their comments have been preserved (Lottin, *op. cit.* pp. 44–7, 50–2, 118–19, 184–8; nos. 47, 48. 54, 158, 231, 232, 234). These passages all express the same point of view: the necessity for the Incarnation (with some qualification), the maintenance of the rights of the Devil, the impossibility of Redemption by man or angel, the 'inconvenience' of the Incarnation of Father or Holy Spirit. This body of contemporary discussion forms the background in the *Cur Deus Homo*.

There remains however one problem. Rivière might not have been tempted to reverse what I believe to be the true story of this borrowing if the Laon fragment had not been ascribed to Radulfus. It was this which probably at once suggested to him a late date. Radulfus, presumably the brother of Master Anselm of Laon, did not become head of the school of Laon until this position was relinquished by his brother. The documents illustrating their careers are unfortunately extremely scarce, but Master Anselm (Ansellus) can be found as chancellor in two charters of 1106–12 and 1115. In the second of these charters Master Radulfus is also mentioned. In 1116

Ansellus had become archdeacon and Radulfus had risen, possibly to the position of chancellor. In 1117 Ansellus died. Whether Radulfus succeeded him as archdeacon or as chancellor is not quite clear: in charters of 1123 and 1131 there is a Radulfus in each of these positions; but by 1134 the chancellor was Ernaldus. On this evidence it seems likely that Radulfus survived his brother by at least fourteen years, and probably died between 1131 and 1134.

In these circumstances, can we suppose that St. Anselm already had a text of Radulfus in front of him in about 1095? To this question various answers might be given: if Radulfus died as an old man shortly after 1131 there is nothing impossible in his being a master with authority by 1095; alternatively, the text might have circulated in the school of Laon before Radulfus's name was attached to it. We know too little to be sure. None of the fragments of the school of Laon can be dated, and we do not know how they came to be written, nor how they were circulated. Perhaps Abelard gives a hint of the way these fragments came into circulation when he describes the pupils joking together after the lecture 'post aliquas sententiarum collationes'. But when Abelard went to Laon in 1112, he found Master Anselm already an old man: 'hunc senem cui magis longaevus usus quam ingenium vel memoria nomen comparaverat'. (*PL* CLXXVIII, 124–5). And we know that by this date the pupils of Master Anselm were to be found far and wide. The school had already had a long summer and its great days were over. On all grounds it is likely that the doctrines and traditions of the school had been fixed well before the end of the eleventh century, and the *Cur Deus Homo* gives us strong reasons for dating one of the extant fragments before 1095.

# EADMER'S REPORTS OF ANSELM'S SERMONS

The chief source of information about Anselm's sermons is the collection of reports made by Alexander. Alexander, however, was not one of Anselm's companions until after his return to England in September 1100. Before this date, and possibly also after it, Eadmer sometimes made reports of Anselm's sermons. The accounts in the *Vita* of Anselm's addresses to the monks of Canterbury in 1079 and 1097 are obvious examples of this. These occasions had a personal interest for Eadmer quite apart from the contents of Anselm's addresses, and it is to this that they owe their place in his biography. The only formal sermon certainly reported by Eadmer is the well-known *liber de beatitudine caelestis patriae*, to give it its title in the printed editions; but there is another piece in Eadmer's manuscript which seems to have a similar origin. They both deserve consideration as examples of Eadmer's reporting.

## I. 'SCRIPTUM QUODDAM DE BEATITUDINE PERENNIS VITAE' [1]

The circumstances in which this sermon was preached by Anselm and reported by Eadmer are described in the Preface to the work: the sermon was delivered in the chapter-house at Cluny either in 1099–1100 or on an unrecorded visit during the second exile between 1103 and 1105, and Eadmer was asked by one of the monks called William to send him a record of what had been said. Eadmer began at once to do what was required, but he found it more difficult than he expected. He kept adding to it, as he did to so many of his other works, and in its final form the sermon in the chapter-house at Cluny has evidently been completed by remarks which he had heard on

---

[1] I give the titles in the form in which they appear in Eadmer's own manuscript. See below, p. 368.

other occasions.[1] The resulting treatise was the most widely read of all Eadmer's works and it had a permanent place in the Anselmian canon. Meanwhile, Alexander's report of the same, or a very similar, sermon circulated independently and was finally printed under the name of Guigo of Chartreuse.[2]

Eadmer's report owed its diffusion to two sources: the copy which he sent to Cluny, and the copy which he himself kept and continued to enlarge. The former was the source of many Continental copies; but the English copies descend from Eadmer's own manuscript. In its original form, as sent to Cluny, the work ended with the words *transituri sunt in societatem demoniorum*; but already by the time that the manuscript of his collected works was written, Eadmer had added a further page.[3] At a still later date, probably about 1121–2, Eadmer added a further instalment on the leaves which had been left blank at this point. Although this addition was made long after Anselm's death, it probably preserved a genuine record of his words, possibly spoken on various occasions and recorded in Eadmer's notes. In his final words Eadmer gives the impression that the work in its latest and fullest form had been read by Anselm and sent to his friend at Cluny; but the manuscript tradition of the work makes this highly unlikely. Here, as elsewhere, Eadmer did not confine himself to words spoken on a single occasion but produced a conflation of relevant thoughts spoken at different times. There can be no doubt, however, that Eadmer's words convey an impression of unity which the work did not possess: 'I have written this' (he says at the end of the work)

as I heard it from the mouth of the blessed father Anselm, in order to satisfy my friend who pressed me to write. I also sent a letter which I have placed at the head of this work in case anyone who contrasted the beauty of the material with the poverty of the language, should think that the material showed Anselm's authorship, but that the language, clouding his insight and eloquence,

---

[1] *PL.* CLIX, 587–8.
[2] *PL* CLXXXIV, 353–64. The tangled history of this literary blunder was first unravelled by Dom A. Wilmart, *Auteurs spirituels et textes dévots du moyen âge latin*, 248–59.
[3] For the original ending, see *PL* CLIX, 601 A. The second recension ended with the words *a diabolo praecipitati depereunt, ibid.* 602 B.

casts doubt on his authorship. Therefore let anyone who deigns to read this work know that Anselm himself often read and heard it, and commended it with his own hand and authority to be read and transcribed for posterity.[1]

Although this may be true of the work in its original form, it cannot possibly be literally true of the work in its final shape. Eadmer's manuscript makes it quite clear that he continued to add to the text of the sermon after Anselm's death.

II. 'ASCRIPTUM DE ORDINATIONE BEATI GREGORII ANGLORUM APOSTOLI'[2]

This piece raises problems of considerable interest and difficulty. It is a sermon, of which the purpose was to promote the celebration of the Feast of the Ordination of St. Gregory. This Feast is a purely Anglo-Saxon one, expressive of the feelings of deep attachment which the old English Church had towards the begetter of its faith. Before the Conquest this Feast was observed on 29 March and closely followed the more usual celebration of St. Gregory's death on 12 March.[3] Like some other local peculiarities it seems to have been suppressed by Lanfranc; and it only reappeared in England in the early twelfth century, in the first place apparently at Canterbury, but at a new date, 3rd September. The older date presumably preserved, on the basis of evidence now lost, the date of Gregory's ordination to the priesthood; the new one certainly represented the date on which he became pope, and this could easily be worked out from the data provided by Bede.

The sermon in Eadmer's manuscript fits well into the circumstances of the revival of this festival, all the more so since it evidently anticipates opposition.[4] But when we ask to whom

---

[1] *PL* CLIX, 604–6.      [2] Wilmart, *Opuscula*, 207–19.
[3] A. Gasquet and E. Bishop, *The Bosworth Psalter*, 33–4, 84, 104–6. The Feast on 3 September is among the early twelfth century additions to the calendar in MS. Arundel 155.
[4] Wilmart, *Opuscula*, p. 212: 'Qui igitur eum (Gregorium) praevium ad caelestia sequi desiderant, ducatus ipsius primordia venerari non abnuant. Nam qui ea sua devotione amplecti nolunt, ipsi sibi testes sunt quod eum

the sermon was preached, and even who preached it, we are faced with a difficulty. In the first place, it was a sermon by someone in authority, delivered to a distinguished gathering; it was also a gathering where Englishmen, if they were present at all, were an exception, for the preacher turns to them and says: 'Eia fratres—forte enim aliqui de gente illa haec me dicentem praesentes auscultant—eia, inquam, vos Angli, fratres nobis in Christiana fide effecti, vobis a deo predestinatum et missum beatum Gregorium pro apostolo suscepistis.'[1] It is difficult to reconcile these words, addressed to Englishmen to whom the speaker was evidently a stranger and newcomer, with Eadmer's position at any time in his life.

I formerly suggested that the sermon might have been preached by Eadmer in Scotland, when he was bishop-elect of St. Andrews in 1120. But I did not then know that, since the piece belonged to the earliest portion of Eadmer's manuscript, it could not have been written after 1116. Moreover, the passage which has just been quoted would more naturally come from someone who was not himself an Englishman, but was speaking in England to an audience in which only a few Englishmen were to be found.

This would exclude Eadmer's authorship of the sermon, but it would fit well with a sermon of Anselm reported by Eadmer. The phrase which he uses to the Englishmen in his audience, 'fratres nobis in Christiana fide effecti' would be especially appropriate to a foreign archbishop in England. The title gives no indication of Anselm's authorship, but in Eadmer's manuscript this is true also of the sermon at Cluny, which undeniably was preached by Anselm. If here also Eadmer was acting as reporter and not as author, all the difficulties disappear. The tone of the sermon is entirely consistent with Anselm's position in England. Also the style and matter of the piece have some striking similarities with other reported sermons of the arch-

ductorem habere refugiunt. Hoc quoniam humana consuetudine et ex divina historia satis patet, plura inde ducere supervacuum existimavimus. Quid etiam ex his colligi possit inferre nolo, ne, si dixero, illos qui eo duce niti renuunt, eo cuius vice functus est niti duce subterfugere, et iccirco Christi qui eum suis ovibus ducem instituit nolle ordinationi adquiescere, videar nimis aliena multorum voluntati proponere.'
[1] Wilmart, *Opuscula*, p. 212–13.

bishop, and one of the images used in it is found in another sermon of Anselm reported by Alexander.[1] Moreover, a distinguished gathering in England at which few, if any, Englishmen were present could always be found at the royal court.

To go on and suggest a date for the sermon is to plunge into the unknown, but there is one date which presents itself as especially suitable. The first mention of the Feast of the Ordination of St. Gregory after the Norman Conquest occurs in a series of charters of Henry I in September 1101.[2] The country had recently been invaded by Robert of Normandy, and Henry, by coming to terms with him in August had escaped a great danger, which might easily have cost him his crown. In all this Anselm had played a notable part. At the beginning of September, the king held a great court at Windsor in the presence of the papal messengers who had brought letters to England earlier in the year on the subject of his dispute with Anselm. Important business was done, including discussions about the papal decrees on investitures and homage. Among the charters which issued from the meeting, the king confirmed the grant of the city of Bath as the seat of a bishopric, and the bishop of Norwich completed the foundation of his cathedral church: both charters were dated on the Feast of the Ordination of St. Gregory. When we reflect that this style of dating is quite unprecedented at this time and represents a break with the known liturgical arrangements of post-Conquest England, and that the archbishop's whole strength at this time was concentrated on securing obedience to the papal decrees, it is tempting to refer the sermon, with its exhortation to renew the ancient bond between England and Rome established by Gregory the Great, to this moment.

At this large and distinguished meeting of the *Curia Regis*, Englishmen, if present at all, would be an exception, and this is the exact situation which the sermon envisages: it was an exhortation to the men of the new régime in England to follow the leadership of Pope Gregory. In the circumstances of 1101, the revival of this old English observance had a new relevance.

---

[1] *MARS* i, 1941, p. 9.    [2] *Regesta*, nos. 544, 547; cf. *HN* 131.

# EADMER'S PERSONAL MANUSCRIPT

Corpus Christi College, Cambridge, MS. 371[1] is the main, and for several works the only, manuscript of Eadmer's writings. With the exception of a single letter and the continuation of one work, it contains—or did originally contain—all his known works. It was evidently his own manuscript, to which he made additions from time to time. The greater part is probably in his own hand, and it provides important evidence for the chronology of his works.

The manuscript is now a volume of twenty-nine quires containing 462 pages, but originally it contained thirty-one quires with (probably) 496 pages. In its original state it had the following works:

1. (Pp. 23–78) *Vita Sancti Wilfridi Eboracensis archiepiscopi et confessoris (Historians of the Church of York, RS*, 1, 161–226; *PL* CLIX, 713–52), written after the death of Lanfranc in 1089 (*Hist. Ch. York*, 1, 225), and probably before 1097, since it does not mention Anselm among the archbishops who had been driven into exile (ibid., 1, 162).

2. (Pp. 78–87) *Breviloquium vitae eiusdem patris* (pr. *Historians of the Church of York*, 1, 227–37), a sermon preached at Canterbury on the Feast of St. Wilfrid, while Aelfwinus was sacrist (ibid., 1, 236). Later, but probably not much later, than no. 1.

3. (Pp. 87–102) *Vita sancti Odonis archiepiscopi et confessoris* (pr. Wharton, *Anglia Sacra*, 11, 78–87; *PL* CXXXIII, 933–44).

4. (Pp. 102–54) *Vita sancti Dunstani archiepiscopi et confessoris* (pr. *Memorials of St. Dunstan*, ed. Stubbs, Rolls Series, 162–222), written after the death of Wulfstan, bishop of Worcester, in 1095 (p. 164).

5. (Pp. 154–75) *Quaedam de miraculis quae idem pater mundo exemptus fecit in mundo* (pr. *Memorials of St. Dunstan*, 223–49) written at about the same time as no. 4.

---

[1] Descriptions of the manuscripts have been given by M. Rule, *HN* pp. lxxviii–lxxxv, and by M. R. James, *Catalogue of Manuscripts of Corpus Christi College, Cambridge*, but their accounts need to be corrected and completed at many points.

6. (Pp. 176–90) *Ascriptum de ordinatione beati Gregorii Anglorum apostoli* (pr. A Wilmart, *Opuscula*, 207–19). On this work, see above pp. 364–6).

7. (Pp. 190–212) *Consideratio Edmeri peccatoris et pauperis Dei de excellentia gloriosissimae virginis matris Dei* (pr. *PL* CLIX, 557–80).

8. (Pp. 212–46) *Vita sancti Oswaldi Eboracensis archiepiscopi et confessoris. ii Kal. Martii* (pr. *Historians of the Church of York*, II, 1–40; *PL* CLIX, 761–86).

9. (Pp. 246–61) *Quaedam de miraculis eiusdem patris* (pr. *Historians of the Church of York*, II, 41–59), written at the same time as no. 8. A great fire at Worcester is referred to (p. 55) which may be the fire of 1113 reported in Florence of Worcester and in Lieber-mann, *Ungedruckte Anglo-Normannische Geschichtsquellen*, pp. 10, 76. The work was written at the request of the monks of Worcester, certainly after 1095; Eadmer's friend Nicholas became prior of Worcester in 1113 and the writing of the work may be connected with this.

10. (Pp. 261–78) *Scriptum quoddam de beatitudine perennis vitae* (pr. *PL* CLIX, 587–606). On this work and its later additions, see above, p. 362. In its original state the work ended with the words *a diabolo precipitati depereunt*, and part of p. 278 and the whole of pp. 279–82 were blank.

11. At this point there were originally ten quires, numbered XVII to XXVI, which have been removed. There can be no reasonable doubt that these quires contained the *Historia Novorum*, in four books, down to the death of Anselm in 1109. It would, in this state, have just fitted into ten regular quires.

12. (Pp. 299–377) *Vita et Conversatio Anselmi Cantuariensis archiepiscopi*. This work occupied five quires, originally numbered XXVII to XXXI, but after the removal of the previous ten quires the numbering was altered to XVII to XXI.

The manuscript was in this state a bulky little volume, and there can be little doubt that Eadmer removed the *Historia Novorum* in order to add to it. The addition increased the size of this work by nearly a third and it would have made the manuscript very unwieldy. Since he was engaged in this work after his return from Normandy in 1119, it is a reasonable inference that the manuscript in its original state was in existence by this date at latest. Probably the works included in it were all written before he went abroad in 1116.

The removal of the *Historia Novorum* reduced the number of pages from 496 to 336, and so the manuscript remained until after Eadmer's return to Canterbury from Scotland early in 1121. He now began adding to it, and several groups of additions can be identified in the course of the next few years:

*Group A.* At the beginning of the volume he added two new quires of ten pages each. The numbering of the existing quires was not altered, so there are now two sets of quires numbered i and ii. Items 1 and 2 are in the same hand as the main part of the volume, but 3–5 are a later addition in the hand which wrote ff 198–208. These new quires contained:

1. (P. 3) *Versus de sancto Dunstano* (pr. *Mem. of St. Dunstan*, 424–5).

2. (Pp. 5–6) *Ymnus de sancto Edwardo rege et martiro* with musical notation (unprinted).

3. (Pp. 6–7) Letter of Nicholas, monk of Worcester, to Eadmer on the mother of King Edward the Martyr (pr. *Mem. of St. Dunstan*, 422–4; Rule, CXXVI–VII). This letter was written in reply to a question of Eadmer, and, since he included its information in his *Life of St. Dunstan* it probably belongs to the time when he was writing that *Life*.

4. (Pp. 7–9) Letter of Nicholas to Eadmer, bishop-elect of St. Andrew's, advising him about the position of the Scottish Church in relation to Canterbury and York (pr. Wharton, *Anglia Sacra*, II, 234–6; *PL* CLIX, 809–12). The letter was written while Eadmer was in Scotland (July–December 1120).

5. (Pp. 10–17) Letter of Eadmer to the monks of Glastonbury about the relics of St. Dunstan (pr. *Mem. of St. Dunstan*, 412–22; *PL* CLIX, 799–808). This letter was written fifty years after Lanfranc's translation of the relics of St. Dunstan in 1070–1, probably therefore shortly after Eadmer's return from Scotland, in 1121.

*Group B.* At the end of the volume he added a new quire (pp. 379–90), numbered xxii, containing the *Miracles of St. Anselm*. The date of this work is about 1123–4.

*Group C.* At about the same time as making this addition, Eadmer filled the blank pages 278–82 in the following way:

1. (Pp. 278–81) He added a new ending to the *Scriptum de beatitudine perennis vitae* bringing it to the end as printed (*PL* CLIX, 606). This still left one and a half blank pages, and on these he began—

2. (Pp. 281–92) *Vita beati Bregowini Cantuariensis archiepiscopi et confessoris* (pr. with omissions in Wharton, *Anglia Sacra*, II, 184–90; *PL* CLIX, 753–60; the omissions are partly supplied in *Anglia Sacra*, II, 76–7). The date of this work is 1123–4. In order to complete it a new quire had to be inserted; this is numbered xvii in a more tremulous hand. There are now, therefore, two quires numbered xvii. Only about half this new quire was required for the *Vita Bregowini*, and on the blank pages was inserted—

3. (Pp. 293–8) the list of chapters to the *Vita Anselmi*.

*Group D.* Finally four new quires were added at the end of the volume, numbered xxiii to xxvi in the same tremulous hand as that which numbered quire xvii. These quires and the two quires added at the beginning of the volume differ from the rest of the manuscript in being ruled in pencil instead of with a hard point, and in being written for the most part in a hand different from the rest of the manuscript. These quires contain:

1. (Pp. 395–415) *De conceptione sanctae Mariae editum ab Eadmero monacho magno peccatore* (pr. *PL* CLIX, 301–18; H. Thurston and T. Slater, *Eadmeri monachi Cantuariensis tractatus de Conceptione sanctae Mariae*, Freiburg, 1904).

2. (Pp. 416–23) *Vita beati Petri primi abbatis coenobii gloriosorum apostolorum Petri et Pauli quod Cantuariae situm est. iiii Kal. Januarii* (pr. Wilmart, *Opuscula*, 354–61).

3. (Pp. 423–4) *Sententia de memoria sanctorum quos veneraris* (pr. Wilmart, *ibid.* 190–1).

4. (Pp. 425–40) *Scriptum Edmeri peccatoris ad commovendam super se misericordiam beati Petri ianitoris caelestis* (pr. Wilmart, *ibid.* 192–206).

5. (Pp. 441–50) *De reliquiis sancti Audoeni et quorundam aliorum sanctorum quae Cantuariae in aecclesia domini salvatoris habentur* (pr. Wilmart, *ibid.* 362–70. Fragments of a continuation of this work have been found in the remains of the great Lectionary of Christ Church in Canterbury Cathedral MS. E42. They are in a later hand than the main body of the Lectionary, but they seem to

370

be by Eadmer. These fragments are printed by N. R. Ker and A. Wilmart in *Analecta Bollandiana*, li, 1933, 285–92 and lxiv, 1946, 50–3).

6. (Pp. 451–60) *Insipida quaedam divinae dispensationis consideratio edita ab Eadmero magno peccatore de beatissimo Gabriele archangelo* (pr. Wilmart, *Opuscula*, 371–9).

None of the works in this last group can be dated, but they probably all belong to the last years of Eadmer's life. The *De Conceptione* in particular can scarcely be earlier than about 1125 and, considering the way in which the manuscript was put together, it is likely that the whole group is late. They probably belong to the years 1124–30.

A glance at this history of changes, excisions and additions is sufficient to show that the manuscript was Eadmer's personal copy of his own works and grew under his direction. The question whether he wrote it with his own hand is not easy to answer. On the one hand there are occasional errors which might indicate unintelligent copying. But an author, through inattention, can make mistakes in copying his own works like anyone else; and, since the same hand wrote the greater part of the manuscript over several years, the probability is that Eadmer acted as his own scribe. The day had not yet come when the rôles of the author and the scribe were clearly distinguished, and in showing an ability to make a calligraphic copy of his own work Eadmer was not different from Ordericus Vitalis and William of Malmesbury. Moreover, we know that he occupied himself on occasion as a scribe,[1] and though there is no certain copy of his work with which to compare this manuscript, the following considerations will show that the hand which wrote the greater part of the manuscript is probably his:

1. With small exceptions, the whole manuscript in its original form is in one hand. The same hand wrote the

---

[1] Besides the story quoted above, p. 251, see Ep. 209 [iii, 25] in which Eadmer is mentioned as transcribing the *Cur Deus Homo* for the monks of Bec. Eadmer added a personal note of his own to Ep. 208 [iv, 117], so he may very well have been the scribe of this and other letters of Anselm. These letters were both written in 1099.

additions which were made at various times during the next
few years with the exception of

(a) the first two quires (pp. 6–17)

(b) the last miracle added to the *Miracula S. Anselmi* (p. 389
lines 6–90)

(c) the greater part of the latest additions to the MS., viz.
pp. 396–423, l. 3.

The original writer however was still at work at the beginning
and end of these additions on p. 395 and pp. 423 l. 5 –460.
All this seems to point to an author at work on his own writings
over a number of years, being able however sometimes, and
especially in his later years, to call in helpers.

2. The hand which wrote most of this manuscript also wrote
the greater part of the main manuscript (C.C.C.C. 452) of
Eadmer's *Historia Novorum*.[1] Here also the hand changed
towards the end. To be precise the original hand wrote the
manuscript to p. 298. In the middle of the eighteenth quire
it broke off in the middle of a paragraph (at the word *occur-
surus, HN*, p. 248, 4 lines from bottom) and a new scribe completed the work, adding three quires for this purpose.

3. The main hand of these two manuscripts also wrote two
fragments of Eadmer's works which were evidently rejected at
some stage in their compilation. These fragments are in
C.C.C. 341 and contain

(a) a leaf of the *Historia Novorum* with many variants from
the definitive text (see *HN* p. 233, l. 5 permissum est –235,
l. 27 consecret)

(b) a leaf of rejected *Capitula* for the *Vita Anselmi*.

When we find the same scribe copying the works of a single
author over a number of years, both in rejected drafts and in
their final form, making corrections and adding to works already
written, the conclusion is unavoidable that the hand of the
scribe is that of the author himself. We may confidently ascribe
this hand to Eadmer, but the question now arises whether he

[1] There is a minute, but over-subtle, description of this manuscript by
M. Rule with facsimiles in *Proceedings of the Cambridge Antiquarian Society*,
vi, 1886, 194–304. Here as elsewhere Rule's theories are vitiated by many
baseless conjectures.

was the scribe only of his own works, or whether other manuscripts in his hand can be found. All the manuscripts we have so far examined belong to the later years of his life: the composite volume (C.C.C.C. 371) to the years from c. 1112 to 1125 or later; the *Historia Novorum* (C.C.C.C. 452) to the period after his return to Canterbury in 1119; the two rejected fragments of the *Vita Anselmi* and the *Historia Novorum* (C.C.C.C. 341) to the same period. But Eadmer had been at work as a scribe thirty years earlier, as his own words (already quoted in another connexion) show:

Cum itaque, post decessum superius nominati patris Lanfranci, quadam die in claustro ex more sederem, occupatus libro quem scribendo inter manus haberem, venit ad me nominatissimus ille cantorum Osbernus. . .[1]

The date of this incident, which shows Eadmer in his role as scribe and confidant of Osbern the precentor, is about 1090. Now in Mr. N. R. Ker's *English Manuscripts in the century after the Norman Conquest* there are reproductions of two pieces of writing of about 1088 which show a remarkable similarity to the handwriting of Eadmer's manuscripts.[2] They are only small fragments, but Mr. T. A. M. Bishop, who has examined them and compared them with Eadmer's hand, tells me that in his view they are the work of the same scribe, and that other examples of his works can be found among the manuscripts from Christ Church Canterbury. We may therefore expect that, just as William of Malmesbury's hand has been detected in a number of Malmesbury manuscripts in recent years,[3] there will soon be a group of manuscripts from Canterbury in which Eadmer's hand has been found. It would be rash to say much about manuscripts which have yet to be located and studied, but two points may reasonably be made. In the first place we know very little at present about the growth of the library at Christ Church Canterbury during its great period from about 1080 to 1130, and little can be known until the work of the main

[1] Wilmart, *Opuscula*, p. 367.
[2] Pl. 5 (second letter of Clement III); Pl. 6a (Profession of John bishop of Wells).
[3] For a list of these manuscripts and an indication of their interest, see Dom H. Farmer, ' William of Malmesbury's Life and Works ', *Journal of Ecclesiastical History*, xiii, 1962, 39–54.

scribes has been identified and arranged in a chronological sequence. In this inquiry the discovery of manuscripts written by Eadmer has a special interest because his active life spans the whole of the most important period, and he is the only Canterbury monk of these years whose life can be known in any detail. He must have been one of the earliest scribes to use the well-known Christ Church hand. This noble local variant of a Norman model was developed at Canterbury when Eadmer was a young man, and when Osbern was in charge of the library. How far they, and other native Englishmen, were responsible for the formation of the new style it is impossible at present to say, but it is significant that Mr. Ker has paid a striking tribute to the anonymous scribe of the early fragments which we may now associate with Eadmer. He saw him as a craftsman of a high order, and his work as an influence of importance in the development of the Canterbury style.[2] This is a line of thought which deserves to be pursued.

The chance of advancing the study of a great library must excuse these minute yet incomplete observations; but reflection also suggests the need for caution. Whatever the interest of Eadmer's manuscripts, it is quite unlikely that they will have the same kind of interest as those of William of Malmesbury. William of Malmesbury was a learned man, and the contents of his manuscripts disclose his peculiar tastes and opportunities. Eadmer was more completely a man of his community, and we may expect his manuscripts, in so far as they contain writings other than his own, to reflect the interests of the community rather than his own tastes. But he was removed from the community for long periods between 1093 and 1109, and again from 1115 to 1119, by his duties in the household of the archbishops. These absences took him away from the day-to-day work of the monastery during the most productive years of his life. During these years he can have made little contribution to the growth of the monastic library except as an author. His work for the library must be sought either early or late in his career, either as a scribe before 1093 or as precentor after 1120. In his middle years, Canterbury gained an author, but it lost a scribe of distinction.

[1] op. cit., p. 29.

374

# INDEX

Abelard, Peter, 79 n., 83; at Laon, 361; theory of redemption, 95–7; contrast with Anselm, 103; school of, 91 n.; correspondence with Heloise, 334

Adela, countess of Blois, 177

Adelaide, daughter of William I, recipient of Anselm's *Prayers*, 36, 37, 42, 46

Aelfric, abbot of Eynsham, 245

Aelred of Rievaulx, contrasted with Anselm, 75

Aelsi, abbot of Ramsey, legend of, 292

Aethelnoth, abbot of Glastonbury, 285

Aethelnoth, archbishop of Canterbury, 235

Alan Rufus, lord of Richmond: plans to marry Matilda, 185; elopes with Gunhilda, 185–7; his death, 187; disputed chronology, 187 n.

Alan Niger, lord of Richmond, brother and heir of Alan Rufus, 188; marries, or plans to marry, Gunhilda, 188; his death, 188

Alcher of Clairvaux, 53 n.

Alcuin, 203; his importance in history of private devotion, 39–41

Alexander III, pope, 339, 341

Alexander VI, pope, 341

Alexander I, king of Scotland, 236

Alexander, monk of Canterbury, author of *Dicta Anselmi*, 200, 220–1, 222 n., 223, 316, 362, 366; member of Anselm's household, 197; witness of Anselm's miracles, 317, 318, 330–1

Alfred, king, his book of devotions, 39 n.

Ambiguity, in *Proslogion*, 65; in *C.D.H.*, 116–21

Anchin, abbey of, 317

Ancilia, wife of Count Humbert Whitehands, 9

Andrew, St; Anselm's *Prayer* to, 40

Angels, fallen, impossibility of redemption, 99 n.

Angels, guardian, 296–7

*Anglo-Saxon Chronicle*, 232, 325; its indifference to ecclesiastical disputes, 142–3

Ansellus, see Anselm of Laon

Anselm, bishop of Aosta (d. 1026), 9

Anselm, abbot of Bury St Edmunds, nephew of St Anselm, 10; monk of Chuisa, 10; protagonist of the Feast of Immaculate Conception, 10–11

Anselm of Laon, his characteristics, 84; his name (Ansellus) 84 n. school of: importance in development of theological discussion, 84–5; contribution to discussion of the Atonement, 87, 357–61

ANSELM, ST, birth (1033) and early years, 3–12; leaves home, 11; arrives at Bec (c. 1059), 12; becomes a monk (1060), 27–30; prior of Bec (1063), 30; abbot (1078), 36, 66; first visit to Canterbury (1079), 217; archbishop of Canterbury (1093), 152–3; does homage to William II, 157; offers an aid, 157; receives the pallium, 155, 300; supports the king, 158; quarrels with the king over knight service, 156, 159; asks leave to go to Rome, 160; first exile (1097–1100), 160–3; stays in Lyons, 161–2; returns to England (1100), 163; refuses homage, 168; but supports Henry I against Duke Robert, 169; agrees reluctantly to his marriage with Matilda, 190; holds Council (1102), 182; second exile (1103–6), 172–9; stays at Lyons, 173–4; threatens to excommunicate Henry I, 174–7;

375

Richard of Clare, abbot of Ely, 168
Richeza, Anselm's sister, 8, 9–10
Ripon: St Wilfrid's relics at, 278
Rivière, J., 87 n., 93 n., 357, 360
Robert, count of Meulan, 174
Robert, duke of Normandy, 152,
    164, 169, 176, 366
Robert, abbot of Bury St Edmunds,
    168
Robertson, A. J., 257 n., 259 n.
Robinson, J. Armitage, 205 n.,
    280 n., 322 n.
Rochester, bishops of: did not
    receive investiture from the
    king, 153; *see also*, Gundulf,
    Ralph d'Escures, Ernulf
Rockingham, council of, 154, 155 n.,
    300
Roger of Beaumont, 37
Roger, bishop of Salisbury, 147 n.;
    sends his nephews to Laon, 84
Roger, monk of Caen and Canter-
    bury, 246
Romuald, St, 28 n., 29
Rooth, E., 210 n.
Roscelin: canon of Compiègne, 78;
    and of Bayeux, 78; and of
    Besançon, 79; in England, 79;
    his heresy, 79; claims support
    of Lanfranc and Anselm, 80;
    Anselm's first reply to, 36 n.,
    78, 80; Anselm's final reply to,
    78–81; attacks *C.D.H.*, 88; his
    historical importance, 78–9
Rule, M.: editor of Eadmer, 298, 372
Russell, Bertrand: convinced by
    ontological argument, 58

St Andrews, bishop of, *see* Eadmer
    bishopric of, 135, 236, 307, 365
St Bertin, abbey of, 317
    Lambert, abbot of, 218
St Davids, bishopric of, 133
St John Hope, W., 260 n.
St Wandrille, 153
St Werburgh, abbey of at Chester,
    78, 337
Saltman, A., 259 n., 337 n.
Saltwood, 257 n.
Samson, bishop of Worcester (1096–
    1112): his character and mod-
    eration, 140, 142

Samuel, monk of Caen and Canter-
    bury, 246
Sandwich, 258
*Sapientia*, 60–1
Savoy, counts of, 8–9
Scepticism, William Rufus's, 145–6
Schmidt, Dom F. S., editor of St
    Anselm: on recensions of *De
    Incarn. Verbi*, 34 n.; on chrono-
    logy of Anselm's works, 36 n.;
    on Anselm's letters, 67 n.,
    199 n.; on the *Dicta Anselmi*,
    220 n.; on the early Canterbury
    collection of Anselm's works,
    238 n.
Schools: at Bec, 12, 14, 30–1, 201;
    cathedral, 78, 94, 96; at Laon,
    84–5, 87–8; absence of in
    eleventh century England, 201
Schütt, M., 326 n.
Segovia, John of, 295
Selden, John, 230
Seneca, *Quaestiones Naturales*, 59
*Servitium debitum*, 108, 110–11, 113;
    of Canterbury, 156 n.
Shaftsbury: Anselm's relations with
    nuns of, 186, 254 n.
Sidonius Apollinaris: importance of
    his description of Theodoric II,
    326–7
Similitudes, Anselm's, 105, 108–9
    the treatise *De Similitudinibus*,
    221–6
Smalley, B., 14 n., 83 n.
Smith, R. A. L., 259 n.
Soul, Anselm's discussions on the,
    224–5; his projected work on,
    206
Southern, R. W., 10 n., 13 n., 14 n.,
    205 n., 206 n.
Stenton, F. M., 159 n.
Stephen, St: Anselm's *Prayer* to, 40,
    43
Stephen of Grandmont, St, 334–5
Stevenson, W. H., 169 n.
Stigand, archbishop of Canterbury,
    312
Stisted, 257 n., 258
Stone, Richard, monk of Christ
    Church Canterbury, 341–2
Stubbs, W., 147 n., 282 n.
*Substitution*, Anselm's views on, 75

Printed in Great Britain
by Amazon

83448188R00235